THE HABSBURGS

THE HABSBURGS

Dynasty, Culture and Politics

PAULA SUTTER FICHTNER

REAKTION BOOKS

Published by Reaktion Books Ltd
33 Great Sutton Street
London EC1V 0DX, UK
www.reaktionbooks.co.uk

First published 2014

Printed and bound in Great Britain
by TJ International, Padstow, Cornwall

A catalogue record for this book is available from the British Library

ISBN 978 1 78023 274 4

CONTENTS

NINE

One Goodbye, Several Farewells 286

Political Chronology

c. 976
German Emperor Otto I makes Leopold I of Babenberg margrave of Eastern March

1156
Privilegium Minus. Margrave Henry II of Babenberg and his Austrian lands raised to ducal status by Emperor Frederick I Barbarossa. Austrian rulers largely freed from imperial feudal obligations in their own holdings. Vienna made government seat

1230–1246
Frederick II the Quarrelsome, duke of Austria. Further consolidation of Austrian lands, with the exception of Carinthia and the Tyrol. Acquisition of territory along Adriatic coast. Extinction of Babenberg line. Otakar II of Bohemia invades Austria

1251
Austrian estates name Otakar II of Bohemia their duke

1254
Peace of Buda divides Babenberg inheritance between kingdoms of Bohemia and Hungary

1265–9
Otakar II of Bohemia enfeoffed with Austria, Styria, Carinthia and Carniola by Richard of Cornwall, co-claimant to title of Holy Roman Emperor

1273
Count Rudolph of Habsburg elected German king by imperial estates

1276–8

Imperial campaign against Otakar II, ending with his death

1282–3

Rudolph I, as German king, enfeoffs himself with Austrian lands

1358–9

Privilegium Maius. Habsburgs take title of archduke, a rank confirmed by Emperor Frederick III in 1452

1379

Intra-dynastic division of Habsburg Austrian lands

1440–93

Archduke Frederick V of Habsburg serves as Holy Roman Emperor Frederick III. With one short interruption, the title remains in the House of Habsburg until dissolution of Holy Roman Empire in 1806

1477

Archduke Maximilian I marries Mary, duchess of Burgundy

1493–1519

Emperor Maximilian I rules reunited Habsburg holdings

1495

Marriage of Habsburg Archduke Philip of Burgundy and Princess Juana of Spain

1515

Double betrothals of Archduke Ferdinand I with Princess Anna of Hungary and Archduchess Mary with Prince Louis II of Hungary

1517

German Augustinian monk Martin Luther challenges papal authority over western Christendom. Beginning of Protestant Reformation

1526

Crushing Ottoman defeat of Hungarians at Battle of Mohács. Upon death of Hungarian king Louis II, Ferdinand I of Austria acquires thrones of Hungary and Bohemia

1529

First unsuccessful Ottoman siege of Vienna

1555

Peace of Augsburg accepts coexistence of Catholic and Lutheran territories in Germany

1618

Defenestration of Prague. Bohemian estates choose German Elector Palatine Frederick v as their king rather than Habsburg Emperor Ferdinand ii. Beginning of Thirty Years War

1620

Forces of Emperor Ferdinand ii defeat army raised by the Bohemian estates at the White Mountain on the outskirts of Prague

1627

Ferdinand ii's Renewed Land Ordinances in Bohemia confirm hereditary Habsburg rule in the kingdom. Estates retain fiscal prerogatives and right to elect monarch should ruling dynasty die out

1635

Emperor Ferdinand ii declares primogeniture rule of territorial succession in the House of Habsburg

1648

Treaties of Westphalia. End of Thirty Years War and Habsburg attempt to re-Catholicize Germany

1683

Second Ottoman siege of Vienna fails. Beginning of Habsburg consolidation of Hungarian crown lands and retreat of Ottoman forces to the southeastern Balkans

1699

Peace of Karlovác. Hungary effectively reunited

1700

Death of King Charles ii of Spain. Extinction of Habsburg Spanish line

1701–14

War of the Spanish Succession. Habsburgs give up claims to Spanish throne. Anti-Habsburg Rákóczi uprising in Hungary

1713

Pragmatic Sanction asserts the unity of the Habsburg lands should Emperor Charles vi not leave male heirs

1717

Habsburg army under Prince Eugene of Savoy begins temporary occupation of fortifications at Belgrade after dislodging Ottoman defenders

1736

Marriage of Archduchess Maria Theresa to Duke Charles of Lorraine

1740

Maria Theresa succeeds her father Charles VI in Habsburg lands. House of Habsburg now House of Habsburg-Lorraine. War of the Austrian Succession (First and Second Silesian Wars). Frederick II of Prussia invades Silesia, part of the Habsburg kingdom of Bohemia

1748

Treaty of Aix-la-Chapelle. Frederick II of Prussia takes possession of Silesia. Signatories acknowledge Pragmatic Sanction. Beginning of major reform of Habsburg administration

1756

Seven Years War (Third Silesian War). Austria launches unsuccessful effort to retake Silesia

1763

Treaty of Hubertusberg. Prussian takeover of Silesia confirmed in return for Frederick II's support of Maria Theresa's eldest son, Archduke Joseph, as Holy Roman Emperor in 1765

1772

First Partition of Poland. Galicia, area around Kraków, parts of Ukraine, added to Habsburg empire

1778–9

War of the Bavarian Succession

1780–90

Reign of Emperor Joseph II. Intense focus on reforming administrative, economic, political and intellectual life of Habsburg lands

1791

Declaration of Pillnitz. Emperor Leopold II and King Frederick William of Prussia raise possibility that they will intervene in revolutionary France where Leopold's sister Marie Antoinette is queen

1792

France declares war on Habsburg monarchy

1795

Third Partition of Poland. Habsburgs receive additional territory around Kraków

1796–7
Napoleon Bonaparte leads campaign against Habsburg lands in northern Italy

1806
Dissolution of the Holy Roman Empire. Habsburg Holy Roman Emperor Francis II becomes Emperor Francis I of Austria

1809
Bonaparte occupies Vienna

1809
Marriage of Napoleon Bonaparte and Archduchess Marie Louise, eldest daughter of Francis I of Austria

1814–15
Congress of Vienna. Habsburg monarchs given presidency of new German Confederation

1848–9
Revolutions take place throughout Habsburg holdings. In December Archduke Franz Joseph becomes emperor of Austria

1849
Suppression of revolution throughout the Habsburg empire. Beginning of Habsburg neo-absolutism

1851
Emperor Franz Joseph declares supremacy of emperor in his New Year's Patent. Administration of Habsburg holdings centred on Vienna

1859
Austro-Piedmontese War

1860
Franz Joseph's October Diploma allows a measure of decentralization in his empire

1861
February Patent establishes an Imperial Assembly elected by regional deliberative bodies in Habsburg empire. Hungary refuses to participate

1862
Treaty of Villa Franca. Franz Joseph cedes Lombardy in northern Italy to Napoleon III of France, who then passes it to King Victor Emmanuel II of Sardinia-Piedmont

1864

Second Schleswig War: Denmark fights Austro-Prussian forces

1866

Austro-Prussian War (Seven Weeks War). End of Germanic Confederation and formal Habsburg political presence in Germany

1867

Compromise of 1867. Dual monarchy of Austria–Hungary established. Common ruler, foreign policy, army and some financial affairs. Hungary internally autonomous. Each half of the monarchy has its own elected legislature

1878

Congress of Berlin. Temporary curbing of Russian influence in Balkans. Austria–Hungary empowered to administer two provinces of the Ottoman empire, Bosnia–Herzegovina, and to garrison the Sanjak of Novi Bazaar

1879

Austrian-Hungarian administration of Bosnia–Herzegovina begins. Lavish public celebration with historical pageants of silver wedding anniversary of Emperor Franz Joseph and Empress Elisabeth ('Sisi'). Mutual defence pact (Dual Alliance) signed between Austria–Hungary and the recently united German empire

1882

Triple Alliance of Austria–Hungary, Germany and Italy

1889

Deaths of Emperor Franz Joseph's heir apparent, Archduke Rudolph, and his mistress Mary Vetsera, apparently in a murder-suicide. Archduke Franz Ferdinand, the emperor's nephew, now next in line for the Habsburg thrones

1898

Assassination of Empress Elisabeth by an Italian anarchist

1908

Annexation by Austria–Hungary of Bosnia–Herzegovina

1912–13

First and Second Balkan Wars

1914

Assassination of Archduke Franz Ferdinand and his wife in Sarajevo on 28 June. Emperor Franz Joseph declares war on Serbia on 28 July. Mutual defence pacts throughout Europe activated

1915

Italy declares war on Austria–Hungary

1916

Death of Emperor Franz Joseph. Accession of Emperor Charles I (Charles IV of Hungary), another nephew of the deceased, to positions of Emperor of Austria and King of Hungary

1917

Emperor Charles allows parliament in the Austrian half of the monarchy to reconvene. United States declares war on Austria–Hungary

1918

U.S. President Woodrow Wilson offers Fourteen Points for settlement of the First World War. In October Emperor Charles issues a manifest that federalizes the Habsburg empire with generous provisions for state autonomy. Emperor Charles withdraws from state responsibility on 11 November

1919

New Austrian republic expropriates Habsburg property and excludes dynasty from the country

2011

Death of Otto von Habsburg, Emperor Charles's eldest son

Usage

❖

THE SPELLING OF place names, proper names, even the name of the entity that the Habsburg ruled, is a linguistic challenge all its own. Central and east central European nomenclature in English-language prose often reads awkwardly at best. Changes of political systems, repeated territorial rearrangements by treaty and inheritance and population movements that often went with them, have conferred multiple identities on many of the dynasty's former holdings. All of these meant something to someone in earlier times, and in some cases still do. For more and more people in the twenty-first century, however, only the most recent designation counts.

While the author has tried to resolve these problems as consistently as possible, flexibility has been observed too. The name Austria, for example, has referred to several locations throughout history. Today it applies to a modest Alpine republic of nine provinces in the middle of Europe. From medieval times to the last decades of the nineteenth century, however, 'Austria' included only the eastern and northeastern reaches of the modern state. Conventionally divided by the Enns river, the region was officially split into what are now Upper and Lower Austria only in 1861. In this book the area is called 'Austria' (Ger. Österreich). Rather than supplying geographical coordinates that most readers will not recognize, the author uses Upper and Lower Austria somewhat anachronistically to situate some sites in the area more precisely. In the course of the sixteenth and seventeenth centuries the Habsburgs gained control of what today is known in English as Transylvania. To Germans, who settled there in the Middle Ages, it is still Siebenbürgen; Romanians, who now govern it, call it Ardeal; for Hungarians, who knew it as a crown land of their monarchy, but lost it after the First World War and still resent the fact, it is Erdély. Thanks more to Bram Stoker and Count Dracula than history, the Latinate Transylvania is accepted as Transylvania for speakers of English throughout the world. For the purposes of this book, therefore, it will be Transylvania rather than Ardeal.

As is normal in modern editorial practice, widely understood anglicizations of place names are used: Vienna instead of Wien, Belgrade and not Beograd, Prague rather than Praha. Constantinople is preferred over Istanbul, because it identifies a metropolis known only that way throughout the entirety of the period covered in almost all of my text. For other cities and geographical locations, particularly those that changed names several times over the lifespan of the Habsburg monarchy itself, the most recent nomenclature prevails. Older usages are appended parenthetically, as in Bratislava (Hung. Pozsony; Ger. Pressburg), for readers for whom they may still be more familiar.

Personal names, especially of major historical figures, and their titles, if any, have been treated in the same way. English forms are the rule: Francis for Franz, Albert for Albrecht, Charles for Karl, Theresa for Theresia, and so on. Franz Joseph, however, remains Franz Joseph; his name not only refers to a single ruler but a man who epitomized an era in central Europe as much as did Queen Victoria in the British Empire. Otakar, Zvonimir, Béla, Leopold and other designations that are foreign to English nomenclature remain as they were born. Authors, artists, musicians and their kind also keep their native names, which often conjure up the character of their work. 'Francis' Lehár takes the lilt out of Franz Lehár; Johann Nestroy, one of world literature's greatest comic playwrights, loses much of his impudent wit when rebaptized 'John'. 'John' also does not get across the intensity of Hungarian national feeling in János Libényi, a man who tried to assassinate Emperor Franz Joseph.

Finding an English name for the Habsburg polity is just as tricky. Here the niceties of recent historiography have become part of the debate. The older term 'Habsburg Empire', once used confidently in the United States by twentieth-century historians such as Robert Kann, Arthur May and Barbara Jelavich, and by Jean Bérenger in France, has been vigorously questioned by scholars who argue that Habsburg rule lacked certain basic features of imperialism. 'Habsburg Empire' also has the considerable drawback of being easily confused with the Holy Roman Empire, the medieval aggregate of German states in which the Habsburg served as emperors from the middle of the fifteenth century to its dissolution in 1806. Where the German 'Empire' comes up in this book, it is capitalized. This author is not altogether persuaded that Habsburg rule lacked basic imperialistic features. But when the term 'Habsburg empire' is used, 'empire' is lower case.

Historians in Britain and in German-language studies have been more comfortable with 'Habsburg Monarchy', used occasionally in this study. Its great virtue is that it implies the narrowly political character that the Habsburg political conglomerate never lost. The problem here, however, is that the Habsburg themselves did not use the term in its formal constitutional sense.

Before the Napoleonic Wars they ruled their own lands under the titles the latter carried with them, that is, as kings of Hungary and Bohemia, and dukes, counts, margraves and so on of the other lands they controlled. From the end of the Napoleonic Wars until 1867 they ruled as emperors of Austria. When that ended in 1867, the Habsburg monarch ruled one half of his lands as emperor of Austria, the other as king of Hungary. A workable title for this arrangement was never found, though two informal ones were and are still used widely: Dual Monarchy and Austria–Hungary. Both terms suggest the fundamental nature of government and administration in the final decades of Habsburg sovereignty; they appear frequently here when appropriate. They do not, however, describe the entity in central and east central Europe that the Habsburgs governed for the prior 341 years.

The easiest solution to the problem, though unfortunately without an easy English equivalent, is the current practice of referring to a Habsburg *imperium*. Close in meaning to the German *Reich*, it denotes the extent of lands and people over which legal and political sovereignty is held. In the opinion of the author, it gets at the reality of what the Habsburgs actually did in their holdings; readers will find it frequently in the text.

Introduction

T
he shot in the Bosnian capital of Sarajevo that killed Archduke Franz Ferdinand of the House of Habsburg-Lorraine-Este on 28 June 1914 set off a month of European backroom manoeuvring as ministers of state and military officials calculated their responses to the incident. When Sir Edward Grey, the British foreign minister, could not persuade his colleagues to continue negotiating, the conflict now called the First World War erupted. When it ended in 1918, the sprawling Habsburg *imperium*, to which the late archduke had been heir apparent and was representing ceremonially in Bosnia, was no more. Historians and journalists still muse on the disproportion between the deaths of two people in an obscure patch of Europe and the worldwide slaughter that followed.[1] But the vastness and depth of the conflict was fully matched by its territorial aftershock. Old states disappeared, new ones emerged. Out of the wreckage of Habsburg-governed Austria–Hungary came large components of European sovereignties known today as Austria, the Czech Republic, Italy, Hungary, Slovakia, Slovenia, Croatia, Romania, Ukraine and Poland.

Few observers in 1914 expected the Habsburg *imperium* to fall apart abjectly four years later. Some thought that, while its structure was in serious need of repair, it could be accomplished through prudent reform. Its virtual self-destruction was out of the question. The dynasty had factored prominently in the continent's political and diplomatic calculus since the fifteenth century and had shown hints of greatness long before. Throughout 600 years or so it had stood down venomous intra-dynastic quarrels, religious upheavals, significant military defeat, revolutions major and abortive, and history-changing shifts in social structure, cultural values and economic systems. Its continued record of sovereign longevity was paralleled by its one-time enemy, the Ottoman sultans, but unique among exclusively European dynasties. Their notorious knack for arranging marriages that opened up territorial inheritances helped. So did their facility in siring credibly legitimate heirs, even when reserves ran dangerously low in the seventeenth century and the first decades of the one that followed. The mighty branch of the family that ruled Spain and its overseas empire in the sixteenth and seventeenth centuries in fact died out altogether in 1700, the chief reason for its comparatively small presence in this book.[2] It was left to their Austrian, and generally far poorer, relatives to manage the family's lands and titles down to the bitter end.

Despite their long ties to the dynasty, many of its subjects cheered the dissolution of Austria–Hungary. Wartime hardship had tried many to breaking point; unresolved national and social grievances dominated the agendas of others. Others, however, brooded over the loss of predictably comfortable lives. However differently they related to the house that ruled them, the removal of the Habsburgs from the European political scene was a defining experience for them all. The same could be said of twentieth-century historians, a substantial number of whom made lifetime missions out of studying the disintegration of the empire and the circumstances that precipitated it. While criticism of this focus is now commonplace, particularly in debates over the role of nationalism and ethnicity in the process, both remain serious factors in the monarchy's history.[3]

Yet, judging the House of Habsburg (more correctly Habsburg-Lorraine from the eighteenth century) from the perspective of the First World War, its run-up and its immediate aftermath, bypasses the central question that its long history poses: how did the dynasty develop and hold together a messily diverse state – polyglot, multi-ethnic, eventually multi-confessional, and culturally parochial – as historical environments in which it ruled changed, sometimes dramatically so. This study proposes at least one part of the answer. Unbroken possession of traditional crowns and titles in Germany, later in Bohemia and Hungary, a process that began in the thirteenth century, certainly helped to legitimate Habsburg rule in times when such artefacts, along with brute force, were the only meaningful expressions of sovereign control. The House of Austria, as it came to be known in the fifteenth century, was not programmatically averse to forcing its government, its values and its faith on its subjects. Rebellious Czechs in the seventeenth century, Hungarians in the nineteenth, Protestants of all linguistic and ethnic backgrounds for roughly 250 years, learned a lesson that could not be forgotten.

But keeping patrimonies together through fear and deportations of outliers sapped treasuries of funds and reserves of public goodwill. The Habsburgs recognized very early that their political, military and fiscal fortunes in part depended on passive cooperation from their peoples, better yet their active respect and admiration. Public belief in the benevolence of their rulers and their appreciation of the general environment they shared with those below them also counted for much. What the dynasty targeted as 'public' was not always the same; some social classes and ethnic communities were occasionally far more supportive, sometimes more problematic, than others. But in all instances the challenge was the same: to associate the House of Habsburg with the changing material needs, values, customs and behaviours of those peoples without compromising the aura of sovereignty that made it one-of-a-kind in its polity. The dynasty's success in mastering this process was an intrinsic element in the story of its lengthy survival; its loss of that mastery parallels its decline.

In burnishing its claims to authority, the Habsburgs linked themselves suggestively to autonomous and quasi-autonomous icons of authority familiar and acceptable to their subjects. The Roman Catholic Church was called upon intensively, so was the military. Both institutions managed their affairs hierarchically, as did the Habsburg monarchy itself, even as its constitutional prerogatives were reduced somewhat in the latter half of the nineteenth century.

The effectiveness of this strategy hinged in turn on the capacity of the dynasty to project these associations as concretely and as widely as possible. It was, in effect, creating for itself a brand name recognized and respected by its peoples and foreign powers alike. The Habsburgs set to doing this very early and only slacked off after the monarchy disintegrated in 1918. The uses of ceremonial space and performance never went out of style; Franz Ferdinand, it is important to note, was killed carrying out one such appearance. The style and content of these affairs, however, changed considerably, as the cultural, political and social circumstances in the dynasty's *imperium* changed too. At first filled with references to religious imperatives and the awesome visual attributes of power, they later stressed the basic humanity of the dynasty, charged with a singular office but conscious of its responsibilities to all.[4] The house and its advisers also became adept at identifying and enlisting media available for the job, beginning with oral transmission in the late thirteenth century. Pictorial techniques, with their unique powers of psychic immediacy, were continually exploited. Statuary, sculpture, painting, engraving, decor, photography, road markers, building plaques and, by the twentieth century, film told viewers about the Habsburgs as rulers and, concomitantly, as human beings.[5] The services of leading architects, artists, composers and craftsmen were often called upon.

The printed word, in literature, high and low, was more difficult to harness: the monarchy never quite gave up on censorship, even when it modified its heavy-handed understanding of it in the second half of the nineteenth century. But the expansion of illustrated mass publication in the nineteenth century was as much a boon to the Habsburgs as a threat. Those who criticized the house in print and picture could be rebutted in print by writers and graphic artists with more favourable views of the House of Habsburg-Lorraine. The dynasty readily used hack pamphlet-eering to get that message across, especially to the modestly educated. It also found a fine writer here and there to convey its message to the liter-ate intellectual. Out of these relationships emerged an intricate interface of coldly instrumental political, economic and social considerations with high and popular culture that would make the House of Habsburg one of history's more memorable public presences, in Vienna first of all, but in more remote corners of the world even today. Musical life would be much the poorer, the offerings of art museums and galleries less compelling, and mass media less well developed without contributions that came from Vienna and the court that ruled it for centuries. Family chit-chat among generations of émigrés, willing and reluctant, would have been very different too.[6]

The coming apart of this long-standing interface, the focus of the final sections of the book, did not stifle aesthetic innovation and the dauntingly talented writers, artists and composers who laboured during Austria–Hungary's final decades. Gustav Klimt, Egon Schiele and Oscar Kokoschka were widely admired in their time. So were writers such as Hugo von Hofmannsthal, and the man for whom he created elegant opera libretti, Richard Strauss. Their counterparts could be found in Bohemia, Hungary, Polish Galicia and the south Slavic lands of the empire as well. Nevertheless, Habsburg perceptions of creative achieve-ment and its uses in the house narrative changed markedly throughout the reign of Franz Joseph. It will take more than this study to prove a straightforwardly causal relationship between so notable a shift and the collapse of the monarchy in the First World War. But as it forswore radical shifts in art and architectural styles, the dynasty was announcing that the distinctively modern had no place in its public self.

ONE

GETTING STARTED

Conventional Ambitions, Exceptional Results

Although functionally illiterate, Rudolph I of Habsburg (1218–1291) was one of medieval Europe's more notable achievers. In an age when land, titles and power were synonymous, he compiled an impressive list of territorial acquisitions and the crowns that went with them. He could not, however, let us know from first hand what he thought about his accomplishments, much less his opinions about his house.[1] Later genealogists linked the Habsburgs with the Merovingian rulers of France in the early Middle Ages. Politically convenient though it was, the claim was never conclusively proven. The roots of his house can be traced back only as far as the second half of the tenth century in southwestern Germany; its first territorial core was a region of the Upper Rhine between the Aare, Reuss and Limmat rivers. Rudolph's ancestors had gradually enlarged these territories by serving as protectors (*Vogt*) of several local religious houses, which were often major landholders. Among them was Muri, a large and increasingly well-endowed Benedictine foundation. Subsequent territorial acquisitions in Swabia, today part of the Federal Republic of Germany, further strengthened Habsburg influence in the region.

As count of Alsace, Rudolph became German king and emperor-in-waiting in 1273. Nine years later he enfeoffed his family with the Austrian lands; from this base his house would eventually rule a substantial portion of central and east-central Europe. These achievements, along with the carefully calculated public presence that he developed to impress himself and his family on their new lands, even his style of faith, would become lasting parts of the Habsburg dynastic template. So would some of his less appealing qualities, such as the cold-blooded opportunism that was especially conspicuous when he made use of all the major powers that new titles gave him. He disregarded treaties and other compacts with his fellow princes to advance his goals. He desecrated the corpse of at least one enemy, King Otakar II of Bohemia. Like several of his successors, he made problematic decisions; at least one of them would haunt his successors for centuries. Nevertheless, enlarging his territorial base and securing it was his lifelong concern; while he was always ready to trim his ambitions to fit the circumstance, on the battlefield and in negotiating, he also retreated to his original agenda, pursuing those goals as soon as he could.

His behaviour, however, was more like that of any number of contemporary German princes than a man on a quest for pre-eminent distinction. He was a German prince and behaved accordingly. Like several of his counterparts, he had used the power vacuum created by the death of the Hohenstaufen Emperor Frederick II in 1250. Earlier Habsburgs had sometimes allied themselves with Hohenstaufen rulers; Rudolph maintained good relations with the dynasty's remnants when they supported his territorial claims and thwarted common enemies. In fact, he took his allies wherever he found them: between 1261 and 1263, for example, he cooperated with the burghers of Strasbourg, who made him commander of their forces in a war against their bishop.

It was, however, Rudolph's administration of his own lands that turned him into one of the more significant territorial princes in the Upper Rhine valley. His reputation for guaranteeing safe passage for travellers through his lands impressed even the important. On a trip through the Habsburg holdings as early as 1260, Werner von Eppstein, Archbishop of Mainz and one of the imperial electors who chose the German king, commended the security that Rudolph had brought to the region. The clergyman became one of the count's most active supporters for the German kingship, an office that conferred regional, even European status, on the Habsburg almost overnight. Should he win election, Rudolph would be in line for crowning as Holy Roman Emperor by the Pope, although whoever held the latter office sometimes refused the candidate. His regional bargaining powers also improved. Strategic marriages with local families in adjacent realms, particularly Hungary and Bohemia, showed him eager to cultivate relations on a more regional level as well.[2]

The Germans who made him their king spoke for some of the medieval Empire's more significant principalities. They, along with Rudolph himself, had improved their territorial positions in the feuding that bedevilled the imperial interregnum. At the same time, however, they had learned that picking the most hapless and distant suzerain they could find (between 1252 and 1273 Richard of Cornwall and Alfonso X of

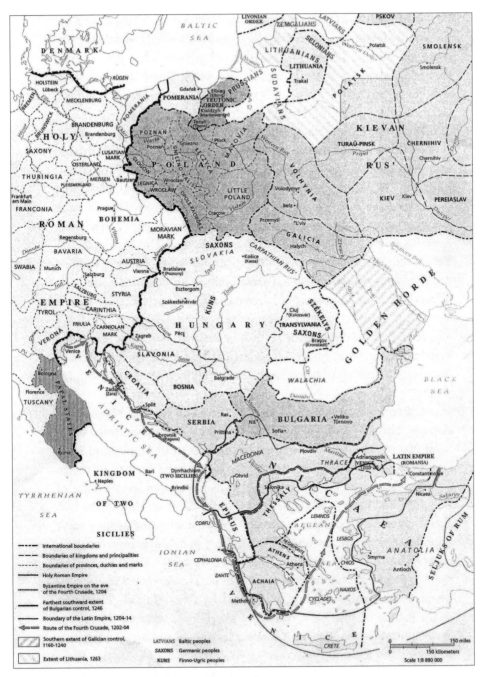

Central Europe, *c.* 1250.

Castile had held the German crown) was the worst way of protecting the holdings of anyone in Germany. The treasuries of even the richest principalities could pay a heavy price. Years of lawlessness had undermined their king's power to defend Germany as a whole. Some lands on which only the crown could charge tolls were now under the control of local German rulers; others had been completely alienated to foreigners.

The Empire desperately needed a suzerain who would recapture some of the fiefs once attached to the German crown and used to finance military undertakings. Deferring to the prerogatives of those who chose him would be useful too. Based on these considerations, Rudolph fitted the imperial German bill of particulars nicely. Aside from his reputation as a pacifier, he was too short of cash at his election to threaten anyone. Even his physical appearance was counter-heroic. The best image we have of him is from a grave plate in Speyer Cathedral: a 'massive aquiline nose' (*magno aquilino naso . . . insignitus*) as an otherwise admiring fifteenth-century historian put it, overwhelms a dourly angular face. It bespeaks a man for whom plodding sobriety was a habit of mind and character. The carver, whether or not he knew it, had chipped out the first known realistic image of a German king or emperor, perhaps because the bearing of his subject was so tightly intertwined with his character.[3]

Rudolph's election as German king surprised some of his contemporaries. He had faced stiff and well-financed competition for the office from two of Europe's wealthiest rulers: Philip III of France and King Otakar II of Bohemia. The latter, who announced his candidacy in January 1273, was by far the more plausible contender. As king of Bohemia, and a very influential vassal of the German Empire, he was also an elector. His realm stood on one of medieval Europe's most important trade routes; revenue spun off from trade and commerce along the way flowed into his treasury. The Bohemian crown also had regalian rights to some of the more productive veins of precious metals on the continent. Otakar made no secret of his assorted riches. Publicly acclaimed as the 'Golden King', he spread gold jewellery, coins and decorative projects around his realm; he also spent lavishly on art, architecture and contemporary learning.[4]

Otakar's territorial plans were correspondingly lofty. As a nineteen-year-old in 1252, he married Margaret of Babenberg, the last legitimate claimant to lands in today's Austria that her family had ruled from 975 to 1246. The unfortunate lady was twice the age of her flamboyant royal husband; siring heirs presumptive did not seem uppermost in his mind.

More to the point was a provision in the *Privilegium minus*, granted to the Babenbergs in 1156 by the Hohenstaufen Emperor Frederick I Barbarossa, that gave the family extensive jurisdictional powers in their Austrian holdings; it also allowed them to observe female succession. Otakar clearly saw his union with Margaret as a way of acquiring the Babenberg inheritance, and he moved quickly. In 1254 he made himself the territorial overlord of the Austrian lands, though most of Styria, to the southeast, was under the sway of King Béla IV of Hungary. By 1261, however, that region had also fallen to the Bohemian monarch, who was now in control of the entire province. Having extracted what he wanted from his relationship with Margaret, he had the marriage annulled on the ground of childlessness. He then married a younger princess, Kunigunde, a granddaughter of Béla IV. His designs received serious reinforcement in 1262 from Richard of Cornwall who, along with enfeoffing Otakar with Bohemia and the margravate of Moravia, also granted him the Austrian inheritance of his first wife.[5]

Otakar and Philip, however, were gravely mistaken in counting on papal support for their campaigns to win the German crown. Rudolph had pushed his candidacy locally, persistently and astutely. He had been very solicitous of the German princes and the welfare of the Empire as a whole. Not only had he a record of subduing disorder and outright criminality, he also formally promised to cancel many unauthorized tolls. Concessions were possible, too. He apparently agreed to forego further alienation of crown properties without consulting Germany's territorial rulers. He would also try to reconvert some of these into revenue-producing assets of the German crown. What territorial rulers themselves had taken over the preceding twenty years or so was not to be touched.[6]

The only exception to this last provision was King Otakar of Bohemia. With a firm economic and territorial base in his kingdom and in parts of the former Babenberg inheritance, Otakar had become worrisome for territorial rulers in central Europe generally. Indeed, the bourgeoisie of Vienna had adjusted to his rule quite comfortably. A small but influential cohort of citizens was now exploiting economic privileges that their Czech territorial overlord had extended to them in return for permission to raise troops in the city to fight the Hungarians. The city's middle class would stubbornly support him as long as they could. Otakar's contributions to the built environment in other areas of eastern Austria had also been quick and impressive. Fortification projects and his munificent underwriting of ecclesiastical construction and renovation invigorated not only economic activity in the region, but its cultural life. Religious foundations and churches, especially around Krems, incorporated Gothic and late Romanesque features that Otakar brought with him from Bohemia and Moravia.[7]

Energy, money and relentless determination had won Otakar territorial prominence in central and east-central Europe. He did not, however, know when to stop. Rejecting Rudolph's election as German king, he refused to renew his oath of fealty as an imperial vassal to his suzerain. Rudolph and the German princes retaliated by dismissing Otakar's claims in Austria. In 1274 Germany's territorial princes empowered their new king to reverse territorial changes in the Empire that had taken place after 1245. Loss of the Austrian lands would substantially weaken the king of Bohemia's influence in the region. Just as alarming for Otakar was leaving disposition of the erstwhile Babenberg inheritance to a king who might become an emperor.[8]

Otakar had overstepped himself in other quarters of central Europe as well. Béla IV of Hungary was eager to cut him down to size. Growing numbers of nobles in the Austrian lands were taking exception to his autocratic style of rule. While the Bohemian king had shared some authority with them at the outset of his reign, he did not intend to continue the arrangement indefinitely. By 1270 he had not only reversed these concessions, but imported officials from Bohemia to enforce his will. The Austrian territorial nobility therefore also welcomed the idea of Rudolph's election as German king, whose theoretical powers made it possible to discipline vassals, Otakar included.[9]

Rudolph exploited all of these anxieties. In 1275 he placed the imperial ban on Otakar for withholding his declaration of loyalty. The elector and king of Bohemia was now an official outlaw in central Europe, legally liable for punishment from his peers and superiors.[10] Open war with the dissident monarch soon followed in 1276, and the German princes charged King Rudolph with leading their side. A treaty in November brought hostilities temporarily to a halt. Otakar had to abandon much of the Babenberg inheritance in Austria to his rival, though the loyalties of Vienna's burghers remained ambivalent. Otakar agreed to accept enfeoffment with Bohemia and Moravia; in return he pledged loyalty to the emperor. The formal ceremony, in which both men performed their ritual duties, was quiet. Nevertheless, the aesthetic subtext of the affair, at least in the eyes of subsequent generations, added up to a public humiliation of the Bohemian monarch. Regaled in all his splendour, the king of Bohemia kneeled before his suzerain. As befitted

1 'The Slaying of Otakar II of Bohemia', from Johann Jakob Fugger and Sigmund von Birken, *Spiegel des Erzhauses Österreich . . .* (1668).

great rulers in history, Rudolph sat, but on a nondescript camp stool. His garb was equally plain; a common leather jerkin was its dominant feature. The message of the contrast was obvious: a wholly modest man had vanquished another who was richer by far but beaten.

Rudolph did not rely on atmospherics alone to complete the job. For that, Otakar had to be thoroughly crushed. Fiscal problems, combined with anxiety among some of the German princes about the extent of their elected king's ambitions, kept Rudolph from acting immediately. In 1278, however, he moved against Otakar again. The showdown between the two men took place on the plains of Lower Austria around Krems on 26 August 1278. Rudolph, who was about 60 years old at the time, entered combat on horseback as befitted contemporary standards of knighthood. He also came close to being killed. His most effective tactic, however, fell so short of ideal gallantry that some observers criticized him for it. Military leaders were expected to disclose the size of their fighting force before combat began. Rudolph kept his reserves hidden until Otakar's troops had weakened to the point where they could be defeated decisively by forces the Habsburg still could bring out. Worse yet, Otakar was not taken hostage but killed by Rudolph's followers without explicit orders from their king (illus. 1). The Habsburg also used his opponent's body to send a crude political message: the embalmed corpse was on display in Vienna for two weeks, long enough for residents who had sided with the king of Bohemia until the end to rethink their political loyalties.[11]

At least some princes had supported Rudolph solidly; Otakar's flawed battlefield tactics worked to Habsburg advantage too. Imperial troops reportedly cried 'Rome, Rome, Christ, Christ!' as they plunged into battle, perhaps encouraging divine favour to assist so pedestrian a king. At the same time, however, some German princes suspected that their new king was already envisioning himself as a prospective emperor rather than a German ruler.[12] If they were right to think that Rudolph was using his conflict with Otakar to ingratiate himself with the papacy, the Habsburg failed badly. The several short-term popes who held the office throughout the last decade or so of his career as king were not hostile to him. Nevertheless, signals between Rome and Germany often got crossed, and the Habsburg never did hold secular Roman Christendom's highest office.

Rudolph fared much better locally. In the autumn of 1278 he concluded a peace with Queen Kunigunde in Bohemia that met all standards of chivalric rectitude and then some. Otakar's widow and her family were left with the Bohemian crown lands on the condition that they would continue as fiefs of the Empire. She was permitted to retain Margrave Otto of Brandenburg, one of Otakar's German supporters, as guardian to Prince Václav, her son and the Bohemian heir apparent. Successive Bohemian kings, however, had to abandon claims to the Austrian lands. Strategic dynastic marriages, a policy for which the Habsburgs would become famous, sealed this arrangement and several more. With nine children, six of them females, Rudolph had a lot to work with. One daughter would wed the Bohemian heir apparent, another would be the wife of the troublesome Margrave Otto, a third would eventually become the bride of Charles 1 of Hungary. A son, also Rudolph, had another Bohemian princess as a consort.[13]

The Austrian Patrimony

As German king, Rudolph I also had a power that gave his family a firm patrimonial stake in the affairs of central Europe: he could grant vassals vacant lands throughout the Empire. In 1282 he bestowed the erstwhile Babenberg inheritance in the Austrian territories on his two living sons, Albert and Rudolph. Though Habsburg exploitation of the royal office for dynastic gain would prompt centuries of criticism in Germany, it would be crucial to the rise of his house.[14] The *Privilegium minus*, which had raised the Austrian lands to ducal status in 1156, allowed their ruler to govern them under local law codes alone. Only he could permit the introduction of extraterritorial practices. The duke's sole military obligation to his king, and sometimes emperor, was to defend his Austrian borders. Succession could pass in both the male and female lines. Should no legitimate heirs be available, the Austrian duke could name someone to follow him. We know these arrangements only from copies, though there are contemporary references to it. But regardless of their formal status, the provisions of the *Minus* would be central to the political evolution of the Austrian holdings, freeing them and their rulers from claims of territorial potentates in Germany and elsewhere. It also helped to detach the Austrian lands from the fiscal and jurisdictional claims of church institutions such as monasteries and bishoprics beyond the former Babenberg holdings as well.

Though not as economically advanced as many regions in western Europe, the Babenberg territorial complex had moved ahead markedly in the twelfth century and most of the thirteenth. Around 1,000 vast parts of the terrain were either completely unsettled or only marginally so. At the moment when King Rudolph bestowed it on his sons, around 500,000 people lived in Austria below and above the Enns river, with another 400,000 distributed over Styria, Carinthia and Carniola. The sole urban settlement, however, was Vienna with between 10,000 and 20,000 people. About a thousand houses crowded upon one another inside the walls that once encircled the modern city's First District. Trade and commerce, however, had become very lively, as had handicraft production. Encouraged by subsidies from the last Babenbergs, the city was also a Danubian commercial centre for both local and extraterritorial enterprise. Merchants from Regensburg upriver, who had won stapling privileges from the dukes of Austria in 1221, were especially active.

Rural folk, however, were not as well off. Though not broadly impoverished, their living standards had declined considerably by the end of the thirteenth century. With the shift to a money economy well under way, the extended fertile plains of eastern Austria were increasingly turned over to grain cultivation of scale. Peasants paid both rents in kind and in coinage to landlords who carried secular titles such as margrave, count and *Vogt*, along with bishops and abbots of cloistered foundations. Until around 1250 landlords had competed for agricultural workers. As populations grew, however, the cost of labour went down and so did living standards. Such conditions were bad news for princes who needed more resources. But the greatest constraint on Habsburg ambition in the dynasty's Austrian patrimony was the system of provincial estates then taking shape. These were deliberative and consultative gatherings of nobles, knights, clerical officials and cities, who met with the territorial ruler when he came to the region and whose wealth was crucial for maintaining defence, commerce and general security in his, or her, lands.

Such people were largely preoccupied with provincial affairs; loyalty to their regnant territorial ruler was correspondingly conditional. They released revenues for military expeditions only when they had to, especially when fighting took place in foreign parts. By the beginning of the thirteenth century they had gained the right to pick their duke in the event he should die without a male heir. It was this very prerogative that justified inviting Otakar of Bohemia to govern the Babenberg patrimony in 1251. It was that same nobility who found the king not to their liking and supported Rudolph's campaign against him in 1278. But the estates had already put a price on their aid, which Rudolph had no choice but to pay. Two years earlier, Rudolph had permitted Austrian noble landlords to fortify castles on their own properties. He had also made it easier for them to bring runaway peasants back to their lands. They could have some input into the use of ducal regalian assets. He also revived a consultative council, dominated by the territorial nobility, that would be the bane of his immediate successors. Thus for all the territorial significance that the Habsburgs now had as dukes in Austria, their provincial estates won concessions that would enable them to remain administratively, juridically and politically autonomous for centuries to come.[15]

Rudolph 1 as Seen by Others

For all these limitations, Rudolph 1 had come a long way thanks to battlefield victory, canny tenacity and sheer good fortune. Legitimating the exclusive hold of one house on a crown, whether hereditary or elective, as was customary in Germany, Hungary, Poland and Bohemia, often called for raw force. More often than not, however, dynasties preferred the somewhat less expensive route followed by Rudolph I in his new Austrian holdings: negotiating their way through local custom into power and negotiating some more to hold on to it. The longer a single house ruled, the more public inertia validated its claims. A story that effectively reinforced the right of one family to rule until it ran out of plausible candidates was crucial, especially when audiences were made up of subjects from all classes of society who were taxed to support such regimes. Established narrative also firmed up solidarity within ruling houses in which disputes over inheritances and matters of policy were routine.

Visual artifices offered ideas about rulers most economically before general literacy made texts accessible to wide audiences. Some of these images were the only way that people would come to know their sovereign as a person.[16] Like most ruling houses, however, the Habsburgs avidly promoted early tales about themselves, along with the illustrative materials that drove these points home. Indeed, they clung to them in some form or other even when the scientific empiricism of modern scholarship forced the house and its propagandists to use legend more cautiously than they had in earlier times.[17]

Despite being an unschooled beginner, Rudolph I was strikingly adept at the job. Indeed, beneath his unprepossessing demeanour was a sharp awareness of the political advantages, both in Germany and Austria, that a positive public image conferred. He clearly understood how to airbrush his own moral lapses. Duplicitous as he had been in 1278, when he kept secret his reserves in battle with King Otakar, he offset the treachery with his notably generous treatment of the widowed Queen Kunigunde. The gesture provided enduring material for a particularly tenacious dynastic legend build around the so-called *clementia habsburgica*, Habsburg magnanimity, a spirit of generosity peculiar to the house.

Rudolph also diligently cultivated his role as a humble man bringing down a dangerously arrogant one, in this case, Otakar II of Bohemia. The message went across particularly well among common people; it also impressed more literate folk, who were very surprised by the humiliating end of the famously wealthy Bohemian monarch at the hands of the impecunious German king. Poets and chroniclers of the time folded the story into their work. In distant England, King Edward I commented on the episode. It proved, moreover, to have staying power. Three of Europe's most gifted writers, beginning with Dante, Rudolph's near contemporary,

2 'Rudolph 1 of Habsburg, the Priest, and the Host', from Johann Jakob Fugger and Sigmund von Birken, *Spiegel des Erzhauses Österreich . . .* (1668).

then the Spaniard Lope da Vega at the end of the sixteenth century, and down to the Austrian dramatist Franz Grillparzer in 1825, incorporated Otakar and Rudolph into some of their work.[18]

The asymmetry of the protagonists, both in manner and material resources, gave the Otakar–Rudolph confrontation its dramatic power. The story also taught a Christian lesson: the inevitable victory of humility, in the form of the Habsburg, over sinful pride represented by the king of Bohemia. No advanced training was needed for European audiences to understand the point in the thirteenth century. But Rudolph was also ready to configure himself and his modest ways at a more intricate theological level. For this he co-opted a legend that seems to have appeared first in medieval Swiss cantons about a chance meeting in 1264 of the

Count of Habsburg and a priest bearing the sacred Host to a dying Christian in need of Last Rites. Rudolph, allegedly out hunting, dismounted from his horse and gave it to the priest to continue his journey (illus. 2). An apparition of the Host then appeared to the Habsburg. When the cleric tried to return the steed the next day, Rudolph would not take it, calling himself unworthy of riding a creature that had borne the body and blood of the Christ. For his part, the priest prophesied that the Habsburgs were destined to govern the world. He also may have taken some practical action to move his forecast along: indeed, with access to the Archbishop of Mainz, he may have urged the latter to promote the Habsburg's candidacy for the German crown in 1273. The story would far outdistance the lessons of the Rudolph–Otakar stand-off in staying power. Friedrich Schiller, perhaps the German language's greatest dramatic poet, moved the theme from a Swiss chronicle into a ballad that was frequently used in school texts; in 1804 a prose version of the story came out in the Austrian lands. Until its monarchy collapsed in 1918, the House of Habsburg and its advocates would use the tale to prove that some force beyond the dynasty itself had chosen it for its position.[19]

Rudolph's more authentic personality also had elements that made it easy to develop an attractive storyline about him. He had a keen sense of humour and a knack for conversing with noble and commoner alike. Around 50 anecdotes about him were in circulation even in his time; several, largely from his years in southwestern Germany, are out and about even today. That most of them lacked a factual base left his contemporaries unfazed. Yet, from what we do know, he seems to have been popular among all the social ranks of his time, especially among ordinary folk. A man in Zurich, for example, cornered him to spill out the woes of his unhappy marriage. As German king, Rudolph was dumbfounded, yet pleased, to learn that a tanner with whom he had taken board and lodging, made enough money in so filthy a job to support an attractive wife.[20]

Rudolph I's notorious modesty – seconded even by his enemies – suggested that he was a model of virtue, especially when his contemporaries compared him with the vainglorious Otakar of Bohemia. Such characterizations and descriptions of the Habsburg's reign in Germany, while he lived and after his death in 1291, frequently came from writers in the Empire's urban centres. The multiplier effect of city environments was considerable, especially when Rudolph enlisted mendicant friars (the Dominicans and, especially, the Franciscans) to help spread his image to literate and illiterate alike. With their mission of ministering to swelling numbers of the urban poor throughout Europe, both orders had access to large audiences that fit Rudolph's designs very well. Franciscans continued to figure prominently in the narrative of Rudolph's career and in the work to publicize it. At the beginning of the fourteenth century a Franciscan monastic chronicler praised the Habsburg for his support and predicted that a reign of peace would follow; he also claimed that a Franciscan lector in Rudolph's camp at the Battle of the Marchfeld in 1278 had spurred the king on in his battle against Otakar, thereby making a friar at least partially responsible for the victory. It was also a Franciscan who developed the legend of Rudolph, the priest and the Host, along with the exemplary piety of the first Habsburg German Emperor.[21]

Poets outside formal clerical circles were somewhat more divided about the first Habsburg German king; some echoed the Franciscan who thought that Rudolph could bring peace to Germany, others wrote him off as just another ambitious and untrustworthy prince and a pinchpenny to boot. Some deemed him knightly, but others saw him as a deal-maker with little taste for valorous combat. Nevertheless, news of his virtues spread quickly to Austrian chroniclers in Styria and urban settlements throughout the new Habsburg patrimony. Rudolph the pious, Rudolph the politically prudent and Rudolph the man of the people would have by far the greater staying power among historians generally through to the nineteenth century and even the twentieth.[22]

Rudolph's efforts to legitimate Habsburg rule both in Germany and the Austrian lands made use of more formal, if equally legendary, media too. While his humbler subjects probably did not give much thought to his ancestry, fellow rulers did. Persistent lineage in a principality or kingdom enhanced a dynasty's proprietary claims to it. With far more ambition than data at their command, Rudolph and his genealogists sought historical figures near and far who qualified as an impressive ancestor. The more remote the progenitor, the more lush the family tree appeared. Egyptians, biblical heroes, Romans, Trojans – a nod to the allegedly Trojan origins of the Franks – and the Franks themselves, all had done something that substantiated the most recent member of the line, King Rudolph I. Several of these constructions were familiar to Rudolph's contemporaries; they continued to have a place in Habsburg dynastic history, including the version studied by its offspring, into the beginning of the eighteenth century.[23] Indeed, decorative genealogies testify even today to the legitimacy of Habsburg lineage (see cover image).

Rudolph I unquestionably added a charismatic dimension into his bland public character. Nevertheless, his policies, as opposed to their results, did not rise above the ordinary. He was not the only German prince of his time with territorial ambitions, nor the only one to call upon some aspect of the religious culture in which all were embedded to shore up his hold on various titles. What was unusual in his case was his success in realizing these goals and conjuring up the aura of personal devoutness that identified his house to this day. He also understood the importance of retaining the cooperation of religious institutions and their representatives, from the popes down to simple friars, begging their way along the roads and lanes in the Austrian lands. Crucial to these achievements had been Rudolph's readiness to take advantage of all promising opportunities, even when he did not have the resources to govern or defend what fortune brought him. He also adjusted quickly to circumstances. He fostered productive relations with realms on his borders through marriage and succession agreements that promised a long Habsburg presence in central Europe. His ascetic private modesty was passed on to many of his heirs as well. The most successful of them found it personally congenial; even more of them found it quite useful in ingratiating themselves with publics that tired of the increasingly sumptuous lifestyles of European rulers as the centuries passed. Not every Habsburg ruler did all of these things, but all of them adopted some or even most of these traits at some point in their careers. In short, Rudolph created a basic template of behaviour for his house that guided its behaviour and public demeanour until the empire came to an end in 1918.

Dynastic Dreams, Dynastic Realities

Rudolph's readiness to compromise, even with those who resisted his whole agenda, paved the way to his acceptance in Austria and neighbouring territories. In at least one instance, however, his flexibility led him into an agreement that turned out to be wholly at odds with his hopes to leave his house with a solid territorial footing. Austrian regional notables much resented his attempt to introduce in his new holdings dynastic testamentary procedures common to his southwestern holdings in the Empire. His grant in 1282 of the Austrian lands, along with Styria and Carniola, to his sons Albert and Rudolph required them to administer their holdings jointly (*zur gesammten Hand*). The practice, in effect, gave males of the same generation equal rights to the lands they inherited from their father. It was not customary in Austrian territories, where nobles vigorously opposed it. Rudolph yielded to their pressures once more by accepting local practice. Spelled out in the Compact of Rheinfeld of 1283, it mandated a form of enfeoffing the eldest son in the house with all of the Austrian patrimony. Theoretically, this would pass down undivided to subsequent senior males born to the line until it expired.[24]

Thus, when Rudolph I died in 1291, his sole heir in the Austrian lands was Duke Albert, who became German King Albert I in 1298. The son shared some of his father's defects, and even outdid them externally. Rudolph was uncommonly homely; Albert was grotesque. Thinking that he had been poisoned, he once had himself hung upside down so that toxic materials would run from his nose and mouth. The therapy was standard for the time, but turned out perversely for him: the rush of blood to the head destroyed an eye, fixing his face into the permanent scowl that would glower from a stained-glass window in St Stephen's Cathedral in Vienna. Like his father, he had ambitions of scale. He hoped to use Germany and Austria as a jumping off point for expansion to the west, south and north of Europe; he briefly installed one of his sons, Duke Rudolph III, as king of Bohemia and married a second, Duke Frederick, to Elizabeth of Aragon. One daughter became the wife of Andreas III of Hungary. Unlike Rudolph I, however, he understood that acquiring land was only a first step to status and power; managing them effectively was equally important. Albert was therefore much concerned to put together a functional administrative apparatus for the Habsburg patrimony. Beloved, however, he was not. His governing style corresponded to his intimidating appearance. Unlike his patient father, he was quick to discipline nobles and city dwellers who disagreed with him.

Nevertheless, it was not dissident subjects but the advantaged position assigned to Albert and his male progeny in the Compact of Rheinfeld that cost him his life. Austrians put off by the intrusion of Swabian custom had been satisfied with the measure. Junior Habsburg males disagreed sharply. Albert I's brother, Duke Rudolph III, was to have been indemnified for acknowledging his brother's pre-eminence; he died, however, in 1290, a year before his father. Johann, Rudolph's posthumous son, believed all his life that his branch of the house had been under-compensated for its sacrifice, indeed even cheated. Albert refused to commit himself, frustrating his nephew even more. In 1308 Johann murdered his uncle, leaving him to go down in the history of his house as Johann Parricida, the Uncle-Slayer. He quickly fled Austria, surfaced in Pisa in 1312 and then disappeared altogether. How he died is not known.[25] In 1309, however, a new German emperor, Henry VII, restored partible inheritance in the House of Habsburg. This, too, would prove to be problematic for a house intent on building its territorial influence.

Before further inheritance troubles arose, however, the Habsburgs did take lasting steps to impress themselves and their rule on the Austrian lands. Albert's immediate successor in the Austrian lands was his eldest, but ineffectual, surviving son, Frederick I. His lone distinction as German king was to serve in a contested co-regency with Duke Louis of Bavaria after the death of Henry VII. But Frederick's brother, Duke Albert II, who took over the dynasty's holdings after the elder Habsburg died in 1330, was arguably the most successful of all the late medieval rulers in the Austrian lands. Crippling arthritis in his extremities, which beset him about the time he took over his patrimony, may have forced him to concentrate on developing the lands that he had rather than pursuing ambitions abroad, such as recapturing the imperial crown for his house. He worked to improve the fiscal condition of the Habsburg treasuries along the lines that the Babenbergs had earlier set down: expanding economic activity in towns, firming up control of the revenues controlled by territorial rulers, and further centralizing Habsburg government of its Austrian patrimony in Vienna by creating a single administrative chancellery there. Like his grandfather Rudolph I, however, Albert II carefully avoided challenging noble jurisdictional and administrative prerogatives unless he had to.

He also, however, had some sense of how to ingratiate himself locally without yielding actual power. Where advisable, he shed his dignity to please an audience. A new duke in Carinthia had to appear in rural garb, leading a steer with one hand and a horse with the other. He would then ask a peasant for the right to rule the territory. Albert II complied, as did yet another younger brother, Duke Otto. And perhaps most pleasing of all to Austrian sensibilities, he used revenues raised in the Habsburg central European patrimony for building projects close to home rather than redirecting them to the dynasty's western holdings. He was especially active in founding churches and monastic houses. A major outcome of the policy was to further the 'Austrianization' policies of his Swabian family. Contemporary chroniclers complained less and less about the Habsburgs' 'foreign' origins. For its part, the dynasty increasingly described the rule of its German domains as 'rule in Austria'.[26]

But territorial princes were routine in German central Europe, even those with the considerable privileges extended to the Babenbergs and, by extension, the Habsburgs in the *Privilegium minus*. Rudolph I and Albert I had been emperors; the dynasty's counterparts in neighbouring

Hungary and Bohemia were kings. Their basic Austrian patrimony was squarely in the centre of Europe, a position suggesting that Habsburgs should have a more significant role in continental affairs. Rudolph I's heirs had yet to establish a compelling basis for arrogating to themselves a more active presence in continental affairs. Daring and imagination were required to create an institutional and cultural structure to announce that the one-time Swabian counts had come to stay in central Europe and deserved a voice among its greater monarchs; Habsburgs normally lacked both qualities.

Albert II left his treasury in unusually good shape. Not one to count on inheritances or negotiations with local estates to fund his government, he had increased his revenues from sources old and new. Ducal revenues in medieval Austria came largely from use taxes: tolls, customs duties, regalian rights in mines, coinage, market privileges, safe-conducts and the like. He collected those vigilantly. He rigorously enforced long-standing sumptuary taxes on Jews whom he took under his protection in return for payment, a privilege that Emperor Louis the Bavarian had granted in 1331 to the territorial rulers in the Empire. He protected the products of his lands, excluding foreign wines, for example, from markets in the Habsburg holdings.

He also left an imaginative eldest son, Duke Rudolph IV, to make use of it. Known somewhat misleadingly as Rudolph the Founder (*Stifter*) – he wanted cathedral status for St Stephen's church in Vienna after 1359, but did not lay its first cornerstone – Rudolph was what most of his ancestors and successors were not: a visionary. Even discounting the early onset of adulthood in societies where lifespans were comparatively brief, he was precocious. He became territorial overlord of Austria in 1358 at the age of nineteen. Education and marriage to the daughter of one of Europe's most spectacularly hyperactive monarchs of the day, Charles I of Bohemia (also Emperor Charles IV in Germany), encouraged his hectic scheming. Charles had persuaded his son-in-law that he had a mission to fulfil and that his house was uniquely fit to realize it. It was, however, more or less up to Rudolph to figure out what this was. He pursued the task fiercely.

As son-in-law to Charles IV, he may have viewed himself as the latter's heir apparent in both Bohemia and the Empire. Nevertheless, he seems to have believed that such goals would be reached through elaborating on the policies of his ancestors. He reinforced the Christian identification of his house abundantly, adding to the personal touch once given it by Rudolph I. On his orders, the tower room of the Vienna

Hofburg and the adjacent chambers where he grew up became a sanctu-
ary dedicated to central articles of Christian belief: the Trinity, the body
and blood of Christ and, for good measure, all the saints. He also
extended the Habsburg patrimonial core, most notably to the Tyrol,
where the dukes of Bavaria renounced claims in 1369. Rudolph cast his
eyes eastward as well. He renewed pacts of mutual succession with King
Louis of Hungary in 1362, and with his Bohemian father-in-law two
years later.[27]

Rudolph IV's regime coincided with two natural cataclysms that
afflicted fourteenth-century Europe: climate cooling and the Black
Death. The first shortened growing seasons and made famine a routine
experience; the second killed in appalling numbers. Between 1350 and
1450 the continent lost roughly one-fifth of its inhabitants. More thickly
settled areas were especially vulnerable. The eastern Austrian lands
would never repopulate themselves in the fifteenth and sixteenth
centuries as fully as did western Europe, challenged by man-made
destruction at the hands of Ottoman raiders and armies dispatched from
Constantinople.

The economic effect of these developments in the Austrian lands all
but forced Rudolph into continuing the fiscal activism of his father.
Indeed, if the generality of his subjects had yet to realize that the Habsburgs
were sufficiently identified with their patrimony to use it as their fiscal
base, he made it amply clear. He banned coin clipping, a practice that his predecessors had let pass, however much it debased their currencies. Other
steps were more imaginative, even radical. Clerical establishments and
local nobles enjoyed wide property rights within urbanized settlements;
they drew substantial incomes from mortgages, even supermortgages,
created on the value of these assets. Rudolph demanded that owners
redeem such instruments, thereby opening up the land beneath them for
sale and development. Such holdings were also now easier to tax directly.
He also broadened the social base from which he appointed the managers
of the programme. In Vienna, the mayor and the city council administered
it. To attract larger numbers of skilled artisans, he tried to curb local guild
restrictions on labour and production that limited work opportunities for
foreigners. Vienna's municipal council was once again called upon, this
time to supervise the protective regulations that local craftsmen enjoyed.
Though the Habsburg residential city was especially affected by such
measures, towns in other Austrian lands felt their impact too.

With epidemic raging all around him, Rudolph also realized that
public health, human productivity and ducal prosperity were reciprocally

linked. He endorsed an order regulating animal slaughter and disposal of the remains. The common man was also a consideration; in order to work effectively, he had to eat. Rudolph empowered the city council to set the price of meat. Predictably enough, none of his economic policies would be quite adequate to his expenditures; he worked his way through the resources that his father had left him and then some. Like Habsburgs before and after him, he borrowed against properties he owned and those attached to ducal office as collateral. Nevertheless, he taught his subjects a lesson that not all of them appreciated, in his own day and for centuries to come: Habsburg rule was of an order that traditional ducal revenues could not sustain; if the family's power were to survive, all of its subjects had to support it materially.[28]

Rudolph iv was also keenly aware that the pre-eminence of his house, domestically and abroad, depended not only on the size and centrality of the lands he controlled, but on his exclusive authority over them. Keeping a tight rein on all who compromised the latter was among his highest priorities, even when it involved rolling back the Church's territorial rights to lands in Austria. Rudolph attacked the problem on two fronts. The bishop who supervised ecclesiastical affairs in much of the Habsburg patrimony had his seat in Passau; his immediate secular suzerain was the emperor and not the Babenberg or Habsburg dukes. Rudolph proposed raising Vienna to a bishopric, with the church of St Stephen as its cathedral. Ultimate supervision of such an establishment would remain in Rome, but a local bishop was more likely to respect a territorial ruler's wishes.

Rudolph's second ploy was more delicate. A homegrown patron saint would confer greater prestige on religious practice in the Austrian Habsburg patrimony, especially if the candidate was a native territorial ruler. Realizing that his subjects, especially noble ones, had often been at odds with his immediate Habsburg predecessors, Rudolph iv turned to the medieval Babenbergs for acceptable nominees. He settled on Margrave Leopold iii, a famously pious figure from the end of the eleventh century who had already become a cult figure at the monastery of Klosterneuburg, not far from Vienna. Johanna of Pfirt, Rudolph iv's mother, was an especially active devotee. The duke called upon Pope Innocent vi to canonize Leopold. Innocent, who had his own political reasons for cooperating, was receptive; in 1357 he ordered a commission to begin investigating the matter, a process that often took decades to complete. Rudolph had no choice but to wait. In the meantime, however, he turned to focusing popular attention on canonized saints who were closely associated with his lands and would therefore give a more Austrian tone to Christian devotions. Rudolph's favourite was St Koloman (Colmán), an Irish pilgrim martyred in 1012 near what is now Stockerau in Lower Austria. Closely associated with the Benedictine abbey of Melk on the Danube, he had long been venerated in the region. Rudolph also sponsored a memorial grave at the monastery for Koloman's remains that closely resembled the duke's resting place in St Stephen's.[29]

Vienna did not become a bishopric and Margrave Leopold was not canonized in Rudolph's lifetime. He did, however, succeed in manoeuvring the papacy into allowing him to create and control an institution that gave Vienna a lasting public testimonial to its status-hungry duke. Indeed, it gave him at least a cultural attribute of a king. Royal seats in the Middle Ages often became scholarly centres; the University of Paris, which dated from around 1253, was the prime example. Rudolph's father-in-law, Charles IV, inaugurated the University of Prague in 1348, the first such establishment in central Europe. King Casimir III of Poland followed with a school in 1364 that developed into the Jagiellonian University in Kraków by 1400.

Rudolph's capital city, to his way of thinking, deserved an equally prestigious facility. Indeed, Vienna was to be rewarded for its loyalty to him. A local institution of higher education would benefit the economies of ruler and subject alike: students would spend their money at home rather than taking it abroad in search of higher education. Indeed, if every detail of his plan had been realized, the incomes of local artisans and purveyors would have risen considerably. Nevertheless, for students to come to a new University of Vienna in large numbers, it would have to offer all the major curricula of the day. Paris had already set a model for Catholic Europe in which faculties of theology were central to advanced study; no university could be great without one. Papal approval was therefore needed. In 1364 the duke requested permission from Urban V to go ahead. The Pope, who much resented Rudolph's steps to curb the financial powers and privileges of the Church in the Austrian lands, was not eager to please uncooperative territorial rulers.

Nevertheless, the university meant enough to Rudolph for him to soften measures that displeased the clergy, and Urban did most of what was requested, but not all: unwilling to dilute the primacy of Paris in clerical education, he would not have theology taught in Vienna. The Habsburg residential city would wait for around twenty years before Rome changed its mind.[30] In the meantime, however, Rudolph turned the absence of papal support for his new foundation to dynastic advantage. The University of Vienna has been known as the Rudolfina for centuries, but Rudolph IV himself turned the establishment into a gift from the House of Habsburg as a whole. According to its charter, his brothers Albert III and Leopold III were empowered to support it, as were their heirs. Though the eldest duke of the house confirmed the university's privileges, they could be altered only following consultation with an advisory commission and the other dukes. Neither pope nor emperor would have any role in the process. The ambitious and energetic duke died, however, in 1365; his immediate successors dropped Vienna's bishopric and the canonization of Leopold III of Babenberg from their list of priorities; both would be accomplished much later. What Rudolph had made clear, however, was that a determined territorial ruler could convert his dynastic holding culturally, politically and even managerially into a launching pad for royal ambitions, if only he had the imagination and fortitude to try.

The Habsburgs Turn on Themselves

All of this was lost on his immediate successors. Rudolph IV died childless, leaving two brothers with little thought other than personal interest and advancement. Both were formally heirs to their Austrian patrimony; neither Albert III nor Leopold III, however, was eager to accommodate the other, though the latter was the more stubborn of the two. The general economic downturn of the fourteenth century had affected both of them adversely, but putting practical control of the dynasty's lands in the hands of one of them would make the other a clear loser.[31]

Rancour between them ebbed somewhat after 1379 when they agreed to divide their patrimony. Albert III and his line received Austria above and below the Enns, the region that was especially orientated towards Bohemia and Hungary, along with the city of Steyr and the Salzkammergut. Leopold and his heirs would be territorial overlords of Styria, Carinthia and Carniola, collectively known as Inner Austria, along with the Tyrol, southwest Germany and some lands more recently acquired along the Adriatic. Although the two brothers did not always see eye to eye on foreign policy, they cooperated acceptably until Leopold's death in 1386. The following year his four sons, dukes William, Leopold IV, Ernest and Frederick, accepted their uncle, Albert III, as their guardian. When he died in 1395, however, fraternal civil war broke out among his nephews, particularly the elder two. Inner Austria, the Tyrol and the Swabian Habsburg inheritance were shuffled and reshuffled for several decades. The Swabian holdings fell into complete chaos. Influence on neighbouring realms weakened as well. During an intricate power struggle around 1400 among the Bohemian church, nobility, King Václav and his brother Sigismund, the Albertine and Leopoldine Habsburg lines would support different sides. With Habsburg territorial management sacrificed to family feuding, the task of keeping order in the dynasty's holdings fell to the estates. Their repeated calls for brothers and cousins to cooperate with one another went unheeded. Only after the middle of the fifteenth century did the dynasty recover some sense of itself as a unity, aided by a dangerous thinning out of Habsburg male progeny.[32]

The territorial and administrative visions of earlier Habsburgs, however, did not wholly desert the minds of their successors, even as they squabbled bitterly. A cousin from the Leopoldine branch in Styria was showing how larger ducal ambitions might be funded and benefit many of his subjects at the same time. 'Iron' Ernest (Ernst der Eiserne) acquired the epithet not for physical prowess, but for his exploitation of the mineral wealth in his lands. After he came into full control of Inner Austrian lands in 1411, he focused on developing rich iron deposits around the Styrian town of Leoben, which he made a centre for mining, manufacturing and trade of the raw metal and goods made from it. To attract investment and managers for these enterprises, he set up in 1415 the first stock company in the Austrian lands. He also made it part of the lives of his subjects in the province; the latter could be shareholders, with the size of their dividends depending both on the profits of the firm and the amount that an individual had put into it. The company was reauthorized at least twice in the fifteenth century, once by Ernest himself in 1421 and again by his son Frederick in 1439 for a further fifteen years. Like Rudolph IV, Ernest appreciated the economic value of cities. He encouraged the development of Wiener Neustadt, today in Lower Austria, and Graz, where he established a mint. He ably defended the southern borders of his patrimony, too, resisting the efforts of the counts of Cilli, known today in Slovenia as Celje, to nibble their way northward. They too were thinking of advancing their geopolitical goals through marriage into the royal houses of Bohemia and Hungary.[33]

The rule of Ernest's second cousin Albert V in Austria, above and below the Enns, also showed that Habsburgs knew how to govern capably when they were not fighting one another. Five years younger than Rudolph

IV had been when he had begun his active career, Albert was declared to be in his majority at age fourteen; but the resemblance between the two men did not stop there. Though Albert's territorial base was far smaller than his great-uncle's, he managed it effectively, even ruthlessly. Recognizing that intrusions of the local estates into the government of the Habsburg patrimony threatened political pre-eminence in it, Albert forced them to retreat, at least for a time. The juridical infrastructure of his lands came under his control when he put his court marshal in charge of it. He then reorganized it for maximum effectiveness. Civil and criminal cases were adjudicated in different tribunals. Nobles and clergy facing criminal charges were tried before a special ducal panel. Like Rudolph IV, he patronized the University of Vienna generously.

Some fiscal and public discipline returned to Albert v's share in the Habsburg patrimony, though his expenses usually outstripped his resources. That Albert's Austrian treasurer customarily took a cut of tax revenues before handing over what remained to his employer did not help. Above all, Albert married well. His wife, Elizabeth of Luxembourg, was the daughter of Charles IV's younger son, Sigismund, who, by the time he died in 1438, was king of both Hungary and Bohemia, and German Emperor. A Habsburg compact of mutual succession finally came to fruition. Signed between Charles IV and Rudolph IV in 1364, it had been renewed in 1437. As Sigismund left no male heirs, the Bohemian estates accepted the Habsburg Albert v as their new king. Hungary had done the same in the previous year. Dynastic success story though this was, it did not last for long, since Albert died of dysentery on the way to confront the Serbs in southeastern Hungary in 1439.

His Austrian lands, moreover, had no reason to appreciate any connections with Bohemia. A good deal of Albert v's career in Austria above and below the Enns had been spent using the resources of the region to contain a destructive religious conflict that spilled westward from his new kingdom. Its inspiration came from an eloquent priest in Prague, Jan Hus, who in the last decades of the fourteenth century set off one of medieval Europe's many cycles of Christian institutional reform. Clerical moral standards were to be improved, something that Albert himself had supported in Austria.

More seriously, however, the Hussites wanted a fundamental and enormously controversial liturgical change: allowing communicants to partake not only of sacramental bread at the Mass, but also the wine, traditionally reserved for the performing priest. Papal authority was thus called into play. In 1415 a Church council assembled in Basel to resolve the controversy. Presiding over the meeting generally, Emperor Sigismund had looked the other way when the body ordered Hus's execution. An explosion of rage took place in Bohemia; Hus had been given safe conduct by Sigismund, and the emperor appeared to have gone back on his word. Albert had cultivated Sigismund, his father-in-law, very carefully and he had made no secret of his sympathy for Orthodox liturgical practice among Roman Catholics. Some of the ire directed towards Sigismund in Bohemia was transferred to Albert, too. Organized Hussite marauders plagued Austria and other German principalities for years to come. Protecting his holdings consumed much of Albert's revenues, regardless of whether he drew them by right from his domains or from taxes. His peasantry suffered especially hard; he drew upon them for taxes and repeated raiding wasted their lands. Poorly trained though they were, he also conscripted them into armies made up of 'noble and commoner alike' from the ages of sixteen to seventy. In the short run, Albert's staunch support of Sigismund paid off dynastically. From 1438 to 1439, under the name Albert II, he was German king and emperor too, the first of his line to have held both titles since Albert I was murdered by Johann the Uncle-Slayer in 1308. But memories of Hussite raiders would remain alive in Austrian popular consciousness for generations, leaving many people with negative opinions about their Slavic neighbours, to the north and east, and about the Habsburgs who had not done an especially good job of protecting their own peoples.[34]

Thus by the fifteenth century at least two of the Habsburgs, albeit in different lines, had proven that some members of the house had sober and practical ideas that might help their family retain a significant niche in European dynastic politics. That Albert v had recaptured the German crown and the emperorship showed that the dynasty could still play an international role. But dividing the family into discrete lines had ignited fraternal wrangling that passed down the generations, reminding observers that no Habsburg spoke for the patrimony as a whole. Fractured among multiple heirs as it was, the entire Austrian territorial complex was open to predators from abroad. Even local commentators deplored the practice; writing at the beginning of the fifteenth century, Thomas Ebendorfer, a contemporary historian, said that the rule of the many was a guide to how not to govern.[35] The notion of dynastic government and its proprietary subtext was not called into question. What remained to be decided was the form of dynastic rule. In the meantime, the Habsburgs had yet to manage their lands consequentially enough to qualify them as more than German territorial princes with significant possibilities, but prone to all the petty weaknesses of the breed. Their subjects responded to them correspondingly, more or less adjusting to these conditions as they found them, using them to advantage when they could and arranging their lives accordingly. Whatever ambitions Rudolph I's successors fostered also had to answer to the requirements of the Austrian provincial estates, who customarily resisted subsidizing the armies of their territorial overlord. If they promised fiscal support at all, they collected it very slowly and only rarely in full amounts.

What the dynasty had excelled in was perpetuating its male lines. Though a source of decades-long fraternal conflict, a continued line-up of legitimate heirs strengthened the Habsburgs' hold on their patrimony even as neighbouring kingdoms lost their ruling houses through contested successions in the fourteenth and fifteenth centuries. Rudolph I's extended progeny would still be in place as ruling house after ruling house died out in Hungary, Bohemia and Poland.[36]

In the meantime, the House of Habsburg would happily remind itself through a brazenly impressive fiction that it was destined for better things. Not surprisingly, its inspiration came from Rudolph IV. It also brought him and his holdings to European attention in a way that all of his energetic economic reforms and religious policies never did. The duke's whole career had argued that he wanted to be a monarch, and he actually tried. Only the emperor could grant such titles and the lands associated with them in Germany. Charles IV, the duke's father-in-law, had often encouraged the young prince's schemes. This, however, was not one of them. Charles was very jealous of his unique status in the Empire as not only an emperor but also as the lone elector who was a king, in his case of Bohemia. He would not see it compromised in any way, notwithstanding its impact on internal family harmony. Relations between the two men would deteriorate badly over the years, in good part as a result of this issue.[37]

With Charles unapproachable on a kingship, Rudolph invented alternatives less humdrum than 'duke', but possibly acceptable to the emperor. He reconfigured titles that his family already had: turning 'Count of Alsace' into 'Prince in Swabia and in Alsatia' was one suggestion, a reminder that the Habsburgs still held lands in the German southwest; 'Duke Palatine of Austria, Styria, Carinthia, Swabia and Alsace' was perhaps even weightier. But he never totally rejected his dream of a kingship. He had a good idea of what he would wear if he held such a title; he even commissioned regalia for it, including a crown ornamented with a cross resting in a bejewelled iron frame that strongly resembled the one worn by his father-in-law as German king. To complicate matters further, he called it the 'Hat of the Archduke' (*Erzherzogshut*), a title unknown in Germany but concocted by Rudolph for male members of his family in one of the more flagrant forgeries of the Middle Ages. This was the so-called *Privilegium maius*, seven documents stitched together around 1358 in Rudolph's chancellery. Among them were two proclamations allegedly issued by Julius Caesar and a third from Emperor Nero declaring Austrians superior to all peoples in the Roman Empire and thereby exempt from all obligations to the Empire itself. Their core, however, considerably expanded the *Privilegium minus*. All imperial lands in Austria were to be turned over to its territorial rulers in perpetuity. Neither the German king nor emperor could claim them or redistribute them, unless they were Church properties. The immunity of Austrian dukes from imperial law was strengthened and succession in both the male and female lines of the House of Habsburg was reaffirmed. Should the duke of Austria choose to accept enfeoffment from his king, he could do so adorned as he saw fit, a declaration that left room for an outfit that might include an iron crown with a cross, along with a sceptre. He would also receive his dignity as a prince, on horseback rather than kneeling before his suzerain as a vassal.[38]

Charles IV called upon Francesco Petrarch, the Italian humanist to whom the emperor was close, to evaluate the revised and expanded *Minus*. The scholar was blunt and brief: the document was written by 'an incompetent, ludicrous ass'. Charles IV disapproved of the text as well, but on more limited grounds: he would hear nothing of the Habsburg's idiosyncratic dress code. He could live, however, with a new title for the Habsburgs in Austria. 'Archduke' fulfilled Rudolph's longing for distinctiveness, and his father-in-law preferred it to 'Duke Palatine of Austria, Styria, Carinthia, Swabia and Alsace'.

Rudolph, for his part, accepted enfeoffment with the Austrian lands in 1360, though not wearing the monarchical trappings he had invented for himself. Most significantly, the *Maius*, bogus or nor, worked its way into the private constitution that the house would be writing for itself over the following centuries. His Styrian nephew, Duke Ernest, would take to calling himself 'archduke', perhaps to enhance his political and military stature in his lands. Ernest's own eldest son, Emperor Frederick III, would legitimize the title once and for all in 1452 with a special ceremony that confirmed the entire *Maius*. His son, Emperor Maximilian I, who put an aesthetic twist on much of what his house did, commissioned an embellished ceremonial copy of the *Maius* that increased its artistic value if not its credibility. He also began the practice of referring to female members of the house as 'archduchesses'.[39] Petrarch, as far as the House of Habsburg was concerned, could have saved his breath.

TWO

The Habsburgs Regroup

A Man of Two Mottoes

By 1440 Habsburgs had been German kings three times, or four if one counts the very contested reign of Frederick I. Emperor Albert II had briefly been king of Hungary and Bohemia. Intra-dynastic malcontent, however, continued to plague the Austrian lands, although the number of dukes to be satisfied was sinking. If the House of Habsburg truly intended to set itself off from the other territorial rulers of the Empire, as Rudolph IV had dreamed, it had to foster some vision of the house that raised it from the conventional to something approaching the unique. None of this appeared likely. Yet, within the space of roughly 60 years, the Habsburg *imperium* had gathered to itself lands never before part of the dynasty's European patrimony in Europe and holdings beyond the continent altogether. It had also discovered more effective ways to declare its new status to audiences not wholly pleased by the development. Circumstance and accidents of birth and death dictated much of the process; the Habsburg knack for making the best of every political opportunity that came its way contributed mightily too.

Nevertheless, developing family unity to a point where it could manage such growth without dynastic infighting remained a trying challenge. In 1436 Emperor Albert II had brokered an agreement between his two living nephews, dukes Frederick V, the elder, and Albert VI, sons of Ernest the Iron in Inner Austria. While both men had equal right to the territory, the compact called for the government of the elder alone. In 1442 Frederick V became King Frederick III in the Empire. The exalted position did not intimidate his aggressive younger brother at all. Fraternal strife eventually broke out between them once again over the Austrian patrimony. Frederick tried to buy off his belligerent brother in 1446 with lands scattered throughout parts of eastern Austria, the Tyrol and what was left of Habsburg Swabia.[1] Albert remained unsatisfied.

Having the imperial crown, however, did give Frederick leverage over more of Europe. At least privately, he thought his family might be destined for greater things. A notebook he kept contains a scribbled acronym, AEIOU, easily read as *Austria est imperare orbi universo* (Austria Rules the Entire World). Scholars have never determined who wrote it, Frederick or someone who had access to the emperor's text, but Frederick would certainly have approved of the idea. Both eager and anxious to shore up his senior status in his house, he persuaded the German princes at his election to support his formal confirmation of the *Privilegium maius*, thereby moving fiction a bit closer to operational fact.

Making his way back home following his imperial coronation in 1442, he visited Philip the Good, duke of Burgundy. A significant territorial ruler in his own right, Philip was an uncle by marriage to Princess Eleanor of Portugal. He suggested his six-year-old niece as a future bride for the Habsburg king when she came of age; ten years later, Frederick, now 37, followed through. He was still making statements about intradynastic leadership, this time very publicly. His journey to Rome, where he was to meet and wed his bride, began in 1451. He took with him his very problematic younger brother, Albert, along with a very important nephew, Prince Ladislaus, the posthumous and only son of Emperor Albert II. Both greeted the bride before she joined Frederick.

Frederick was also showing the results of carefully cultivated relations with the papacy. He had supported the elections of Eugene IV, then Nicholas V, both of whom brought to an end the contested pontificates that had divided the western Church between 1328 and 1439. Eugene's gratitude had been especially rewarding. He gave Frederick lifetime power to nominate important bishops in the Inner Austrian lands, most notably Gurk, and Brixen and Trent in northern Italy. The Habsburg could also recommend personnel for church visitations in his lands and distribute 100 clerical benefices as he saw fit. The Pope also agreed that Frederick should be not only German king, but also Holy Roman Emperor.

Thus Frederick came away from Rome in 1452 with a wife and Christendom's highest secular office; he would be the last Habsburg ever to receive the imperial title in the papal seat. Successive popes cooperated with him on imperial business too. Eugene's successor, Nicholas V, accepted the emperor's feudal suzerainty over Lombardy, long a contested matter between Frederick's predecessors and the papacy. Frederick was also permitted to recruit excommunicated mercenaries, meaning Hussites, to put down Duke Albert's sedition in Austria. Though he was technically the sovereign of Christendom, Frederick had yet to win or coerce support from his brother's many followers and from those who believed that the emperor was violating Prince Ladislaus's claims in the Austrian lands. Driving home the point that Frederick was maltreating relatives from the diminishing second branch of his house, the estates paraded a daughter of Emperor Albert II through the streets of Vienna in beggars' rags.[2]

The new emperor certainly looked like a man destined for great things; he was tall, with a striking mane of blond hair that fell to his shoulders. He also respected the scholarly standards of the contemporary Renaissance. He could read and write himself and clearly believed that a good monarch was an educated monarch; he drew scholars to his court, and not only because they added to the prestige of his establishment. His biggest catch would be Aeneas Sylvius Piccolomini. One of the master humanists of his time, who would become Pope Pius II, he would serve Frederick in several capacities: he finalized the marriage contract between the Habsburg and his Portuguese wife; he also escorted her back to Italy. Piccolomini's first job was to tutor the emperor's two young Habsburg wards, his cousin Duke Sigmund of the Tyrol and Prince Ladislaus. Piccolomini warned the young princes that most of the great rulers in the past were versed in the classics: princes without such training were, in his opinion, crowned 'asses'. He also urged Ladislaus, whose mother was the queen of Bohemia, to learn Czech and Hungarian if he ever hoped to converse with his subjects in those realms.[3]

Yet, the official motto that Frederick had adopted at his election as German king, 'Fortunate is the man who forgets what is no longer to be changed' (*rerum irrecuperabilium sum[m]a felicitas est oblivio*), was psychologically and procedurally closer to the reality of the man and much of his career than was AEIOU. He was a soul of disparate and often contradictory parts. He combined great ambition – a feature that troubled other rulers – with consistent underperformance, thereby opening himself frequently to contemporary ridicule. German princes and untitled observers alike accused him, as they once had Rudolph I, of worrying far more about his house than the Empire or even the Austrian lands as a whole. He had little feel for the niceties of public life and the expectations that people had of him.

Should representational needs leave him no choice but to conform, Frederick put on a good show. An appropriately grand entourage went with him to Rome for the imperial coronation, and he enthusiastically donned a bejewelled and gold-trimmed surcoat for the baptism of his first son in 1459. Magnificence, however, did not come easily to him. He endured, rather than enjoyed, the lavish entertainments that his status required.[4] His tight-fistedness was legendary, but disappointing to those who hoped to profit from his public appearances. He bought chicks to raise for his cooks when he came to a diet in Nuremberg in 1486, rather than supplying his entourage through local vendors. His known passions were solitary: gardening, cultivating fruit trees and collecting unusual stones. All in all, he came over to his kindest critics as somewhat eccentric; to a less generous French envoy at his court he was torpid, melancholy, miserly, timid and consumed with anxiety.[5]

Much of whatever energy he had would go into bringing his Austrian patrimony under his control. When Frederick and his bride returned from Rome in 1452, Austria above and below the Enns were still turbulent places. As early as 1440 some members of the local nobility had begged Frederick to enfeoff them with abandoned castles to prevent bandits and mercenaries who moonlighted as vandals from occupying them. Some of the latter were in the pay of the disgruntled Duke Albert, Frederick's brother. A meeting of the regional estates in 1441 had criticized Frederick's ineffectiveness heatedly; at one moment several members cried out 'Crucify the king of the Jews!', an allusion to his refusal to pay off some of his debts by taxing Jews disproportionately. His notebook indicates that he resented the confrontation bitterly.[6]

Even his imperially validated *Maius* got him nowhere in Austria for at least twenty years. Local estates, defending partible inheritance, would not acknowledge the arrangement. Dissidents briefly cornered Frederick and his wife in 1452 behind the walls of their residence in Wiener Neustadt. While still insisting that he alone was responsible for governing the entirety of the Habsburg lands, he had no choice but to give in to his opponents, again and again.

Good fortune, however, began to drift Frederick's way, though incrementally. Ladislaus died in 1457, probably of the plague. The following year the Habsburgs reconfigured their Austrian holdings once again, this time among Frederick, his brother Albert VI and their cousin Sigmund in the Tyrol. But Albert remained as intransigent as ever. He called upon earlier house compacts to validate his status as a legitimate heir to the entire Habsburg inheritance. Frederick's feeble response was once again to call upon the *Maius* and its seniority provisions.

Open warfare between Frederick and Albert for control of Austria above and below the Enns tormented the entire region between 1461 and 1463. The local estates and Vienna had shifted support to the younger brother, though the ruthlessness of his troops made many think twice.

At one point in 1462 Frederick again barricaded himself, his wife and a young son, this time in the Vienna Hofburg, to protect themselves against local dissidents who were not beyond drawing and quartering their captives alive. A year later, however, Duke Albert vi died, perhaps of the plague. His body was dumped summarily into a grave sequestered for victims of the disease.

No longer challenged by a younger brother or bothersome nephews, Frederick was the sole claimant to the Habsburg patrimony. The lone exception was the Tyrol, which Duke Sigmund administered, together with what remained of the Habsburg holdings in Swabia. But the easternmost regions of the dynasty's holdings had little reason to thank its territorial overlords for much of anything. Decades went by before its towns and rural settlements recovered somewhat from intra-dynastic hostilities and looting mercenaries hired by both sides. Decades of conflict with the expanding Ottoman Empire, seated after 1453 in Constantinople, would deplete all of these lands sadly.

But even as the sultans were fixing their sights westward, Frederick faced a greater threat from a Christian near-neighbour. He had never renounced his family's claims to the strategically significant thrones of Hungary and Bohemia. Prince Ladislaus had some claim to both, but estates in both kingdoms would eventually vote for ethnically native houses. George of Podiebrad, who belonged to the moderate Hussite faction known as Utraquists, ruled in Prague after 1459. The very aggressive house of Hunyadi controlled Hungary. There King Matthias launched in 1458 a programme of solidifying his position in central Europe at the expense of the Habsburgs, among others. He also had his eye on Bohemia and the imperial title. In 1462 he would drive the beleaguered Frederick and his family from Vienna to Wiener Neustadt, where Frederick stayed for a month until Podiebrad arranged his release.

Frederick recognized his opponent as king of Hungary in the following year, but Matthias was relentless. By the early 1480s Frederick appealed to the imperial diet for aid, arguing that Matthias's seizure of Austrian lands would be an incursion upon the integrity of the Empire. The German princes were not very sympathetic. Matthias occupied Vienna in 1485 and made it his residence. He clearly intended to take all of the Habsburg lands where he could. A sarcastic pastor in Carinthia, Jakob Unrest, noted that the letters AEIOU could also be read as 'First and Foremost Austria is Lost' (*Aller erst ist Österreich verloren*). In 1487 Frederick fled Vienna again, this time to his preferred residence in Linz where he would while away his time mulling over astrological and mathematical problems along with bizarre fixations such as mouse droppings, according to local gossips.[7]

Good fortune saved Frederick once more. His Hungarian rival died in 1490 without male heirs. But though Frederick and his heir apparent, Maximilian I, born in 1459, tried to enforce a succession agreement signed between the emperor and the late king of Hungary in 1463, they failed egregiously. Called upon to supply funds for these campaigns, the Austrian lands and the German princes who had responded deeply resented the two emperors' self-serving pressures. The throne went to the Polish ruling house of Jagellon, which was clearly entering into the competition for dynastic pre-eminence in central and east-central Europe, having acquired the Bohemian throne following the death of George of Podiebrad in 1471. Though succession agreements with the Habsburgs remained in place, they had yet to be taken seriously.

Frederick's house in the Austrian lands was still well placed to grow eastward, with the programmatically aggressive Matthias now out of the way. On balance, however, the emperor's career in his patrimony alone, filled as it was with internal conflict and personal humiliation, had done little to ingratiate his house with his peoples and kingdoms abroad. Local commentators and foreigners insulted him. His endless financial short-falls left him pawning property and incomes. When that option ran dry, he clipped coins. Peasant uprisings were frequent, and the estates in Austria, above and below the Enns, and in the Empire itself took umbrage at his reliance for many years on a squad of advisers from Inner Austria, the 'Styrian Wise', as Piccolomini snidely dubbed them.[8] Nor would he ever do much to protect the southeastern parts of his lands, Carinthia in particular, from Ottoman raiders who appeared periodically in the area in the latter decades of the fifteenth century.

Resignation and the capacity to forget bad moments, the advice of his personal motto, suggested that Frederick could live with defeat, at least on a psychological level. He did have some natural qualities that gave him some standing with his peoples. His unassuming demeanour, if not his imposing physique, was a throwback to Rudolph I; public reaction was correspondingly positive. Some praised his modesty, his generally virtuous ways and his ascetic habits. He drank sparingly at a time and in an environment where temperance was an asocial statement, at least when German princes got together. His piety was never in ques-tion, probably the result of training he received from his Polish mother, Cimburgia of Mazovia, who was reputedly very devout. Frederick's commitment to unitary sovereignty over his lands and closely controlled management of them was equally unwavering.[9] Most importantly, failure in big things did not keep him from enhancing the status of his house in smaller ways. He revived the title of archduke for male members of his family, along with the pretentious special crown that Rudolph had designed for them. Frederick III also took to calling the Habsburgs the 'House of Austria', a distinction that accompanied the dynasty's many offspring wherever they went on marital assignment to Europe and the New World.

Like Rudolph I and Rudolph IV before him, Frederick also knew how to manipulate titles and the powers and privileges attached to them. He understood that not all of them were constitutionally equal. The elective kind, he observed in his chaotic notebook, gave local estates too much influence; hereditary monarchs were much freer to discount the prerogatives of local representative bodies.[10] But regardless of its constitutional idiosyncrasies, should a crown be available, Frederick went after it. His commitment to his imperial German title was a cardinal example. Its authority had clearly diminished over the centuries. The office, however, was still crucial to those hoping to develop a larger imperium in Europe. Even strivers like Charles IV in Bohemia and Matthias Corvinus in Hungary, both serious competitors of the Habsburgs, saw advantages in the position and wanted it badly.[11] At the very least, emperors could still verify and confer titles throughout the Empire and the land rights associated with them. Frederick's many successors would take the lesson to heart; beginning with Frederick, the Habsburgs would relinquish the office only once and briefly, in the eighteenth century, until 1806 when Napoleon Bonaparte deconstructed the entire edifice in rearranging Germany more advantageously for himself and France. But as long as they had it, the Habsburgs exerted whatever influence the emperorship gave them, especially when the dynasty could improve its own standing. Success at this game called for patience and a clear understanding of one's goals. Passive by nature, Frederick was made for such work. Indeed it was the imperial title, combined with luck once again, that helped him pull off one of the major dynastic unions in European history.

Habsburgs and Burgundians

Frederick III and his lonely and misplaced wife, Eleanor of Portugal, produced five children before the empress died in 1467. Two of them survived to adulthood, both psychologically scarred by the political turbulence that had humiliated and physically threatened their father several times over. One was a daughter, Archduchess Kunigunde, who would bring a strong sense of Habsburg status to her marriage with the duke of Bavaria, Albert IV. The other was a boy, Maximilian, born in 1459. The name, familiar from Roman antiquity, was very new to Habsburg family nomenclature, which through the fifteenth century was top heavy with Germanic Fredericks, Alberts and Rudolphs. The boy's birth took place only six years after Constantinople had fallen to Sultan Mahmoud II. A mercurial soul, Eleanor had wanted to call her son Constantine; she hoped that he would grow into the man who would recapture what Constantine, emperor of Rome, had made a Christian seat. Frederick had a more conventional, though equally pious, suggestion. He believed himself to have once been saved in battle against the counts of Cilli by a local saint, Maximilian of Lorch. The emperor's wish prevailed. Maximilian it was.[12]

Maximilian would become one of the most eloquent and extroverted advocates his house would ever have, but it was his dour father, the emperor, who positioned him to play the role. Among the unruliest areas of late fifteenth-century central Europe were the German-speaking cantons of what is now Switzerland, where marauding bandits from all of the southwestern Empire and parts of the Tyrol had taken refuge. The Habsburgs still had patrimonial holdings in the region governed from the Tyrol by Frederick's cousin Sigmund; so did the dukes of Burgundy. Overlords in what is today Belgium, The Netherlands and northeastern France, they had developed an impressive territorial conglomerate out of an appanage assigned in 1363 by a French Valois king, John II, to one of his younger sons, Duke Philip. Ultimate suzerainty over several of these principalities belonged historically with the German king, but this was not rigidly enforced.[13] Frederick, Sigmund, and the duke of Burgundy (after 1467 Charles the Bold) all had an interest in getting the bothersome cantons under control. A dynastic union between the houses of Valois-Burgundy and Habsburg was a first step to that end. Frederick began looking to Burgundy for a bride for his son in 1463; the then regnant Duke Philip III (the Good) had a six-year-old granddaughter, Mary, who had excited the nuptial imaginations of several European houses – Spain, England and France, most notably – but she had yet to reach a marriageable age. Philip died in 1467, but his son and heir, and Mary's father, Duke Charles I, had good reason to cultivate Frederick a bit more. The duke wanted to be a king in his lands, and only the emperor could make him one. Charles may have been thinking about

3 'The Marriage of
Maximilian I and
Duchess Mary of
Burgundy', from
Johann Jakob Fugger
and Sigmund von Birken,
*Spiegel des Erzhauses
Österreich . . .* (1668).

trying for that office as well. Frederick therefore dealt with him warily,
even though the latter had much to offer. Negotiations between the two
houses dragged on for ten more years, only to be resolved when Charles
was killed in battle against the Swiss in 1477. Mary, who was then twenty,
was his sole heir; it was she who opted for Maximilian rather than the
competing French dauphin.

Once the archduke arrived in Burgundy, the couple found themselves altogether compatible. She loved riding and hunting and so did
he; a quick wedding took place (illus. 3). Two children followed in short
order: the boy was called Philip; the girl was Margaret, after several
earlier females in the Burgundian family tree. Once the son of one of
Europe's most fiscally strapped rulers and now consort of the heiress to

57

one of Europe's most economically productive regions, Maximilian had become a central player on the European political stage. Contemporary rulers, who had hoped to use a marriage with Duchess Mary to advance their own dynastic agendas, quickly challenged the sudden expansion of the House of Austria's influence. The Habsburg took up arms almost immediately, defending the enviable role that his father had created for him. The king of France, Louis XI, who had yearned for Mary as a daughter-in-law, was especially irritated. Parts of Burgundy, notably Flanders and Artois, had come out of Valois France and the king wanted them back.

The initial territorial conflicts set off by the Burgundian marriage endured until the 1490s. They would, however, fuel international dynastic conflagrations or hostilities until the end of the Napoleonic Wars in 1815. Maximilian would spend a good deal of his young manhood defending his prerogatives from foreigners and from factions in local estates and municipalities. Many among the latter refused to accept his succession through inheritance as their ruler after his young wife died following a fatal tumble from a horse in 1482. In the opinion of many dissidents, the legitimate heir was already Archduke Philip, born in 1478.

Frederick's handiwork had certainly given his dynasty a sharp political profile abroad. Defending Habsburg interests in the Netherlands, nominally part of the Holy Roman Empire, did about as much for Emperor Frederick's standing in Germany as had his unsuccessful campaigns in Hungary. His peoples in Austria were not impressed either. In Carinthia, Jakob Unrest, the most extensive contemporary commentator we have on the appearance of Ottoman raiders in fifteenth-century Austria, criticized the Habsburg–Burgundy marriage for diverting funds and attention from anti-Muslim defence.[14] For his part, Frederick was far more absorbed in keeping the imperial office in his house. He spent considerable time and money in the 1480s persuading the electors to accept his son as German king, which they did in 1486, thereby raising the likelihood that he might become an emperor like his father. And control over the entirety of the Habsburg Austrian patrimony came to Maximilian in 1490, as the childless Sigmund of the Tyrol voluntarily resigned his land to the major line of his house. Frederick thus lived to see the Habsburg Austrian patrimony reunified in a way that it had not been for roughly 150 years. He died in 1493.

For a man who had spent a good part of his life swallowing one indignity after another, Frederick had not done all that badly by his house. His reign as emperor would be the longest in the history of the title – 53 years, if one includes his time as elected German king. His

4 Detail of the sarcophagus of Emperor Frederick III (*r.* 1452–93) in St Stephen's Cathedral, Vienna.

confirmation of the *Privilegium maius* underscored the dynasty's distinctiveness and the sense of solidarity that went with it. That he left so few children was dangerous in any polity where status and authority were transferred through inheritance. In the case of the late medieval Habsburgs, however, the presence of only two living offspring, and but one son, opened the way for Frederick to bring a unity to his family's German-speaking patrimony that it had long lacked. He had actually added more titles to the house escutcheon, at least one of which, the Burgundian, was a major step towards giving the Habsburgs a consistent base from which to conduct European dynastic politics of the early modern era. The crowns of Hungary and Bohemia escaped him, but he had never given up on the succession agreements that made him a plausible candidate for both thrones.

He thought well enough of his achievements to remind posterity of him, indeed to give some thought to how it should be done. His sarcophagus stands to the right of the high altar of St Stephen's Cathedral in Vienna, where a side altar normally should be. A massive construction of red marble, its sides swarm with patterns and figures that, taken singly, say something about the values and beliefs he pondered, but in the end give no sense how he prioritized them. On the sides just below the cover plate are the coats of arms of ecclesiastical establishments that he founded, supported, or both. Below these is an intricate interweaving of assorted persons, among them monks praying for him. Around the register below squirm a series of reptilian forms, some clutching prey in their claws or mouths, which have been taken to represent Frederick's sins. A death's head is there too (illus. 4). The lid is more secular: the imperial crown and Rudolph iv's suggestive remodelling of it for personal use stand out, but the image of Frederick himself is the most intriguing. Its most prominent feature is the luxurious mane of hair above and around the face. It suggests strongly that a ruler of vigour and manly resolve lies within. Whatever his shortcomings, Frederick was not ready to underscore them for future critics.

Trying Father, Difficult Son

Sovereigns and their heirs have often been ill-matched, but Frederick iii and Maximilian i were a particularly dissonant couple. Where the late emperor was deliberate to a fault, the son was prodigiously imaginative, recklessly overconfident and impulsive. Fellow rulers had trouble taking him seriously, as did sharp-eyed, neutral commentators such as Machiavelli. For much of Frederick's life there was always someone attacking his lands or his claims to them, but he seemed to think only of peace, sometimes at any price. Maximilian prided himself, with some reason, as a military leader and expert in the technology and organization of war.[15] Organization, however, did not always lead to accomplishment; he suffered as many serious and humiliating setbacks as had his father. Common burghers in Bruges captured and held him for a time in 1488; in 1499 he accepted the withdrawal of the Swiss cantons from the Holy Roman Empire after being beaten by what he scorned as a band of peasants. He generated plan upon plan to rationalize the administrative structure and fiscal resources of his Austrian patrimony and Germany. Few, however, were realized in his lifetime, and the changes that he did make did not last long or were bitterly opposed, especially by local estates.

Repeated cycles of hope followed by loss, along with the frenetic pace at which he operated, flattened him emotionally several times. Nevertheless, unlike his father, Maximilian always recovered the *joie de vivre* and creativity that he expressed most durably in his lavish patronage of art, music, the dance and on the chase. Frederick took little interest in such distractions; his happiest moments were apparently spent with his solitary hobbies and in decoding messages that came to him in dreams.[16]

Maximilian, for his part, spent a lifetime thinking about audiences, real and virtual, and performing for them in any way he could.

He was also ready to challenge his father's authority in matters of dynastic policy. Frederick had hoped to marry Archduchess Kunigunde more advantageously than to a duke of Bavaria, Albert IV. Maximilian was close to the latter and supported the arrangement actively. The couple wed in 1487, leaving the emperor furious. Frederick also disapproved of Maximilian's choice of Bianca Maria Sforza, as a second wife. The son prized her as the moneyed offspring of an Italian dynasty of warlords who had a central position in Italian politics. They had controlled Milan since the middle of the fifteenth century, but to Frederick they were a 'family of shoemakers' and he rejected the entire proposition as a misalliance.[17] Continuing to cultivate the relationship behind his father's back, Maximilian married Bianca Maria in 1493 after Frederick had died.

Father and son did, however, agree on most dynastic matters, especially when it involved adding more titles to Maximilian's name. Frederick knew that the more of these that the House of Habsburg controlled, the safer its future would be; Maximilian thought much the same way and he did not object in the least to new offices that his father found for him or thought should be his. The Burgundy marriage was one of the happiest moments in Maximilian's career, so much so that he later allegorized the journey that took him to Duchess Mary in *Theuerdank*, one of the semi-autobiographical accounts of his activities that he commissioned and supervised. Ever pressing for recognition of Habsburg claims to the kingship in Hungary, he would go to war there briefly in 1506, when a succession was once again questionable, taking the opportunity to clear away from eastern Austria the remaining vestiges of King Matthias's occupation. Though the popes refused to crown him emperor, he used the distinction anyway as elected German king. He took the prerogatives of both offices very seriously, defending imperial claims in Italy as well as in lands that kings of France insisted belonged to them.

As a marital tactician, Maximilian equalled his father and even outdid him. Persistently challenged by France, he looked to the rulers of Spain, Isabel of Castile and Ferdinand of Aragon, as allies and as partners in the dynastic unions that sealed such relationships. King Ferdinand blew hot and cold on formalizing family ties at any specific time, but by 1495 he gave in. Two of his immediate progeny, Prince Juan, the heir apparent to Castile and Aragon, and Princess Juana would marry Maximilian's legitimate offspring, Archduchess Margaret and Archduke Philip, respectively. At the very least, a Habsburg would be the consort to the future Spanish monarch, whose realms had begun to reach across the Atlantic.

The ensuing scenario did not work out quite that way. A few physically passionate weeks with his new wife left the frail Spanish prince dead. The Habsburg princess was now but a royal widow; her brother, however, would live long enough to sire progeny who peopled a Habsburg dynastic chain that stretched from central Europe to the Iberian Peninsula until the beginning of the eighteenth century. Ferdinand of Aragon, who only died in 1516, was much disappointed by this turn of events, but could not alter it. He would be followed in Spain by Philip and Juana's eldest son, Charles, who by 1521 was King Charles I of Spain and on the way to becoming Emperor Charles V in Germany. With Habsburgs to the north, south and east, the French geopolitical environment could not have been more precarious, just as Maximilian had intended. Looked at another way, however, he and the accidents of nature had set the scene for decades of dynastic conflict that strained the resources of most rulers in Europe, the Habsburgs included.

Project Maximilian

By the beginning of the sixteenth century Maximilian had extended Habsburg influence far beyond what even his most ambitious ancestors had envisioned. Unlike his father, however, he was acutely sensitive to the growing need for great houses to confirm their status publicly by championing behaviours and values that marked them as princes and rulers. Rudolph I and Rudolph IV had known this; Maximilian not only followed in their footsteps but overran them. Maximilian's conventional credentials were excellent, and he rehearsed them frequently and in many public settings: German king and emperor, head of his house, devout Christian. Holding the title to all of the Austrian lands guaranteed his access to even the lowest ranks of his local subjects who might look to him for support should all other resources fail. A typical example would have been Sofia, a self-described 'poor, miserable, disconsolate widow with seven children' who also, as she informed her Habsburg ruler, taught young girls. Regrettably, there were all too few of the latter, and she needed financial assistance.[18]

But driving many of his activities was a deeply personal concern: 'whoever fails to create the memory of himself in his lifetime, will leave no memory after his death. Such men are forgotten with the tolling bells. For this reason, whatever money I spend on my legacy, will not be lost.'[19] The sentiment itself was a commonplace among European rulers in Max-imilian's time and even earlier. Nevertheless, Emperor Maximilian's dec-laration has a visceral quality to it, though why is unclear. Not until much later would Habsburg rulers leave detailed personal testimonies about the principles that guided them, and even then not regularly. This included Maximilian: he dropped his early stab at an autobiography because his Latin was embarrassingly bad – 'soldiers' Latin' (*Soldatenlatein*), he called it. Aeneas Sylvius Piccolomini had once noted that fame-seekers gener-ally thought that a glorious life on earth guaranteed a glorious stay in eternity, and Maximilian may have been one of them. Perhaps he hoped that he could savour the reputation he left with the living, if only from a distance beyond the grave. Or perhaps he felt his reputation and that of his father needed shoring up after the complex trials and triumphs that his family had gone through for almost two centuries. What we can say with confidence is that he did not stint when pursuing his agenda. Towards the end of his life the hostelries and tradesmen of Innsbruck refused to sell to the emperor's entourage or to house it because the emperor had so many creditors after him.[20] Political and military expen-diture accounted for much of his perpetual shortfalls, but so did his outlay on the art, music and literature that celebrated his achievements and those of his family.

Unlike the public-conscious Rudolph I and Rudolph IV, Maximilian had access to technical resources that made it far easier for him to turn his self-images and those of his family into widely available cultural property. Some of this would fade like the funeral bells of his credo, but much of what he commissioned and sometimes supervised would mark the minds and memories of the audiences he eagerly sought. Maximilian was in the first generation of European monarchs with access to movable type and techniques for reproducing graphics; he quickly adopted the printed and illustrated page to explain himself and his house to contemporary and future audiences. We still have roughly 1,000 images of Maximilian I, ranging from portraits to prints, along with countless texts about him. The pictures alone were often reprinted in different publications. His target audiences were not always the same; the two larger autobiographical works, *Theuerdank* and *Der Weisskunig*, projections of what he wanted to be and what he was, were geared towards the learned and powerful of his time. But there were also more modest folk who understood things through the 'eye and mouth', as Maximilian put it, and he wanted to engage them too.[21]

Maximilian's formal education had been spotty, in good part because he hated it so much. Though he genuinely regretted his lack of formal learning later in life, he never forgave the pedantic bearing of the tutor who made him the recalcitrant pupil that he was. It did not help that he was instructed from the age of nine in maxims from contemporary manuals on the upbringing of exemplary princes, all of which only called to mind his deficiencies. None of these experiences, however, shook his selfconfidence. To contemporaries, Maximilian was a man in constant motion, a quality that he and the secretaries who assisted him transferred to his surrogate in *Der Weisskunig*. There he was not just busy, but omni-competent: as a ruling prince and military leader, of course, but also as a diligent student, hunter, fisherman, carpenter, cook, a patron of arts and learning, even a necromancer. The more subjects interested him – angling, the chase and weaponry – the more eager he was to put his mastery of them on display in print and pictorially. Much of this was self-serving fantasy. Yet the contemporary ideal of the good monarch was a man who knew everything, and from that perspective Maximilian was an impressive performer.[22]

Der Weisskunig would be published in its entirety only in 1775. Maximilian, however, had other texts to remind his subjects of his activities, his achievements and the persona he constructed from them. He made at least one virtual appearance on stage. Conrad Celtis, the most notable humanist whom Maximilian brought to his court, reworked one of the Habsburg's military victories in 1504 into dramatic poetry performed that year by students at the emperor's 'College of Poets and Mathematicians' in Vienna. He persuaded important writers of his day, among them Sebastian Brant, the author of *The Ship of Fools*, to write about him. His name came up frequently in broadsides, panegyrics, even folk songs, which, if they dealt with contemporary events, contained bits of hard news that audiences welcomed. They were also useful for polish-ing Maximilian's image. 'Women suffer, churches fall/the king will avenge them all', promised one text written during a particularly trying conflict that the emperor got into over a succession question in Bavaria in 1503. Maximilian's invitations to diets were also published and widely read because they often had news about current wars. Reports of victories and major diplomatic triumphs were folded into imperial decrees. Between 300 and 400 such documents circulated throughout the Habsburg patrimony and all of Germany, to be posted outside city halls or read from pulpits. Need overrode social distinctions; recruiting in 1494 for the knightly order of St George, established by Frederick III to contain Ottoman aggression, Maximilian asked all ranks of society to participate – prelates, aristocrats, municipal officials, burghers and common folk.[23]

Some of his most important autobiographical projects called for more than the printed page. The historical details of Maximilian's life, especially military events, were carefully selected and re-spun a bit, if necessary, to fit into two of the most grandiose visual projects that he sponsored and supervised: the woodcuts for a triumphal arch (*Ehrenpforte*) and an equally dazzling triumphal procession, the *Triumphzug*, both begun around 1512 under his auspices.[24] The quality of the artists he engaged to realize these images bespoke the seriousness of his intentions. Among them were Hans Burgkmair, Albrecht Altdorfer and, above all, Albrecht Dürer. From sketches to finished products, their work for Maximilian would be reproduced again and again.

Nor did his memorializing programme stop with himself. He was but a recent addition to a genealogical tree that had to be researched and for-mulated for serious political purposes. Competing claims for lands where traditional dynasties had died out or where succession disputes raged were routine in fifteenth- and sixteenth-century Europe. Many rulers, great and small, routinely justified their territorial claims by generating constructions of their lineages, often shamelessly far-fetched, to prove that their families had rights in lands that they were eager to acquire for strategic and eco-nomic reasons. The House of Habsburg was prominent among them; it still had territorial unfinished business in Bohemia and Hungary where there were always competitors for the imperial office should it fall vacant.

Maximilian sponsored several genealogical projects that would per-suade all naysayers that the Habsburgs were sufficiently well connected and venerable to justify whatever claims they advanced. Indeed, his quest for claims to historical pre-eminence turned genealogy into a central element of his court culture. Some of the suggested ancestry was patently absurd; one claim linked the dynasty to the ancient Egyptians, for example. Maximilian himself appears to have understood that he needed a reasonably plausible bloodline for it to be politically useful over a long stretch of time. In 1498 he ordered his first court historian, Ladislaus Sunthaym, to explore more factually the backgrounds of the dukes of Burgundy and the Habsburgs. He would be delighted when another scholar who served him, Jacob Mennel, found that the Habsburgs them-selves could be linked to the Frankish Merovingians, thereby giving the dynasty's candidates for the German crown added status. During one wakeful night just before his death in 1519, the emperor listened to Mennel read through his findings once again.[25]

Before he died, Maximilian and his researchers had also identified a hundred martyrs, popes and saints as Habsburg forebears. These added gravitas to the sacramental aura the dynasty had assigned itself from Rudolph I on. The illustrations for Maximilian's *St George Prayerbook* show sanctified Habsburg ancestors in heaven. In fact, the emperor created for himself a variant of Rudolph I's legendary Eucharistic epiphany. Lying prostrate after a serious hunting accident, Maximilian saw his life closing and gave himself up to Christ. An angel bearing the Host brought him bread, a sign that heaven had a special place for the Habsburgs. Furthermore, Maximilian recovered. More crucial yet to the House of Habsburg's Christian identity was the connection with Burgundy. Duchess Mary's Frankish lineage made her and her progeny direct descendants of Clovis, the Frankish king who had been anointed by God. Her paternal ancestors had already exploited the point; Maximilian would continue to stress it.[26]

Maximilian thus elaborated the visual and literary vocabulary that his family would use to describe and think of itself in decades to come. He would pass on to his grandson, emperor Charles V, not only the imperial office but the custom of portraying Habsburg rulers on horseback, an image that would be before the dynasty's subjects until Habsburg rule ended in Europe for good. Although historians and countless classroom teachers have credited Louis XIV of France with first personalizing himself as a Sun King, Maximilian clearly associated himself with the radiant Sun on the *Ehrenpforte* with the motto 'What the sun is in heaven, the emperor is on earth' (*Quod in coelis sol hoc in terra caesar*). Taken up in the propaganda of his great-great-grandson, Rudolph II, German Emperor from 1576 to 1612, it would then move to France, to be appropriated by Bourbon kings. He joined contemporary rulers in his time in allowing himself to be embodied as Hercules, the classical archetype of power. His successors continued the practice well through the eighteenth century.[27]

Maximilian's sojourn in Burgundy also impressed upon him the tactical value of a splendid court and an elaborate administrative staff that incorporated many regional nobles, where he could watch their moves more closely. Unlike the tight-fisted Frederick III, Maximilian's Burgundian in-laws were also generous and discriminating patrons of art and music: the great Netherlandish portraitist Jan van Eyck was a chamberlain to Duke Philip the Good. They also developed an outstanding chapel choir and orchestra that increasingly blurred the distinction between sacred and secular music. Maximilian imitated them slavishly. Some, in fact, thought that he spent more time diverting himself, aesthetically and erotically, than he should have.[28] But what he saw and heard in Burgundy, then imported to Vienna and Innsbruck, left his successors a cultural infrastructure that would become a fixture in the Habsburg identity, first at the court, and later far beyond. Most immediately responsive would be some members of the Austrian estates. However much they centralized the administration of their provinces, local nobles began modelling their households and behaviour on standards set by Maximilian, particularly at his preferred seat in Innsbruck.[29]

A Singular Identification in the Making

Maximilian's projects for self-memorialization were largely unfinished when he died in 1519, the *Ehrenpforte* and *Triumphzug* included. For all of the imagination and effort he put into the programme, his contemporaries in the Austrian lands, Germany and the rest of Europe had serious reservations about him as a ruler and as a man. Fellow princes supported and then abandoned him at will, depending upon what role they saw for him in their own agendas.[30] In an age of monarchical over-spending, he had one of the worst credit ratings in Europe, Yet he was quick to distribute vast sums of borrowed money among the imperial electors as they considered the claim of his eldest grandson, Archduke Charles, as their next king and, as it turned out, emperor. While he was publicly far more gracious than his taciturn father, his arrogant commandeering of rural lands and streams for his hunting and fishing parties often enraged the local peasantry.[31] He never would make much headway in meeting a responsibility that threatened to take his Austrian patrimony right out from underneath him: reversing the westward thrust of Ottoman sovereignty.

Maximilian's Austrian lands, along with Hungary to the east, lay directly in the path of various sultans' armies and raiding parties as they edged up the Danube valley in the fifteenth century. Frederick III and his arch-rival Matthias Corvinus of Hungary had been clear on the danger they faced. One factor behind the Hungarian ruler's interest in the imperial crown was the hope that he could enlist Germany directly in defending central Europe against the forces from Constantinople. Corvinus's father, John Hunyadi, made a European reputation for himself in 1456 when his forces repulsed an Ottoman attack on the fortifications of Belgrade. Nevertheless, although the sultans seemed likely to persist in their westward drive, popular concern about the serious danger to all the Austrian Habsburg patrimony lagged for decades. Writing in the fifteenth century, the Austrian historian Thomas Ebendorfer saw the problem as a Christian issue, and not a specifically local one. Nor did Austrians directly affected by Ottoman raiding, especially in Carinthia, think that the Habsburgs could defend them at all. Jakob Unrest, for one, whose parish experienced Ottoman pillaging first hand in 1473, looked to local militias and not Frederick III to protect the region.[32]

From the standpoint of dynastic background, Maximilian was far better positioned than his father to legitimate himself as a defender of Christendom and his family's holdings. Mary of Burgundy's forebears had sizeable records of fighting in medieval Christian–Muslim conflicts, including efforts to recover the Holy Places. Not all of it inspired great confidence, especially an episode that involved Duke Philip I and his son and heir, John the Fearless. Hoping to contain Ottoman expansion, John reached Nikopolis in Greece in 1386. With notions of knightly single combat for God and for Glory in their minds, his Burgundian cavalry met an ignominious end. Refusing to wait for reinforcements from imperial troops under Emperor Sigismund, they slashed their way into the Ottoman ranks, only to be surrounded and badly beaten. John was captured and remained an Ottoman hostage for around two years, when he was released upon payment of a hefty ransom raised by his father. Nevertheless, none of these setbacks significantly weakened the Burgundian crusading ideal.[33] The notion carried over to Maximilian's court astrologer, Johann Lichtenberger, who divined that the Habsburgs were fated to wipe out the Turks. Maximilian's union with a Carolingian bloodline was certain to produce a second Charlemagne.

Crusading had been more or less forced on Frederick III. The fall of Constantinople prompted Aeneas Sylvius Piccolomini, now Pope Pius II, to send the emperor a consecrated sword and the command to prepare a Christian offensive. Frederick was in theory Christendom's secular protector, but he was in no financial position to follow up. In fact, few seemed to take the Ottoman threat seriously, even when he tried to alert his Austrian subjects. In 1467 he founded the Order of St George to serve as the nucleus of future anti-Ottoman campaigns. His subjects were notably uninterested, even when he permitted them to donate to the cause in lieu of fighting. Money from men and women was welcome. Unperturbed, Frederick would argue in 1486 for Maximilian's election as German king in 1486, declaring the title would position him all the better to organize a crusade against what the era knew as 'the Turks'. The Order of St George did not yet seem prepared to help. Maximilian, who continued to support the organization after his father's death, reached

5 The Chain of the Order of the Golden Fleece, founded by Philip III, duke of Burgundy, in 1430.

unusually far out into society for support, with equally dismal results. In 1494 he offered to give gold and silver crosses to commoners in return for one year's service in an anti-Ottoman crusade. Few responded, even fewer asked to join the order.[34]

Maximilian had certainly internalized the family injunction to vanquish what his family would call the 'hereditary enemy'. Indeed, the job had been assigned to him even before birth. The *Weisskunig* synchronizes the future emperor's gestational stages in the womb with movements of the Ottoman armies.[35] He adopted the ornamental features of the crusader, too; he was regularly depicted wearing the necklace of the Burgundy Order of the Golden Fleece (illus. 5). Established by Duke Philip the Good in 1430, its selective noble membership was dedicated to anti-Ottoman offensives that would ultimately return to Christian control the holy places in the Middle East. On Duke Charles the Bold's death in 1477, Maximilian became the head of the brotherhood; the office is still reserved for the senior member of the House of Habsburg.

Membership in the order also brought Maximilian more closely into the orbit of his Burgundian relatives who, despite the notorious humiliation of John the Fearless, had authentic credentials as crusaders. It also aligned Burgundian and Austrian interests more closely. The emperor's youthful alter ego, pictorialized in *Theuerdank*, speaks for both dynasties in costume and in purpose. Wearing the pheasant-plumed headdress of a knight of the Golden Fleece, he leaves on a crusade, at the behest of Princess Ehrenreich, Duchess Mary of Burgundy's stand-in:

Just a few days ago,
The enemy, out of arrogance,
Spilled much Christian blood,
And sorely tried my lands and peoples,
With looting, murder and fire.
My territories lie in such a way.
They border on the unbelievers.
Such danger and hostility
Tears away at Christendom.[36]

Although technically the 'my' of her declaration refers to her Burgundian inheritance, the events she is recounting suggest problems in contemporary southeastern Austria. For Maximilian and his secretaries, it was a distinction without a difference.

Typically for all of his autobiographical undertakings, Maximilian enlisted a legion of artists and writers to publicize every aspect of his anti-Ottoman agenda. His poet laureates eloquently concurred that any war to free Christians, the holy places and Constantinople from Muslim rule was a just war. Panegyrists, hired and independent, ritually promoted him and his dynasty as militant advocates of their faith. The outcome was foreordained. Maximilian appears in Hartmann Schedel's widely circulated *Chronicle of the World* at the head of a triumphal parade in Rome celebrating his conquest of the Turks.[37]

The task was not without its pleasures for the emperor. Among his favourite poses were those of a knight errant-warrior or the leader of military forces. The challenge from Constantinople allowed him to cast himself in these roles as much as he wanted. Artists cooperated repeatedly. Albrecht Dürer worked a lone Christian knight girding himself for battle, clearly a surrogate for the emperor, into a prayer book; Maximilian would dedicate the finished product to the Order of St George. The image reappeared in quasi-secular contexts as well. A woodcut of 1508 by Hans Burgkmair, possibly ordered by Maximilian himself, shows the emperor outfitted with the necklace of the Golden Fleece and a pheasant plume on his helmet, ready for combat against the Turks. Should that not be enough to assure him of victory, he found reassuring portents in current events that had no connection with his court at all. Triumph over the Muslim foe seemed imminent to him in 1512 after the discovery in

Trier of what were alleged to be Jesus' cloak along with the remains of St Matthew the Apostle, who was supposedly buried in Germany.[38]

Yet for all of his faith in his God, the chosen mission of his house and his military prowess, Maximilian was better at dressing as a crusader than performing as one. He neither sponsored nor undertook any such an enterprise. The outcome of all of his efforts amounted to little more than 'frustrated intentions and thwarted ambitions', as one close student of the emperor's self-imaging has put it.[39] Defending Christendom, from the papal perspective, had long been a collective, rather than individual, responsibility of all the faithful, particularly rulers. Maximilian himself endorsed the idea, but found it hard to persuade some of his counterparts to give up their own plans to use the Turks as a cover for their ambitions. King Charles VIII of France used the Ottoman menace as one excuse to invade Italy in 1494. Campaigning for his election in Hungary, Matthias Corvinus had reminded local estates of the same threat as he urged them to think more of the integrity of the kingdom than parochial noble interests.[40] Europe's monarchs suspected that Maximilian hoped to use Habsburg victory over the Turks just as opaquely. They were right. At the end of the fifteenth century Maximilian was using the Ottoman menace to promote a comprehensive administrative reform in Germany that would mandate funding for military commitments more systematically. Not so coincidentally, it would also enable him to defend his Austrian patrimony more effectively. Even as his life drew to a close, he conjured up prospects of a crusade that had obvious political advantages for his dynasty. Working between 1517 and 1518 to assure the votes of the German electors for his grandson Charles V, already duke of Burgundy and king of Spain, Maximilian pointed out that the young Habsburg possessed resources great enough to begin the long-postponed Christian offensive against the Turks.[41] Left unsaid was that the prospect of victory over the sultans' forces would put much of Europe under Habsburg sway.

In the absence of unconditional victories, Maximilian relied on conventional diplomacy to contain Ottoman expansion throughout central Europe as best he could. Preserving Hungary as a buffer against armies coming up the Danube valley was crucial if he hoped to maintain the integrity of his Austrian patrimony. Any terrain the sultans occupied in Hungary would compress the distance between the core holdings of the Habsburgs and the Ottoman-occupied southeast. Under permissive Jagellonian rule, the Hungarian court had also become a listening station for information about the Ottomans and other significant rulers in central and eastern Europe. Never having held the crown of St Stephen for any length of time, Habsburg rulers wanted at the very least to foster mutually cordial relations with the man who wore it. The kings of Poland, the senior branch of the Jagellon dynasty in Kraków, were not programmatically averse to negotiating flexibly with the Porte, the Ottoman court.[42] But neither, as other European monarchs suspected, was Maximilian. Should it look useful, he was ready to cut territorial deals with the Ottoman regime that rearranged southeastern Europe to mutual advantage. He also considered military policies that stressed defence against the Turks rather than the glorious offensives that had been a staple of Christian culture for centuries. Towards the end of his life he was thinking of organizing various crusading orders, including the Teutonic Knights, the Knights of St John and the Order of St George, into a single force that would at least repel Ottoman marauding and invasion. This too fell through for financial reasons, though his successors would develop a variant of it very soon.[43]

Maximilian was keenly aware that he was leaving unfinished a task with which he had identified himself publicly, frequently and very visibly for much of his life. He did his best to substitute other Habsburg associations with territorial grandeur for the great victory that never came his way. He drew heavily, if fantastically, on his familial connections with Spain, Portugal and their overseas holdings. Both the *Triumphzug* and the *Ehrenpforte* bear coats of arms for 'the islands', probably a reference to Habsburg holdings in the Atlantic and South Atlantic. The lands and inhabitants of Asia had a place in his schemes as well. To demonstrate the breadth of their emperor and patron's *imperium*, Altdorfer and Burgkmair invented the 'People of Calcutta' (*Kalikutischen Leut*) around 1512. Generically outfitted as Indians or in the 'Moorish fashion', as Maximilian instructed, they appeared in plans for the *Triumphzug*. Such people, 'from nations far and wide' and 'conquered by the Emperor', as Maximilian directed the explanatory text to read, reinforced his dynasty's claims to world rule. He was, as usual, overstating his case; Portugal, with colonial outposts in parts of India, was indisputably the homeland of his mother; its kings, however, had never recognized the sovereignty of German emperors. Nevertheless, panegyrists for Suleiman the Magnificent, Maximilian's arch-rival in Constantinople, had forecast a global empire for the Ottomans and their faith, and Maximilian could not let such ambitions go unchallenged.[44]

Remarkably, he acknowledged not only his achievements but also his shortcomings in print and pictorially. Chapter 117 of *Theuerdank*, composed late in his career, shows only a picture of a knight off to do battle with the 'unbelievers'. The page for an explanatory text is blank. Nevertheless, by the end of his life he was setting the stage for a future Habsburg victory over the Ottomans. Though Hungary had eluded his grasp and that of his father, Maximilian continued to think that the kingdom belonged to him. He knew exactly what would be his once he or one of his heirs governed the realm: a section of the *Ehrenpforte* displays the coats of arms of Croatia, Bosnia and, somewhat vaguely, Dalmatia. All bore some relationship to the Hungarian crown; all three, at Maximilian's death, stood in the Ottoman sphere of influence. It was now up to the emperor's progeny (*Sippschaft*), reads the legend on one panel of the arch, to protect the territory that the Habsburgs now governed and capture others conquered by the Ottomans. To this end, Maximilian had undertaken and actually completed a major first step. In 1515 he had engineered a double betrothal for two of his half-Spanish grandchildren. Archduke Ferdinand and Archduchess Mary would marry Princess Anna and Prince Louis, the offspring of King Vladislav of Bohemia and Hungary. The penultimate panel on the *Ehrenpforte* shows the emperor hovering solicitously over all four children. The legend promises that the unions to follow from this arrangement would be of great benefit to Christendom. As with the final page of *Theuerdank*, the last panel is left open for the text that they will create. Clearly he was charging his successors with ridding Europe of the Ottomans. He was also predicating that defeat on a continued Habsburg presence in central and east central Europe and expansion of the dynasty's holdings. It was equally clear that the broadening of Habsburg influence in Europe would take place largely at the expense of Muslim sultans and their own universal dreams.[45]

It seems also likely that Maximilian's counter-Ottoman strategies were now being dictated by the emperor's practical side. The familiar image of the lone knightly defender of Christendom is absent from the final panels of the *Ehrenpforte*. Though Romantic Austrian writers, searching for patriotic heroes in the nineteenth century, fictionalized Maximilian as 'the last of the knights', the emperor seems to have abandoned the fantasy.[46] The *Ehrenpforte* implies that if the House of Habsburg were to defeat its 'hereditary enemy', it would begin with firm control of strategic crowns, particularly in Hungary. Effective military leadership and disciplined armies would also help. Maximilian himself had realized this in his more realistic moments, but never been able to follow through. It was up to future generations of the dynasty to convince a suspicious Europe, their own subjects, even themselves, that they deserved the job to which they had nominated themselves.

There is no more eloquent testimony to Maximilian the man, his outsize imagination, his disappointments and his legacy to his family than the cenotaph and mammoth bronze statues that surround his intended burial site. Located in the court church complex in Innsbruck, the emperor began planning the installation around 1502; design got under way in 1509. Like so many of his projects, it would not be completed in his lifetime. Forty historical and legendary figures, among them King Arthur and Theodoric, the fifth-century founder of an Ostrogothic kingdom of Italy, were to surround the grave site; 28 were completed by 1583. Nor is Maximilian buried there. His real tomb is in the far more subdued chapel of St George in Wiener Neustadt, now attached to the Austrian military academy. But the Innsbruck layout to which he hoped posterity would look represented Habsburg self-promotion of a very high order. Dürer supervised some of the earliest work; other contributors were not of that class, but very skilled. Many of the finishing touches were done by Alexander Colin, a major sculptor from the Netherlands who was commissioned by Ferdinand I, Maximilian's grandson.[47] Though realization of his ideas was spotty, Maximilian unquestionably knew how to think big. Should his successors actually drive the Ottomans from central Europe, he had shown them how to tell the world all about it.

THREE

CHAMPIONS OF FAITH AND FAMILY

A Man, a House, a Place

Though he wished all of humankind to recall him warmly and well, Maximilian left his dynasty a problematic legacy. The immense debt load he had piled up would be the nucleus of fiscal burdens handed down to Habsburgs for generations to come. On the other hand, his testamentary provisions for the Habsburg Austrian patrimony did much to ensure the family's survival. His son, Philip I of Spain, had died in 1505, leaving two male heirs, Charles and Ferdinand. The former, after 1515 ruler of Castile and Aragon, after 1519 German emperor, would have vast resources if he managed them wisely. He held territorial titles in the family's less wealthy Austrian patrimony as well.

Ferdinand's maternal grandfather, King Ferdinand of Aragon, had thought about promoting his namesake as his successor, but never quite figured out how to do it. Finding an appropriate title for the youth became Maximilian I's problem. His solution was thoroughly conventional: his will ordered division of the Habsburg patrimony in central Europe between the two brothers. A further agreement between Charles, Ferdinand and their advisers, who hammered out the details in 1522, assigned Ferdinand virtually all of these holdings. Charles nominally retained title to all of these lands; his career, however, quickly drifted towards defence of the offices in the Burgundian Netherlands, Spain and Italy conferred on him by both sides of his family. As the New World opened up, Maximilian's dreams of universal empire seemed briefly in reach.[1] But even Germany, where he was emperor, would take second place to his Mediterranean concerns. Should Charles appear in central Europe at all, it was in moments of crisis, and he skipped some of those too. By his death in 1558 governance of the Habsburg holdings in central and western Europe had been functionally divided between Charles's son, Philip II, and his uncle Ferdinand, though only after fierce quarrelling over which of the two branches of the dynasty would offer the next family candidate for the German emperorship. Even after that was settled the Habsburgs, both German and Spanish, claimed the totality of the dynasty's patrimony until the first decades of the eighteenth century, when the Spanish line died out.

Ferdinand spent his childhood with his mother in Spain; as an adolescent he was sent to the court of his aunt Margaret in Mechelen to remove him far from the Spanish throne that he always hoped would come his way. To keep his progeny eligible for the position, he would eventually introduce the system of cross-cousin marriage that both branches of his family made notorious. But his stay in the Netherlands left him well educated; it also put him in touch with the thinking of the great Netherlandish humanist Erasmus of Rotterdam, who was resetting scholarly standards for biblical criticism and Christian practice.[2]

He was not, however, the German ideal of a territorial ruler. Habsburgs were very familiar in central and east-central Europe, but Spanish Habsburgs were quite another breed. The young prince spoke barely a word of German upon his arrival. He did not help his cause by importing several Spanish advisers and courtiers, who were likely to influence him more than regional nobles and notables. The latter routinely expected to have access to their local prince and even served in his court. The common people of his lands had their differences with Ferdinand's entourage, too: the Spanish soldiers who accompanied him to Linz for his wedding to Princess Anna of Hungary in 1521 insulted town residents, who avenged themselves with their fists and whatever else was available.[3]

His reign also began on an ugly note, a leftover from his grand-father's domestic administrative reforms. Anticipating that he would be out of his patrimony as often as he would be in it, Maximilian had begun arranging for officials to act for him before provincial deliberative bodies. The latter, accustomed to dealing personally with their territorial ruler, were implacably hostile to surrogates, especially when extraordinary taxation was at issue. Opposition from the estates of Lower Austria and municipal authorities in Vienna was especially stubborn. Ferdinand reacted swiftly and punitively, and by 1523 the dissidence had subsided. Many of his subjects found it hard to forgive the execution of prominent figures in the resistance, the mayor of Vienna included.

It was a most unpromising start to a career as a territorial ruler. Yet Ferdinand would manage it in ways that raised the profile of the House of Habsburg to levels his ancestors had never reached, domestically and even abroad. Like his grandfather and his great-grandfather, he took

Central Europe, *c.* 1570.

every title he could to enhance his own position and that of his house. His responses to the daunting circumstances he faced became formative moments in the development of the lasting and spectacular pan-European identity of his house, which would be fixed by around 1700. Ottoman raiders and armies moved relentlessly towards Ferdinand's patrimony during his reign; the Protestant Reformation came to the Austrian lands about the same time. The first threatened his control of his patrimony, which included Hungary and Bohemia by 1527; the second promised to segment his peoples into confessional factions that made governing them more problematic than any prince wanted. Neither of these issues was settled in his lifetime. Indeed, the two questions would become interrelated in ways that complicated the Habsburg position in Europe significantly. Against the Ottomans, he became one of Christendom's notable, if accidental, defenders. In the case of religion he managed to keep the House of Habsburg Catholic, no small accomplishment when the faith of his eldest son wavered. A territorial division he required of his three archdukes split their resources badly but ensured the survival of the faith in at least some of the Austrian lands. It also provided the house with a useful cadet line in a moment of dire need. The forced Catholicism exercised by some of his immediate successors won the dynasty few friends among Europe's Protestants in the sixteenth and seventeenth centuries. Nevertheless, it made what was becoming the Habsburg empire easier to control, politically and culturally.

Developing a Political Identity

Ferdinand's Austrian patrimony was minuscule compared to the realms his brother controlled. The debts he inherited from his grandfather made it necessary for him to manage what incomes he had more efficiently; he therefore began centralizing his government more systematically, following lines laid down by the late emperor. He was, however, willing to make some concessions to traditional regional prerogatives, and the various offices he set up – a chancellery, a court council and a rudimentary central finance bureau with provincial subsidiaries – met with the open hostility that Maximilian provoked in the Austrian lands. The structure left by Ferdinand persisted in the Austrian lands until well into the eighteenth century. It also became the model followed by other German rulers in organizing their own establishments.

Equally pressing was the need to validate his credentials as a worthy member of his house, locally and abroad. He began by underscoring the future that his Austrian grandfather had assigned to him. Though we are not sure of the audience he had in mind, Ferdinand ordered 700 reproductions of Dürer's *Ehrenpforte* woodcut that suggested his political future.[4] He continued efforts to keep his ancestors in the public eye, resuming work on his grandfather's unfinished cenotaph in Innsbruck.

Dreams of Spanish crowns notwithstanding, he turned immediately to making his patrimonial share in central Europe the proving ground for his career. Basic and reliable information was apparently important to him; he was committed enough to want information about them at his command. His court historian, renowned humanist Wolfgang Lazius, was assigned to write a history of Austria. A scholar committed to working from primary sources, Lazius scoured regional monasteries, including Gurk in Carinthia and Göttweig and Lilienfeld in Lower Austria, for suitable documentation. Leaving a receipt, he quietly transferred these materials to what would become the court library in Vienna.[5]

Popular perceptions of leaders' characters and the degree to which they were comfortable with their subjects played a significant, if informal, role in the legitimizing process. From the standpoint of private behaviour, Ferdinand was, by contemporary standards, an unusually admirable figure. Maximilian I had gone to extraordinary lengths and spent vast sums of money in publicizing his variants of himself. Ferdinand was as conscious of his exalted status as his grandfather. Unlike the latter, however, he was not given to self-advertisement; he was energetic, disciplined and intellectually nimble, but also as cautious and circumspect as his grandfather was self-confident and extroverted. He had expensive tastes, but he offset them with a simple personal lifestyle that characterized many Habsburgs in generations to come. Through the last decades of his life he ate only one meal a day and drank sparingly. His personal morals were those of a model Catholic layman; his marriage to Princess Anna of Hungary and Bohemia was a dynastic success story: husband and wife were devoted to one another and proved it with an impressive array of legitimate progeny, fifteen in all. He deeply mourned her death from a postpartum infection in 1547 and had no interest in remarrying.

He did, however, make quite clear that he and his house were in Vienna to stay. The city became his capital in a way that it had not been either for Frederick III, who had endured some of the worst moments of his life in and around it, or Maximilian I, who preferred the recreational opportunities available in the Tyrol. It was Ferdinand who made the first efforts, partial though they were, to remodel the medieval and dingy Hofburg, which would become synonymous with Habsburg rule. The entrance to the inner court, the black and dusty-red Swiss Gate (Schweizer Tor) built between 1552 and 1553, bears his name and numerous titles, including prince of Spain. As he rose in status, he allowed the general public to enjoy his advancement. After becoming German emperor in 1555, he sponsored increasing numbers of house and public celebrations, or mixtures of the two, that brought him, his family and some of the values they represented to the city's residents. His children also gave the city an occasional festive treat. Entrances, even of archdukes, could be memorable occasions. Maximilian II and his Spanish wife returned to the city from the Iberian Peninsula in 1552 with an elephant. A gift from the king of Portugal, it left spectators gasping. The dynasty's weddings were both private ceremonies and municipal entertainments. The formal nuptials took place before a core audience made up of the family, appropriate officials and court personnel, and a select number of invited guests. The entrance of the bridegroom and the arrival of the bride, on the other hand, could be seen by the public; such affairs were organized, designed and paid for by the city of Vienna itself. Public enjoyment of lavish celebrations for dynastic rites of passage would spread to the provinces too. Seven years after Ferdinand's death in 1554, the marriage of his youngest son, Archduke Charles, and Princess Mary of Bavaria was repeated in Graz with red and white wine flowing from a town fountain.[6]

As useful as such conventional gestures may have been, they addressed Ferdinand's minor problems only. Sultan Suleiman II the Magnificent had taken Belgrade and its fortifications in 1521 and was edging ever westward. On 25 August 1525 Ottoman forces clashed at Mohács in southwestern Hungary with those of Ferdinand's brother-in-law, King Louis II. The battle ended in an ignominious defeat for the king, who died after falling from his horse when retreating from the conflict. The two crowns that Louis held – Hungary and Bohemia – were now vacant.

The date coincided with the anniversary of another major moment in Habsburg history: Rudolph I's triumph in 1278 over Otakar of Bohemia at the Marchfeld. Though perhaps not taking his distinguished predecessor as a model, Ferdinand was as quick as Rudolph I to capitalize on an opportunity long sought by his family. After protracted negotiations in both kingdoms, along with a short military campaign in Hungary, where a significant faction of the estates had elected a native claimant, Ferdinand ruled both realms by 1527. His success, particularly in

Hungary, came not so much from his own qualities, but from his ties to his brother. Surely, as the reasoning went among some of Hungary's magnates, a brother of King Charles I of Spain, Charles V, German emperor, and Charles II, duke of Burgundy, could count on fraternal help in keeping their kingdom whole and Christian. The results fell far short of their expectations.

As an elected king in at least part of Hungary, sometimes referred to as royal Hungary, and in Bohemia, Ferdinand was now more than a junior archduke with more important close relatives in Spain. Culturally and politically, both kingdoms had histories and constitutional practices all their own; Ferdinand was especially uncomfortable with the idea of elective monarchy. Adapting to such procedures yet maintaining his controlling position would be among his lifetime tasks. Ferdinand had taken up arms in Hungary to subdue his local opponent, John Zápolya, but he clearly preferred to pursue his basic goals without provoking the antagonisms that military measures leave in their wake. Court appointments, from the lower levels to the highest, often soothed the affronted political status and financial well-being of local notables when foreign rulers brought their own agendas, administrative styles and service personnel to their new realms. Ferdinand accepted the need to make adjustments here; in Bohemia, for example, he removed deeply resented German managers from silver mining operations. In a more innovative vein, he appreciated the role of language in bringing a ruler closer to his peoples. Even as his German remained a work in progress, he made an effort to develop some facility in Hungarian and Czech. Maximilian was even more linguistically versatile, though how fluent he was in languages he reportedly knew is uncertain. More important for future ties, however, was the cadet school that Ferdinand established to acquaint his three sons with the idioms of their father's patrimony; noble boys from all of the Habsburg realms were invited to Vienna where they conversed with the young archdukes, who picked up elements of the Slavic and Magyar vernaculars through repetition and association.

Ottoman expansionism, however, was Ferdinand's most persistent concern. He had been raising the alarm on the Ottoman threat almost from the moment he had arrived in Austria. A good part of his life would be spent on convincing Christian rulers, his brother included, to resist Ottoman campaigns. Suleiman's expansionist visions, more than a little ironically, had opened the way for Ferdinand to hold two royal crowns that his ancestors had coveted. But the defeat at Mohács and the sultan's occupation of Buda now put the young Habsburg squarely in the path of Ottoman advances that would surely move on to the Austrian lands. The Ottoman ruler, indeed, had actually hoped to take Vienna in 1525, but postponed the campaign until the weather would be better and logistics fully prepared. His return trip in 1529 brought him to the walls of the city, but once again hostile conditions, disease among his troops and the defenders' stubborn resistance persuaded him to retreat. Ferdinand, who was away from the city trying to drum up some aid for his beleaguered capital, had yet another narrow escape.

The aborted siege of Vienna gave residents a taste of what many in Europe thought would follow Ottoman conquest. Returning to the city on 1 December 1529 after an extended diplomatic mission, Sigismund von Herberstein, a sober and trusted emissary of both Maximilian and Ferdinand, was shocked by what he saw:

> Its appearance had changed completely. All of the outlying districts, which were not that much smaller than the city proper, were razed and burned down in order to keep the enemy from taking his comforts within them, and most of all in order to allow wares to be brought in through one narrow passage. The enemy had done the same thing throughout the entire region for the same reason; one could rarely look as far as a crossbow could shoot, without spotting a human corpse, a dead horse, pig or cow lying about . . . from Vienna down to Wiener Neustadt. It was pathetic.[7]

Avoiding catastrophes through good fortune and the steadfastness of others translates poorly into legends of dynamic leadership. Some of Ferdinand's best-known and most articulate contemporaries had nothing but scorn for his behaviour during the siege of 1529. Hans Sachs, sixteenth-century Germany's master of occasional verse, was one. In one short poem, 'A Tyrannical Deed of the Turks that Took Place Outside Vienna' ('Ein tyrannische that dess Türken vor Wien Begangen'), the poet has Suleiman threatening to hunt down Ferdinand, supposedly hiding in Linz. In Sachs's 'As the Turks Camped Before Vienna' ('Wie der Türke vor Wien lag') Ferdinand not only dismisses a local Viennese delegation begging him to defend the site vigorously, but also says that he will yield the city to the Turks. In Sachs's longest account, 'The Ottoman Siege of Vienna' ('Historia der türkischen Belagerung der Stadt Wien'), the poet attributed Suleiman's retreat to the bravery of local defenders and, most importantly, providential concern for Christendom. For the faith to survive, divine intervention would again be necessary. No role is assigned to Ferdinand at all. A contemporary Austrian memoirist, Georg Kirchmair, said much the same thing, though he thought that Emperor Charles v could have been more helpful. Lazius, the court historian, stressed the contribution that sturdy walls and lookout towers had made to saving the city.[8]

Still other writers and publicists, in central Europe and elsewhere, began looking far more positively at Ferdinand, the Habsburgs and even the Austrian lands as Christendom's defenders. The siege of Vienna in 1529 began the city's transformation throughout Europe into an emblematic arena of Muslim–Christian hostility. Its name appeared in titles of numerous pamphlets, poems and eyewitness accounts of the event published throughout the continent. Though failing to mention the Habsburgs once, Sachs's poem on the 1529 struggle abounds in mentions of local landmarks where action took place: city gates, the Danube, religious houses and, perhaps most memorable of all, the bells in the tower of St Stephen's Cathedral that rang as the Ottomans withdrew.[9] At least 37 works on the sultan's failed campaign, mostly in German but also in Italian, French and Latin, came out between 1529 and 1530 alone. Sensationalism drove more than one author; Archbishop Vincenzo Pimpinella in eastern Calabria produced the exemplary 'On the Great Turk's Siege of Vienna, Austria. The Horrors of Cruelty and Unusual Torments Used by the Turks against Christians, as well as Bestial Savagery against Domestic Animals and Things. Mines, Tactics, Furious Assaults of the Turks and Descriptions of their very Powerful Army'.[10] Some were allegedly eyewitness accounts; some were second-hand journalism; some were in rhyme. Among the latter was a piece by one Christoffel Zell who, though never present at the scene, insisted on being known as the author. Printed in Nuremberg, it was to be sung to a familiar hymn tune. To make sure that readers knew exactly what Suleiman's target had been, one newsletter provided several historical variants of Vienna's name, including three possibilities in Hungarian. Illustrations in several texts, some of which reproduced in detail the contested sites in the city, also added to the immediacy of place.[11] At the very least, the 1529 siege gave residents enough distaste for Ottoman rule for the whole scenario to be invoked publicly in church homilies when Suleiman was organizing another offensive in 1532.[12]

Ferdinand himself received a notable endorsement in the pamphlet *Vienna Austria the Noble City under the Siege of Sultan Suleyman the Magnificent with a Huge Army. With Gratitude to the most Powerful*

Emperor Charles and his Renowned and most Invincible Brother Ferdinand, the king of Bohemia and Hungary, published in 1530. It marked an upward step in esteem for someone whom Suleiman was calling the 'Little King'.[13] In fact, Ferdinand had formally carried out at least part of the mission that his grandfather had assigned to him on the *Ehrenpforte*: defending the Habsburg Austrian patrimony and the small chunk of northern and eastern Hungary to which he now had claim. He had also established himself as a plausible champion of his faith. Looking back after twenty years on the outcome of the Battle of Mohács and the 1529 episode, Lazius had been persuaded that Ferdinand alone was positioned for these roles. He had also, in the scholar's opinion, performed for his subjects a service once rendered by the progenitor of the House of Habsburg. Rudolph I had defeated a tyrannical Otakar II of Bohemia; Ferdinand had vanquished an equally despotic sultan.[14]

Though he clearly suffered a setback in 1529, Suleiman's expansionist designs did not change. By 1531 Ferdinand was preparing for the long haul, psychologically and tactically. Crises often made him eloquent; threats to his new crown in Hungary made him all the more so. Writing in his native Spanish to his brother, he set out the situation in broad strokes:

> [the Kingdom of Hungary] so noble, large, productive and wealthy and so many guiltless souls, and so much Christian blood, and many men and women, boys and girls, images of the living God, should under no circumstances fall into the hands of the Turkish tyrant, an enemy and scorner of God as well as humankind. Such a thing would diminish and damage the honour of our Lord and his holy faith and good and sacred laws, both divine and human, and bring hardship and restrictions on public peace and liberty to trouble [us] now as well as those yet to come.

In fighting for Hungary, he would be working to save 'the Faith, the Fatherland, Liberty', and 'their children and households'. An 'honest death' in such a fight was preferable to servitude.[15]

While Ferdinand's main worry was his personal survival as a territorial ruler, his references to offspring and dwellings were not empty formalities. He needed the active support of all segments of the societies he ruled. Fully aware that many of his subjects, particularly peasants, had yet to consider Ottoman landlords worse than their Christian counterparts, he thought that some would willingly surrender the kingdom to the sultan once and for all.[16] Indeed, Ferdinand's rival for the Hungarian crown, John Zápolya, had retreated to his homeland of Transylvania after being vanquished by the Habsburg in 1527. There he resumed his role as governing prince of the territory, but only after establishing himself as a vassal of the Ottoman ruler.

Far more rhetorical firepower, visual as well as verbal, was needed to impress the virtues of the House of Habsburg and the nefariousness of the Muslim Turks on Hungarians, Austrians and Europe at large. Efforts in the dynasty's German-speaking lands to overcome popular indifference to the alleged horrors of Muslim rule had started in the latter decades of the fifteenth century, particularly in religious settings. Around 1480, for example, the cathedral church in Graz had commissioned a depiction of the three torments – Hunger, Pestilence and War – each with its own embodiment: locusts, plague and the Turks. Until the Hungarian disaster at Mohács and the siege of Vienna, the Turks had been troublesome only in Carinthia and Styria. They now, however, appeared ready to move much further into central Europe; Ferdinand and his immediate successors had far greater numbers of people spread over a much wider territory to defend, many of whom had never given much thought to the problem. Raw sensationalism, tempered by some elements of truth about the Ottoman armies and Ottoman rule, was a formula calculated to arouse the public and to keep its anxieties high for every appearance that the so-called 'Turk' chose to make.[17]

The alarmist intonations and imagery of Ferdinand's letter to Charles therefore previewed the norm for Habsburg constructions of the enemy from Constantinople throughout the dynasty's holdings for the next century and a half. News of Christian leaders being impaled after the Battle of Mohács and the frightful moments of the siege of 1529, when the sultan's armies had allegedly brutalized residents of the city as they fled, circulated in broadsides and newsletters all over central Europe. The number of such publications exploded throughout the German-language community in the sixteenth and seventeenth centuries – 8,000 to 10,000 according to one serious estimate. Although not all of them dealt with Ottoman–Christian confrontations, many did under emotionally charged headlines such as 'Terrifying News', 'Pathetic News' and 'Happy News'. The Austrian lands, Bohemia and Habsburg-controlled regions of Hungary were increasingly ornamented with grisly reminders, written and pictorial, of the Turks and their surrogates: Turks performing the biblical Massacre of the Innocents and turbaned figures torturing Jesus along the way to Calvary were among the more suggestive examples. That Ottoman behaviour sometimes matched these images made the latter all the more plausible. The mention of the sites of these atrocities in the titles of reports in printed newsletters and broadsides all but confirmed the factuality of the texts. It was highly likely, for example, that an encounter with Ottoman forces had taken place in Komárom (Ger. Komorn) in 1595 when a local schoolmaster published a long lyric poem on the subject called '[A] True, Detailed, and Actual Description of the Nature of the Siege of the Imperial Border Fortress of Komorn in Lower Hungary by Sinan Pasha, the Grand Vizier of Sultan Murad, the Turkish Emperor in Constantinople, the Foe of all of Christendom after the [Ottoman] Surrender of the City of Raab'.[18] They also did much to persuade contemporaries that the Christian and Habsburg causes were inseparable and just.

The Habsburg identification with this mission would never sit equally well at all times in varied populations that often wearied of shouldering the costs of their own defence and suffered as much from the marauding of unpaid Christian troops as from Suleiman's raiders. Hungarian serfs often preferred absentee Muslim landlords to the resident Christian variety; and aristocrats in the southern regions of the kingdom were far more interested in protecting their own properties than they were in the theological sensibilities of those with whom they bargained. But people in all social and economic stations had sound reason to fear and resent the Ottomans too. Nobles who had to turn over their holdings to the Ottomans in Hungary, villagers taken in captivity from their homes, refugees who had drifted into Hungary from Serbian areas in the Balkans, all had their grievances with Muslim rule and wanted it ended by whatever means possible. The accidents of territorial alignment and battle had virtually forced Ferdinand I and his family into the job. No one could say that the Habsburgs were innocent of ambition in central Europe, but they would have preferred to realize it by negotiating with less committed opponents than Suleiman II. Nevertheless, regardless of which side had the stronger moral position and territorial claims in the region, many subjects of the House of Austria had a real stake in its survival. As this relationship developed, their respect, even admiration for Habsburg rule would grow. The sixteenth-century Hungarian humanist Johannes Sambucus was indeed very close to Ferdinand and his eldest son, Maximilian II. He was also a thoroughgoing patriot of his native Hungary. Nevertheless, he said that among the regional rulers of central Europe the Habsburgs were the rulers most likely to drive back the Turks. Ferdinand and Max-imilian II, he said, were good rulers; they respected laws, maintained public peace and knew when to fight. All these opinions he bundled into his widely circulated study of emblems that went through several printings until the end of the sixteenth century.[19] Though Ottoman aggression had complicated Ferdinand's career mightily, it had given him a wonderfully useful way to persuade his subjects to keep him on the job. His ceaseless travels to all corners of his land in search of mili-tary funding were a constant reminder that he was trying to defend them. Because the problem never quite went away in his lifetime, he was in a position to deliver a credible message again and again, remind-ing the peoples he now ruled and even other members of his house that they really needed him.

Divisions from Within

Ottoman conquest was by itself an existential threat to Ferdinand I as a territorial ruler. Worse yet, it overlapped with what proved to be over time an even more intractable problem for European monarchs of his day, politically and militarily.[20] Ruling princes routinely assumed that prince and subject had to be of the same faith for government to function effectively. Though he probably was not the author, Ferdinand I's grand-son Archduke Matthias summarized the view exquisitely in a memoran-dum from 1504: 'it is impossible to govern a sound polity where religions differ, because for subjects to obey authority they must trust and love it; where religion is not uniform, government is not respected.'[21] Religious pluralism undermined public deference to authority and provoked wars among Christians themselves. Enmities churned up by sectarian dissidence vexed Catholic and Protestant rulers alike.

To demonstrate his proposition, Matthias pointed to the sixteenth-century German Reformation, a spiritual and political convulsion that began working its way through Germany's numerous principalities shortly before Ferdinand I arrived in Habsburg Austria. Inspired by a fiercely pious Augustinian monk, Martin Luther, it was a frontal attack not only on ever-present problems with clerical corruption, but on the structure and theology of papal authority as well.

Ferdinand never denied the Catholic Church, the papacy and the clergy were in need of moral improvement. In the Netherlands he had absorbed the central programme of a Catholic reform movement, identified with Erasmus of Rotterdam, which called for new standards of scholarship and personal behaviour throughout the Church hierarchy. Ferdinand, however, was genuinely devout and thought that Luther, his followers and the dissenting persuasions that soon spun off from their movement were in profound error. Indeed, he thought that his own salvation hung on reversing evangelical gains made by Protestants among his own peoples. He also, however, needed external funding to pay for his campaigns, offensive and defensive alike, and for armies against the Turks. Time and again he made such requests to the princes of Germany and his Austrian estates. In both cases, the price they exacted included concessions to the new evangelical reform. The conflict forced him reluctantly into several compromises with Luther's followers and others who had broken from the Church of Rome to establish movements generically denominated as Protestant. Though Pope Paul iv fumed mightily, Ferdinand brokered a peace at a meeting of the imperial diet in Augsburg in 1555 that provisionally recognized Lutheran and Catholic territorial churches in the Empire until its princes agreed to restore a single, though revitalized, Catholic faith.

Within his own lands, Ferdinand's defence of Roman Catholic orthodoxy was more vigorous. In his early years he drove more radical Protestants from his Austrian lands, especially those who were convinced pacifists. Wholeheartedly convinced that the survival of his faith depended upon good preaching and effective teaching, he brought a new order, the Jesuits, from Italy to Vienna in 1551. There they founded their first college in central Europe; another was opened in Prague in 1555. Ferdinand wrote the introduction to a new Catholic catechism, prepared by the Jesuit Peter Canisius and published in 1555. Administrators and advisers with Protestant leanings served at his court. But he drew a sharp line between needs dictated by politics and the souls of his family members. Indeed, he was concerned enough about the spiritual welfare of the latter to forego good relations with his offspring in order to set things right.

Ferdinand's eldest son, Maximilian, was a difficult person. Intellectually sophisticated and well educated, he was also prone to overstepping the moral standards of his faith, indulging as a young man in bouts of heavy drinking, womanizing and general frivolity. Ferdinand called him sharply to task for such behaviour in 1547, pointing out the danger not only to the young man's frail body but to his public reputation.[22] Where father and son did clash bitterly, however, was over the younger man's apparent attraction to Protestant reform.

Headstrong young prince though he may have been, Maximilian never explained his attraction to evangelical doctrine in detail.[23] Father and son in fact agreed that practice and learning in their church were in need of serious reform. Nevertheless, Ferdinand persisted in viewing Luther and his followers as symptoms of Catholic practice gone astray, dangerously so when the disruptive cleric argued that the Turks were God's punishment on a sinful people and not to be countered aggressively. Maximilian, however, would repeatedly neglect formal requirements of his faith, such as regular confession and appearing in public religious processions. That many in his family deplored his behaviour, including his wife Mary, the sister of King Philip II of Spain, made no apparent impact on him. In a codicil to a will he had written in 1554, Ferdinand reminded his son of the prosperity that had come to the House of Habsburg as observant Roman Catholics. Members of their family were connected to every throne in Europe, with the exception of Scotland. The New World had come under their control as well.[24] At a tense conference in 1552 with his father and brothers, Maximilian vowed to remain within the Church of Rome, which he did. But Ferdinand would never trust Maximilian's Catholic loyalties enough to grant him governance of the entire Habsburg patrimony. Rather he would undo one of the most notable achievements of the grandfather who had charged him to protect the integrity of the Habsburg lands. He re-divided the dynasty's central European holdings, now augmented by Bohemia and Hungary, among his three male heirs. Maximilian received the lion's share: Bohemia, the part of Hungary under Habsburg rule, and what is today Upper and Lower Austria. He would also succeed to the German emperorship, a position that Philip of Spain, Charles V's son, was ready to yield. The Tyrol, along with what was left of the Habsburg territories in Swabia, would go to the second son, the impeccably Catholic Archduke Ferdinand. Archduke Charles, the youngest brother, was equally unshakeable in matters of faith, so much so that his father thought that he might be a Catholic and a consort to Elizabeth of England at the same time. The youngest archduke received Inner Austria: Styria, Carinthia and Carniola, now part of Slovenia.[25]

After Ferdinand's death in 1554, Protestants continued to have important privileges in the lands that fell to Maximilian. He granted Lutherans in Bohemia and Lower Austria the right to worship as they saw fit, although he successfully denied their appeals to build churches. The careers of both his brothers, as their father may have suspected, were far more to Catholic liking. The evangelical reform never put down deep roots in the Tyrol; the younger Ferdinand's task in Innsbruck was to maintain a solidly Orthodox confessional environment, and he did it very well. The Jesuits were especially active there, supported generously by a strictly observant nunnery in Hall under the direction of Archduchess Magdalena, Ferdinand I's third daughter and a dauntingly pious lady.

Archduke Charles and his very devout wife Mary, a Wittelsbach princess from Bavaria, contended with altogether different circumstances in Styria and Carinthia. Here the teachings of Luther and his followers had won many converts in towns and cities. They also had strong support from important members of a regional nobility that guarded its political prerogatives jealously and had no intention of relinquishing such powers, even for military necessities. Around 1578 local estates blocked Charles's efforts to raise a peasant militia against the Turks, arguing that only they had the right to recruit such forces.[26] Latitudinarianism was the farthest thought from the minds of both husband and wife. Nevertheless, Charles followed a path already worn by his father and elder brother: temporizing with the Protestants in the local estates in order to raise funds for military undertakings, chiefly against the Turks. But before his dynasty could apply itself wholeheartedly to this enterprise, it had to resolve a familiar, yet very serious question about its future, the more privately the better.

From Crisis to Crisis

The death of Maximilian II in 1575 left his court in Vienna in some disarray. While his brothers cultivated their own establishments in Graz and Innsbruck, his eldest son, Rudolph, succeeded him in Austria, Bohemia and royal Hungary. As Rudolph II he was also German king and emperor. In adulthood, his reclusive preoccupations and behaviour made him the object of public curiosity that he is to this day. As a child and youth, however, it was the dynamics of Rudolph's educational and religious environment rather than his eccentricity that made him interesting, even important. He was a prime example of the strains that contemporary religious factionalism took on family solidarity, sovereign dynasties included.

Maximilian II's confessional ambiguities troubled not only his wife and his father, but his cousin Philip II in Spain. With Ferdinand in the lead, all three decided that a future emperor was best educated at an indisputably Catholic court; in 1553 Rudolph and his brother Ernest were dispatched to the establishment of their maternal uncle and paternal second cousin in Madrid for their schooling and upbringing. The letters that Rudolph sent to his father are those of a dutiful though aesthetically sensitive child; his reports indicate that his lessons were heavy on languages and history, Habsburg genealogy included. Recreational outings came up too; excursions to the airy royal summer retreat in Aranjuez, 'truly a pastoral setting', were among Rudolph's favourites. He did not like hard work, a trait that would bedevil his adult career. He was also conscious of his high status: he described himself and his brothers as 'well-born boys'.[27] Returning to the German-speaking regions in 1571 to prepare for the imperial election, he struck people as stiff and supercilious – 'Spanish', the Germans called him.

Just why he shifted his court from Vienna to Prague in 1583 is not clear. A sumptuous coronation in 1575 had made him king of Bohemia, of course, and Emperor Albert II's short reign in the realm from 1438 to 1439 set a precedent for Habsburg residence there as both kings and emperors. Vienna was far less hospitable to Rudolph in several ways. He disliked being so close to his politically engaged mother, the dowager Empress Mary, who could be an intrusive pest, but she had returned for good to Madrid in 1581. Protestants certainly did not trust him; they were sure that anyone with his Spanish education was sure to oppose their evangelical reform altogether. Never the most courageous of men, he might have thought that Luther's supporters threatened his life. He had seen at first hand in 1577 how rancorous and violent religious divisions in Vienna could be. During an Ascension Day procession in which he and his brothers were walking, a nasty fight broke out between their bodyguards and Lutheran milk sellers. Vienna's exposure to Ottoman invasion may have also worried him.[28]

As the years went by, Rudolph avoided confessional controversies far more than he confronted them. He shrank from most conflicts with Protestants. The Royal Castle at Prague, Hradčany, became not only his administrative centre but his personal cultural retreat.[29] By 1595 a Venetian ambassador was reporting on behavioural oddities that were embedding themselves in his character. Unlike his father and his uncle Philip, he had little patience for routine work and the details of foreign affairs. Ministers, not the monarch, handled most of these matters. On the other hand, he seized every opportunity to discuss works of art and natural curiosities and did so at tiresome length. His frequent visits to artists were notorious; he observed them and even worked with them on occasion. He also painted privately.[30]

6 The crown of Emperor Rudolph II (r. 1567–1612).

Nevertheless, reluctance to inflame confessional hostilities and apathy to the business of ruling did not weaken his concern for his house, its place in history and his commitment to displaying it publicly. Whether he was neurotic, schizophrenic or just victim to the psychic and physical effects of the tuberculosis that probably killed him, he kept up on a grand scale the public and private ceremonial rituals of his house. Though he drifted away from his Spanish relatives, Rudolph used the worldwide reach of his family's collective holdings as evidence for the grandeur of his house and his place in it. With the death of Philip II in 1598, he may also have wanted to give visual testimony to a shift in the dynasty's centre of political gravity from Madrid to Vienna. A crown that he privately commissioned for himself pictorially declared that his branch of the house had as much claim to 'worldwide rule' as did the

Spanish line (illus. 6). On the four fields of the crown are scenes of his three coronations in Frankfurt, Hungary and Bohemia and, as we will see, his victory over the Turks.

His court also embodied internationality. Artists, writers and intellectuals whose ideals were far more humanistic than narrowly confessional were welcome; so were officials from Germany and Bohemia alike. From 1595 on Rudolph asked his ambassador in Spain several times for artefacts live and dead from the 'Indies': seeds of exotic plants, Aztec feather crowns, rare minerals, wildcats and parrots. Many ended up in Curiosity Rooms (*Wunderkammer*) and menageries in Prague and Vienna, where they gave content to his personal dynastic reveries and, he hoped, the imaginations of guests he sometimes invited to inspect his latest purchases. Among Rudolph's several fantasies was one that used common interests in art to promote good relations among princes. In fact, lesser German territorial rulers did learn something from him. They looked to the staggering collections of paintings, sculpture and precious stones that the emperor was assembling as models for displays of their own to awe guests with their munificence and taste. For all of his preoccupations with his own magnificence, he did not begrudge the same urges in his subjects. Rudolph often appeared at wedding festivities for members of highly placed noble families in Bohemia, some of which featured tournaments that he had funded.[31]

Rudolph spent profligately to broadcast his attributes of power to his contemporaries. By his death in 1512, his debts, swollen by extended episodes of warfare, came to 12 million florins.[32] It is difficult to judge his impact on his intended audiences, but at times he could be intimidating. Watching him chide a Bohemian nobleman who had asked his king's forgiveness for some offence, a correspondent for the widely circulated *Fugger Newsletters* cryptically observed that 'one does not take rulers lightly; their hands are long and one should not open one's mouth too carelessly'.[33] Residents of Prague had good reason to appreciate his lavish ways. His establishment in the city fed and clothed a legion of minor service personnel, regardless of what they knew and thought of their eccentric master. Rudolph's kitchen staff typified his lavish tastes: the master chef got 500 florins and one errand boy. Other employees included a record keeper, a purchaser, a grinder (*Zuschroter*), a personal cook, six regular cooks, two pâté makers, seven sous-chefs, eight general assistants, three porters for storage areas, two men to carry provisions from markets, a woodcutter, a baker, a confectioner and a door guard. All received free meals.

If the message behind Rudolph's propaganda circulated beyond his immediate surroundings, however, this was achieved not through closely supervised galleries and rarely worn crowns, but through oral transmission. Central to this process were clergy preaching in their pulpits.[34] The Catholic Church had good reason to support one major aspect of Rudolph's foreign policy. Tempted by a perceptible downturn in Ottoman political and military fortunes at the end of the sixteenth century, Rudolph launched an offensive against them in 1592. Explaining the move in the first of his patents that same year, he followed the language and message of his predecessors closely. At the same time he intertwined far more explicitly Catholic Christian practice, loyalty to the dynasty and the well-being of all. As they inflicted harm on Christian princes, the sultans' forces also routinely abducted men, women and children. Behaving as a good Catholic Christian was not only an act of loyalty to the dynasty, but a duty to one's self. Defeating the Turks required God's blessing, a favour not bestowed on sinners or on Protestants who had once been told by Luther to accept the Ottoman menace as a form of divine punishment for their sins. The German reformer had rethought that piece of advice after the Battle of Mohács, but no matter. Rudolph's mandate called for all his peoples to engage in the regular prayer of Catholic orthodoxy and to participate in religious processions.

The many times that Habsburg propagandists reiterated these injunctions suggests that their target populations remained stubbornly reprobate. But common people had reason to listen to them seriously, wherever they heard or read them. Official patents often included crucial practical information such as mustering orders and recruitment notices for defensive duty on the borders. They also reinforced the idea that their emperor and territorial ruler was defending not only his lands but Rome's version of Christianity, which was humankind's sole hope for salvation. Commands to pray and parade also came with specific organizational directives. Obedience was also expected. In 1500 the citizens of Vienna were ordered to group themselves by social and economic class – the emperor's advisers first of all, followed in order by the university, the local magistracy, the city patricians, home-owning citizens, and finally the guilds – each to pray consecutively for specific periods of time. The guilds were also charged to punish members who refused to participate.[35]

The effect of this increasingly close association of religious and dynastic enterprise had political benefits for the dynasty throughout its lands. The close link between faith and state that was celebrated in Rudolph's military successes gave the dynasty a religious, as well as a constitutional position in royal Hungary that would prove invaluable in short order. In the meantime, all of the homilies that common folk heard in their churches and the broadsides that the literate could read seem to have had the broad-based emotional impact that both Church and state were promoting. A temporary victory in 1598 of the emperor's forces over the Ottomans at Győr, close to the Hungarian–Austrian border, sparked a spontaneous outburst of popular elation in Vienna that surprised even clergymen who habitually demonized the Turks from their pulpits.[36]

Rudolph was confronting the Ottomans at one of several periods in their history when internal difficulties were plaguing the regime in Constantinople. Both he and, even more, his house were very fortunate. Indeed, the emperor's commitment to driving the forces of Islam from central and east central Europe coincided with a fissure in the House of Austria itself. Spearheading the trouble was one of the emperor's younger brothers, Archduke Matthias. Ambitious for titles and honours that his junior status had denied him, he used Rudolph's 'government-at-a-distance' in Prague to ingratiate himself with the estates of Lower Austria, among whom the Protestant reform had made serious inroads. In return for their acknowledging him as their territorial overlord, he agreed to allow evangelical worship to continue. He repeated these concessions in Hungary and the margravate of Moravia where local deliberative bodies also accepted him as their ruling prince. By 1512 he would assume the title of King of Bohemia. Rudolph, who had desperately tried to hang on to that throne by acknowledging Protestant rights in the kingdom, was left monarch in Germany alone, where he may have reigned but hardly governed. Deeply embittered, the emperor died in that same year, stripped of all but one of the offices that he had carefully incorporated into his own imagery. Mourning for him took all of these circumstances into account. His body was briefly on display in the royal audience chamber of the Hradčany palace. A double eagle emblazoned on his bed-cover was the only visual reminder of his former powers.[37] Though he left several offspring sired illicitly, he had no legitimate heirs.

With his brother dead, Matthias became emperor as well. While he had good administrative and political instincts, his reign was an un-inspired holding action, preferring compromise with both Protestants and Turks to serious confrontation. His most serious failing, however, at least from the standpoint of his house, was his childless marriage. As Matthias became visibly more frail in 1517, his remaining brothers, Maximilian and Albert, who also had no children, decided for the sake of their dynasty to abandon all claims to ruling the Habsburg patrimony.

Their preferred candidate for the job was their eldest nephew in Graz, Archduke Ferdinand, who had already proven his vigour by siring a male heir. Matthias demurred at their choice, but typically gave in.

With Ferdinand of Styria becoming Emperor Ferdinand II in 1519, the tone of Habsburg relations with Protestants changed dramatically. The dynasty's agenda grew increasingly tied to Catholic doctrine and practice when required to explain and justify its government and its policies. Urban VIII, whose pontificate stretched from 1523 to 1544, was more critical of the regime in Vienna than propagandists ever said.[38] But by Ferdinand II's death in 1537, the special relationship of Rome with the House of Austria had become very apparent. It would also become synonymous with repression and violence in the minds of contemporaries and generations to come.

Nevertheless, recovering Austrians for the Church of Rome was a massive undertaking. Confessional demographics alone explained the problem. By 1585 nine out of ten nobles in Lower Austria were Protestant; so were three-quarters of urban residents and one-half of the peasantry in Upper Austria. In Ferdinand II's Inner Austria, around 70 per cent of the population was Protestant; only five of the 135 nobles of Styria remained Catholic. In the more recent Habsburg acquisitions, the confessional situation was even less auspicious. By 1580 less than 15 per cent of the population in Bohemia was Catholic; in Moravia the figure stood at 35 per cent. At the turn of the seventeenth century, only one in ten of the local nobility in Habsburg Hungary had remained with the Church of Rome; the number of ordained clergy had dropped as well. Only Croatia and Carniola had Catholic majorities, in part because many local men belonged to an anti-Ottoman border guard. Begun by Ferdinand I, it expected dynastic loyalty from all who served.[39]

Unlike his immediate ancestors, however, Ferdinand II of Styria proved to be more willing to use force if there was no other way to restore his personal confession to his lands. He was certainly thoroughly grounded for the task. He had been raised in the observant household of his parents and never forgot their model. Jesuits played a central role in his strictly Catholic education. Unusual for his family throughout its entire political history, he left the court in Graz for higher education at a college and a university. Both of them, however, were Jesuit establishments in the Bavarian town of Ingolstadt, so that he was not likely to stray from the precepts of his faith.

He had also matured in a philosophical context that made fearing God and cultivating the goodwill and admiration of a monarch's subjects prerequisites for effective government. Though also commonplaces of the times, Ferdinand may have encountered them through Giovanni Botero's *Reason of State*. Published in 1589, during Ferdinand II's formative years the tract was circulating around courts in Munich, Madrid and Graz, as well as at the papal establishment in Rome. Two copies were in the archduke's private library. The author had a sunny moral perspective on Habsburg state-building through the centuries; the angelic blessing bestowed on Rudolph I after the Habsburg refused to remount the horse that had borne the Host was, in Botero's view, the moment at which the dynasty's rise to greatness began. Forgetting, apparently, the warfare that the Burgundian marriage of Maximilian had set off, he praised the House of Austria for expanding its holdings through non-violent nuptial unions rather than outright conquest.[40] Such principles conformed nicely to the Habsburg reading of themselves, and Ferdinand II was not the sort of person to reject them. But they had a truly perplexing side. How could he persuade those who refused to change their confessions without using raw force? And even if formally reconverted, would they admire and respect him and the house he led?

He did have imperial law on his side. The Religious Peace of Augsburg in 1555 allowed Lutheran reformed practices in German principalities where rulers had formally adopted them. The Habsburgs, as imperial princes with territorial overlordship in the Austrian territories, were arguably empowered to compel all of their subjects to follow Catholic rites. A tentative start had been made in Vienna: in 1581 Bishop Melchior Khlesl, acting as rector of the city's university, ordered that degrees be awarded to Catholics alone. With Matthias's off and on support, he set about re-Catholicizing Upper and Lower Austria. Ceremonial broadcasting of the programme was part of his strategy. In 1599 Khlesl guided a pilgrimage of 23,000 people from Lower Austria to a site at Maria Zell in Styria. By 1617 the procession had become an annual event.[41]

Bloodless methods of restoring Catholic uniformity to the Habsburg lands did exist. Reconverting the nobility through appeals to self-interest did not necessarily involve bloodshed; many succumbed to the tactic quite readily. A Habsburg territorial ruler could promote the careers of Catholic officers at his court and not appoint Protestants at all. He could legitimize a nobleman's children. Only he could grant titles of nobility, even though other nobles could propose candidates. Only the territorial ruler could confer the lesser title of knight. Ferdinand restored several aristocrats and families with lesser titles to the Church of Rome this way.

Demographic accident also worked in his favour: a substantial number of noble families in Austria and Bohemia died out through the sixteenth century, giving the Habsburgs the opportunity to replace them with loyal Catholics. By 1610 the proportion of Catholic to Protestant nobility was beginning to rise in Upper and Lower Austria and in Bohemia. They often required their immense agricultural labour forces to follow suit, thereby speeding up the re-Catholicizing process enormously.[42]

Nevertheless, many of the Protestant communities in the Austrian lands held very stubbornly to their faith. For them, Ferdinand and his advisers re-spun Botero's lofty ideals of Catholic Habsburg rule somewhat more prescriptively. As God's singular perfection foreclosed worshipping him in different ways, so God-mandated rulers on earth could command obedience only from a people of one faith. Ferdinand, along with his successors, might have to forego at least temporarily the love of many of his peoples in the interest of containing Protestant teachings, or better yet, eradicating them.

The Styrian estates were still heavily Protestant in 1595 when Ferdinand II succeeded his father and two uncles who governed Styria as regents. As territorial ruler, he moved swiftly and often ruthlessly to restore the pre-eminence of Catholic belief in his lands, first among the common people, eventually against the nobility. Protestant preachers and schoolmasters, many of them from other German principalities, were summarily driven abroad. Substantial numbers of their congregants also removed themselves and their families to lands that were confessionally more hospitable. Those who remained faced often brutal treatment at the hands of a church and a government that insisted upon conformity in matters of faith. From the Protestant perspective, the symbolic high point of Ferdinand's efforts to restore Roman Catholicism in his lands came in 1600 with the burning of 10,000 books in the centre of Graz. Their content allegedly had evangelical leanings. Pockets of resistance, however, endured in towns and in the countryside. Only after Ferdinand II flatly forbade Protestant teaching and worship in 1628 was Catholicism securely established in Inner Austria.[43]

Taking on Europe

Ferdinand's reputation as a fierce advocate of Roman orthodoxy spread rapidly. In Hussite Bohemia, Utraquism had become a recognized form of Christian worship. Lutheranism had also taken root, along with some

smaller, but fervent evangelical movements. As part of his election concessions in 1617 he promised to observe privileges given to Protestants
by Rudolph and Matthias. Nevertheless, the estates remained on edge
over the chance that he might soon turn to authoritarianism. They did
not wait long to express themselves. In 1618 they defied their new
Habsburg ruler by pitching two of his spokesmen in Prague out of a window in the Hradčany castle. They then elected another king altogether,
Elector Frederick v from the Rhenish Palatinate, a Calvinist to whom
the Peace of Augsburg did not apply. He was also the son-in-law of James
I of England, whom some of the rebels mistakenly hoped would come
to the aid of Protestant co-religionists. They also contacted fellow evan-
gelicals in the Austrian provinces, particularly in the northeast, to create
a front that would stave off the root and branch re-Catholicization of
Bohemia that a new Habsburg government threatened to bring.

Ferdinand lived up to his advance billing. Legally, he had a strong
argument for his actions. The estates had rebelled against him, thereby
unilaterally abrogating any promises he made to Protestants when he came
to the throne. Military measures were clearly in order. The Bohemian
opposition collapsed in 1620, disastrously beaten by Habsburg forces
near the White Mountain (Bílá Hora), which stands on the outskirts of
Prague. Frederick fled haplessly to the evangelical United Provinces.
Monarch once again, Ferdinand brought to an end a constitutional
debate over rules of succession to the Bohemian crown that had pre-
occupied the land for decades. Rule of the kingdom would be hereditary
in the House of Habsburg. But he otherwise proceeded with considerable
caution, letting stand ceremonial requirements such as formal coronations. He also left largely untouched the fiscal prerogatives of the
estates.[44] His campaign to restore Catholicism to the kingdom prompted
roughly one fifth to one quarter of the realm's aristocratic and well-
to-do middle-class families to abandon their holdings altogether and
reconstitute their livelihoods abroad. Rather than upending the kingdom's long-standing political structure completely, however, Ferdinand
replaced them with Habsburg loyalists, who often received émigré
properties as well. Once he had reconstituted the nobility as a Catholic
stronghold he let constitutional arrangements rest as they stood.

Ferdinand and his Catholic spokesmen clearly wanted to avoid all
appearances of tyranny. Important aspects of the campaign to make
Bohemia Catholic again were more affairs of intellectual and spiritual
persuasion than raw force. In dealing with traditional Bohemian
Utraquists, who continued to think of themselves as Catholics, albeit

with a serious liturgical difference, restoring them to the papal fold often took the form of stressing links between the two confessions. More gentle yet was a hard-to-miss visual programme to remind Ferdinand's Bohemian subjects of the faith they were supposed to be following. By the beginning of the eighteenth century their homeland was awash with churches, religious ornamentation, statues and the like, all testimony to the restoration of the Church of Rome and its culture in the kingdom. Ferdinand joined in the aesthetic spirit of the undertaking as well, allowing himself to be portrayed as a champion of his faith with the sword in one hand and the scales of justice in the other. More active devotional experiences such as pilgrimages were widely available too.[45] The campaign extended to the entirety of the Habsburg monarchy, leaving the impression that if it was united at all, it was in religion.

However, many German princes, particularly the Protestants among them, viewed the Habsburg emperor's victory over the Bohemian rebellion in 1520 and the confessional and political advantages he took from it as troublesome indeed. Their concerns, along with those of Lutheran Denmark and Sweden, and the French, who were always eager to downsize Habsburg influence, converged in the vast pan-European struggle called the Thirty Years War, which ended in 1648. While inspired as much by territorial and political rivalries as by religious conviction, it made the Habsburg commitment to defending the Catholic faith a subject of international public scrutiny. Examined in this context, Ferdinand made some ill-advised moves. A series of successful campaigns in Germany during the 1620s encouraged him, as German emperor, to issue an Edict of Restitution of 1629. While the measure continued to allow Lutheran religious rites in territories ruled by princes of that faith, it required the return of Catholic church properties that had been taken over by Protestants after the agreement reached at Augsburg in 1555 was in place. As for evangelical movements other than Lutherans, they could convert, flee Germany, or stay and face the possibility of execution.

From that point on, Ferdinand's drive to enlarge the Church of Rome's position in the Empire sputtered, then died altogether, as opponents emerged from all corners of royal Europe to curb his Catholic mission and settle territorial scores of their own as the fortunes of combat permitted. Even the deeply Catholic Spanish branch of his house, with geopolitical interests of its own in the conflict, thought that the Edict was politically counterproductive.[46] Nor were his subjects prepared to sacrifice their blood and treasure on defending the House of Habsburg and its causes indefinitely. An all-too-conspicuous example was the public reaction to his apparent approval of the assassination in 1634 of one of his most gifted commanders, Albert von Wallenstein. A fiercely ambitious man with vast territorial holdings in northeast Germany, rumour at court had it that his concerns mattered more to him than the fate of Catholicism. Some said that he wanted to be king of Bohemia, others that he planned to ally himself with Sweden to protect his own lands or that he hoped to become emperor himself. Nevertheless, he was also known as a champion of peace, if such could be negotiated advantageously with an enemy. It was a message that war-weary folk beyond the court wanted to hear; his sordid end produced spasms of outrage in Vienna.[47]

Much taken aback, Ferdinand's regime went very public to justify the deed. By the turn of the seventeenth century the dynasty had been using the pages of the public press to advance their policies and to explain them. Khlesl had recommended the policy to Archduke Matthias during the dynastic quarrels that roiled the house in 1610; Ferdinand II himself had issued several pamphlets to justify his measures in Germany. A court newsletter, the Vienna *Öffentliche Postzeitung*, was reporting in various regions of the monarchy about the dynasty's various campaigns. The public antipathy to the Wallenstein affair made Ferdinand's government all the more aware of the need to spin their side of controversial stories in print. A flood of literature came out of the court to persuade some of his generals, his estates, the peoples of his patrimonial lands and Germany at large that he was not the Spanish-style tyrant whom critical pamphleteers were describing. They insisted that Wallenstein's execution-style slaying was fully in order. A court-sponsored 'White Paper' on the subject was also circulated, though Ferdinand would not allow it to be reissued, as some of his advisers recommended.[48]

Redesigning the Pieces

The idea of bringing the Thirty Years War to a close had, in fact, crossed the minds of major belligerents since the conflict began in 1618; agreements had been reached, but many of them only postponed discussion of difficult issues to a day that never seemed to come. Ferdinand II himself contributed to the final settlement, withdrawing in 1635 much of the Edict of Restitution. Yet when he died in 1637, the war had eleven more years to go. His successor, Ferdinand III, was, like his father, a devout Catholic. He continued to hope that the conflict would end favourably for his house and the Church of Rome, and explored a variety of angles by which he might abandon the field without a decisive victory. That satisfaction was denied him. The two treaties signed in Westphalia that terminated hostilities in 1648 largely reversed what was left of the Edict of Restitution. It also added Calvinism, yet another offshoot of the Protestant reform, to the recognized religions in the Empire. Nevertheless, he would be able to accommodate private belief and morality to public cravings for peace more serenely than his father. While he spread confessional uniformity throughout his own lands, he resigned himself, as emperor, to religious territorialism in Germany and concentrated on shoring up what constitutional powers were left to him. The dynasty would continue to use the supra-dynastic connotations of the imperial office to rally support to its other causes until Napoleon brought the entire system to an end in 1805. He would also do much administratively and visually to, as one of his orders put it, 'enhance the reputation of our court'.[49]

The Westphalia settlements were not wholly disadvantageous to the Habsburg Roman Catholic cause. The Habsburgs remained authorized through the Peace of Augsburg to require their subjects to follow their faith. They did not rule all of central Europe, to be sure, but their consciences could rest secure in the certainty that they were doing their best to ensure the return of the lands they directly governed to the Church of Rome.

Their tactics, however, and the image of the dynasty that emerged from them seriously compromised their reputations as rulers both at home and abroad long after the confessional antagonisms of the sixteenth and seventeenth centuries had moderated. Cooperation between the Spanish and Austrian branches of the house was spotty throughout the entirety of the Thirty Years War, especially when Madrid was unable to deliver on the subsidies that they promised for the central European front. Nevertheless, the Spanish Habsburgs had an infamous link to merciless suppression of Protestantism in the Netherlands. Alleged Spanish brutalizing of indigenous peoples in the New World added more detail to the picture. The stereotype was settled on the central European branch of the dynasty when behaviour in Vienna suggested it. A notorious example was the so-called 'dice-casting' on the Haushammerfeld at Frankenburg in Upper Austria, occupied with Ferdinand II's approval by his cousin Duke Maximilian of Bavaria since 1620. Here, following a large-scale public protest against the installation of a Catholic preacher in 1625, Maximilian's governor, Count Adam von Herberstorff, brought together around 5,000 people from the region. Among them were various notables, including magistrates and guild members. These he separated out from the mass and divided into pairs, each of whom would cast dice with one another to determine who would be executed. Seventeen of them would be hanged, four from a linden tree where they had gathered, and the others from the towers of their parish churches. Their heads then went on public display.[50]

Ferdinand II had not proposed this scenario, though he did eventually endorse it. Protestants, however, had reason to suspect that he and his house would replay it to forestall thoughts of apostasy. The regime of his son and successor tried offsetting this image by pointing to episodes in the war in which the Habsburg peoples vigorously supported the dynasty. The city of Prague's staunch defence against the Swedes during the siege of 1648 was reworked as a tale of the population's loyalty to the Catholic Church and the ruling house, a subtle move that sidestepped the unpleasant fact that a rebellion in that city had set off the entire conflict. It also gave Ferdinand III a chance to show off his streak of genuine magnanimity; he acknowledged the support of the local burghers by ennobling the city councillors and students who had blocked the passage of Swedish troops on the Charles Bridge, thus saving the New Town. In 1649 the city received a new charter that gave it a special place in the Bohemian estates.[51]

Still, as eager as the dynasty was to minimize unfavourable publicity, it was not ready to experiment with formal confessional toleration, nor to cease impressing on its subjects the creed they were expected to profess. Protestant hostility to Catholic processions in 1577 had intimidated Rudolph II; his immediate successors put their faith on display fearlessly and frequently. Public veneration of the cross, a staple of Habsburg religious self-identification since Rudolph I, went on in many settings throughout the Thirty Years War and after. A Carmelite monk bore a crucifix before the Catholic army at the Battle of the White Mountain. In 1622 Ferdinand II ordered his entire court to take part in the Feast of the Eucharist procession, including himself. His confessor, the Jesuit William Lamormaini, described him 'walking hatless with a miserable crown of roses around his head and a lantern in his hand, he serves his lord every year, who is borne around triumphally'. Nor, reported the cleric at another time, was the emperor afraid to fall back on family legend to express his devotions. Should Ferdinand encounter a priest bearing the Host to administer extreme unction, he followed the praiseworthy example of Rudolph I. He immediately sprang from his carriage and kneeled in a reverent posture, even on filthy ground, prayed for his salvation and accompanied the clergyman to the ailing parishioner. Ferdinand III could be emphatically Catholic as well. During the seventeenth century an erstwhile last redoubt of Protestantism in Vienna, the castle of the Jörger family in Hernals, today the seventeenth city district, would be torn down. It was replaced by a cross and a replica of Mount Calvary, which would soon in turn become a pilgrimage site. Prescribed penitential processions to the installation started at the Corpus Christi altar in St Stephen's Cathedral, binding together two of the Habsburg's most consistent devotional icons: the Host and the cross.[52]

Veneration of the Virgin Mary intensified too. Site upon site throughout the monarchy was occupied by visual reminders of her significance in the dynasty's past and the history of its peoples. Between 1622 and 1624 a church, the Church of the Virgin of Victory, was erected where the Battle of the White Mountain had taken place. Bohemia's Hussite past, at least in Prague, was systematically marginalized. A statue of the Hussite king George of Podiebrad holding a gold chalice, the emblem of the Hussite reform, was removed from the facade of the Týn Church. Once a Utraquist centre, it now featured an image of the Virgin in a radiant crown. The Virgin could be used to express more political messages as well. In 1650 her statue appeared on the spot in the Old Town Square where 'rebels' had been executed in 1621. The process lagged somewhat in Hungary because of the tripartite division of the kingdom that lasted until the beginning of the eighteenth century. A serious start, however, was made under the inspiration of Peter Pázmány, the primate of Hungary and Cardinal-Archbishop of Esztergom. Born to a Protestant family, he had converted to Catholicism as a youth, become a Jesuit and taught at the University of Graz as well as in Rome. Taking to heart his order's commitment to the improvement of clerical intellectual standards, he founded two seminaries in royal Hungary and a university with a theological faculty at Nagyszombat (now Trnava, Slovakia); the latter was transferred in 1777 to Buda, where it would grow into the modern University of Budapest. Pázmány also founded a Jesuit institute for Hungarians in Vienna that closed only around 1975. Most important of all, his powerful preaching and writing returned several of Hungary's leading noble families, and the vast servile labouring class that attended them, to Catholic practice. Though sincere belief was an ideal that both Ferdinand II and Ferdinand III had internalized, those proselytized on behalf of Church, state, or both, often disregarded the relationship of inner conviction to conversion. But, at the very least,

Habsburg confessional policy had made it very difficult for the dynasty's peoples to be anything other than a public Catholic.

Nor did the dynasty always have to use death threats and loss of property to promote such behaviour. The role of the Habsburgs, either as emperors or simple archdukes, in championing Roman Catholicism against Muslims and Protestants throughout central Europe was stressed repeatedly from pulpits throughout the dynasty's lands. Important subjects were exposed to this message, from time to time in settings free from the constraints of ritual formalities. Theatrical performances could be especially helpful. The Habsburgs were not pioneers here; the Bavarian Wittelsbachs of the sixteenth century were the first German princes to dramatize the interface of their princes with Christian and Catholic religious culture. Performances took place in Jesuit schools and other auditoriums controlled by the order. Married to a Wittelsbach himself, Ferdinand II in Styria used his court theatre early in his reign to promote similar themes. Schools run by local Jesuit communities quickly followed suit. A Graz staging of a drama drawn from the story of Joseph and his brothers cast the young Ferdinand as the former. In one episode, the archduke's siblings kneel before him, dressed as monarchs from all over Europe, along with his uncle, the then Emperor Matthias. Filled with many more scenes of homage to Matthias's successor, the piece took several days to perform. Another production, staged for Ferdinand's coronation in Bohemia in 1517, the Prague *Constantinus*, recalled that Rudolph I had legendarily seized a cross at his coronation when no sceptre was available. None too subtly, a cross emerged from a heavenly cloud during an onstage crowning. Politics themselves were very explicit; an oath of fealty to Ferdinand was the centrepiece of one scene. Productions throughout the seventeenth century continued to enact public declarations of loyalty to the dynasty and its representatives.

The interlocking relationship of Church and state was especially well integrated into *Pietas victrix*, the work of Niklaus Avancini, a Jesuit dramatist and philosopher. Completed around 1659, it showed the Habsburgs as partners of the papacy in restoring and defending the Catholic faith as well as their legitimacy in their own lands. Some updating of the message had, however, taken place. Germany, where the Westphalia settlements had formally ended any idea of a uniformly Catholic central Europe, was not mentioned. The Habsburg vision of the dynasty's relationship to the Church of Rome changed noticeably in subsequent performances of the work. Unlike the Wittelsbachs, who focused on glorifying faith alone, the Habsburgs were promoting themselves as

Catholicism's foremost champions. Given the setback in Germany, the only proof of their Catholic commitment that they could exploit was what they had done to reconfessionalize their own lands. They had done their duty as rulers according to standards exacted by their omnipotent single God. With the exception of Hungary, where the dynasty would never rearrange the confessional map to its complete satisfaction, Roman Catholicism prevailed throughout the Habsburg holdings.[53]

A Decisive Victory

While Protestants no longer threatened the internal unity of the Habsburg monarchy, it still faced serious military challenges from abroad. Louis XIV of France had resolved to round out his borders, some of which fronted upon western Germany. Equally worrisome for the dynasty's central European branch after 1550, the Ottomans were mobilizing. Inspired by an ambitious succession of grand viziers, the Albanian Köprülü, they were likely to come to Vienna again.

Ferdinand III's successor was Leopold I, who became German emperor in 1658. He had unexpectedly come to the office; his elder brother, who would have been Emperor Ferdinand IV, had died of smallpox in 1654, leaving Leopold next in the line of male inheritance. He was, in some respects, a most unlikely candidate for the job. Profoundly homely, fervently pious and more than a little timorous, he would happily have remained in the cloister where he was preparing for clerical office. He was also uncommonly musical. For all his deficits, however, he did have some appreciation of the need to cultivate the goodwill of his peoples interactively. He would draw the Viennese municipal authorities increasingly into devising celebratory arches and other props for dynastic celebrations such as coronations. He occasionally even visited subjects in workaday settings. When in the Styrian capital to receive the province's oath of fealty in 1655, he was serenaded by a chorus of miners who also gave him a tour of their underground workplace.[54]

Most crucially, however, it was on Leopold's watch that the Ottoman drive towards the west was checked for good in 1683. The Habsburg's personal leadership was itself lacklustre; having cobbled together an international army from several corners of Europe and won substantial financing from the papacy, Leopold fled the Hofburg with his family before the sultan's army besieged his capital in July. The Viennese scolded him roundly and publicly for abandoning them for safer quarters, first in Linz, and then Dürnstein, somewhat closer in Lower Austria.[55] His allies complained too. The fortifications of the city had, however, been much enlarged and strengthened after the Turks last appeared before its walls in 1529. These installations, plus a vigorous defence, substantially determined the outcome of the confrontation. For all of Leopold's absentee management, when the Turks began to retreat on 12 September in deep disorder, the victory was his. The city walls once again played a major role in Habsburg triumphal propaganda. The decisive contribution that King John Sobiesky of Poland and his forces made in the struggle received far less mention.[56]

Moreover, the pushback of the Ottomans from central Europe had just started. After Leopold's armies drove the Ottomans from Buda in 1685, his reputation, along with that of his house, rose even higher, most remarkably in Protestant Germany to the north. Historically the imperial estates had been reluctant to join any cause that smacked of Habsburg self-interest, but even these warmed to him, while the Hungarians momentarily stopped criticizing Leopold's reluctance to prioritize liberation of their kingdom over keeping Louis xiv out of Germany.

A man who would never allow himself to be depicted in military uniform found himself cast as a mighty hero. In Prague, not long before the seat of rebellion against Habsburg rule, the counts of Sternberk commissioned one of the most spectacular ceiling paintings in Europe for the Troja Palace to commemorate their sovereign's victory over the Turks. An appreciative Leopold moved the Sternberks to a higher rank of nobility. Once scorned for his hasty departure from Vienna before an Ottoman advance, the Habsburg was now depicted as Hercules.[57] Though he never quite lost his unprepossessing demeanour, he appears to have accepted his Greek alter ego, perhaps because Charles v had favoured the image, and Leopold respected family precedent. He was known to address his ancestors as he contemplated their likenesses in his coin collection. Artefacts and texts extolling Leopold flooded much of the continent, especially in Catholic regions. Fearing the awesome power that the emperor's victories gave to his house, rival rulers, even Catholic ones, tried to keep news of the Turkish fallback to a minimum. One of the emperor's envoys to Louis xiv, Count Wenzel Ferdinand Popel of Lobkowitz, was perhaps the most tactless. He took with him to Paris a spectacular gold medal struck in 1685 memorializing the removal of the Turks from Buda. Leopold was depicted as Joshua, controlling both the moon, understood as the Ottomans, and the sun, in this case the current king of France. Another image of the sun on the reverse side clearly referred to the Habsburg Emperor. Not only did the count show it around to the king of France's subjects, he also sponsored a spectacular fireworks display along the Seine in 1685 to remind Germans in Paris of what the Habsburgs and their allies had achieved. The Bourbon government registered its objections. For its part, the House of Habsburg admitted Lobkowitz to the Order of the Golden Fleece.[58]

Even in Italy, which had a long and often tempestuous relationship with German emperors, Leopold and his dynasty enjoyed positive public attention and approval. Avid interest there in the progress of the Ottoman wars from 1683 to 1699 was creating an audience on a scale that would make public journalism a central component of the peninsula's literary culture. Excited by events that bespoke the revitalization of Christendom at the expense of Muslim imperialism, readers in Venice, Bologna, Ferrara and Lucca snapped up books, pamphlets and broadsheets on the subject. Venetians, who were close to regions ruled by the Porte, were especially drawn to coverage of battles against the Turks in Hungary. An alert regime in Vienna licensed a well-known Vienna publisher, Johann Van Gehlen, to open a branch there. Gazettes, imported directly from Vienna then pirated and issued under the imperial double eagle, were especially popular sources of information between 1684 and 1690. In them readers found stories about Christian forces on the attack, whose battle cry of 'Viva Leopoldo!' so intimidated frightened Turks that they converted on the spot. Leopold and his administration both encouraged the publicity; they also acknowledged it materially. One of the best-known Venetian military gazette writers, Giacomo Torri, assembled reportage on the Turkish wars to appeal to the emperor, his 'particular lord and patron', who duly responded with a salary.[59]

Military prowess, moreover, was but one card that Leopold could play to establish the Habsburgs as a power to be reckoned with. With the number of newspapers increasing markedly throughout Europe, he and his government created a succession of court journals that told Habsburg subjects about the man who ruled them. Foreigners could also learn more of him. Leopold was happy to send histories of himself around his lands and abroad. Though immediately accessible only to the literate, these works, or parts of them, were probably read aloud, thereby reaching more general audiences. Writers quite independent of his court, however, culled these works for information about the emperor, especially within Catholic circles.[60]

Far more to his natural taste was his programme to celebrate the newfound might of the House of Habsburg through patronage of arts.

Leopold never had first-rate painters and sculptors to serve him; those whom he commissioned did well enough at the basic job of rendering him and the members of his family, but little more. What did spread his fame was the overall quality of the professional music and musical productions he sponsored. Like his father, Leopold was an active amateur composer, with around 234 secular and religious works to his name. Performed for church festivals and theatrical entertainments at his establishment, they did not impress all of their audiences; foreign ambassadors, whose presence was required at these affairs, were occasionally quite critical. One of the emperor's scores, however, was outstanding: the solemn *Il lutto dell'Universo*, performed at court in connection with Passion Week observances and revived to much acclaim in Vienna during the final decades of the twentieth century. Like his immediate predecessors, he promoted Italian musical models in his establishment, even in the face of nativist popular opposition. Under his patronage, Italian opera set down deep roots in Vienna where it would have a long stay. His sons, Joseph and Charles, were also accomplished musicians and patrons of music and art.[61]

Leopold died listening to music, an eloquent acknowledgment of his lifelong devotion to the art. His commitment, however, was more than aesthetic. Like newspapers, he often used musical entertainment to highlight the accomplishments of his rule. He was very concerned that the texts for his own works, as well as those he commissioned from other composers, particularly for operas, contained appropriate references to the House of Habsburg. To ensure that everything met his standards, he served as supreme impresario of his establishment, especially as a young man. He insisted on controlling the hiring of composers, librettists, singers and musicians, all of whom were selected to enhance his imperial status and international reputation, along with that of his household and government. With the same intentions, he ordered his personnel to behave decorously, perhaps to differentiate his court morally from that of Louis XIV, where sexual license was allegedly rampant.

Leopold calculated the effect of his court theatricals carefully. Widowed twice, he occasionally called upon one of his three mothers-in-law for help, but it was the emperor who scheduled performances, deciding who could attend them. He then mediated controversies that arose between the invited and those left out. Ambassadors and courtiers did not like to be snubbed. To make sure that his image reached other parts of Europe, he sent copies of the texts that he and others were setting to music to his relatives abroad. Legates serving abroad were sometimes directed to circulate these materials where they were posted. Should there be demand for more copies, Leopold forwarded them happily. He was also very selective in choosing items from his collections of *objets d'art* for reproduction and distribution at home and abroad.[62] Just what effect these tactics had on their targets – foreign dignitaries and local courtiers who ideally would take up Leopold's imperial message and spread it when they returned to their homelands – is hard to say. At least one Ottoman ambassador was clearly impressed by what he saw during a visit to the Vienna court in 1659. Those watching him closely at a performance of *Il Pelope geloso* ('Pelops the Jealous') described him as staggered by the lavish grandeur of the whole affair and the ceremonies that went along with it.[63]

Leopold also extended his august presence to his people beyond the confines of his court. As a young man, he was an active participant in the equestrian ballets that his reign would make famous. Often performed on open land in front of the Hofburg, these affairs gave his larger public a glimpse of him.[64] Commoners also frequently spotted him at fairs and public theatrical occasions. He and his house figured in contemporary educational programmes, not only in Vienna but also in Graz, Linz, Klagenfurt and Ljubljana (Ger. Laibach). The sons of aristocrats and the high bourgeoisie were taught to respect, indeed venerate, the House of Habsburg. School dramatic presentations that made divine will and the achievements of the dynasty virtually coextensive were performed in Latin, a language not accessible to all. By the end of the seventeenth century, however, a more socially diverse public was attending these affairs, drawn by entr'acte entertainments in German, as well as the exciting visuals and special effects that often accompanied them. Leopold came off very favourably in all of these. In return, he not only financed productions of some of the plays written by Jesuits, but also visited performances to hear celebrations of himself and his family at first hand. Not to be outdone, other orders, including the Ursulines and Augustinians, also put together such occasions. When Leopold and his consorts were not in the audience, however, references were made to his house rather than to him.[65]

Nor did the Habsburgs allow young men taking high academic degrees to forget who ruled them and had spared them from Muslim conquest. Noble pages to the emperor at the University of Vienna, which Leopold personally patronized, effusively dedicated their theses to him. Students at the University of Graz did the same. Encomiums to the emperor prefaced faculty publications throughout the monarchy too. The

7 Carl Blaas, *The Battle of Zenta*, 1860s, fresco in the Pantheon in the Arsenal, Vienna.

Society of Jesus, with establishments all over central Europe, helped to spread such texts around, even in lands where the Habsburgs did not act themselves as the local territorial ruler. Sometimes a play showing Leopold in a favourable light might be performed on stages quite independent of any religious or pedagogical sponsorship.[66]

Even if Italian libretti and Latin dramas were impenetrable in most quarters, a broad range of Leopold's subjects had reason to appreciate these celebrations of grandeur and the power they embodied. Printers flourished as an avalanche of texts came their way from the court. A regime that had successfully demonstrated real power drew to it people who furthered that might, together with individuals who had some claim to might themselves. The imperial presence benefited those much lower on the social scale as well. In 1550 roughly 45,000 people lived in Vienna and the districts immediately beyond its walls. Fifteen years later, the emperor's personal household and offices of state, along with the establishments of his wife and his children, were employing around 1,500 men and women. This figure, moreover, does not take into account the families that many of Leopold's employees were supporting. His court expenditures, moreover, had risen to 250,000 gulden, almost all of which went to local producers, vendors and service providers. The general public seems to have settled into this situation quite comfortably: court fashions in dress were beginning to take hold of Vienna and its adjacent countryside.[67]

The man who would have happily remained cloistered for the entirety of his adult life, shunning all active military engagement, had reassured Christian Europe on one very important point: the Turks and the faith that they embodied for contemporaries could be beaten.[68] The slaughter inflicted on Ottoman forces in 1697 at the Battle of Zenta, in southeast Hungary, made the point unambiguously; depictions of the episode would be a staple of Habsburg military iconography for centuries to come (illus. 7). By 1699 they were driven from the kingdom for good, and retreated through the Balkans. They had not been completely vanquished, but their territorial influence had taken a lasting hit. Although Leopold was never an active hero, his funeral in 1705 was fit for one. Vienna was offered a dramatic public spectacle in which both dynasty and local subjects played their role. Catafalques, highly decorated temporary monuments to commemorate the late emperor, were designed by leading architects and set up in five churches throughout the city. According to custom, the procession from the Hofburg to the imperial crypt below the Capuchin church took place at night. More than a thousand people, including residents of military homes, religious houses and almshouses, took part or faced punishment. The whole affair was intended to announce locally and abroad that a great man had died. His catafalque or *castrum doloris* in the church of St Augustine depicted his Habsburg ancestors in characteristic poses along with references to his victories over the Ottomans and the French, topped by his apotheosis. Leopold would have been gratified to know that the message did indeed spread: images found their way west, for example, to the German bishopric of Würzburg and south to Florence in Italy.[69]

Within 100 years the Habsburgs had withstood a succession crisis of their own making, restored confessional unity to most of their patrimony, driven the Ottomans from Hungary and even helped to temper Louis XIV's territorial appetite for Germany. Though the Westphalia settlements freed territorial rulers in Germany to conduct their own foreign policies and religious affairs, the House of Austria still retained the title of emperor and significant legal functions connected with the imperial crown. At Leopold I's death, the status of the Austrian branch of his house had achieved something of the worldwide status that his ancestors, beginning with Rudolph I, had cherished for their house. Militarily and confessionally, he had realized goals that had eluded his influential relatives in Spain. He had certainly grown more confident about impressing this turn of events on his subjects in Vienna. Triumphal arches erected in the city to celebrate the election of Joseph I, Leopold's eldest son, as German king and emperor-apparent in 1690 appropriated all of the conventional symbolism in European political iconography to make the point: Joseph as a Sun King and Leopold as Jupiter appear in one; Joseph seated alone with laurel wreath and sceptre in hand, the

Roman pose of supreme majesty, is in the other. Put another way, the younger Habsburg rules the sun and the secular world, his father is supreme on Olympus.[70]

Leopold had realized the mission that Maximilian I had put upon his family: to drive the forces of Islam out of central Europe. Ferdinand II and Ferdinand III had reassured the Roman Catholic Church a major place in Europe. The militancy with which the House of Habsburg had enforced the latter did not meet with universal approval. Nevertheless, it did give the dynasty something approaching cultural unity in the lands it ruled. Maximilian had taught his house another lesson as well: whatever the accomplishment, celebrate it in all available media. In the midst of such triumphalism, however, some qualifications were in order. The impact of these artifices did not depend alone upon the court's ability to manipulate them as propaganda. Leopold, his artists, architects and advisers were working in a context in which monarchs were expected to represent themselves rather than to explain themselves. Certain types of monarchy were in bad repute among rulers themselves; Ferdinand II had wanted very much to muffle accusations of tyranny. Nevertheless, kingship as a form of government was rarely questioned. Nor were the confessionally framed mandates of their rule. Exalted imagery and immense expenditure were normal by-products of so singular an office, even less vulnerable to criticism in the context of proven military and diplomatic effectiveness. Within this setting, the Habsburgs had carried on adequately, at worst, and remarkably well at crucial moments. By Leopold's death, however, the very circumstances that created that context were undergoing fundamental change. Leopold had handed on to his family a polity that made them very important indeed. Retaining that position, however, would require the House of Habsburg to exchange Baroque grandeur for something far more modest, in politics and in lifestyle.

FOUR

New Tactics for New Times

AEIOU: Ideal and Reality

A string of imperial victories over the Ottomans in the first decades of the eighteenth century inspired some Catholic clergy in the Habsburg lands to declare that world rule of the House of Austria was imminent. The house had toyed with the idea since the fifteenth century when it began incorporating such imagery into its iconography. Such dreams passed quickly, however, with the extinction in 1700 of the Spanish branch and the shift of its vast overseas empire to rulers from a cadet line of the French Bourbons. Even the glory of turning back the Turks lost some of its propaganda value by the mid-eighteenth century as the administrations in Constantinople and Vienna grew increasingly nervous about Russian ambitions in the Balkans and around the Black Sea.

The remaining branch of the House of Austria, however, had serious economic and political problems to solve without taking on the whole world. By 1700 they had devoted two and a half centuries to persuading their peoples from the most impoverished to the wealthiest that paying for defence against the Ottomans and Protestantism was to their material and spiritual advantage, regardless of the economic hardships taxation brought with it. Within the Habsburg lands and outside them, the integrity of the dynasty's patrimonies was challenged and rechallenged by estates and institutions anxious to retain their traditional prerogatives. A major noble uprising in Hungary in 1705 was quelled by 1711 with the Habsburgs still on the throne in the kingdom, but only after making significant constitutional concessions to the rebels. Foreign monarchs hoped to expand their borders at the expense of the House of Austria too, an ambition that appeared easier to realize when the house was faced with the possibility of a female succession. Wars set off by this issue plagued almost all of Europe throughout the eighteenth century.

The Vienna Habsburgs would hang on, but only after substantially altering some of the cultural and administrative devices that had brought them through crises in the previous 200 years. The dynasty would modify its close identification with the Roman Catholic faith, its understanding of its duties to its public, and the imagery that tied it to its peoples. It would also adopt attributes of a real-life family, far closer to the world at hand, rather than adjuncts for God. Political circumstances remained uppermost in the minds of the Habsburgs and their advisers, but their approach to them was increasingly shaped by exterior social, cultural and even economic considerations.

That monarchs bore a unique responsibility for the material well-being of all of their people was a commonplace in European political mythology. The definition of well-being, however, was a matter of perspective. The House of Austria had construed this in several ways to suit their purposes. The most consistent source of revenue came from ever increasing taxes on impoverished peasantries, especially in the Austrian lands. These moneys were often collected and sent to Vienna by noble landlords, who were not beyond shifting the cost of these burdens on to their agricultural labour force.[1] The representational costs of the court – a steadily rising figure from the fifteenth century on – were arguably as much a part of the protective function of princely government as outright military expenditure. Money was secondary to the importance of impressing and intimidating foreign dignitaries, and maintaining order and respect in the larger population.

Such difficulties were not unique to the central European Habsburgs; their Spanish relatives, along with French and British monarchs, had wrestled with them too. Their answer had been mercantilism, the monopolizing of natural treasures such as precious metals, along with agricultural commodities and the market potential of lands beyond the European continent to the benefit of distant royal treasuries. With no navy or extensive coastline, the Vienna branch of the House of Austria had played only a minor role in overseas commerce. Leopold I's government had considered turning southeastern Europe into a Habsburg trading preserve even before the Ottomans were tamed, but it had never pursued the idea consistently.

The answer, according to Philip von Hörnigk, in his *Österreich über Alles, wenn es nur will* (*Austria over Everyone, if It Only Wants to Be*) was autarchy. The first edition of his book came out in 1684; revised at the beginning of the eighteenth century, it was reissued fourteen times. The author argued with some passion for turning the Habsburg lands into a closed production and trading system; foreign commodities and finished products could be imported only if they were clearly needed or if the population adamantly refused to give them up, such as spices from India. But otherwise people might have to settle for second-rate merchandise, at least temporarily. The monarchy's subjects would also have to spend more time in productive labour than they had in the past. In the end, however, the scheme would rescue them from the poverty and material devastation brought on them by decades of war with the Ottomans and the kings of France.

It was in the interest of rulers to impose this programme on their peoples. But princes had to change their behaviour too. Indeed, they had to impose on themselves the very discipline that they were forcing on those below them: shunning foreign products. Leopold I was a transgressor of scale; he allegedly told a minister at the celebration of his second marriage that there was not a thread on him that had come from his own lands.[2]

Protectionism was no stranger to Habsburg policy. Archduke Rudolph IV had done it in the fourteenth century; so had Albert II before him. Leopold I was already thinking of it in terms of public interest. When in 1672 he conceded to one Christian Sind the exclusive right to manufacture wool in Upper Austria for 30 years, he was thinking in terms of general usefulness.[3] Hörnigk's mercantilism, however, added a radically new dimension to the relationship of Habsburg princes and their peoples; the House of Austria, by the beginning of the eighteenth century, was firmly linked to its subjects territorially and confessionally. Mercantilism added a third fundamental tie: economic benefit. No longer was the government collecting revenue simply to meet emergencies large and small and to sustain its own lifestyle, but to advance a programme that would satisfy the material needs of both princes and ordinary mortals.

Carried to its logical conclusions, the mercantilistic formula had radical implications for the structure of values that had long informed the sociopolitical structure of the Habsburg lands. The house itself, along with the nobility and high ecclesiastical dignitaries, had been the chief market in the Habsburg lands for the imported products that distinguished them from plain folk. New categories of deference might also be in order. Hörnigk, for example, argued for honouring tradesmen such as major retailers (*Verleger*) and artists as a way of helping merchants, even wealthy ones, overcome their conventional stereotype as swindlers.[4] Such notions clearly called into question the exclusivity of the aristocracy and its special relationship with the Crown. It also had serious implications for the laboriously constructed reputation that the House of Habsburg had acquired by the end of the seventeenth century. The aura of Catholic quasi-sanctity that the dynasty had acquired by driving Protestants and Muslims from their lands would fade somewhat as the ranks of the preferred opened up to the middle classes for whom wealth rather than birth was their claim to recognition.

Getting Down to Work

The challenge of synthesizing these imperatives productively fell initially to Leopold I's second son, Archduke Charles, who took all of the Habsburg titles left to him following the very short reign of his elder brother, Joseph. After 1711 he was Emperor Charles VI in Germany, Austria and Bohemia, and Charles III of Hungary. Philosophical speculation was not his strong suit. Nevertheless, the fate of his dynasty was much on his mind. He had been in the Iberian peninsula since 1704 as part of the Habsburg military effort to keep Spain out of the hands of Louis XIV and to promote his own candidacy for the Spanish throne, once the childless last male in the Habsburg Spanish line had died. The Bourbon successor in Madrid, Philip V, ended those hopes. Much disappointed, Charles returned to Vienna to take up the duties of his house there.

With no surviving children of his own by 1713, and facing the possibility that he might never have a male heir, he did not want the Habsburg patrimony to pass from his line. The House of Habsburg had never formally precluded female succession – its women were more attractive marriage partners as a result – but had never called one to any of their thrones either. His late brother had two daughters; to keep them from claiming their dynasty's holdings, their uncle had to demote them in the line of succession. This Charles formally accomplished through negotiations with each of his provinces, who promised to accept his offspring, male or female, as their legitimate ruler upon his death. Equally important, he or she would receive their family's lands undivided. The policy, known as the Pragmatic Sanction, also marked a step towards future centralization of the monarchy and more efficient government. Provincial fealty ceremonials were in any case disappearing during Charles VI's reign; the Hungarian estates saw the implication of this thrust right away. They did not accept the prospect of a female ruler until 1723, and only after they were assured that their traditional privileges would continue, including the right to approve rulers at their corona-tions. The legitimate and Roman Catholic heirs of Leopold I and Joseph I would remain eligible for the position, but it was less clear what would happen after that.[5]

With the assent of his lands secured, Charles threw himself into coaxing promises from other European states to respect the arrangement. Most went along; the exceptions were Bavaria (where Joseph II's younger daughter, Maria Amalia, had married Elector Charles Albert), and the recently created king of Sardinia-Piedmont, Victor Amadeus (who coveted Italian territory that had passed to the Austrian Habsburgs following the War of the Spanish Succession). In keeping with the cynical self-interest that drove contemporary state relations generally, the Hohenzollerns of Brandenburg-Prussia signed on, but would change their minds very soon.[6]

Scholars have faulted Charles VI for paying more attention to narrow dynastic problems than larger matters of state. In order to win over the king of England and the Dutch United Provinces to the Pragmatic Sanction, he curtailed the Atlantic trade that the Habsburgs had begun cultivating in the Netherlands.[7] Looked at more expansively, however, his record of advancing his dynasty's interests, synchronizing them with his subjects' concerns, and expressing the results compellingly, was impressive indeed.

Like his father and his elder brother, Charles realized that the future of his house and the material well-being of his people were closely linked. Perhaps more by accident than design, his reign coincided with a pros-perous surge in the economy of his lands. Even conspicuous grandeur served economically benevolent ends. The end of the Ottoman wars brought an explosion of building and construction-related employment to Vienna, where the landed magnates of the Empire flocked to build palaces that often outstripped the elegance of the Hofburg. Prague and even Graz shared the boom. The regime by and large tolerated the com-petition; even if such structures were testimonials to noble and ecclesi-astical eminence, they bespoke a system of values shared by the dynasty and some of its mightiest subjects. All of this activity employed and paid for a large labour force that had been promised, as early as the sixteenth century, such work would begin once Ottoman looting and confiscation had been stopped.[8] For those who needed to be reminded of what Vienna had withstood in 1683, the city's grim fortifications were still standing.

Though his court numbered around 10,000 people and cost a corres-pondingly vast sum of money, Charles did not identify himself and his dynasty with monumental housing alone. As summarized later in the eighteenth century, his intent was to leave behind him buildings and artefacts that honoured God and his own might – the Vienna Karlskirche, dedicated to St Charles Borromeo, was his classic contribution – and to better the general welfare. His elaborate court library was intended as a testimonial to his support and respect for the learning that would further this process.[9] The main cupola is decorated with an orb bearing a discreet 'VI' between trumpeting angels and two gilded eagles.

Charles's good intentions also included broadly inclusive economic policies. His government encouraged a noteworthy expansion of trading and production facilities throughout many areas of his patrimony. Iron mines were opened in Temesvár County, then located in southeastern Hungary, now a part of Romania. There he settled a colony of artisans to turn ore into marketable products. Interregional transportation arteries – canals, roads and bridges – were built or improved. Charles was particularly interested in reviving trade and commerce with Italy; he vigorously supported the development of Trieste on the Adriatic as a commercial seaport, making it a centre for the shipment of iron. Existing industry also received government support; in 1715 Charles renewed the private licence of the Linz wool factory, first privileged by his father in 1672.

For all their religiosity, the Habsburgs had not called attention to their heavy patronage of several churches constructed in Vienna in the seventeenth century. The name of Ferdinand II over the entrance to the Jesuitenkirche is so exceptional as to be virtually unique.[10] Charles VI was far less self-effacing in any of his projects, ecclesiastical or secular. A major highway initiative in Wallachia to the east was called the Via Carolina. His subjects began responding in kind. In 1728 the citizens of Trieste erected a public monument to the emperor to thank him for his contribution to the local economy. The estates of Inner Austria commissioned another such tribute, in German, not Latin, and embellished with the signature Golden Fleece. Placed on the Semmering Pass, the road along which Charles planned to develop north–south trade and other business activity, it reminds passers-by of his efforts to improve roads and commerce in the public interest.[11]

His understanding of the public good and its contribution to the concerns of his house went far beyond straightforward economic development. Here, too, he was quick to let his subjects know where such benevolence came from. In Rijeka, Croatia (It. Fiume), where he also planned to develop a harbour, he erected a military hospital that soon served as a quarantine station used to block the spread of infectious disease from the Balkans. An inscription on the facade noted that the facility had been funded from the emperor's private resources. Some improvements testifying to the largesse of the House of Habsburg remained unwritten. Charles's street lighting programme for Vienna was extended to Prague, Osijek (Hung. Eszsék), Linz and Graz, to be turned on only for imperial visits. Benefits or potential benefits had to be spread widely through the monarchy. A good part of Charles's schemes for economic development were prompted by the need to make the Habsburg armies more effective. The benefits of these measures too were spread far beyond his regime's capital in Vienna. To counter the horrendous sanitation in camps and fortifications, water conduits were laid down throughout his lands; they were especially important in Hungary, where supplies were widely contaminated. Educational reforms in Charles's military also gave an important segment of his subjects advantageous skills. Vienna had long looked abroad for field engineers, but was finding it difficult to locate enough of them; in 1717 Charles established an academy to prepare military engineers. The emperor also opened the way for his nobility to become practically acquainted with agronomy and surveying, knowledge that benefited both trainees and the monarch's treasury. Land measurement played a key role in the comprehensive reassessment of taxes that Charles planned to carry out. Nor did he locate such institutions in Vienna alone. Young surveyors attended a facility that their sovereign set up in Neukirchen in Upper Silesia; military schools (*Ritterakademien*) were opened both in the capital and in Liegnitz, Bohemia, to prepare young men for the army and civilian administration.[12]

Unlike his Habsburg predecessors, Charles also gave thought to the family life of the men who fought in his name. Once they left the dynasty's active service, many common soldiers and even low-grade officers had wretched existences. Rulers took no responsibility for mercenaries once they became veterans. Popularly stereotyped as beggars and vagabonds, they often became petty criminals out of necessity. By the second half of the seventeenth century, officers themselves, along with some of the clergy, were funding private charities to care for them. In 1694 an almshouse for military invalids was set up just outside the walls of Vienna. Soon to become the nucleus of a vast general hospital, it would be the largest such establishment in Europe.

Honouring and supporting those who had fought against the French and the Turk was also an opportune way to put an altruistic cast on

Habsburg rule. If nothing else, such behaviour brought Charles, and by extension his house, directly into the lives of the peoples as no ceremonial appearances ever could. He substantially enlarged the Great Almshouse to accommodate 3,000 people; it also fed an additional 600 discharged and impoverished soldiers. People with some future before them also benefited from the facility. A study room was made available for 58 poor students who also received bed, board and an allowance for personal expenses. Financial support for these privileges came through a pawnshop that Charles licensed in 1713 and renovated, along with imposts drawn from public contributions that came from many sources, from other charitable foundations to the fees paid to the government by coachmen in return for the right to continue standing their vehicles just outside Vienna's gates.

Neither recipients nor passive civilian spectators were allowed to forget the source of most of this largesse. Fortresses, barracks, hospitals for the wounded throughout the Habsburg *imperium* from Vienna and Pest, to Belgrade and Alba Iulia, now in Romania, proclaimed the Habsburg role as defenders of Christendom and their lands against the Turks and other enemies. They were generally run in military fashion, though residents could bring their wives and offspring with them. Theoretically they were still liable for service, but the dynasty was indisputably grateful for their help.

Charles vi's other charitable activities similarly combined dynastic considerations and public needs. Still mindful of his connections with Spain, its erstwhile provinces in the Low Countries and those acquired in Italy in 1713 through the Treaty of Utrecht, he founded a Spanish hospital in Vienna in 1718. Eligible for care were Spaniards and all who came from the 'Spanish Provinces': Sicilians, Milanese and Netherlanders, and families in which wives, mothers or grandparents had roots in those lands. Space was available for 90 ailing people; there were also separate sections for men, women and the mentally disturbed. Funds came from Habsburg Sicilian and Milanese incomes – all a way of underscoring Charles's relationship to a once-glorious branch of his house. The facility admitted many who had fought with him in the War of the Spanish Succession as well. He also persuaded, through example, other well-to-do individuals and families among his subjects to attend to the needs of the less fortunate. Capitalizing on the inclination among aristocrats and the wealthy to mimic the behaviour of the court, he asked them to cooperate in charitable activities that enhanced his state. Charles vi initiated construction of the Hospital of St John Nepomuk, opened in 1723, for aged and infirm

workers, servants, maids and young orphans. He did not, however, endow
it. Monies for this and similar facilities that opened in 1724 and 1726
came chiefly from the donations of the pious. Open for both residents
and those who came to them only for food, further such establishments
continued to be erected in Vienna throughout his reign.[13]

Restating a Position of Power

For all of his efforts to reach out to the general populace, Charles never
abandoned more formally traditional ways of reminding his subjects who
ruled them. He made that amply clear to Jakob van Schuppen, the new
director of the court academy for painting and sculpture that the
emperor opened in 1726. Part of the programme was to grant access to
allow a more general public to view rooms containing the paraphernalia
of might and power, a privilege once available by invitation only. The
interior of the academy could be visited and viewed free of charge, an
opportunity that Anton Höller, a contemporary professor at the University of Vienna, declared was 'to the benefit of the common welfare as well
as the personal advantage of many'. But the most serious duty of court
painters was to reinforce and publicize Charles's authority and his virtues
and those of his house.[14]

Charles did indulge himself expensively, though not in every building under his control. The ramshackle Vienna Hofburg, which had been
the despair of his fifteenth- and sixteenth-century forebears, remained
as dreary as ever, despite Leopold I's extension of one wing. Charles's only
serious modification of it may, however, have been the greatest public
service he ever rendered: the court show horses that perform in the
Spanish Riding School continue to enchant paying publics from the
world over.[15]

Nevertheless, grandiose buildings throughout the monarchy attested
to his might. Some of these structures were the working headquarters of
his officials, an interesting contrast to contemporary France where the
splendid building and the functional building were being designed on
quite different structural and decorative principles.[16] Pious though he
was, Charles also worked dynastic dreams and purposes into the ecclesiastical architecture that he sponsored. He was especially devoted to the
veneration of St Charles Borromeo, a key champion of Catholic moral
and intellectual reform in sixteenth-century Italy, and a remote Habsburg
relative by marriage. The outcome of the emperor's commitment was one

of Vienna's most striking ecclesiastical structures, the Karlskirche. Its audaciously eclectic exterior, which brings east and west together along with touches of Roman imperial grandeur, summarized and embodied Habsburg world pretensions. Charles's armies had pushed far into the Balkans, capturing Belgrade in 1718. Such a record made him a second Constantine, at least to his architects. Two oversize Trajan spiral columns outside the church projected strength. They may also have been an allusion to the pillars of Hercules, by now a very familiar figure in Habsburg iconography.[17]

Memorializing St Charles Borromeo had practical political uses as well. At one stage in his missions he had been in direct contact with the clergy and nobles of Hungary. Furthering his memory was a cause in which both intractable Hungarian aristocrats and the dynasty could find common ground. Hungarian prelates were pleased as well. One part of the emperor's programme to rebuild Hungary in areas that Ottomans once occupied was the construction and reconstruction of Catholic churches, monasteries and convents; the same agenda was introduced to eastern parts of the kingdom, including Transylvania, where Calvinism had flourished.[18]

Charles, however, left more than buildings to guarantee a generalized posterity of his house. Since the early part of the seventeenth century Habsburgs had been interred in the crypt beneath the Capuchin church not far from the Hofburg. After 1717 when an altar was added to the vault, Charles opened the space for daily public viewing. Souvenir hunters pilfered ornamentation and vandals damaged the sarcophagi; Charles's grandson, Emperor Joseph II, closed the site down in 1787. When it was eventually made accessible to small groups it attracted more than its share of ordinary, and not-so-ordinary, sightseers: a fellow emperor, Napoleon Bonaparte, for one, and the imperial-minded American statesman Theodore Roosevelt.[19]

In 1733 Anton Holler, a university professor in Vienna who praised Charles for making his art academy accessible for public viewing, published an elaborate tract on Charles VI's building activities, sacred and secular alike. All of them spoke of Charles's determination to leave a lasting imprint of himself, his family and the inviolability of Habsburg rule on their peoples. Prominent references to the House of Austria often appeared on facades and interior walls alike. The strategy was not new: sixteenth-century Jesuit aesthetics recommended looking, rather than analysing and verbalizing, to understand the world and the life that lay beyond it for the contrite.[20] The message of dynastic sovereignty got through even to those who had long tried to qualify it: the high nobility. Many were as eager as their ruler to pictorialize their self-importance and that of their family; indeed, the architects, artists and scholars patronized by the latter also worked for them. All were eager to pictorialize their self-importance, along with that of their family, to the point where here and there they seemed to forget that they owed much of their status to Habsburg rulers. Adam von Schwarzenberg lavished far more attention at his Vienna garden palace on the achievements of his own family than to his Habsburg connections, even though it was Charles VI who had made the nobleman his High Stable Master in 1722 and raised him to the rank of duke in 1723.

Yet Schwarzenberg and his kind never went too far, contenting themselves with mimicking some features of the imperial style, while at the same time acknowledging their debt to their ruler and his centrality in their careers and in European affairs generally. Philip Lorenz, Count von Daun, fought at Zenta with Eugene of Savoy in 1697. He defended Turin against the French in the War of the Spanish Succession in 1707 and was Charles VI's viceroy in Naples-Sicily in 1707–8 and 1713–19. Charles VI conferred a princely title in Italy on him and in 1712 he was inducted into the Order of the Golden Fleece. The ceiling decorations in Daun's Vienna palace celebrate his role as viceroy, but also the peace that the emperor had brought to the region.

Eugene himself, the statesman-general who drove the Ottomans back through the Balkans, had become genuinely popular, yet he was exceedingly careful in all of the self-referential iconography that embellished his residences to appear as a servant of the House of Austria. The Habsburgs in the role of Hercules was a protected piece of iconography for the dynasty. While Eugene appropriated the topos of the hero for his Belvedere residence, he made plain that his Greek surrogate's conquests were in the name of the House of Austria and that Hercules-Eugene was subordinate to the various classical gods as rulers who represented the Habsburgs. The one statue that did clearly depict Eugene himself as Hercules was banished to the servants' dining room in the basement of the Upper Belvedere. He professed not to like it. Eugene also incorporated the Habsburgs symbolically into other decorative touches around the grounds of the Lower Belvedere. In one balcony corner Jason appears stealing the Golden Fleece, a reference to Leopold I's reconquest of Hungary from the Turks and the return of the order's emblem to Christendom, thereby avenging the Ottoman capture of one of Leopold's ancestors, John of Burgundy, in the late fourteenth century.[21]

Yet as much as Charles's initiatives helped, practically and culturally, to consolidate the hold of his family on his lands, one crucial problem remained to be tackled: the prospect that a female would be defending the Habsburg patrimony. Women had come to European thrones before, of course, but they were often associated with weakness that left their realms open for the taking. Indeed, it was just this possibility that drove Charles to arrange the Pragmatic Sanction. But anticipating problems, and inventing measures to forestall them, was one thing; getting others to respect them scrupulously was quite another. All of this became painfully apparent sooner than anyone anticipated. Charles vi died suddenly and unexpectedly in 1740; while lithe and quite good looking as a young man, his inner gourmand had long since claimed his face and figure. In likelihood it also killed him. The culprit, allegedly, was a dish of poisonous mushrooms. His successor was indeed a woman, his eldest daughter Maria Theresa, who was 23 at the time. It was not long before the king of Prussia, Frederick ii, challenged the integrity of the Habsburg monarchy by invading Silesia, a fiefdom of the Bohemian crown, in 1740. This set off episodes of warfare that would reorientate the diplomacy of Europe dramatically by 1763. Maria Theresa never recovered the province. Nevertheless, the rest of the Habsburg patrimony remained hers, in part because she quickly adopted every mechanism available that legitimized her rule – she was crowned in both Bohemia and Hungary – and because her extensive bloodline gradually convinced contemporaries that she was indeed a rightful successor to her father.[22] All the constitutional ambiguities that accompanied her rise to monarchy, however, plus near ceaseless struggle on the battlefields of Europe, forced her into a lifelong programme of reconfiguring the relationships between her house, and especially herself, and its peoples, and the very essence of monarchy itself. Out of this came a set of behaviours that defined the core of the dynasty's view of itself, and which the dynasty, with some adjustments, would present to its realms until the very end. It also assigned her a persona that remained both a political and cultural referent for Habsburg rulers of the future and their subjects.

Little about Maria Theresa was truly magnificent. Her education had been problematic. The Habsburgs had historically paid close attention to the education of the men in their families; although Rudolph i could neither read nor write, Rudolph iv, Albert iii and Frederick iii could do both. The sons of Ferdinand i and Maximilian ii had excellent educations; Leopold i was deeply concerned that Joseph i be conversant with a variety of disciplines. Maria Theresa, however, had been trained far less broadly. Deeply pious even as a young woman, she became even more so as her life wound down to its finish. While the clash between faith and real-world issues often stressed her conscience, she retained the air of sincere piety that most of her subjects expected from their rulers. Beyond that, her formal schooling was thin. She had familiarized herself with topics important to ladies and gentlemen of her rank – above all religion, but also music, dance and some whiffs of geography and history. French she wrote and spoke passably; she had some training in Italian, Spanish and Latin as well. All of them she scattered artlessly throughout her German, as did many members of her court. Reminiscences of the practice are still to be found in commonplace *Wienerisch*, an idiom that the empress readily slipped into, as long as it did not breach her homemade standards of good taste.

Her apprenticeship in day-to-day statecraft – military and foreign affairs, along with administrative management – was even more hit-and-miss; her father, she said, bore responsibility for that one. Nevertheless, crucial personal traits offset some of these deficits: above all, the serious persistence that was seemingly bred into her family. More specifically, hers was a steely independence that betokened great self-confidence and resistance to the manipulation of others, along with instinctive prudence. Above all, she was as realistic about herself and her relatives as she was about the people who served her. A political testament that she dictated in the 1740s rehearsed in detail the failings of Charles vi's advisers and soberly laid out the constitutional weaknesses of Habsburg territorial administration. Forceful reform coming from the monarch was essential, but officials dedicated to the preservation of the dynasty's interests were essential to carrying her programme forward. Here she was both fortunate and as good as her word. Count Frederick William Haugwitz, who was the presiding officer over a newly reorganized fiscal department, pushed some of her early administrative changes to their conclusion. His successor, Prince Wenceslaus Anton Kaunitz, backtracked on some of Maria Theresa's more controversial domestic initiatives, but was of immense service in maintaining the influence of her monarchy abroad. In another detailed memorandum, apparently meant for her successor, she could not have been clearer on the need to have capable advisers: finding them was the chief concern of any ruler.[23]

Her husband, Duke Francis of Lorraine, whom she married in 1736 and who became German Emperor Francis i in 1745, was perhaps her most useful adviser in her early years. He had not been her father's first choice, but she had held out until she got her way. Their marriage led to a change in the name of the house, from Habsburg to Habsburg-Lorraine (some family members still use this formally today). He more than met his obligation to promote the dynasty's survival; twelve of his children survived their parents. His other major service to generations of Habsburgs to come was fiscal. An active supporter of technically useful scientific advances, he was also a canny developer of properties he acquired privately. Incomes from these and other investments threw off a yield large enough to allow him to establish a private fund designated to support the family in the future.

The marriage itself, however, had troubling implications for Habsburg pre-eminence in the new lineage, particularly given Maria Theresa's role as a female head of her house. She was at pains, therefore, to establish at the very least a form of equality for the two dynasties. The Ancestors' Gallery in the Innsbruck Hofburg shows Maria Theresa reaching back in history to this purpose. While acknowledging Charles's origins in Lorraine, it shows that husband and wife had common ancestors in Alsace.[24] Less officially, she celebrated her forebears publicly too. Under her patronage Maximilian I's largest single literary contribution to his memorialization, the autobiographical fantasia *Der Weisskunig*, was published in full, including striking woodcuts by Hans Burgkmair. Architectural style was used to remind passers-by that her house had been on the scene even earlier. The renovation of the court chapel of the Hofburg got under way in her reign. Its stripped-down, Gothic details recalled the age of Emperor Frederick III, who had sponsored construction of the original building, and also of Rudolph IV.[25]

Like all members of her house, Maria Theresa valued titles; in her case they became something of a fixation because they were grounded in a real political problem: no one was quite sure what to call her, especially in Germany. Her private opinion of the imperial crown office was not very high: she called it a 'duncecap' (*Narrenkappe*). The Holy Roman Empire had never had an empress, and was not eager to change that tradition. Here, again, balanced compromise was her solution. Francis of Lorraine became Emperor Francis I in the Empire. If anyone called Maria Theresa an empress she did not contest the matter unduly. Nevertheless, she refrained from using the title prominently after her husband died in 1765. Keeping her political connection in Germany, she came up with the folksy 'Kaiserin Wittib' (Dowager Empress). As a queen in Bohemia and Hungary, she was called both *Regina* and *Rex* in constitutional Latin, and apparently answered readily to both.[26] Beyond that, this issue more or less came to rest. Well into the nineteenth century, archduchesses and archdukes of the House of Austria both carried the Latin title Archidux Austriae.

Motherhood, Imperial-style

Where Maria Theresa clearly excelled, however, was in creating a family and managing as much of its behaviour as she could in preparing them for future dynastic roles. Her sizeable brood itself became her clearest public testimony to her capacity to rule. At the very least, other European rulers might add a Habsburg to their family marriage plans. The dominant subjects of the hundreds of family portraits she commissioned were her offspring. Many of these images were sent to other ruling houses for inspection in the later stages of dynastic nuptial bargaining. She also carried their likenesses with her on her travels. She cared mightily about getting them just right, turning herself into the ambitious and overly protective bourgeois mother that was becoming a familiar stereotype in her time. She rejected a portrait of her daughter, Marie Antoinette, the queen of France, because it made the young woman more a noblewoman than a queen.[27] Her concern for her progeny, their welfare and their role in the perpetuation of the political survival of her house was tireless.

Maria Theresa said in her first political testament that Divine Providence, and not personal volition, had singled her out for the job that she now held.[28] Nevertheless, her voluminous correspondence with her offspring makes plain that Habsburgs might be born, but also required fine-tuning for roles that people from all classes of society would watch. Ever on the lookout for opportunities to situate them strategically through marriage or in the Church, she not only calculated her brood's futures down to the last detail, but told them how to do it. She could be insultingly intrusive, chiding her daughters for everything from being boring to misunderstanding the male psyche. She found fault with their religious habits, their public demeanour and their intellectual preferences. Their spousal and sexual performances worried her too; where children were not forthcoming, she strongly recommended sleeping in the same bed to encourage intimacy.[29] Her greatest coup was the wedding in 1770 of her youngest daughter, Archduchess Marie Antoinette, to Louis XVI of France. She then coached the fourteen-year-old queen from afar on how to behave as a royal consort and a member of the 'illustrious' House of 'Lorraine and Austria'. Her first letter to a still bewildered child gave the latter detailed instructions on behaviour. It was to be reread every month. By 1776 the empress told her offspring to take their mother as a role model. The image carried over into official documents as well. A mandate on some property questions in Lower Austria was issued in her name as *Landesmutter* in 1771.[30]

Most of these wiles were meant to help her children negotiate the various court societies that would be the primary concern of the young archdukes and archduchesses as they matured. Above all, her children were to cultivate a level of dignity consistent with their unique positions. She routinely scolded any behaviour ill-befitting their standing in the European dynastic firmament. Their roles in the House of Habsburg forbade Leopold to lapse into the vulgarities of 'little people', Ferdinand to consort with actors and other theatrical folk, or Archduke Maximilian to use commoners as confidants.[31]

Nevertheless she was keenly aware that the society she ruled had many constituencies whose respect she much enjoyed when she received it. As far as her own relations with lower-level court personnel were concerned, she did little to change traditional practice: she regarded them as part of an extended court family to whom she and her successors owed lifetime support.[32] Nevertheless, the message that the dynasty was theoretically and practically answerable to a more general common good had been circulating at her father's court. Maria Theresa accepted the notion, but wrestled emotionally and intellectually all her life to reconcile it with dynastic concerns and, in some instances, her faith. The results were expressed elliptically but clearly in her first testament:

> dear as my children were to me, so much so that effort, concern, trouble, and work for them took precedence over myself. Nevertheless, as the common and first mother of [my] lands I would always put their general welfare before that of my offspring should my conscience tell me to do it, or that their well-being required it.[33]

She would also make it plain that her motherhood extended to all the 'nations' she ruled.[34]

The benevolent connotations of maternal imagery smoothed over the gross differences between the two concerns, at least in her own conscience. She urged on her own daughters the role of bridging the divide between ruler and servant at the courts into which they married. She recommended that Archduchess Carolina treat her loyal servants as a mother would her children. It could be exploited for political advantage, too. Maternal fecundity, underscored in several of her portraits and in a twelve-volume *Teresiad* by Franz Christoph von Scheyb, would promote the dynasty's survival and prosperity.[35] One of the high points of her career as mother-in-chief was an appearance before the Hungarian estates in 1741with the infant Joseph ii before her bosom. The kingdom's nobles received her dramatic appeal for aid against Frederick of Prussia with gratifying enthusiasm and promises of help, though the fiscal follow-up never quite met expectations.

In Search of Talent and Loyalty

Motherhood, however, would not fully bond the empress with her peoples. She fully realized that economic and social measures were called for as well. Some of her efforts were clearly easier for her than others, especially those that fell within the more or less traditional duties of rulers. Combating infectious disease was one. After a near-fatal attack of smallpox in 1767, Maria Theresa invited the physician Jan Ingen-Housz, born in the Netherlands but working in London, to Vienna. There he vaccinated not only her own children, but also 65 other youngsters. When the tactic proved effective, she knighted him. Her house also acknowledged the youngsters who participated in the experiment. At a celebratory dinner at Schönbrunn in 1768, the empress's own offspring served food to their colleagues.[36]

The empress had gone against the recommendations of close advisers by implementing the programme. The move highlighted her independence and tenacity. She was protecting her people, regardless of the novelty of her experiment. She was also, however, ready to revise major institutional practices with long and powerful cultural and social roots in the monarchy, even if she risked upending conventional understandings of her subjects' roles in dynastic policy. Few Habsburgs depended more upon their army to keep their crowns than Maria Theresa. Silesia, lost by treaty to Frederick ii in 1763, had a profitable textile industry that made the region one of the most productive lands of her monarchy. With its tax revenues now flowing elsewhere, she and her councillors had to think long and hard about improving the defences of the Habsburg holdings against further aggression. A more dedicated and well-prepared officer corps was much in order. Unlike their Prussian counterparts, the Habsburg nobility had never treated high military office as their exclusive preserve. A few noble families close to the court frequently held top commands in the army, but as a group their members typically preferred administrative posts either locally or in Vienna. Habsburg officers were therefore socially quite heterogeneous even before Maria Theresa succeeded her father. In 1740, men of noble and common origins were almost equally represented.

Diversity by itself, however, did not guarantee that talent would be available for command positions. The empress and those who counselled her realized that they not only had to identify promising young men from all classes of society, but they also had to be trained and retained in her service. She therefore increased opportunities for qualified people from all backgrounds to serve as officers and rewarded them in ways calculated to develop both their gifts and their loyalty to her house. Privileges within the military reward structure also had to be revised more inclusively. Maria Theresa did this in the compromising way that became her administrative style: rather than abolish distinctions, she expanded the number of people eligible for them. They also were tied more directly to the Habsburg establishment. By early 1751 all officers were *hoffähig*, formally eligible to appear at court. Hunting privileges, a hallmark of aristocratic life and of sovereign rights too, were granted more widely, as were noble titles for service: by 1757 all those who had held ranks in command for 30 years were benefiting from the privilege.

Talent, to become useful, also required learning and discipline. A military institute to train officers opened in Wiener Neustadt in 1752; by 1759 there were places for 400 students. Its special charge was to train the sons of Habsburg officers, young nobles from families whose finances fell short of their bloodlines, and sons of the dynasty's civil servants. Although military commissions were still available for a fee, aspiring but poor subaltern officers were charged nothing for their education. Those who needed to remedy academic deficiencies before entering could attend a preparatory school in Vienna.

An officer's family received benefits too. By the end of the eighteenth century some regimental schools were available for children on sites where their fathers were posted. Youngsters received an elementary education along with some vocational instruction: weaving and knitting for boys, equipping them for work in the growing textile industries intended to replace those in Silesia, and household skills and manners that would qualify girls to be governesses in the homes of the wealthy. Maria Theresa's Christian scruples forbade taking a major step further by conscripting common soldiers outright on the Prussian model, which she called a form of slavery. For the foreseeable future, local estates continued to raise troops for Habsburg armies when needed. But the higher ranks of the army increasingly represented what the dynasty wanted its people to see: a visible demonstration that people and ruler were working together to preserve the integrity of the sovereign's holdings. The spread of barracks throughout the villages, towns and cities of the Habsburg lands kept local populations of all social ranks in contact with the army and the multiple functions it would assume. These ranged from keeping order to public entertainment until the monarchy collapsed in the twentieth century.[37]

Maria Theresa paid her officers miserably. Nevertheless, she was exceedingly generous in acknowledging good performance through public honours that also linked recipients explicitly to the dynasty. The Military Maria Theresa Order for meritorious service was created in 1757. Featuring secular insignia rather than traditional Christian emblems, it underscored the recipient's specific relationship to the house and the government it exercised. Awardees were automatically ennobled, with rights to request baronial rank. Exceptional courage in combat, and not religion, birth or family background, was the only qualification considered.[38]

Nor did the empress exempt her own house from her modification of class distinctions among her subjects, especially in matters of style. The empress had a casual side, especially in private. She once chided a son-in-law, Albert of Saxony-Teschen, for addressing her in a letter as 'Madame' rather than her much preferred 'Mother', and for signing himself with his full name and not 'Albert'. While punctiliously formal in essential ceremonies, she brought to her surroundings quasi-bourgeois, though not vulgar, touches that her successors exploited more fully in the century to come.[39] Her establishment lost some of the grandeur of a court to become more of a home, a change that neatly matched the maternal image that she was cultivating. Her artistically gifted daughter Archduchess Maria Christina caught something of the atmosphere in her gouache reworking of a Netherlandish domestic scene into a portrayal of her parents' off-duty lifestyle (illus. 8). French courts of her day had very little private space, but even her grandfather, Leopold I, had arranged living quarters of equal size for himself and his empress. His granddaughter followed the pattern and expanded it substantially. Her summer palace at Schönbrunn had rooms dedicated to state, family and private affairs; the chambers of the empress and her husband opened onto a large communal area through which they easily gained access to their children's quarters. The modest size of the empress's rooms made them genuinely homely; largely absent were the celebrations of the dynasty that adorned walls and ceilings in the palace's halls of state. The

8 Archduchess Maria Christina, *The Imperial Family*, 1762, oil and gouache on paper.

double bed in the imperial bedchamber was so conventionally intimate that visitors took note of it.[40]

She was also ready to take on the Church, the very institution that the dynasty had once attached to itself to justify religious and military policies that rid the Habsburg patrimony of divisive Protestants and Ottoman armies. The empress's intense Catholicism was sometimes indistinguishable from outright bigotry. She would never allow Protestants to teach in public schools. The superstition-ridden religious practice in her lands, however, bothered her. So did the conditions of monastic and clerical life, which, she believed, were endangering not only the Church but the spiritual welfare of her subjects. Monks who spent more time on their private pleasures than preparing laymen for the afterlife disturbed her considerably. Her first testament called for action.[41]

Sheer accident advanced her general agenda. The wars that sapped her finances in the first half of her reign also forced the government to limit subsidies for renovating monasteries, convents and churches in her lands. Both Maria Theresa and her husband encouraged plainer struc-tures. They also supported programmes to simplify devotional and cere-monial practices that would cost less and increase public understanding of the Catholic faith at the same time. Royal restraint was especially noticeable in Hungary, where numerous ecclesiastical building projects were in progress to make up for years of neglect and decline during the Ottoman occupation, along with some Christian destruction during early eighteenth-century uprisings in the kingdom.[42] Maria Theresa also pressed to shift the thrust of clerical training. Improving educational standards overall was a major goal; the most controversial side of her programme, however, was to encourage novices and monks alike to exchange the contemplative life for the parish and charitable service that the generality of the faithful required. That, however, was about as far as her conscience and her political instincts allowed her to go. Her abolition of the Jesuit Order in 1770 was not prompted by deep conviction but by the need to keep in step with contemporary rulers who were minimizing clerical input into government. Nevertheless, she never folded such behaviour into her image, public and private. Attacking church institutions, even cautiously, had no place in the aura of devout motherliness she was cultivating. During her reign, spectators in Hungary watched her and members of her family many times as they joined elaborate pilgrimages in which the local nobility and high clerical officials took part. A second version of her testament in 1756 dropped the issue of Church reform altogether.[43]

Getting Basics in Place

Perversely enough, it would be one of Maria Theresa's most successful and sincere contributions to the public good and the interests of her house that eventually forced changes on the Church and its cultural patterns to which she was unshakeably attached. The state of basic education in the Habsburg lands worried her deeply. We know little about elementary instruction in the medieval Austrian lands. The curriculum depended on what a teacher brought to it and not a fixed lesson plan. The intrusion of the secular authorities was not unknown, but rare. Appeals for special funds to keep schools going were made to local rulers, but they had no fixed responsibility for primary training generally.[44]

By the end of the fifteenth century the dynasty began to play a more direct role in schooling, at least among the privileged classes. Some members of the Austrian nobility were adapting for their own use didactic manuals presented to Maximilian I on how best to conduct his future career.[45] It was, however, the Protestant Reformation that turned education into a serious affair of state, a *politicum*, as Maria Theresa called it in 1774. Catholic and Protestant princes alike found it in their interest to keep a close eye on what was being read and taught in their polities. Indeed, it was the empress's concern for sound religious practice among her subjects that prompted her to address the issue of public education generally. She was herself an active reader, though what she truly preferred was devotional literature, which she insistently forced upon her children and their spouses. She even admired publishers, giving titles of petty nobility to two leading figures in Vienna, Joseph Kürzbock and Johann Thomas Trattner, a one-time gooseherd.[46]

As was true in her ecclesiastical agenda, the empress was an unlikely advocate of educational improvement. She had little tolerance for scholars and artists who pursued their vocations as ends unto themselves. Even as she urged a broader curriculum at the University of Vienna, she was hoping to produce better trained officials rather than great scholars. In fact, her scorn for the latter was complete:

> Should I see these men of learning, these philosophers more happy and content with their private lives, I would change my mind. But unfortunately daily experience makes me think otherwise. There is no one weaker, more cowardly than these great minds, no one is more fawning and more beside themselves at the slightest mishap. They are bad fathers, sons, husbands, ministers, generals, burghers. Why? They are without firm foundation; their entire philosophy, their principles derive from their own wills.

She was equally dead set against Archduke Ferdinand inviting Wolfgang Amadeus Mozart to the former's court in Parma. One should avoid, she argued, taking on more personnel than needed. Mozart was among the 'useless people' swarming around like 'beggars'. Worse yet, the composer had a big family, a broad hint that Ferdinand would end up supporting them too.[47] She also believed that reading and artistic pursuits were just a higher level of distracting her own children and everyone else from mischief; idleness in anyone was among her chief bugaboos.[48] One of her favourite paintings was a double portrait of her eldest sons Joseph and Leopold cooperating in some nameless, but serious, enterprise of state. She installed it in Schönbrunn on a wall where visitors could never overlook it. Individual studies of her offspring in a set of engravings made by Jean-Étienne Liotard of Geneva show most of them at tasks that presumed serious prior education or training in the useful arts: reading, writing, surveying, painting, lecturing from a book, playing musical instruments, embroidering, winding yarn and the like.[49]

The practical uses of education of all kinds, however, were quite a different story. The empress's children received good musical instruction;

Joseph and Leopold played instruments, and the former also composed in his off-hours. Their mother made serious use of their training. For special occasions, her offspring doubled as entertainers. In Christoph Willibald Gluck's *Il Parnaso confuso*, put on at Joseph's marriage in 1765 to Maria Josepha of Bavaria, the future emperor sang with three of his sisters; Leopold, who would eventually succeed his brother, played the continuo passages.[50]

Regardless of her prejudices and misgivings, however, she was convinced that the prosperity and happiness of her peoples, and the survival of her monarchy too, all hung on the expansion of primary schooling among her peoples, male and female.[51] As in all of her more successful reforms, she did her best not to offend vested interests, such as the very Church that she wanted her subjects to understand more clearly. She asked progressive clergymen to advise her and carry out the programme. A Premonstratensian monk from Silesia, Ignatius Felbiger, designed the elementary school component. He had already worked for the new territorial ruler of the province, Frederick II of Prussia, who needed a catechism to convince local Catholics that they owed their loyalties to state as well as Church. Maria Theresa accepted the formula without reservation. The following colloquy, which appeared in the manual for Catholic teachers that Felbriger published in 1768, might have been written by the sovereign herself:

Q: Who is subject to the power of the ruler?
A: Everyone.
Q: Why must everyone submit to authority?
A: All power comes from God.
Q: From whence comes the power held by the ruler?
A: This power comes from God.
Q: Whom does God ordain?
A: Everyone who holds authority. Because all who exercise
   authority are ordained by God, subjects must be
   submissive, loyal and obedient, even to a ruler not
   of our religion. This was taught by the Apostle Paul,
   who himself lived under the pagan Roman emperors.
Q: What does it mean to resist authority?
A: They will suffer eternal damnation.

Children, moreover, were to take these injunctions deeply to heart; lip service would not do.[52]

Few government programmes would ever serve both dynasty and its people so advantageously. State schoolrooms allowed the House of Habsburg-Lorraine to drill the young on their civic and moral duties, even as boys and girls learned skills that prepared them for useful and productive lives. Felbiger also ensured that pupils throughout the monarchy heard the same lessons. His government-sponsored 'Normal Schools' would tell future instructors how and what to teach. The first one, which gave basic pedagogical training in reading, writing, arithmetic and the catechism, opened in Vienna in 1771 to considerable public fanfare. Institutional infighting slowed their expansion to the dynasty's other lands for a time, but by 1776 every capital of the monarchy had its own college of education. To make sure that children truly grasped their lessons, a subsequent state mandate required that elementary schoolbooks should be written in the appropriate local vernacular.

It was impossible to remove the parish clergy from the classroom in grammar schools because teachers were paid abysmally and steered clear of the job. The actual numbers of pupils who took advantage of the system grew slowly: relatively urbanized parts of the monarchy had the highest rates of attendance, rural mountain settlements the lowest. Only a third of the monarchy's youngsters were attending school in 1780, with boys far outnumbering girls. By 1800 the total number of children taking basic schooling had expanded and the ratio of males to females had closed to three to two.[53] Maria Theresa could therefore be reasonably sure that she had initiated serious and meaningful change that was in the best interests of both herself and her monarchy. Felbiger and another clergyman, Gratian Marx, who worked with the government on secondary education, shared her misgivings about the social mobility such training might encourage. Dynastic monarchy to all three of them was a hierarchical operation and a condition of effective rule.

The empress, however, was generally reluctant to move too radically in any of her reforms, educational or otherwise. Dynastic monarchy was a hierarchical construct with a system of protocols that required a ruler to enforce it. Maria Theresa, along with some of her nobility, clearly wanted to give Habsburg subjects the schooling that made them publicly productive and privately more comfortable. Neither she nor her officials intended to inspire large-scale socio-economic changes that would expose dynastic rule to criticism, the Habsburg variant included. Though the school ordinance of 1774 called for her subjects to be freed from the 'darkness of ignorance' (*die Finsterniss der Unwissenheit*), it also recommended a curriculum 'appropriate to class'.[54] Benevolent motherhood, it would seem, went just so far. Nevertheless, where public school instruction was concerned, the empress could say quite honestly that she had taken account of the needs of both her people and her house, and that was quite enough.

The Theatre and the General Good

The Theresan School Ordinance had a strain of idealism running through it: the empress's concern for schooling girls as well as boys was a case in point. But equally important from the dynasty's point of view was to have in place a manageable agent for fixing dynastic messages in impressionable heads and providing Habsburg governments with a reliable pool of civil servants. The effectiveness of the programme as a whole, however, depended upon cooperation in all corners of the general public. Predictably, there were those who refused to see the programme's benevolent side. Some felt decidedly threatened. The Church establishment resisted any state encroachment on its control of education, both theological and secular. Even segments of the common folk, the announced beneficiaries of school reform, grumbled. Throughout the rural hinterlands of the Habsburg holdings, parents needed their offspring at home to do routine chores and work in the fields. School fees seemed onerous too.[55]

At the core of the new educational agenda was a clear quid pro quo: the state would give its peoples the training they needed to achieve greater prosperity, even though the process would require accustoming themselves to daily labour, rather than the seasonal regimens of the countryside. At the very least, they would probably be worrying less about existential challenges. Famine, for example, was still familiar in most of Europe.

But what if the all-providing mother chose to make pleasure itself an obstacle to remedying the educational and cultural deficiencies of the empress's peoples and enhancing the renown of her house and its monarchy? Here, for all of her concern for the well-being of her peoples, Maria Theresa would find people who not only resented her machinations, however sincerely intended, but openly resisted them.

Like her seventeenth-century ancestors, Maria Theresa realized that the public stage had an educational function too. Vienna itself had few theatres of scale. It was not until 1745 that public concert life in the city got under way, and only after 1831 did the city have a hall dedicated to such affairs. Throughout her reign, Maria Theresa herself used her court theatre and the arena of her father's new riding school for quasi-public performances. The house figured prominently in many of these. The impresarios who organized the affairs duly acknowledged the generosity of the ruling dynasty, an understandable move as they could not put such crucial patronage at risk. It was equally serious if they had no access to auditoriums in noble residences. One musical entertainment for the empress in 1758 included an interlude commending the dynasty for its support of the arts. This was followed by a gilded transparency of a temple, in which the monarchy's peoples acclaimed the 'Fame, Crown, and Name of our Sovereigns'. Shortly after this came a sequence, replete with classical mythology, in which Archduke Joseph, costumed as a heroic Telemachus, was the central figure.[56]

Most people, not only in Vienna but throughout the monarchy, experienced the theatre in less august settings. Urban stages throughout the Habsburg lands had developed a comic tradition in which performers commented freely on every conceivable subject: political, social, scatological and sexual. Word choice and pronunciation were often crudely regional. Actors who mastered such delivery and the gestures that underscored it were idolized by audiences. Cultivated foreigners who attended these performances both laughed themselves silly or sat in stunned amazement as trousers were dropped; Lady Mary Montague from England was one of them. Local elites liked them too, Maria Theresa's husband for one.[57]

Habsburg rulers formally controlled places of entertainment. Along with Lower Austrian local authorities, the government censored theatrical productions, though erratically. Theatres could be shuttered or reopened by the dynasty for any number of reasons, prominently among these being dynastic funerals and the mandatory public mourning that followed. Nevertheless, the court also understood the popularity of the comic stage. It had even encouraged such performances to reward public fiscal self-sacrifice during Eugene of Savoy's expensive Balkan campaigns.[58]

In her younger days the empress had visibly enjoyed the theatre and music.[59] By 1750, however, the prudish strain in her character was coming to the fore, making her relentlessly hostile to public comic theatres. For one thing, they drew far larger audiences than the court-sponsored theatre she established in 1741. For another, she detested coarse speech, not only in her sons but wherever it could be heard. She also took umbrage at the suggestive body language that reinforced it. On a much higher, critical level, she was listening to critics who wanted to use French social comedy, which usually took place in upper-class settings, as a model for refining the vocabulary, delivery and behavioural conventions of the German-speaking stage. The empress even had an audience with the leading German advocate for such reforms, Johann Christoph Gottsched, when he and his wife visited Vienna in 1749.

Maria Theresa banned the free-speaking stage and its salacious antics between 1752 and 1754. The policy was widely resented and ignored. She backed off far enough to concede differences between acceptable and unacceptable stage language. But in 1765 she transferred responsibility for overseeing theatrical productions from the municipal administration of Vienna to the court itself, where the new standards of literacy were taking hold. Unable to discriminate between the permissible and the forbidden, however, the members of a new supervisory commission threw up their hands at the job.

Maria Theresa remained adamant. Supporting her strongly was Joseph von Sonnenfels, her cultural factotum, who recommended censorship. Playwrights were ordered to submit written texts to bureaucrats who inspected them prior to performance and suggested emendations. Theatre people were generally furious. Actors, once free to say whatever came into their heads the moment they appeared on stage, now had to memorize lines out of fear that they would overstep the regime's linguistic standards. Some of them, including the most popular, flatly refused to conform and retired. Managers complained about losing such people; audiences loved them too and stopped patronizing the stage.[60]

By 1770 Maria Theresa had transferred oversight of the theatre to her son and heir apparent, Joseph II, who was now her co-regent. He had also been German emperor for five years. The cultural battle over the comic stage would continue through her reign and his, with serious consequences for intellectual and aesthetic concerns throughout the Habsburg lands. But the reactions to his mother's high-minded efforts to reconfigure popular preferences and behaviour should have warned him that dynastic notions of the common welfare could not be readily enforced beyond what was demonstrably necessary or generally acceptable. Too close a personal identification with such measures might be dangerous too. If sufficiently aggrieved, it seemed, the very public to whom the Habsburgs had extended the benefits of self-improvement could strike back.

Maria Theresa accomplished what she did by proceeding with utmost caution in remedying conditions that she thought were problematic: the material and legal conditions of peasant life, fiscal structures and minis-terial appointments. She found it hard to fire anyone. Such an approach clearly helped her and her immediate family to weather the military and political challenges the dynasty faced following Charles VI's death. Her grasp of the arts of the possible had a long history in her house. Nevertheless, not all of its members were masters of the discipline. A compelling example was her otherwise highly gifted successor.

Doing Good Comprehensively

It is hard to say how much of Maria Theresa's rhetoric in a second testa-ment was formulaic, idealistic guidance for Joseph II. The document remained secret until he followed his mother in 1780. In any case, he may never have read it. Relations between mother and son were tense, even tempestuous. Sometimes he simply threatened to quit his co-regency. It is hard to say which of the pair irritated the other the more. The son often seemed less bothered by the empress's cautious approach to local and foreign politics than by his secondary status in her regime. The job turned out to be an exercise in frustration. While it forced him to focus on the Habsburg lands themselves, he was unable to do much about them. She was fully empowered to act without consulting him and sometimes did; she also set aside his initiatives at will. German imperial policy was just as vexatious. Joseph as emperor had supreme command over the Habsburg army, which figured heavily in international affairs. It was his mother, however, who retained ultimate responsibility for the latter; when she sought advice, she turned to councillors more frequently than to her eldest son. Even after she turned theatres over to his direct supervision, she intervened now and again. For her part, Maria Theresa fretted ceaselessly about Joseph's selfconfidence, his frequent liberal inter-ventions in religious and cultural affairs, and his sarcasm, which was especially withering when directed at his intellectual inferiors.[61] Com-promise rarely satisfied him, though in some instances he had no choice.

He and his mother did, however, agree in principle on some impor-tant issues. Though Joseph was unwilling to push any economic agenda that might interrupt the revenue flow to his army, he was as certain as his mother that the family empire and its populations had to be economic-ally more dynamic. He retraced and elaborated on the measures that Maria Theresa and her advisers had taken to raise the productivity of their peoples and improve their material lives: suppressing contemplative monasticism and nunnery, furthering public education, refining public taste, addressing the harsh legal and economic constraints on peasants throughout the monarchy, and governing his lands in a more rational and centralized fashion. Most important of all for his dynasty and its administrative future, he extended meritocratic principles more widely among his subjects, thereby introducing them to the egalitarian values that would take hold throughout Europe in the following century. His military public relations also took up where his mother left off; by 1790 two-thirds of his officer corps were of commoner background, and he created a medal honouring bravery among ordinary troops. And like his mother he acquired a profiled parental image, which even made its way into contemporary music. Some texts for Mozart's Masonic and military scores call Joseph's concern for common soldiers fatherlike.[62]

He also, however, took steps that his mother would never have made. While economic concerns forced the empress to curb ceremonial excesses at her court, she had been sufficiently mindful of her exalted status to display it lavishly many times. Normally her travels with officials and members of the house, even to their hunting lodges, were vast public spectacles. There was a ceremony for everything. Her cortège was arranged to remind audiences of the social pecking order that governed the court and, implicitly, the world at large. Should the party stop in a town, salvos were a mandatory welcome, along with pealing church bells and a short address from the highest local official, with or without the gate key. The population was rounded up to shout 'Vivat!'

Joseph declared outright war on much of this behaviour, even before he ruled much of anything. Ceremony, he thought, kept him from knowing the lands of the monarchy better. While his mother was still alive, he had often travelled incognito throughout his lands. Local officials were sometimes offended when he preferred modest inns to the more luxurious quarters they could offer him. His passion for simplification carried over to his court. The Spanish cloak of state (*spanisches Mantelkleid*), worn for formal court appearances, was not obligatory after 1784. Such customs, Joseph said, no longer helped monarchs to control the nobility, another of his goals, and only distracted attention from the business of state. His preferred military uniform for public appearances, a custom that he may have taken from the Prussian king, Frederick II, but possibly from his father, Emperor Francis I. Most of his successors continued the style.[63]

Joseph also substantially modified the Habsburg court ceremonial brought by emperor Charles V to his establishment in Spain in the mid-sixteenth century. Imitated in varying degrees by several European sovereign houses, it set up a dense firewall of lower personnel around the monarch and his family, who called upon these people night and day for services. Sumptuous jewellery and clothing, elaborate carpets, baldachins, steps and platforms, various levels of genuflection and bowing, terms of address – all set rulers off as a special order of humanity.

In Spain access to the king and his consort, and such matters as who could sit on a cushion with the latter, and who had the privilege of wearing his hat in audiences with the king, were strictly defined. The number of rooms one traversed to reach the monarch depended upon an individual's status. The higher one's rank, the nearer one started en route to the royal presence. The Spanish ruler ate alone. His court colour code swathed everyone in black, at least by the time Philip II died in 1598. All other colours were banned, but since his dynasty was frequently mourning relatives or fellow monarchs, convenience may have trumped personal preference for many. Not all of these protocols governed in Vienna, but many did, including the succession of chambers to negotiate before meeting the monarch. Hunting and riding were the only moments when Habsburg rulers dispensed with many of these formalities, even into the twentieth century. At Ischl, his summer residence, Emperor Franz Joseph often cast aside his uniform for lederhosen and a woodsman's feathered cap.[64]

At least outwardly, Maria Theresa respected the niceties of rank. Some merely bothered Joseph: some he truly detested. Genuflection of any sort and kneeling before the monarch had stopped by 1787. Men of his court took to wearing army uniform and styling other clothing on military lines. He also allowed the public to see a more human dimension of their ruler's character. After his time, Habsburg rulers made fixed public appearances for only two religious occasions – Corpus Christi and the Maundy Thursday foot washing – along with funeral processions and festivals for the various secular orders established by Maria Theresa and his father. Such limitations did not mean that Joseph was no longer on view to his subjects, either in Vienna or its suburbs. He was seen frequently on the road, either on business or for holiday travel, at public celebrations of military victories, at services in the five churches where he chose to worship, and when strolling through the gardens at his Vienna summer retreat in today's Augarten. There he, and occasionally his ministers, mingled with the general populace, very much embodying the inscription over the gate, 'A place for recreation dedicated from their admirer to all people.'[65]

Subjects in other regions had the same opportunity. One of the longest-lived images of Joseph shows him in a Moravian field pushing a

plough commandeered from a reverent local peasant. Travelling throughout his lands and at headquarters in Vienna he received as many public
visits, deputations and written requests as a single human being possibly
could. Petitions for his consideration may have numbered well into the
thousands. He did not hide himself even when while at work in the
Hofburg. Any crackpot could enter the *Controleurgang*, a corridor outside
his official quarters. In 1772 Count Charles von Zinzendorf, a major figure
in Joseph's government and its diarist-in-detail, saw the emperor chatting
with a man about the date of the coming Apocalypse. Beggars were all
about, too. In fact, Joseph occasionally added a common touch to the
polite society that surrounded him; for a musical performance in 1786 at
the Habsburg suburban retreat in Laxenburg, Joseph brought in between
300 and 400 residents of the neighbourhood, even providing rides for
the local children. The unaccustomed company, some conspicuously
dirty, put off a number of elegant guests quite visibly.[66]

To see that his peoples spent their time and energies productively,
he scaled back the number of dynastic festivities for which they attended
church services many times a year: Habsburg birthdays and name days,
heretofore celebrated with special church services, were collectively observed on New Year's Day. Other house-specific occasions were gradually
shifted to the private spaces of the Hofburg. Protocols for court functions
also loosened. When Joseph ordered the court theatre to focus on developing German-speaking culture generally, seating arrangements according
to social rank were modified to attract paying audiences. Many such
changes took place without major controversy. Some, however, caused
him considerable grief. His disregard for traditional public coronations
and the vows to uphold local political and administrative structures that
were part of them would spark one of the most incendiary domestic
issues he faced in his career.

Joseph's distaste for ritual and ceremony also extended to one of the
Habsburg court's most theatrical public spectacles: dynastic funerals. By
the middle of the seventeenth century these were rivalling fireworks and
operatic extravaganzas as court-sponsored general entertainment. They
also gave the dynasty an opportunity to dramatize on a massive scale the
sociopolitical system that governed them. The dynasty as a whole was
on full display, part of a divine order that included nobles attached to the
inner circle of the court, members of the Order of the Golden Fleece and
its female counterpart, the Order of the Crossed Star, along with the four
highest court officials. Privy councillors and chamberlains, nuncios,
ambassadors, magistrates of the city of Vienna and representatives of the

university also took part. All of this Joseph had witnessed at his mother's obsequies, and he did not like it. Regardless of the tension between them, he mourned her deeply and the mood might have prompted the drastic simplification he brought to the burial customs of his house. Public interments were to change, too. In 1784 he recommended that his subjects be put to rest in wooden caskets that could be reused in the future.[67]

The Indispensable Habsburg?

Such measures and many more powerfully affected the material and cultural life of the Habsburg monarchy, just as Joseph intended. Vienna benefited most from his initiatives, but other areas were not neglected. After mandating street lighting for his capital in 1776, he extended the service to the crime-ridden thoroughfares beyond the city walls. New police stations and court facilities added to the security of these regions. Perhaps the most widely appreciated and used facility of all was his Vienna General Hospital, opened in 1754 and largely funded from his personal resources. He planned, though never realized, similar facilities throughout the entire monarchy.[68]

Joseph also did much to turn Vienna into the European cultural capital that emperor Leopold I had once sought to create. In fact, Joseph cared as much as the latter about the arts, music, literature, including poetry, and the theatre. In his youth he had studied not only music but also some acting. He talked endlessly about what he saw, read and heard with interlocutors who had no choice but to listen helplessly. Like his great-grandfather, he personally oversaw the aesthetic environment at his court, especially its musical side. He sought out librettists, composers and performers and frequently attended rehearsals. His preferences reoriented Viennese opera forever. The ponderous Italian *opera serie* that graced the punctilious establishments of his ancestors were not for him. From 1778 to 1783 only comic operas with German-language texts were given in his German National Theatre. He also willingly shared his musical resources with other theatres in Vienna. The National Theatre orchestra, acknowledged to be the best in the city, had the emperor's permission to play for other local performances when he did not need them.[69]

Maria Theresa had sincerely wanted learning as well as the arts to flourish in the Habsburg lands. Joseph II did too, so much so that he fashioned his policies with unusual caution to reach his ends. He lifted many restrictions on writers and publishers, in part to encourage the print trades in Vienna but also to allow the circulation of ideas that would add substance to intellectual life in the monarchy. The theatre, however, continued to make him edgy. He recognized hostile social criticism in plays when he read them: he ordered alterations in the German translation of Beaumarchais' *The Barber of Seville*, put on at the popular Theater am Kärntnertor in 1785. The emperor also forbade certain topics in scripts: no prostitutes (even though he called upon them for his personal comfort habitually), no grisly crimes or unspeakable acts, no boudoir escapades, no unpunished wrongdoers. No social class was to be demonized or trivialized in stereotypes, including peasants. The latter were even allowed to be shown in revolt, as long as monarchy itself was held harmless. Nevertheless, the effect of all these reservations was considerably offset when he limited the scope of his censors' authority to Vienna. What was forbidden in the capital could be performed elsewhere in the monarchy.[70] He also, to his eventual regret, allowed new theatres to open.

Caroline Pichler, who presided over one of Vienna's significant intellectual salons in the early nineteenth century and was an astute judge of cultural developments, had high praise for Joseph's musical and theatrical enterprises. In her opinion, the level of skill that Joseph demanded at his court theatre prepared young singers to be prima donnas in lesser houses throughout the continent. His stage also acquired an aura of emotional and intellectual seriousness that bourgeois audiences, including herself, were beginning to expect. Important musical figures appreciated the attention paid to music in Vienna as well. The young Ludwig van Beethoven made a very brief visit to Vienna in 1787, possibly taking a few composition lessons with Mozart. At home in Bonn in 1790, he was engaged to set to music an *Ode on the Death of Joseph II*. By 1792 he was ready to make the Habsburg capital his permanent headquarters.[71]

With few exceptions, these initiatives had roots in the policies of his mother, even his grandfather Charles VI. But Joseph brought to their initiatives a transformative philosophical agenda that sharply departed from their values and their political calculations. His Edict of Religious Toleration in 1781 shared his mother's goal of encouraging all members of the monarchy's society to work productively. It was, however, a sharp rebuke to her devoutly held Catholic beliefs. She tried to convert Protestants wherever possible; Joseph allowed them to worship freely in his lands and, with some limitations on size and design, to have their own churches. Jewish subjects received corresponding concessions, tailored to fit the differing conditions of Jewish life in the regions of his lands. Joseph, pleased as he undoubtedly was to be viewed by soldiers as a father figure, far preferred to be known as a first servant of the state.[72] His lifelong role stood in the secular here and now, where the needs of his subjects and his administration set performance standards, and not his Maker. His claim to 'firstness' arose from the unique responsibilities he bore in this world, and not from some inscrutable dispensation of Providence. Within this frame of reference, he therefore was prepared to move more radically than his mother ever would to adjust the position of organized Catholicism in his realms. And when he moved, he moved ruthlessly.

His reforms of the extensive Catholic monastic network in the Habsburg lands was a case in point. Whatever changes Maria Theresa had made to synchronize the religious obligations of cloistered communities with the welfare of the monarchy were piecemeal at best. Joseph attacked the problem frontally, both in words and deeds. He had a fifteen-year record of criticizing monasteries and nunneries even before he succeeded his mother in 1780. Not only had some become excessively rich, but they routinely lured people into taking orders before the age of sixteen, a standard set for the age of reason established at the Council of Trent more than 200 years before. The practice drew the young and strong away from the labour market; it also diminished the likelihood that even the brightest of boys would prepare for government service. While the emperor did not reject clergymen as teachers, he wanted them to train good and useful subjects.

The implication was clear: the needs of the state and its chief servant required as much attention as did the scrutiny of one's soul, even in cases where the call to the cloistered life had been sincerely felt. Joseph came down even harder on mendicants, especially Franciscans. Begging, he thought, subverted market discipline, discouraged personal responsibility, and furthered idleness and even disorderly public behaviour. Worse yet, the brotherhood pandered to popular prejudice and superstition. Though he was never able to remove the order from his realms altogether, Joseph did convince many members to adapt themselves to his clerical ideal, as pastors who actively attended to the spiritual welfare of their parish communities.

As radical as these measures were, progressive churchmen in the monarchy did support them. Popular approval was there, too. As for charity, it was best handled by the state. A print of 1783 shows Joseph II and St Peter, hand in hand on a hilltop, calling the common people to worship. Standing around are layfolk with sacks of money in their hands. A chest at the bottom of the picture is full of devotional paraphernalia such as rosaries and priestly garb, packed away because they are no longer needed. Thus would the state alone, epitomized by its first servant, provide for public needs. Costing two and a half florins, a hefty price for the time, the image sold thousands of copies.[73]

Yet Joseph never quite understood that such programmes could grievously injure the innocent too. The closure and secularization of religious houses forced both day labourers and artists to look elsewhere for employment. Looking to the allegedly benevolent state for a living had a downside all its own. Politically energetic monarchs and their advisers were far quicker to shift aesthetic paradigms than Church foundations, where eternal truth framed artistic decisions. An exemplary victim was Franz Anton Maulbertsch, one of the great colourists in the history of European painting. His early frescoes and painted ceilings were done mostly for monasteries and churches throughout the monarchy. He worked just as easily in worldly settings and taught in the Imperial Academy of Engraving after receiving a commission from Maria Theresa to allegorize the science, learning and industry that she was promoting in her lands. In 1769 he was restoring the ceiling of the Hall of State in the imperial library, a complex representation of the dynasty's support of learning. Nevertheless, he received no further engagements after 1777, even though he worked continually to please his rulers. By the 1780s he had begun painting allegories of education and, by implication, the rational process; in 1785 he produced an etching celebrating Joseph's Edict of Toleration. But he had become the victim of a different set of aesthetic values that had been introduced to the court: the censorious Joseph von Sonnenfels deplored all art that required a classical education to understand. Painting, like the Habsburg emperor, should be true to nature and easily accessible to all.[74]

Joseph allowed some monastic establishments to continue as before, especially when they broadened the range of their mission and their links to the emperor's ideals. Architecturally among the most beautiful was the Premonstratensian house of Strahov in Prague. Threatened with closure, the canons of the order built a 'philosophical library' in addition to its theological counterpart, established in the previous century. More suggestively, a bust of Joseph adorned the entrance to the new building. The emperor duly left the house untouched. When he backtracked a bit to help those among the cloistered clergy, particularly nuns, who were virtual strangers to secular life, he drew upon money sequestered for

Church missionary activity, which Joseph clearly disliked. Maria Theresa had financed her Catholic missionary work among Protestants through a religious fund set up for the purpose. Joseph restructured it to receive the revenues paid on properties and assets of dissolved monasteries and cloisters in Austrian lands. The proceeds were dedicated to providing pensions for once cloistered nuns and monks who no longer resided in these establishments, but lacked the means to live independently. The remainder went into furthering new parishes, the work of parish clergy and the like. In cases where a former monastery was converted into barracks, the army paid rent into the Religious Fund. As at Strahov, the policy showed state and Church working productively in the interests of both institutions. The foundation to this day supports Catholic religious activities in Austria.[75]

As was true with clerical charity, such policies were well received in circles inspired by the anti-clericalism spreading through eighteenth-century Europe. Opinions on the subject were expressed very freely, and sometimes quite indelicately, especially after 1782 when Joseph eased the censorship that had kept these ideas out of open public discussion. His greatest weakness, however, now began to come to the fore: his inability to appreciate the strength and variety of the interest groups that might resist his measures, well meaning and reasonable though they seemed to him. Churchmen throughout his lands badly missed the protection the state had once given them now that they faced a newly liberated press, filled with anti-religious diatribes. By 1783 a papal nuncio in Vienna, Giuseppe Garampi, was comparing the situation to the upheavals of the Reformation. He claimed that books favourable to the Church were actually being denied publication and that people had been heard to say that 'Jesus Christ . . . having given useful service to the House of Austria for many centuries, deserved to have his salary reduced' and to be retired.[76] The Church of Rome tenaciously opposed Joseph's efforts to turn the Catholic establishment into one among several government responsibilities: theological faculties, for example, were to be attached to universities and general seminaries were to be run by the state. Popes had historically been ready to compromise with secular institutions in moments of necessity, but this was not one of them.

Nor did public criticism always find fault with the ecclesiastical hierarchy. Distress over the emperor's attacks on the Church and its officials had been rising in the more remote provinces of his monarchy. Once again, his ideology had not served him well. Having turned Habsburg rule into an explicitly secular undertaking, he had sacrificed the spiritual attributes of his office that his forebears had traditionally stressed. Not all of his subjects, however, saw replacing God's appointed sovereign with the ruler as an avatar of the public good, as defined by Joseph and his advisers, as an equal exchange. His relentless worldliness, at least as some read it, skimped on the religious dimension inherent in sovereignty. Even Joseph's revised mission for parish clergy stressed their practical responsibilities. In the Austrian Netherlands, now Belgium, the public had not been all that hostile to regular clergy in the first place. Local monks and nuns were seen as important components in the charitable and economic life of a province.[77] Dissatisfaction with the emperor's treatment of local religious institutions would become the complaint of many in the anti-government upheavals throughout his lands that accompanied Joseph's troubled last years.

Having expanded freedom of the press, Joseph spent much time brooding over the perverse outcome of his magnanimity. Archduke Leopold had once said that his brother hated being criticized; Joseph now heard it night and day. He hired people to write favourable comments about him in newspapers that treated him unkindly. The common people, his professed centre of concern, thought better of him than other constituencies, but even they had palpable grievances. Joseph decreed an end to serfdom in 1781. By 1783, however, the detailed conditions he set as part of the reform bitterly disappointed the peasants who had expected much more generous treatment. With the goal of giving farmers small plots of their own, rates of compensation to former estate owners for rents and work services were reckoned according to multi-variable calculations that took into account the size and quality of the plots and what was produced on them. Although the programme never went fully into effect, it enraged many of the prospective beneficiaries, especially when they believed that they would be performing as much unpaid labour as they had in the past. Some even rioted.[78]

That was not all. Maria Theresa had persuaded the estates of her lands to provide more regular support for her fighting forces. Nevertheless, these bodies still had important functions locally and were not about to yield them to a central administration. Joseph's pursuit of increased administrative efficiency was bitterly contested. His efforts to introduce German as the official language of government business was hotly contested in Hungary, whose nobility preferred Latin, at least in their official documents. It was, in their opinion, the idiom of rulers. Nor did they like their monarch's scheme to divide the realm into equally sized districts: they much preferred their traditional Hungarian counties, in which their families had long held such offices as sheriff. In short, Joseph's self-image as the first servant of the state looked to them like a disguise for the absolute monarchy that had been anathema to Hungary's ruling elites for centuries. In fact, they were not altogether wrong: Joseph did take a positive pleasure in the powers he enjoyed.

Joseph II clearly misjudged the public appetite throughout his monarchy for programmes in aid of the general welfare. He ended his life bemoaning the 'appalling ingratitude' he had encountered. Whether he was speaking as a cruelly disappointed father or a peevish servant of his state, his feelings befitted both roles. But the emperor had brought many of his troubles upon himself, just as his mother had feared he would. Boundless and misplaced self-confidence blinded him to the possible flaws in his thinking and behaviour. As Derek Beales, Joseph's consummate modern biographer, has put it, 'his aim was to work for the good of his people while paying little or no attention to what they themselves wanted'. The state he professed to serve was not some autonomous entity but a composite of interests, wants and desires that were ready to fight back more vigorously than he thought possible.[79] For his part, Joseph struck back like the threatened monarch he was. Creating a formal Ministry of Police in 1789, he applied the intrusive censorship he had recommended for the stage to many more forms of public activity throughout his patrimony.

Archduke Leopold, who was serving as Grand Duke of Tuscany through much of this period, had deplored his eldest brother's tendency to congratulate himself as a man of the people simply because he talked to impoverished, occasionally deranged supplicants who found their way to the corridor outside his office in the Hofburg. It never seems to have occurred to the emperor that they wanted money from him, not suggestions for changing their lives. He also badly underestimated his power to limit the prerogatives of the traditional elites – the nobles and clergy – in his realms and, in the end, it was they who most effectively frustrated him.

Nevertheless, his calculated openness did have the effect he intended; humble folk did, for whatever reason, turn up outside his workplace to see an emperor who made himself available to them informally. A literature of sorts rose up about his behaviour, such as the little book *Joseph II Outside his Office: Various Scenes from Today's Government*.[80] His ideals and handiwork, as contested as they often were, synthesized public policy goals that had been under discussion in the offices of the monarchy for a century. They would shape and reshape his dynasty's empire and the role of the House of Habsburg in it more substantively than he may have ever anticipated, particularly in his embittered last days. The state bureaucratic apparatus, the part of Habsburg rule that gave subjects some hands-on contact with the regime until 1918, was in good part his creation. Its officials and subordinates would become not only instruments for the perpetuation of his personal legacy but for the continuation of Habsburg rule generally. He also laid the foundations of the public persona adopted by his house until it left the political stage in 1918. Long reliant on Christian Catholic practice and policy to validate its position on this earth, the Habsburgs had now taken it upon themselves to answer to the needs of people from whom they were demanding great changes in productivity and lifestyle. While this step may have contributed to his immediate problems – it is far easier to criticize a demystified monarch than a self-proclaimed agent of God – it contributed more than a little to the ability of the monarchy to shift gears effectively in the revolutionary social, political and economic environment that was taking shape in France and threatened to drift elsewhere.[81]

Joseph died on 20 February 1790. His most intimate legacy to his house was a lesson in monarchical manners. His know-it-all ways, his savagely witty, often sarcastic tongue, combined with his utter confidence in the unique significance of his position, lessened him as a person. The same traits made enlisting the cooperation of others all the more problematic. His successors all had flaws. Almost to a man, however, they were unfailingly circumspect and polite.

Joseph had the elaborate Habsburg funeral that in life he had deplored. At the end, however, he managed to snub ritual and tradition. His sarcophagus in the crypt of the Capuchins is a far cry from the ornate resting places of his parents. Starkly plain, it contrasts strikingly with the immense tomb chest nearby where Maria Theresa and Francis of Lorraine recline, both physically and in relief on the cover.[82] As a very visible champion of simplicity, he had set in motion major changes that altered the monarchy in the minds and eyes of its subjects, culturally and operationally. His policies became referents for political and social change in the Habsburg lands thereafter. They would help to make Vienna a musical and artistic centre for those who cared about such things. The immediate results of his initiatives were disappointing. But his successors would have cause to thank him for the suggestions.

FIVE

REVOLUTION, RECOVERY, REVOLUTION

The First Servant as Monarch

The German imperial crown and rule in the Habsburg patrimonial domains fell to Joseph's younger brother Leopold, known after 1790 as Emperor Leopold II. As intelligent and economically progressive as his elder sibling, and also a target of maternal scolding, he contributed far more to the survival of his house than did Joseph. The latter's carnal lusts, at least within the confines of marriage, were largely exhausted on Isabella of Parma, his unresponsive first wife. He loved her deeply, but dynastic maternal service and the serial pregnancies that came with it were clearly not for her. She died three years following her wedding; her replacement, a Bavarian princess, did not excite Joseph at all. Leopold, on the other hand, to quote Joseph, was a 'first-rate population-maker'.[1] Survived by ten legitimate sons and a couple of daughters, he guaranteed the presence of his house in European territorial politics until 1918. His flock of illicit offspring was also sizeable.

Leopold shared Joseph's liberal sympathies and goals; his political radicalism outstripped that of his brother by far. Not long before he took over in Vienna, he confidentially told his sister Maria Christine that rulers generally should have constitutions to follow.[2] Unlike Joseph II, he performed his first assignment as a territorial ruler brilliantly. Governing the Habsburg holdings in Tuscany, he turned the region into a model of eighteenth-century economic and juridical rationalism. His newly efficient police force tightened security. Such success, however, depended as much on the cautious, sometimes devious way he introduced his policies as on their content. It also underscored one reason for his brother's apparent failure. He too expected serious institutional change to provoke automatic resistance that had to be countered by propaganda of his own. Nevertheless, his positive reputation on the peninsula survived intact. Even as pressures for an independent Italian national

153

state were increasing in 1832, the city of Pisa dedicated a monument to him.[3]

Like most members of his house, Leopold did not confuse principle with necessity once he came to positions of power. He quickly cancelled some of Joseph's most resented reforms, but continued onerous practices such as censorship to maintain order in the Habsburg lands. Though he disliked traditional rituals as much as his predecessor, he restored and used them when he thought they enhanced his authority and the esteem attached to it. At the same time, he recognized that he had to update these affairs in ways that ingratiated him with his subjects. He revived formal coronations in his various lands, but modelled them after folk festivals. He commissioned August Wilhelm Iffland, a popular German dramatist, to write a play about a king who recovers his throne. The end product, *Friedrich von Österreich*, dealt with Emperor Frederick III, certainly not the most illustrious of Habsburg forebears. His career, however, paralleled Leopold's in one significant way: both began their reigns facing very restive populations. The work ends with Friedrich weeping at his failure to do more for his people than he might have. It also recalled a moment from Leopold's imperial coronation in Germany where he had broken into tears during his communion ceremony. Such scenes confirmed the humanity of monarchs, a position that Joseph had frequently championed, but only when he said it and not his critics.[4]

The Habsburg lands might have been more prosperous and just places if all that Leopold needed to convince his subjects to reconsider his brother's social and administrative programmes were sympathetic presentations of himself. The dramatic political changes taking place in Europe at the outset of his reign ruled out the luxury of such political experiment for all ruling dynasties, even the most well meaning among them. Joseph II was not altogether surprised by the revolutionary upheavals that began in France in the summer of 1789. Indeed, he, along with supporters in his government, thought that the *Ancien Régime* in Paris was suffering the consequences of its notoriously feckless behaviour. Nevertheless, in 1789 he had ordered his ministry of police to quiet any signs of local sedition.[5]

More immediately worrisome for both Joseph and Leopold was the fate of their sister Marie Antoinette, the queen of France. They also feared that regime change in France would weaken diplomatic ties between Bourbons and Habsburgs. Nevertheless, the increased radicalization of revolutionary forces in France, following the clumsy attempt of Louis XVI and his wife to flee the capital in 1791, awakened Leopold's fears

Central Europe, *c.* 1815.

about the ideologizing of his peoples.[6] Though he died before Marie Antoinette's public execution in 1793, he lived long enough to take two important counter-revolutionary steps: committing his regime to war against France in 1791 and putting seditious thinkers under even closer surveillance.

Whether such moves were prudent is an open question, but Leopold had good reason to behave as he did. None of the organized opposition that his ancestors had confronted – religious, political or military – had questioned monarchy as such. French revolutionary goals raised an altogether new challenge to the hereditary foundations of dynastic authority and to the hierarchical structure of society that placed monarchs at its pinnacle. The ideal state for the radicals of Paris was based on the oneness of humankind. States organized on this principle did not respect ranks, distinctions of birth, or even religion. While it was not clear in Leopold's lifetime that the French would abolish monarchy – the first revolutionaries had turned a compliant Louis XVI into a constitutional king of his people rather than the proprietary overlord of France – Leopold would never countenance changes in his status forced upon him from below. He had to push back hard, and not simply by displaying his august presence in religious processions, at worship and in triumphal parades. Systematic manipulation of public opinion was crucial to his strategy.

From the standpoint of technical resources, Leopold was better situated to defend his positions than many of his ancestors. One of Joseph II's lasting legacies had been his development of Vienna as a centre of the print trades.[7] Leopold himself founded periodicals to spread the idea that his rule was beyond criticism. He also kept a close eye on those likely to be reading material dangerous to the House of Habsburg-Lorraine. State employees, high school teachers and university professors were ordered to censor their students. They were also asked to publish kind remarks about the dynasty.[8]

The immediate result of this policy was bitter and often very open conflict in academic and other institutional settings between partisans of the liberal Enlightenment, inspired by the record of Joseph II in the early phases of his reign, and those who thought such programmes should be judiciously tempered. Leopold's own government split on the issue, with the emperor, on the whole, opting for the latter side. In the time he had left before his death in 1792, he began a full-scale campaign to encourage 'Patriotism', by which he meant loyalty to the monarchy among his subjects. Leopold did not give up promoting material bonds between ruler and people; civil servants and academics, for example, were directly commended for outstanding work. But a deep mistrust of the public from the lowest orders to the highest animated his thinking. A 'Patriotic Society' that he founded to speak for his position was a covert intelligence agency as well. The reading he selected for the members suggests that their chief job was to keep the regime informed about groups of people known to have thwarted Joseph II, prominent among whom were the nobility, civil servants and academics.[9]

Demystifying and Remystifying

Though it had not been their intention, Joseph II and his brother had become masters of their people rather than their servants. While the House of Habsburg had long required acceptance of established social and political order from their subjects, its prerogatives in churches and traditional ceremonies conferred a recognizable spiritual dimension on the entire arrangement.[10] Joseph and Leopold, on the other hand, were demanding obedience for the sake of the dynasty alone, an argument that was losing strength in revolutionary times.

The flashing wit and arrogance that Maria Theresa once deplored in Joseph and Leopold was wholly lacking in Leopold's eldest son, the new Emperor Francis II. Nevertheless, he was as intolerant of public dissent and criticism of the monarchy as both of his immediate predecessors. In 1794 and 1795 the police force he inherited from his father and uncle brutally put down democratic opinion in Vienna and a more nationally focused progressive movement in Hungary. Throughout much of his eventful reign, which ran from 1792 to 1835, he was on the defensive, as he worked to protect Habsburg rule in central and east-central Europe from challenges both real and occasionally imagined.

Consistently defeated in war with Napoleon Bonaparte between 1800 and 1814, Francis's personal pride took some heavy hits. The image of grandeur and might that his family had cultivated for several centuries suffered too. The political status of his dynasty also changed fundamentally. After 1803 the Franco-Corsican conqueror redesigned the internal boundaries of the Germany over which Francis was still presiding. The latter did manage to manoeuvre Napoleon out of the title Holy Roman Emperor, but the imperial office was in the end abolished. Bonaparte was forced to devise a new distinction for himself, Emperor of the French, which he held from 1804 to 1814.

As a consolation prize Francis received the title Emperor of Austria, a construction that covered his entire family patrimony. Neither man overly emphasized religion in assuming their new title. For his coronation portrait in 1806, Francis would wear Rudolph II's private *Rudolfskron*, an artefact from family, and not German, history. It would, however, serve as an imperial crown for his successors. He had, in effect, participated in the destruction of the highest title that the German lands collectively carried. He was certainly thinking of an imperial future for his family, however, as he explained the logic behind his new distinction. Habsburg rulers had to be emperors in order to maintain the respect of other European rulers. To merit the distinction, they also had to rule vast stretches of land.[11] In fact, the new position of his house did confer major advantages. The term 'Emperor of Austria' effectively united for the first time the Habsburg realms throughout central and east-central Europe.

Napoleon had not finished with Francis quite yet. In 1805 he chipped Dalmatia, Istria, Venetia, Tyrol and Vorarlberg away from the Habsburg holdings. He also did something that the Ottoman sultans could never do: occupy Vienna militarily. Though his troops soon withdrew, they returned in 1809 when, by the terms of the Treaty of Schönbrunn, Francis not only accepted his imperial enemy's rights as a conqueror in the Habsburg lands in Italy, western Austria and the German southwest, but experienced a symbolic humiliation of the worst order. Bonaparte had brought all of Europe's major dynasties to heel on the battlefield. Nevertheless, the ambitious Corsican was still wary enough of the Old Regime to want not only a son, but one with a heavyweight lineage that would help to legitimate his own. He had even visited the crypt of the Capuchins where the extensive ancestry of his prospective bride stretched entombed before him.[12] Urged on by his new councillor on foreign policy, Prince Klemens von Metternich, Francis agreed to marry one of his daughters, Archduchess Marie Louise, to the provincial Corsican adventurer. The young lady, who duly gave birth in 1811 to the longed-for male heir, hated the arrangement; other members of her family deplored it too. Still, it removed the French from Francis's capital city, albeit with a respectable haul of artistic and other cultural valuables culled from the Habsburg collections.

The reversal of Napoleon's fortunes after 1812 and the death of his son in 1832, after passing a sickly youth under close watch in Vienna, considerably improved the Habsburg position. The Congress of Vienna, a gathering of all of Europe's monarchs or their official representatives, which met between 1814 and 1815, restored to the House of Habsburg-Lorraine much of the terrain that Napoleon had seized. The most notable loss was the Austrian Netherlands, eventually to be renamed Belgium. But the challenge of dynastic self-defence during more than fifteen years of warfare had been something of a public relations problem in itself. Nor had all of the political notions that Napoleon had seeded around Europe been completely uprooted. The response from Vienna to all such concerns would, in fact, substantially revise the bonds that the dynasty used to coordinate its interests with those of its peoples.

In matters of governance, Francis was a rigid soul. Nevertheless, when the public face of his house was at issue he was ready to follow directions taken by his father and his uncle Joseph, if these promoted his rule. As a young man Francis had, in fact, admired the latter deeply. At his 1792 coronation in Frankfurt for the soon-to-be aborted German emperorship, past protocols were certainly observed. The underlying message of the affair was that life was better on the east bank of the Rhine than the west. Nevertheless, with the French revolution still going on, he looked for ways to make himself more publicly appealing. Like Joseph, he adopted contemporary fashions that betokened cultural and social change. His physical appearance, noticed widely in the press of the day, suggested that a ruler from a venerable dynasty was capable of reaching out to popular modes. The era of wig-ridden court formality was over. The new emperor wore his blonde hair long, a custom that Romanticism had revived in Europe. He continued to dress down. As a young man Francis wore knee breeches; as adults, he and his male relatives preferred bourgeois trousers.[13]

His return to Vienna from Frankfurt also had distinctly public-spirited overtones. The triumphal arches that normally went up in central sites on such occasions were notably absent. Featured instead was the model for a structural redesign of the site around St Stephen's Cathedral that many residents had wanted. A far more spacious layout replaced nondescript small shops and dwellings. Indeed, from the earliest moments in his career, Francis worked hard to impress Vienna's citizenry with the sincere goodwill of his house. A set of wars launched by Joseph II at the end of his reign had been immensely expensive and widely unpopular. Anticipating invasions from the French revolutionary army, Francis resolved in 1792 to support Habsburg military efforts with his own funds for two years. The gesture moved Vienna's people to raise contributions of their own. All civic corporations, guilds and other local organizations donated money to their new territorial ruler, even melting down some of their possessions for precious metals that could be monetized in the cause. Francis thanked their spokespersons at a ceremony in the Hofburg on 7 April 1793, presenting them with a silver trophy cup embellished with his likeness and an inscription recording his gratitude for their service. Ruler and the ruled then sat for a ceremonial banquet, at which the mayor toasted the emperor and his consort. The population of his city also continued to be generous. Five years later, 15,000 men responded to his call to arms, once again in expectation of a French assault. Though the threat did not materialize, Francis had a medal struck for each man who had volunteered; they could wear them at festive occasions. As late as 1809, the practice of private contributions to emergency militias was still followed in Vienna.[14]

Like Maria Theresa in her progressive moments and Joseph II, Francis was committed to furthering the material well-being of his lands. He was very reluctant to resurrect the inefficient commercial and fiscal practices that his grandmother and uncle had cashiered. Defeating Napoleon had left the government with an enormous public debt to pay off. Vertiginous inflation erased part of that, but for manufacture and trade to thrive, the monarchy required a stable currency. With that established, Metternich, social and political conservative though he was, unveiled his Josephinian side. He applied himself to introducing market-friendly principles into the material lives of Habsburg subjects and to encouraging exports from which he hoped to grow state revenues. Responding to pent-up demand at home and abroad, which the wars with France had suppressed, the economy of the Habsburg empire righted itself quite impressively. Though taxes were onerous, prosperity came back, particularly in eastern Austria and Bohemia, where a manufacturing infrastructure was already in place.

For all of these progressive flashes, however, liberals at Francis's court were outnumbered by conservatives eager to mobilize the emperor for the task of scaling back the influence of the Enlightenment and Bonapartist adventurism on European cultural behaviour. One of the most reactionary steps urged upon him came from a circle of Catholic German Romantics who came to Vienna around 1810. Their goal was to recreate the Holy Roman Empire under Habsburg rule, and return the Church of Rome and the institutional structure on which it was built to philosophical centre stage on the continent. To all of this, Francis initially turned a deaf ear. Though personally devout, he was reluctant to bring economically unproductive monastic life back to his patrimony. After 1801 he gradually allowed suppressed houses in Hungary to reopen. It was not until 1827, however, that he cleared the way for contemplative orders to establish new quarters in his realms. From then on, his religious policies took a consistently traditionalist course. More important religious houses in Austria received a new role in higher education. Symbolically most important of all, the Jesuits were permitted to work in a land that had not been open to them since 1773.[15]

Such a reversal reinforced his already close-minded outlook on government and society. Fearing that revolutionary liberalism and egalitarianism would spread, he had willingly continued his father's war against France. Censorship tightened accordingly. Like-minded segments among his peoples supported him; established elites throughout his lands were as put off Jacobin ideals as he was. Popular opinion grew increasingly wary of revolutionary morality too. The execution of Louis XVI and his queen in 1793 shocked Vienna's society at large. But the most effective and intimidating weapons at the regime's command were its police force and spies. The latter turned up in public and more selective settings alike, often bribing servants to eavesdrop on social gatherings in private homes. Obedience to a monarch who sanctioned such restrictions was placed ahead of imagination, initiative and even experience in government appointments. A conversation between Francis I and Count Joseph Wallis, an officer in the Bohemian royal government, whom the monarch wanted as a finance minister, says it all:

> 'Count [Wallis, said Francis], I am going to reward you for your faithful services. O'Donnel is dead; I have designated you as his successor.'
>
> 'Your Majesty . . . will most graciously condescend to consider that I am entirely ignorant in this department, as I have never paid the least attention to it.'
>
> 'That is what I want; never mind, you will learn it, everyone to his business. You were a faithful Supreme Burggrave; you will be a no less faithful Finance Minister.'

Whatever his other flaws, Wallis knew himself well; he performed his job dismally.[16]

Cultural affairs as a whole were tightly constrained. Maria Theresa and even Joseph II were promoting higher standards in thought and speech when they tried to sanitize the common public stage. With the French Revolution and the blood-soaked Terror between 1792 and 1794 in mind, Leopold, and then Francis, ordered that both the theatre and books should be closely scrutinized for political dissent as well as off-colour comic language. Regulations drawn up for Hungary in 1795, but applicable throughout the Habsburg dominions, struck the words 'liberty', 'freedom' and 'enlightenment' from scripts. Themes linked to tyranny and despotism were suppressed. On the premise that rulers should never abdicate their thrones, Shakespeare's *King Lear* was recast in Vienna to end with the beleaguered monarch still exercising royal powers. Because its heroine queen faced execution on stage, Frederick Schiller's *Maria Stuart* was forbidden outright. In December 1794 the government ordered that all foreigners, some of whom might be posing as artists, should be turned back as soon as they crossed the border.[17]

Seeing Things the Habsburg Way

For all of these measures, however, Francis's monarchy remained home to a post-Josephinian intelligentsia. Men and (even a scattering of) women alike, their world view was shaped less by familiar Catholic dogma than Voltaire's humanistic universalism and British philosophical empiricism. Both outlooks had egalitarian implications that Prince Metternich, a major voice in the Habsburg regime until 1848, and Francis were committed to discouraging. On the other hand, the former was both a realist and a cosmopolitan; he strongly believed that the good name of Habsburg rule required the regime to show intellectuals at home and the media abroad that Francis was not completely in thrall to repressive obscurantism. The challenge was inventing tactics that preserved the integrity of serious thought and creative art and writing, yet kept texts and pictures free of radical implications.

The government's greatest test came on the domestic front. Public loyalties occasionally wavered as the Napoleonic Wars dragged on. Bonaparte's early victories in Italy and central Europe raised serious doubts about the military capacities of the Habsburg regime and, by logical extension, its fundamental viability.[18] Nevertheless, the ideological inspiration that supposedly drove the upstart Corsican's armies suggested its own counter-strategy: if Bonaparte's men were fighting in aid of French-generated ideals of equality and fraternity, Habsburg armies should go into battle inspired by a territorial patriotism that identified the monarch as a supreme father of his peoples (*Landesvater*). This move was made more credible by his 'Austrianization' after the dissolution of the Holy Roman Empire in 1806. It was a notion that was simple, familiar and consistent with his new title. It was also not excessively tied to

Catholicism, although Francis took that allegiance to heart far more than did some of his key, though worldly, advisers. The emphasis was on identifying regional interests with the dynasty's defence. As part of the campaign, one of the emperor's younger brothers, Archduke John, who had taken his student reading of Rousseau quite seriously, was to form local militias that would rescue their province, rather than the holdings of distant foreign monarchs. At least once the policy appeared to work when, in April 1809, there was an uprising in the Tyrol against Napoleon's Bavarian allies, who were occupying it. The rising was led by a local pro-tégé of Archduke John, Andreas Hofer, who had been named 'the chosen commander of the House of Austria'. Hofer enjoyed some initial success, but was executed when Napoleon retook the region later that year.

Nevertheless, indigenous resistance movements had their downside, especially for the House of Habsburg. The cultivation of provincial pride could inspire individual lands in the monarchy to dispense with the dynasty altogether, an idea that disturbed Francis's government in Vienna. Less dangerous from the dynastic standpoint was a campaign to impress upon his subjects their centuries-old ties to the House of Habsburg-Lorraine and the benefits that they had derived from the connection. Political systems, monarchical or otherwise, were to be legitimated not through conquest or religious mandates alone but through the experience of a complex common history. The very longevity of a polity became the justification for its continued existence. The horrors of the French Revolution had graphically shown the evils that might befall societies that forget their past. Establishing a database that confirmed the temporal persistence of ties between the Habsburg peoples and their rulers became the order of the day for Francis I's regime.[19]

New approaches to history suggested methods to further this programme, but Vienna had little faith in its chief advocates. For a start, they were German and Protestant, rather than reliably Catholic and familiar in the Habsburg lands. They also were attracting attention throughout Europe, putting them beyond the reach of Francis's thought police. Johann Gottfried Herder was a philosopher, cultural ethnologist and general man of letters; the other, Leopold von Ranke, was a classicist turned historian who held forth during much of his career at the University of Berlin. Both were interested in the singular identities of the world's peoples, whose fundamental cultural and historical differences expressed the will of divine providence. Although Metternich and his supporters had no problem attributing the durabil-ity of the Habsburg monarchy to the hand of God, too much searching for the reasons behind this made them very uneasy. Their preferred historical narrative made the dynasty its central focus and kept silent on the unfolding of the Creator's plan, particularly when ethnically, linguistically and politically distinct groups seemed to be the result. Controversies arising from speculation about providential design also upset the internal harmony that Francis and his government were promoting.

Both Herder and Ranke, however, were fierce advocates of research techniques that the Habsburg regime found usable, yet met standards for scholarship that were taking hold elsewhere in Europe. Arguable conclusions about the course of political or cultural history were the product of carefully assembled empirical databases. This was a position that the Habsburg government could tolerate after some tweaking. The government would cooperate with writers and scholars who concentrated on gathering and editing materials that added verifiable positive detail to narratives of Habsburg rule. Cooperative intellectuals would often find a comfortable niche in Francis's regime. They could also preserve their disciplinary integrity. With the modern study of history in its formative stage, the process of uncovering, authenticating and ordering documents became a respectable and exciting enterprise for some first-rate minds and researchers.

The regime relied at times upon inherited texts to recall the story of Habsburg monarchs and the benefits that they had brought to their peoples. As late as 1819 a birthday panegyric that Joseph von Sonnenfels had dedicated to Maria Theresa in 1762 was reprinted as a rhetorical model and a lesson for high school students. From it they would appreciate the centrality of the monarch to all facets of life in the empire. But Francis's government also promoted a vast new historical literature based on exacting critical standards, particularly where chronology and credibility of documents were at issue. Joseph von Hormayr, a Tyrolean historian and publicist embodied the programme throughout the Napoleonic and post-Napoleonic eras. For part of his career he was also the official court historian. His *Momente aus der vaterländische Geschichte* ('Moments in Patriotic History'), *Archiv für vaterländische Geschichte* ('Archive for Patriotic History') as well as his *Taschenbuch für die vaterländische Geschichte* ('Pocketbook for Patriotic History'), which combined crucial dates in Habsburg history with explanatory texts, were exemplary products intended for as large a public as possible. Hormayr's *Österreichischer Plutarch* offered substantive biographies of Habsburg rulers and a few of their significant commanders.

9 Johann Peter Krafft, *Entry of Emperor Francis I into Vienna, 1814*, wall painting for the Vienna Hofburg, *c.* 1828–36.

As part of an effort to align the histories of Bohemia and Hungary with the government in Vienna, Hungarian and Bohemian heroes were also included.[20]

But persuading the Habsburg peoples to continue their relationship with the dynasty called for material more immediately compelling than fragmentary papers and manuscripts resting in archives. A programme in Vienna to publish historical picture books that combined illustrations and text had begun in the early decades of the nineteenth century. Written to acquaint children and adults with the story of the Habsburgs and their assorted virtues, the genre would create an unbroken history of its own, written and drawn by scores of imitators even beyond the collapse of the dynasty's state in 1918.[21]

Paintings of the dynasty enacting some of its now legendary past were adapted to modern sensibilities. References to contemporary politics were there as well, at least for those who looked really hard. An especially popular and widely reproduced scene, now on display in the Upper Belvedere Gallery in Vienna, depicts Emperor Rudolph I's encounter with the priest carrying the Host. Painted by Ludwig Ferdinand Schnorr von Carolsfeld in 1828, it was much prettified to conform to contemporary style; the haggard progenitor of the Habsburgs was anything but cherubic. Nevertheless, the piece has several important messages. The Habsburg association with religion is cast benignly. The clergyman and surrounding rustics are appropriately reverent, and Rudolph is very gracious. Yet it is the behaviour of two horses on the canvas that transmits an important subtext. The steed Rudolph is handing over is quiet; another held by peasants in the background, however, appears to be uncontrollable. The message is subtle, yet clear; the Habsburgs bring peace where commoners cannot.

For all his disdain of republicanism, however, Francis I's most effective tactic in visual propaganda was based on painting in revolutionary France: identify historical events that dramatically affected both government and the governed and spread the message as widely as possible through galleries and public buildings, and out to specific audiences. That the emperor himself was a sophisticated judge of the plastic arts helped his cause. He commissioned one of the finest historical painters in central Europe, Johann Peter Krafft, to create three outsize encaustic murals for the Audience Hall in the Hofburg, each of which illustrated major episodes in Habsburg history. The first, done around 1828–36, recalled Francis's entrance into Vienna in 1814 as he returned from Paris, the signatory of a treaty that virtually ended the Napoleonic Wars (illus. 9). While the event was more current than historical, Krafft was working from the premise that, when future generations looked back on the Habsburgs, they would remember this moment. From the immediate standpoint of the dynasty that made the Hofburg both office and principal residence, these images reminded both family members and visitors, the more important the better, that Francis had the approbation of his people from all social classes. While the emperor is prominent in white military coat with a red–white–red sash across his chest, his subjects are as much on display as their monarch.

Both Schnorr von Carolsfeld and Krafft were from Germany, but inspired enough by Habsburg tradition and a victory over Napoleon to accept commissions in Vienna for memorable work that met the dynasty's political specifications in the required genre. The style and themes of such works spread to the eastern lands of the monarchy too, most notably to Hungary, where political incorporation into the post-Napoleonic Austrian empire remained imperfect. Krafft also designed and executed a historical cycle for the Hungarian National Museum between 1820 and 1825. Intended to emphasize the interrelationship of the kingdom with the House of Habsburg, one piece celebrated Francis I's coronation in 1792. Another portrayed the Hungarian hero Count Miklós Zrínyi defending the fortress of Szigetvár, bravely but in vain, against the Ottomans in 1566. The episode illustrated Hungarian service in the Habsburg defence of Christendom, precisely the mix that Francis's regime wanted. Reviewing an exhibition of Krafft's oeuvre in this vein, a commentator noted that such images could quicken the patriotic sentiments of the young, another high priority on the dynasty's agenda. For the rest of the century Hungarian painters did indeed copy the scene many times. As for Francis himself, he and his wife were pleased enough to engage Krafft for the Hofburg cycle. Francis also made him director of the imperial gallery.[22]

Dynastic history also entered high theatrical culture, mediated by one of the great dramatic poets of the German language, Franz Grillparzer. A full-time civil servant – at one point he supervised the court treasury records – he quarrelled with his emperor's censors time and again. Nevertheless, the story of Habsburg rule inspired two of his finest plays: *König Ottokars Glück und Ende* ('King Otakar's Good Fortune and End'), a dramatization of Rudolph I's thirteenth-century encounter with his royal Bohemian rival; and the more historically complex *Ein Bruderzwist in Habsburg* ('A Conflict among Brothers in the House of Habsburg'), which reworks Rudolph II's bitter travails with his male siblings. One can only assume that Grillparzer was genuinely drawn to the House of Habsburg and its Austrian patrimony and not writing as a mouthpiece of the regime; the elegant poetic language in both plays argues for genuine inspiration rather than crass careerism. Perhaps the most famous example is in *Ottokar*, as Rudolph hears a description of the lands that await him:

> It is a good land,
> Befitting a prince who makes it his own.
> Where else have you ever found such beauty?
> Look around you, wherever you can see,
> It laughs like a bridegroom face to face with his bride!
> With gleaming green meadows and golden seed,
> Embroidered blue and yellow by flax and saffron,
> Flavoured with sweet blossoms and noble herbs;
> Down broad valleys it stretches,
> Lush bouquets of flowers wherever it goes,
> Contained by the Danube's silver ribbon! –
> Hung to the very top with golden grapes,
> Ripely swelling in God's sun, shining bright,
> All crowned by dark forest, the hunter's delight.[23]

The back story of *Ottokar*, however, reveals how tricky the process of historicizing the Habsburgs and their ties to their lands could be. Grillparzer finished the manuscript and delivered it to the censors in

1823. The plot places Rudolph in a uniformly favourable, though historically plausible, light: an austere and cautious character adept at using the legalities of the Austrian ties to the German Empire as leverage to remove Otakar from the one-time Babenberg patrimony. He respects titles and the rights and honours they convey. He is just. He is ambitious but not arrogant. The Austrian lands are what he wants, not all of central Europe. And he has an appealingly folksy side; one scene shows him hammering out dents in his own helmet. The author also crammed in the story of Rudolph, the priest and the Host, and mention of the king's substitution of a crucifix for a sceptre at his coronation in Aachen.[24]

Nevertheless, the work ran into heavy official weather before arriving on stage in Vienna. Part of the plot revolves around the unhappy forced marriage of Margaret, the last Babenberg claimant to the Austrian lands, and King Otakar. To some of Francis's censors, this sounded all too much like the recent miseries of the daughter Francis handed over to Napoleon. Best, they thought, to avoid all depictions of humiliating moments in the monarch's recent past. Moreover, Grillparzer was no admirer of Bohemian Czechs. His King Otakar has a low opinion of his subjects; thick-headed and unimaginative, he calls them at one point. Worse yet, the play has an unflattering subplot that revolves around the Bohemian noble house of Rožemberk; in Grillparzer's hands this is a reptilian nest of courtiers bent on winning the Bohemian crown for one of their own. It was only upon the urging of his wife, Empress Karolina Augusta, who read the play and liked it, that the emperor allowed its performance.[25]

The role that the empress played in getting *Ottokar* to the theatre suggests that the Habsburg regime would, and did, let talent have its way upon occasion. The more typical approach of the dynasty to keeping major free spirits productive, but within acceptable limits, was to make them clients. A prominent example was Joseph Danhauser, called by some the Hogarth of early nineteenth-century Austria. A mordant critic of the profiteering that enriched Vienna's bourgeoisie after the Napoleonic Wars, he turned the contrast between wealth and poverty into a lifetime preoccupation. Nevertheless, he owed his career to the ruling dynasty. Trained in historical painting at the Vienna Academy of Fine Art, Danhauser also worked there as a fact checker for works based on themes from the past. He also paid the dynasty back, collaborating with the Archbishop of Eger in Hungary for an exhibition on Rudolph I in 1826.

In fact, as long as their ideas and images remained politically and intellectually uncontroversial, artists, writers and composers had little to fear from the regime. Music had the easiest time of it. Members of the imperial house and the resident great nobility of Vienna heavily patronized Ludwig van Beethoven, his fits of revolutionary spleen notwithstanding. Writers and artists avoided censure by encouraging audiences to idealize the humble side of life rather than to revolt against it. A representative and technically polished example was Ferdinand Waldmüller, whose microscopically observed and brilliantly coloured canvases celebrated the commonplace and the humble folk who embodied it. The densely detailed fiction of Adalbert Stifter reflected what he called the 'Gentle Law' (*das sanfte Gesetz*), which made quietude almost tactile. Much of his work, collected and published in his *Bunte Steine* ('Many-coloured Stones') in 1853, turns the artefacts and rituals of daily and domestic life into moral lessons acceptable to all but the perverse in his age.

Finding aesthetic inspiration in the familiar encouraged concentration on the subtleties of human character and individual interaction with social roles theoretically fixed for eternity. Even the Austrian popular comedy, which outlasted all schemes to sanitize it in the second half of the eighteenth century, took a more introspective turn. Sly innuendos and improbable high jinks still prevailed in these performances, even when their authors were two masters of the Viennese farce, Ferdinand Raimund and Johann Nestroy. At the same time, their works began moving from diverting entertainment to classical popular comedy, a change that brought their plays to the stages of more prestigious local theatres in the latter third of the nineteenth century. Raimund was especially caught up with issues of self-knowledge and accepting one's true place in society. Presented as a pair, both concerns were exemplary additions to the list of political and moral norms espoused by Francis I's regime. Nestroy covered something of the same ground, while bringing to it a socially critical tone that intensified as his career went on. For him, just about everyone, regardless of class, had his or her price. Like Danhauser, however, his most frequent comic targets were feckless nobles and the arrogant newly rich, and not the dynasty. Many characters in his plays are absorbed in defending themselves against their fellow man, rather than against a government that posed few difficulties if one obeyed it. Spontaneous, and often hilarious, parodies of upper-class and moneyed bourgeois behaviour were, in fact, less socially dangerous than they superficially may have seemed. They trivialized so much, from cultural developments to political and social problems, along with eccentricities of character, that the ideological implications embedded in them faded into nothingness.

It is hard to say whether political quietism in the post-Napoleonic Habsburg monarchy was the outcome of convinced philosophical inwardness, a longing for private pleasure after the public upheavals at the turn of the nineteenth century and the sacrifice they exacted, or simply a survival tactic in a closely monitored environment. That the mood existed and guided behaviour, however, is unquestionable. The stormy emotionalism and brooding relationship with nature that characterized European Romanticism heavily influenced literature and art in Hungary and Bohemia. It was largely absent from the Austrian lands and Francis would never have to deal with the agony that this culture would spawn. As far as his own regime was concerned, it was accomplishing his purpose: to foster cultural habits that he and his house could live with and not to appear overly reactionary in doing so.

The Good in Pleasure and Practice

As intimidating as Francis, his spies and his censors could be, the emperor would live to be known as Francis the Good. One reason was that his public rarely saw his peremptory side, especially in his Austrian domains. For all of his discriminating taste in art and as a collector of valuable maps, engravings and studies of natural history and geography, he nevertheless had an unforced common touch that his propagandists sought to link with his house as a whole. To emphasize the point, in 1822 the Academy of Fine Arts in Vienna unveiled a painting by Karl Russ showing Emperor Maximilian I visiting an artisan's shop.[26] Francis required no ancestral icons to prove that he was at ease with all classes of people. Like his grandmother and his father, he conversed by preference in Austrian dialect and its Viennese variant. Seen on the street and portrayed with wife and children in bourgeois trousers and muslin, he and his Habsburgs were credible representatives of an Imperial First Family rather than chosen agents of God.

Changes in the character of his court, not always on his initiative, reinforced the more human side of the dynasty. The great nobility, the proprietors of the vast Baroque city palaces in Vienna, increasingly drifted back to their landed residences. Some of these families simply wished to return to lifestyles associated with the pre-Theresian monarchy when aristocratic prerogatives still shaped local life. Others had decided to commit themselves to advancing the culture and economy of their homelands more intensively than they could from a distance. The middle-class bureaucrats sought out by Joseph II and his mother became far more central to Francis's administration. More than 50 per cent of the new service nobles he created were military officers; 29 per cent were highly placed civil servants. Others were high-achieving commoners: 11.5 per cent were bankers or industrialists specifically commended for their service to the state. Roughly 6 per cent were artists, musicians and scholars. The development had an ironic twist: even as the dynasty and several members of the traditional nobility affected middle-class styles and social customs, the bourgeoisie adopted aristocratic values of their own. From the standpoint of Habsburg public relations, however, the levelling of class behaviours was just the effect Habsburg propagandists wanted. Dynastic portraiture itself captured the shift. Francis appeared as a model for diligent civil servants supposedly at work throughout the monarchy. His most widely circulated image was Johann Stephan Decker's *Emperor Francis I in his Workroom in the Vienna Hofburg* (1826), a sovereign at a tidy bureaucrat's desk poring over papers on behalf of subjects to whom he was as responsible as they were to him.[27]

Posing as the chief civil servant of his lands was not out of line with roles that both his father and his uncle Joseph had scripted for themselves. Nor was his depiction of himself as the benevolent father of his peoples unfamiliar; his grandmother Maria Theresa had cultivated it to the hilt, albeit from female-specific perspectives. Francis, in fact, came close to treating patriarchal authority as an attribute of sovereignty. The hyperfeminized portrayal of women in his time, with wives docilely gazing on husbands, fathers and children, reinforced the idea. But images of Francis the *pater familias* endured long after his death in 1835: in 1867 Francis Isidor Proschko, a patriotic man of letters, addressed Francis as 'Father' in a poem.[28]

Francis and members of his family-in-chief worked hard to spread their presence around the peoples with whom they shared a virtual household. Members of the dynasty travelled widely in the Habsburg lands and visited subjects in all ranks of society. Appearances in humble dwellings and workplaces expressed Habsburg concern for the less fortunate. A contemporary lithograph shows Francis as *Landesvater* surfacing unexpectedly with his wife and daughter, Archduchess Leopoldine, in an orphanage. Between 1826 and 1834 he made 67 trips around his lands to receive welcomes under triumphal arches, review parades in his honour and sponsor shooting contests and other events open to all, even when the official purpose of his travels was to attend conferences. For its part, the court that travelled with him was unfailingly generous when

10 Friedrich August Brand, *An Area in the Vienna Prater around 1785, c.* 1785, watercolour sketch.

praising spectators for their modest demeanour, discipline and orderliness. Empress Karolina Augusta was painted in 1817 visiting Kolozsvár (Rom. Cluj), far to the east in Hungary. In 1838 Anton Ziegler, one of the more important history painters of contemporary Vienna, showed Francis's eldest son and successor, Ferdinand I, helping local flood victims in Buda and Pest.[29]

Francis reactivated his uncle Joseph's programme to make their house a major benefactor in civic causes, even when popular ceremonies had to be dropped. As late as the eighteenth century, the rendering of fealty to new territorial rulers in Lower Austria included distribution of bread and meat to the crowds. Free wine helped to wash it down. At his provincial installation in 1792, Francis directed funding for refreshments to be redirected to specific charities.[30] Indeed, where general civic improvement was at issue, Francis outdid his uncle in many respects. Joseph had turned the grounds of a former imperial hunting ground, the Prater, into a public park, but a transverse roadway lined with chestnut trees was reserved for aristocratic and imperial carriages. Certain buildings for imperial business and pleasure activities were also sequestered. Francis opened the latter, not only for public viewing, but for public use (illus. 10).

Joseph had also installed part of the dynasty's art collection in one of the two Belvedere palaces, formerly occupied by Eugene of Savoy. Organized didactically, it was meant to introduce the history of painting to selected visitors.[31] Francis, however, opened the dynasty's massive and priceless holdings of art and artefacts to visitors casual and scholarly alike. The imperial collection of minerals, gems, precious stones and objects made from them, such as tobacco containers, were made accessible to serious students or connoisseurs of these materials. Upon application to the director, the collections of coins and medallions, which were

11 Carl Goebel the Younger, *The Marble Gallery in the Belvedere Palace, c.* 1876, watercolour.

reproduced in numbers for propaganda under Leopold I, were now open to both cultivated amateurs and professional scholars. Restrictions were few and reasonable: swords and walking sticks were forbidden in the galleries. Contemporary primness was also a consideration: '*ganz natürliche*' ('all-natural') images, especially nudes, were curtained off behind green taffeta, although 'modest persons' (*bescheidene Personen*) could have a peek upon request. The target audiences, however, had been reinvented; materials that had once reaffirmed the importance and discriminating taste of the Habsburgs in their own eyes, and those of competing monarchs, were now to perform this mission for the dynasty's general public and to educate it in the process. By 1876 viewers from all corners of society – bourgeois and rural, male and female – would be mingling in the galleries (illus. 11). Francis also moved several sections of his collections to other facilities in the city and nearby suburbs.[32]

Nor did Francis's concern for art and public understanding of it stop with the great masters of the past who were so important to his ancestors. Contemporary painting had to receive its due as well, because the dynasty had programmatic uses for it. Many of the new paintings he bought to install in the Belvedere came from the historical school that would depict the dynasty so nobly. To encourage local artists of this kind as well as others, the emperor appointed Joseph Rebell to the directorship of the imperial picture gallery and to a professorship in the Academy. The public was also kept abreast of what they could see; Francis provided exhibition space where contemporary artists could display and market their products. He both permitted and belonged to the Club for the Encouragement of the Plastic Arts, founded in 1830. By the following year it had 1,431 subscribers, whose dues went to artists for their paintings; these would then be raffled off to members, who were entitled to purchase one or more tickets. Similar groups were set up in Budapest, Prague and Trieste. Through such arrangements, the well-to-do urban residents of the monarchy learned that art was something of value as well as something that was decoratively desirable.[33]

The two court-sponsored theatres, the Burgtheater and the Theater am Kärntnertor, had been open to a paying public for some time, though the loges in the former were fully subscribed by nobles who spent at least part of the year in their Vienna residences. The imperial house had also maintained its unique presence in these houses with separate boxes in each of them. On occasions when members of the dynasty actually attended, the entire audience had to remove their hats. Francis, however, did not consistently keep the general public at arms' length from his headquarters and residences: he brought large-scale popular entertainment to halls in the imperial Hofburg itself. The two *Redouten* (redoubts) in a wing of the complex were turned over to festive public balls for 'the better elements of society', as one commentator put it, from the day after New Year's Day until Ash Wednesday. At first permitted only on Sundays, the ballrooms were soon open for a fee every third day during the prescribed period. Refreshments were also to be had at a price. The proceeds went towards financing the support of the court theatres and, with a nod to the upcoming penitential season, the city poorhouse. Theatre managers elsewhere in the city themselves sponsored spectacles honouring the monarch and his house. In 1832 the director of the commercial Theater an der Wien, Carl Carl (the stage name of Karl Andreas von Bernbrunn), put on a gala to marked the fortieth anniversary of Francis's accession to the throne. The following year he celebrated the day with a public carnival evening, complete with special decorations.[34]

Francis also continued Joseph II's tactic of readapting dynastic property for public enjoyment. Constructed and used by Maria Theresa in the summer, the imperial suburban residence at Schönbrunn had quickly fallen into disrepair when her eldest son and successor Joseph II found a comparatively modest hideaway in the Augarten. Francis, however, frequently moved at least the younger members of his family once again to his grandmother's retreat for the hottest time of the year. He also allowed sections of the grounds and gardens to be used for public recreation. For those bent on combining a stroll with eating and drinking, he installed a canteen in a side building that was open at noon and in the evening. The arrangement itself was intended for people of modest means, but with the palace now often occupied by the imperial family, the neighbourhood became a gathering place for people of all classes. Some of the city's wealthy residents built summer homes in the adjacent villages of Hietzing and Penzing. Less luxurious quarters were available for those who could rent for only a week or so. Overnight guests could not bed down in them, but people of limited means could invite friends and relatives for a stroll and a repast in the palace park.[35]

It was, however, at the Laxenburg palace, Francis's favourite residence in the Vienna area, where the emperor most effectively combined the didactic with the pleasurable. Modelled and remodelled on its original foundations, which dated from the fourteenth century, the centrepiece of the complex was the Franzensburg (Fortress Franz). A replica of the original Swiss Habichtsburg, it was ornamented with artefacts and fragments from other castles, monasteries and medieval buildings generally. The emperor spent a good deal of his time in the space that housed the last large picture gallery of Habsburg-Lorraine ancestors. Open to the public when Francis was in residence during the summer, it recalled the distant Habsburg past and the dynasty's impressive longevity. All of its male members, from earliest times to the present, were clad in medieval costume.[36] The entire installation was an arch example of anachronism, even in an era that accepted medievalizing as a cultural commonplace. Nevertheless, as a graphic image of the continued Habsburg presence in Europe and its lands, it was very compelling.

The process of being good also required Francis to situate himself and his family in more responsible activities. Here, too, he followed the example of his uncle. Joseph II had firmly associated his house with benevolent public works projects large and small. His Allgemeines Krankenhaus (General Hospital) was the city's largest building at the beginning of the nineteenth century; he had also founded a modest but welcome lying-in home, where women could give birth anonymously. It was not free, except to the most impoverished, who had to donate some service to the facility in return for care, but clients from all over Europe availed themselves of its services.[37] Both establishments fit well within the emperor's programme to develop a large, healthy and service-ready population for his state. The hospital treated the sick and injured; the maternal shelter curbed infanticide, at least in theory.

Francis's public policies had the same thrust. Moreover, unlike some of his uncle's more intrusive schemes, they met widely perceived and immediate needs. Inflation throughout the Habsburg empire in the early nineteenth century had tipped once self-supporting families into near-penury that many were ashamed to declare. For people whose incomes were still too high to qualify them for charity, the court founded a Benevolent Institute (Wohltätigkeitsanstalt) in 1804 that helped cover costs of illness, childbirth, rent and firewood for minor civil servants and other middle-class residents of Vienna. Funding came from a share of the ticket sales for theatrical and musical performances, but also from the ruling house itself along with other wealthy donors who supervised the programme. When the provincial government of Lower Austria refused in 1803 to finance a rescue service for drunks, victims of violent crimes and those found freezing to death, Francis stepped in with a contribution from the dynasty's private treasury, built up through revenues drawn from assorted private family inheritances, patrimonial properties and the return on equities. This, along with an anonymous donation from a Moravian cavalier, sufficed to get the service off the ground. Four years before his death, the emperor and his wife appeared in newspaper supplements visiting sewer construction sites, a project undertaken to prevent the recurrence of a devastating outbreak of cholera in Vienna between 1830 and 1831. Approving commoners stood in the background.[38]

Indeed, Francis had done great good, even in the opinion of those who deeply resented, feared, even hated his monitoring of intellectual life. His outward air of bourgeois simplicity and respect for middle-class family ways helped, all the more so because he seemed to enjoy it. The expatriate author Charles Postl (Sealsfield), otherwise an unforgiving critic of the regime, conceded that, 'As a father of a family, he deserves praise: there is not a more decent and respectable family in the empire than his own.' The emperor's material support of his people did not end with charity. Although his court establishment was huge – 3,000 people at its height – the growth in the payroll largely came from additional minor service personnel such as daily labourers and people connected with provisioning. He also cut back on extravagant festivities. If his court stressed authority at all, it was in its revival of some of the punctilious etiquette that Joseph II had abandoned.[39]

What may, however, have clinched the epithet 'good' for him was the stately imperial anthem 'Gott erhalte' ('God Save'), which was first sung as a matter of course during his many public appearances. With a melody based on a song written by Joseph Haydn, which the composer then folded into one of his string quartets, the first two lines were 'God Save Francis the Emperor / our Good Emperor Francis'. Sung throughout the empire long after he died, in many languages and in settings ranging from classrooms to public ceremonies and funerals, it would fix Francis and his house in his subjects' memories as few other artefacts ever would.[40]

History in the Eyes of Others

The Habsburgs would exploit the theme of imperial benefactors and appreciative subjects from the Napoleonic Wars to the end of the empire. Francis I was followed as emperor of Austria by his eldest son, Ferdinand I, who had already appeared performing charitable activity in the name of his house. A flood in 1830 that unleashed untold misery along the Danube inspired a picture of him in a skiff picking up a stranded eleven-year-old orphan. Many reproductions of the episode soon appeared. A work by Anton Ziegler, one of the major Habsburg *Historienmaler*, shows him in involved in yet another flood rescue, this time in Buda and Pest in 1838.[41]

In truth, if one were looking for a transparently well-meaning soul among Habsburg rulers from first to last, Ferdinand would be in a class by himself. His good nature was apparent even in his teens; he was also inclined far more towards music and natural history than the business of war and policing. On becoming emperor in 1835, he granted amnesties to inmates of the Špilberk, a political prison just outside Brno. He had been epileptic from childhood, however, and the illness limited his formal schooling and made him generally unpredictable. His father had deep reservations about the young man's fitness for rule but put these aside to endorse him, persuaded by legitimist arguments from Prince Metternich and the finance minister, Count Franz Anton von Kolowrat. Though they despised one another, they would run the monarchy's affairs throughout Ferdinand I's reign. Still another opinion on who should follow Francis, though, was growing louder. This belonged to Princess Sophie, the wife of another of Francis's sons, Archduke Francis Charles. A Bavarian Wittelsbach, she was opening her lifetime campaign to make an emperor out of Archduke Franz Joseph, her first son – the sooner the better.

Ferdinand I would have been a problematic monarch in the most placid of times. It was his great misfortune, however, to come to power at one of the most explosive moments in the history of an empire that by 1850 was governing roughly 36 million people. The benign glow that his father had tried to cast over his house through personal charity and association with homely cosiness had not warmed his peoples equally. Francis's regime had a pronounced middle-class bias that not all appreciated. He reactivated some of Joseph II's land reforms, including the redistribution of some noble properties. Traditional agricultural economies were rearranged accordingly, both for landlords and labour, but not everyone was wholly comfortable with the change. Around one-third of all such holdings in Lower Austria had been shifted to bourgeois ownership and converted to agriculture of scale. Taxes were kept low for major industrial entrepreneurs, who profited directly from satisfying consumer demand that the Napoleonic Wars had suppressed.[42] They were also the prime beneficiaries of tariffs that kept foreign competition at a distance. Such policies were intended to foster entrepreneurial activity that would enrich the state. They were also supposed to lull the monarchy's middle classes into forgetting revolutionary ideals left over from the upheavals in France. Written constitutions and representative government were not preconditions for prosperity under Habsburg rule; at least this was what the regime wanted its subjects to think, especially its wealthier ones.

The dynasty had also tried to erase another political and cultural by-product of the French Revolution and its Bonapartist aftermath: nationalism. Habsburgs from the Renaissance on, almost without exception, had aspired to centralize their governments, largely for fiscal and military reasons. More often than not, they had been forced to compromise such aspirations with their provincial estates, who characteristically acted as guardians of territorial privileges and revenues. Even in Bohemia, where coordination of the realm's institutions with policy coming from Vienna had been most successful, regional representative bodies in each crown land had a strong voice in fiscal affairs. Except for religion, the House of Austria had also allowed local culture and social practice to stand as long as the sovereignty of the ruler remained intact. Even in confessional matters, Habsburg governments had relented from time to time when necessary: for example, orthodox Serbs in Hungary, refugees from the Ottoman occupation of their land, had been given cultural and religious autonomy towards the end of the seventeenth century.[43]

Nor was the polyglot linguistic map of the dynasty's empire a philosophical problem for governments in Vienna throughout most of the early modern era. For the Habsburgs and their cohort sovereigns throughout Europe, possession of titles alone legitimated rule. From the standpoint of dynastic government alone, identification of a monarch with only one tongue within a linguistically diverse realm was not a self-evident disqualification for royal office. Maria Theresa might possibly have had no inkling of how combustible an issue language could become when her officials decided that schoolchildren learned best in the vernaculars they heard at home. Czech would be one of the three obligatory languages to be studied at her military academy. Her son, Leopold II, was equally at home with practical multilingualism in his lands; he established a chair for the study of the Czech language at the German-dominated University of Prague.[44] Beginning with Ferdinand I, several Habsburg rulers tried to learn enough of their peoples' languages to establish some form of identity with them. Policies from Vienna, however, were often made and executed by ministers who used court languages that came from all over Europe: German, Italian, French and even Spanish. In fact, neither Francis nor Metternich had principled objections to nationalism as a purely cultural phenomenon. So long as they did not question the prerogatives of the sovereign house, local historians, anthropologists and philologians could study and write as they pleased.

Nevertheless, experiments with explicitly regional defence forces during the Napoleonic Wars had convinced the chancellor that the strategy could be politically dangerous. He had opposed Bonaparte's message of national liberation before 1815; after, he remained one of its most dogged and militant opponents. He was at his most consistent in Italy. Between 1820 and 1848 the Habsburg regime dispatched armies five times to the peninsula to rescue shaky legitimate governments from domestic revolutionary pressures: the Bourbon kings of Sicily, the papacy and, last but not least rulers in the cadet Habsburg line in Parma and Modena. Such moves only further alienated local liberals, many of whom were calling for a single Italian state.[45] National questions arose in environments that the regime controlled tightly. The government in Vienna had supported university chairs in theology for teaching the young to respect and uphold the status quo. In Prague, however, Professor Bernardo Bolzano, among the more original philosophical spirits of his time, used his lectures to explore the rational side of man and his capacity to create a better society. From these discussions he formulated an argument for equal treatment of the kingdom's Germans and Czechs. Neither the Pope nor the House of Habsburg welcomed such notions; he lost his academic position. Nevertheless, his views had a considerable influence on the early phase of the Czech national movement.[46]

Nor had the regime effectively met economic needs specific to individual lands of the monarchy. In Hungary, Count István Széchenyi was one of a few prophetic voices in his class calling on its members to focus on bringing the prosperity to their kingdom that Vienna had yet to provide. Fearing that his nation would eventually be absorbed into the far larger Slavic and German populations on its borders, he looked to England as a model for agrarian and commercial reform. Crucial to his schemes was the expansion of railways, a policy that would improve the incomes and living conditions for one of central Europe's most exploited peasantries. Not coincidentally, it would also bring relief to aristocrats whose lifestyle often left them debtors in perpetuity. While he did not question the status of the Habsburgs as rulers, he was in effect advancing programmes long recommended by the dynasty, but shifting them to local hands.

The generous economic considerations that Franciscan absolutism extended to the empire's middle classes had yet to turn them into reflexive supporters of the ruling house. Bourgeois liberals had a challenging list of intellectual discontents yet to be stilled. Restraints on the press and free speech inconvenienced them personally; they also made the monarchy they obeyed sound embarrassingly backward abroad. Though such people acknowledged the authority of the ruling house, they obeyed its cultural policies selectively, keeping abreast, as best they could, of ideas circulating in more enlightened regions of Europe. They began to refine some ideas in case liberal reform should ever come to their homeland. The Vienna Legal-Political-Reading Association, established in 1841, smuggled progressive literature from the West, including the New World, into the empire for study and discussion. Comparable clubs in Graz and Innsbruck did the same. When a group of leading writers, academics and intellectuals had asked the regime in 1845 to curtail censorship sharply, even a few liberal aristocrats approved.[47]

Ferdinand's government and the venerable ages of those who ran it had become the stuff of private jokes among the self-selected intelligentsia. Grillparzer's mordant epitome of the regime said it most economically:

An old man (Count Kolowrat)
An old woman (Prince Metternich)
An old bachelor (Archduke Louis)
Such men bear what is our crown,
So that an old child won't fall down;
Shouldn't things remain the same,
Where the senile play their games?[48]

Popular resentment of the regime mounted exponentially between 1840 and 1848. Every complaint had some bearing on material circumstance, although the content of each depended on the class of society from which it came. The landed nobility resented any tax policy of the government that favoured bourgeois capital formation at the expense of aristocratic and peasant income alike. The middle classes, at the forefront of industrialization, were increasingly impatient with anachronistic restraints on enterprise such as guild regulations, which had outlived Joseph II's campaign to scuttle them. To increase the size of the labour pool and advance commercial agriculture, they also wanted the end of serfdom, once and for all. More productive farming would supply manufacturers with basic commodities, especially the cheap food that workers needed to survive. In fact, workers themselves were becoming restless, particularly in Vienna, where their numbers were growing dramatically. Charity alone was not enough to temper the hardships built into the boom-and-bust cycles of early industrial capitalism: overproduction followed by inventory reduction and the unemployment that came with it. Adding to such misery was the potato blight that had taken hold of central Europe by 1847, leaving many humble folk facing starvation, but with a cause to vent their ire on their government.

A serious contributing factor to all of these grievances was the monarchy's fiscal behaviour. The scenario was all too familiar. The expenditure of Habsburg governments in the post-Napoleonic era had always outrun current revenues. To make up the difference, the regime taxed and taxed again. Though the empire's middle classes had not suffered unduly since 1815, they resented both the policy and the chronic imprudence that it represented. The nobility balked at repeated requests for increased funding, as did the common masses, whose livelihoods depended on what trickled down from the incomes of their landlords or employers. In 1845 the estates of Bohemia and Moravia demanded the right to approve government budgets; with little movement in Vienna in that direction, they flatly refused to pay a new impost in 1847. The diet of Lower Austria petitioned the government similarly in 1845–6, asking to review government budgets with authority to sanction any new taxes. Obviously worried about lower-class restiveness, they also proposed introducing an income tax, lowering consumption levies and the complete abolition of serfdom. A recently created agricultural credit bank would be available to grant credit that would encourage greater agricultural productivity.

News from Paris of an uprising in February 1848 against King Louis-Philippe, a leftover from a cadet line of the Bourbons, transformed petitions and popular unrest into revolution in Vienna. Class-specific discontent initially dominated the agenda. On 13 March a demonstration organized by students, but including non-academic middle-class radicals and even some workers, demanded the end of censorship and the introduction of a constitution that provided for some form of popular representation. While no one questioned the sovereignty of the ruling house –protesters took Joseph II's establishment of freedom of the press as their precedent – they did ask for the removal of all ministers hostile to revolutionary ideas. The pigtail worn obligatorily by court officials to set them apart from other mortals became an emblem of misrule and the need for reform. Another large demonstration the following day repeated the call for the lifting of censorship.[49] The regime caved in immediately. The aged Chancellor Metternich, who epitomized for many all that was wrong with Habsburg government, was dismissed; he quickly fled Vienna, first to England, then Brussels. He returned to the Habsburg capital in 1851 and spent the remaining eight years of his life there in an elegant residence where he ruminated and pronounced on topics great and small.

Ferdinand promised on 14 March to end censorship, restore freedom of the press and begin work on a constitution. In the midst of wild public jubilation, the emperor himself appeared in public, weeping quite openly. Humanizing displays, however, did not increase popular respect for him. Snide stories about his simple-mindedness made the gossip rounds almost immediately. One reported that he initially responded to the unrest by asking if such behaviour were permissible. On 15 March he supposedly asked, sourly, if he were the emperor or not. That he may have ordered no one to be shot won him some popular acclaim, but not for long.[50]

In fact, his government never stopped fumbling politically. Constitutional proposals prepared by the regime alternated between one- and two-house parliaments, neither of which wholly satisfied the revolutionaries. The court that 'granted' the bicameral version on 25 April was in flight to Innsbruck by 17 May. The Vienna Writers' Club delegated some of its members to go to the Tyrol and persuade Emperor Ferdinand to return to his capital city. Their spokesman was a leading contemporary dramatist, Frederick Hebbel, who had transferred his residence from Germany to the Habsburg lands. His prestige, apparently, did not count for much. He and his colleagues were very disappointed by the monarch, finding it impossible to move him beyond empty formalities. The regime eventually did return in August; Hebbel liked to think that his mission had been more persuasive than it seemed at first. By October, however, Ferdinand had decamped to Olomouc in Moravia. A revolutionary mob had bludgeoned to death Count Theodore Latour, the minister of war, then hung him from a lamp post near his office. The emperor was taking no chances.[51]

By July 1848 delegates to an assembly had been selected; its most immediate accomplishment would be a vote on 7 September to abolish the remnants of serfdom. Emperor Ferdinand accepted it two days later. The move substantially calmed peasant unrest, especially in the Austrian lands. By this time, however, Bohemia, Hungary and the Habsburg Italian principalities were engulfed in revolutions displaying distinctively national thrusts that threatened the integrity of the empire far more than the niceties of constitutional structures in Vienna.

Though Ferdinand did not want to shoot anyone, the House of Habsburg had used force in the past to quell internal dissent, as Protestants, Bohemian rebels and recent Italian liberals knew well. It called upon the military once again to keep the empire together. From the perspective of the dynasty, the results were gratifying. By 1849 revolution had been suppressed in Prague and Vienna by Field Marshal Albert von Windischgrätz. The aged Joseph Radetzky had done the same thing for Italy.

In Hungary, however, the constitutional situation became seriously out of hand almost from the outset. It also took a year longer to resolve. Close to autonomy even in the spring of 1848, the revolutionary government had asked the imperial army stationed in the kingdom to pledge its loyalty to the local regime. Officers and men faced a genuine dilemma. The head of state was still a Habsburg, King Ferdinand v, who was also Emperor Ferdinand i of Austria. Should Hungary be at war with other Habsburg lands, the lone ruler of all these realms would be fighting with himself![52] By 1849 resistance in the kingdom had turned into demands for outright independence. It ended only when Vienna enlisted help from Tsar Nicholas i of Russia and a Croatian force led by Joseph Jelačić, who had a national agenda of his own: to disengage his homeland from the Hungarian crown and place the former kingdom directly under Habsburg dynastic rule. The climactic Austrian mop-up of the Hungarian revolutionary militia and their political sympathizers was shockingly brutal; the episode was quickly added to the central narrative of Hungarian history.

Regrouping at the Core

Though the Habsburgs had survived the mid-century upheavals as a ruling house, they had not done so with great glory. Liberal public opinion had soured after the court's flight to Innsbruck in May 1848. For some such behaviour was all too reminiscent of Louis XVI and Marie Antoinette's ill-fated plans to save their positions by escaping to Varennes in 1791. Nevertheless, even as the revolution was in full swing, the dynasty and its advisers were asking themselves crucial questions. Among them was how to restructure Habsburg family protocols to deal with the emergency now confronting them and to recover their traditional status when the crisis had passed. One of the more widely reproduced images of Francis I had been his skeletal face on his deathbed in 1835. Beneath this was a passage in his testament that confirmed his eldest, but mentally questionable son as his successor. The intended message of continuity and legitimacy in his line was clear. The dynasty had reconfirmed the mechanics of this four years after his passing. A private house compact of 1839 had established a comprehensive set of rules for Habsburg guardianships, marriages, ranks of prospective spouses and the like. It had also conferred the job of overseeing these arrangements on the head of the house.

Under normal circumstances, this would be the eldest son in a given generation, usually the current ruler. In the face of revolutionary challenge, however, Ferdinand's relatives and advisers were reconsidering ironclad rules of succession that put the survival of their house and their empire at risk. Though she had been more open to liberal opinion than other members of the court, Princess Sophie feared that her hapless brother-in-law might sign the empire away. His promise in the early days of the Vienna uprising to constitutionalize the monarchy alarmed her, along with other family members. It also worried important military figures such as Field Marshal Windischgrätz, who would soon play a central role in bringing the upheaval to an end. She began working on Archduke Francis Charles, her husband and Ferdinand's youngest brother, to renounce his rights of succession in favour of their son, the eighteen-year-old Franz Joseph. At the same time, she vigorously promoted Ferdinand's abdication. With the outbreak of violence in Vienna in March, her sister-in-law Archduchess Maria Anna advised Ferdinand to think about abdication too. He proved to be uncharacteristically stubborn; he respected the legitimist scruples of his father and defended them tenaciously. He also seemed confident of his people's support.[53]

Ferdinand's several changes of residence in 1848 made it easier for him to resist being marginalized at his own court. By the beginning of December, however, he was ready to give in. On 2 December 1848 he turned the throne over to his nephew, Franz Joseph I, who was declared to be in his majority, though in reality he was three years away from it. 'Be good', Ferdinand said, 'it's all right' – even though it was not, either for him or for his brother. The latter, who was generally regarded as a nullity, was just as reluctant to step aside. Strict legitimists did have an argument on their side: according to Charles VI's Pragmatic Sanction, the Hungarian estates should have been consulted before Archduke Francis Charles was discounted as a successor. The Bohemian estates would soon raise related issues too. These were, however, not immediate problems; the circle that pushed both men aside wanted someone in the imperial office whose political record was as yet unwritten. Ferdinand had made too many concessions; Archduke Francis Charles was too closely associated with his regime. Having promised nothing, Franz Joseph could more easily disavow commitments made by his predecessors.[54] Franz Joseph it would be, and for a very long time. He would leave the scene only in 1916.

A Midpoint Perspective

Structurally considered, the House of Habsburg had survived periodic encounters with revolutions and their aftermaths during the first half of the nineteenth century reasonably well. Their territorial holdings were only marginally smaller; the most significant loss at the Congress of Vienna in 1815 had been the Austrian Netherlands. What the dynasty in Vienna might have done with a presence on the Atlantic coast is a question for the 'What If' school of history. Nevertheless, its rulers still had a right of way through Italy to important sea lanes. The abolition of the German Empire and the imperial title that went with it forced a major change in the House of Habsburg-Lorraine's self-perception. Nevertheless, its leading role in the German Confederation at the Vienna conclave had softened that setback too. While largely a peacekeeping body within the several principalities and kingdoms that were cobbled together out of the former Holy Roman Empire, the ruler of the Austrian empire headed it. Metternich would use the arrangement to great effect in driving up support for counter-revolutionary measures between 1815 and 1848. To be sure, monarchs generally were an endangered species, as Jacobin and Bonapartist France had proven. Even though Napoleon I had conferred imperial status on himself, the political framework within which he was working differed sharply from the one that the more venerable lineages of Europe had traditionally used to legitimate themselves. That the Austrian Habsburgs and the Russian Romanovs, serious competitors in the Balkans, cooperated in driving Napoleon back to France and crushing revolution in Hungary was a measure of how vulnerable kings and emperors thought themselves to be.

For all that, compared with the French Bourbons, the Habsburgs had played the survival game quite deftly. Aided from the late eighteenth century on by increasingly sophisticated print and pictorial techniques, they had credibly positioned themselves as ready and willing to coordinate their interests with public needs, for example by the abolition of serfdom, without fussing unduly over religious allegiances and time-honoured privileges of rank. They had also continued to receive private petitions from subjects and often responded to them. Beneath much of the rhetoric in 1848 ran the hope that the dynasty might revive the progressive benevolence of Maria Theresa and, especially, Joseph II. Indeed, the belief that the dynasty might resume these behaviours may have contributed to the quick fading after 1848 of revolutionary ideals in the monarchy, once militant hostilities ended.

Clearly the Habsburgs had some public image rebuilding to do after 1848. They were not altogether without articulated and talented supporters. Some of the most graceful pens and paintbrushes of the Habsburg domains stood behind the monarchy and its favourite images, both up to the events in Vienna that March and afterward. Others were just deeply suspicious of its more extreme critics. The widowed Empress Karolina Augusta commissioned Leopold Kupelwieser, one of several talented artists she sponsored, to create frescoes for the assembly hall of the Lower Austrian estates in Vienna one day before revolution broke out in the city. Taking as his theme the virtues of the House of Habsburg-Lorraine through history, he worked on throughout the revolution.[55] Like Adalbert Stifter, Franz Grillparzer found mass movements suspect; national activism in Bohemia and Hungary bothered him greatly. Against such causes, he concluded that the Habsburgs would have no defence other than the army and the person of the emperor himself. He hoped that better education would help the monarchy's peoples to accept the pre-eminence of Germans and German culture in the monarchy, but also glumly predicted that nationalist causes would co-opt all of history and literature. Unsurprisingly, his efforts to write a couple of plays with Hungarian and Czech themes fell considerably short of his greater achievements.[56]

More auspiciously for the monarchy, some of its writers trivialized revolution as a political genre by satirizing it, among them the sharp-tongued and exceedingly popular Johann Nestroy. His take on the 1848 turmoil, *Freiheit in Krähwinkel* ('Freedom in Crow's Corners'), performed every day during July 1848, mocked both the Old Regime and the principles of the revolutionaries. When Pfiffspitz, the editor of the local newspaper, tells an activist named Eberhard Ultra that such upheavals would never come to the village, the latter replies:

> ULTRA: Who told you that? All conditions for revolution, every-
> thing that excites human outrage in the greater world, are here
> in miniature. We have a tiny absolute government, a tiny unac-
> countable ministry, a tiny bureaucracy, a tiny bit of censorship,
> sovereign debt that exceeds our tiny powers to master it. There-
> fore, we have to have a wee bit of revolution and through a wee
> bit of revolution get a tiny constitution and finally a smidgen of
> freedom.[57]

Successful defence of the house and its rule in 1848, however, did not prove that it would never face such a crisis again. Superior force aside, the dynasty owed much of its survival to the accidents of history. The goals of the dissidents had been formed over time in quite different contexts. Peasants and the revolutionary middle classes in Bohemia and the Austrian lands, Vienna particularly, could not cooperate for long on important issues. Once the government made clear in 1848 that all vestiges of serfdom would be abolished, whatever hostility the vast rural underclass had towards the monarchy subsided. While bourgeois liberals were generally eager to have more formal oversight of government decisions, especially in fiscal matters, they were not comfortable with redistributive economic programmes. Talk of greater material egalitarianism heard in the working classes and among student agitators in and around Vienna and Prague alarmed even convinced political and legal democrats. Yet no regime could reasonably expect its opponents to be in disarray all the time. The court itself had been more than a little alarmed by a sign placed near the Hofburg during the revolution that designated the complex as 'national property'.[58] Even painters known for celebrating the House of Habsburg in the post-Napoleonic era had gone rogue. Anton Ziegler, who had dedicated his career to inspiring love of country and its dynasty, joined the Vienna Revolutionary National Guard in 1848.[59]

Francis I's formal declaration of his new title as emperor of Austria in 1804 had been a massed affair; Johann Peter Krafft gave him a prominent place in his painting of the scene, but the crowd surrounding him competes for the viewer's attention (see illus. 9).[60] The evidence of 1848, however, suggested that this crowd had begun to divide sharply in pursuit of several agendas. Even important nobles, whose families had always been lured back into cooperation with the dynasty's monarchs, were looking for a way to bring greater autonomy to their home provinces and regions.

A core of these several agendas had survived under decades of Habsburg post-Napoleonic repression; one more setback in the wake of the 1848 upheavals might silence them for a time, but not eradicate them and their spokesmen for good. The eighteenth-century Habsburgs had constructed for themselves a public image attuned to a secularizing society no longer in need of protection from Ottoman marauding and Protestant schismatics. Demonstrators throughout the monarchy in 1848 were asking the ruling house to reset its relations with its peoples yet again, increasingly disparate though the latter were.

SIX
CONSTRUCTING COMMITMENT

Removing Doubts and Revising Values

H oping to speed her eldest son to an emperorship, Franz Joseph's mother began bypassing the Habsburg dynastic management code early on. Shortly after his birth in 1830 she asked to celebrate it at Schönbrunn in a style reserved for heirs apparent. Though Metternich, ever the legitimist, balked at that, she eventually won special status for the infant as the first nephew of the prospective Emperor Ferdinand I (illus. 12). Franz Joseph was thus baptized at the court in Schönbrunn, a custom usually reserved for future rulers.[1]

Unorthodox though his succession would be, there was nothing strikingly unusual about Franz Joseph either as a boy or mature man. Rudolph IV *der Stifter*, Maximilian I, Joseph II and Leopold II were imaginative and in some ways brilliant. They were, however, exceptions that underscored the rule. The most successful of Franz Joseph's predecessors were notable for steadfast pursuit of their interests, conscientious attention to duty, commonsense opportunism and their general conviction that God, not luck and strategic thinking, had given them what they had. Their most consistent operational principle could not have been more straightforwardly simple: acquiring territories and titles for a variety of reasons, then defending them tenaciously on battlefields and in diplomatic negotiations.

Judged by these standards, the young emperor Franz Joseph represented his house very well, and then some. Unlike the uncle he had displaced, he was mentally intact and gifted with an unusually good memory that eased his way through a blurring array of public situations. His education at the hands of some very fine teachers emphasized duty and discipline, reinforced by a heavy dose of religious indoctrination. Like several of his predecessors, he had also studied a few of the languages spoken in his lands, some of which he handled quite comfortably.

12 Ferdinand
Waldmuller, *The
Child Franz Joseph*,
1832, oil on panel.

He had a playful side that he never quite lost, especially when he was writing to his siblings or sketching. Nor was he totally in thrall to his mother. She was not at all happy that he chose to marry the striking Princess Elisabeth of Bavaria in 1854, rather than the bride's older sister whom Sophie had picked out for her son. Most important of all, he had an unshakeable commitment to his patriarchal duties in his house and his responsibilities as a ruler.[2]

He had come to power, however, in a constitutionally suspect way that would dog him for some time. Not since Emperor Rudolph II was shunted aside by his younger brothers at the beginning of the seventeenth century had the Habsburgs so summarily dismissed one of their own from imperial office. Some of the dynasty's subjects were primed to complain vigorously. Resentment of government from Vienna after 1848 was so entrenched in Bohemia that Franz Joseph skipped a formal crowning there. Politicized Czechs responded by constructing a cult of the disgruntled Ferdinand I as the last legitimate claimant to the Crown of St Wenceslaus. He furthered his case by transferring his residence to the

13 Franz Joseph I (*r.* 1848–1916) in a Corpus Christi procession, 1900.

kingdom. The issue even found its way into music, previously among the least politicized of the arts in the monarchy. Shortly after Franz Joseph became his sovereign, Bedřich Smetana, among the most significant composers in the Czech national style, wrote an *Anthem to the Bearer of the Czech Crown*. The title tactfully avoided naming the Habsburg currently ruling the kingdom, but made clear that the central attribute of rule was embodied in the traditional Bohemian royal regalia and not the house that wore it. That the disgruntled Ferdinand I resided in the kingdom until he died in 1875 added credibility to his cause. The act of passing over Archduke Francis Charles in favour of his eldest child for the imperial office also troubled conservatives. A Catholic periodical, the *Österreichischer Volksfreund*, noted that the process had ended with the unnatural arrangement of a son ruling his father. Unlike Bohemian national legitimists, however, they piously accepted the step as further testimony to the special grandeur that God had bestowed on royal office.[3]

Franz Joseph continued to exploit theatrical aspects of Catholicism to enhance the sacral aura in which his house had enveloped itself for centuries. Indeed, his appearance in the Corpus Christi procession of 1849 formally began the receremonialization of legitimate Habsburg rule (illus. 13). The image he wished to embody was of a ruler whose grandeur was tempered by the humility and piety that made him one among millions of simple Christians. He further underscored the point during Easter Week in 1850. On Maundy Thursday twelve elderly and

14 'A Pauper after Maundy Thursday Foot Cleansing', from Max Herzig, *Viribus Unitis. Das Buch vom Kaiser* (1898).

poor men were brought to the festive hall of the Hofburg and given a meal. When they had finished, the younger archdukes cleared the dishes away. A kneeling Franz Joseph then cleansed each pauper's feet, after which they returned home in imperial coaches, somewhat the richer spiritually and for the twenty silver coins awarded to each, along with souvenir silver beakers and saucers (illus. 14).[4] The practice endured until the end of the monarchy in 1918.

The emperor held fast to the religious orthodoxy that his mother and tutors drilled into him. He firmly supported the basic doctrinal and institutional positions of the Roman Catholic establishment, which had suffered substantially in the monarchy's lands under Joseph II and even the pious Maria Theresa. In 1855 Franz Joseph accepted a concordat with the papacy that returned to the Church a controlling role over its physical facilities, fiscal arrangements and personnel in the Habsburg lands. The appointment of local bishops was again largely in papal hands; anti-clerical measures left over from the eighteenth century were abolished. The clergy also retained a significant role in primary school instruction, although only over Catholic children in religious education.

Nevertheless, the scrupulously Catholic emperor and his advisers recognized after 1848 that religious institutions of every confession no longer commanded reflexive obedience from a public that had become far more pluralistic – socially, economically and philosophically. 'Liberal' was a synonym for 'anti-clerical' in middle-class urban circles throughout much of the monarchy. Attitudes of more humble folk had changed too. In the countryside, especially in the more western regions of the monarchy, the total abolition of serfdom after 1848 had made the peasantry physically and intellectually more independent. They attended church services less regularly. Clerical careers, a time-honoured way for rural men to move a rung or two up the social ladder, became less attractive. Enrolment in Catholic seminaries slipped sharply throughout much of the nineteenth century as public facilities displaced monastic schools that had once trained boys through the lower secondary level. Urban industrial labourers took social democracy's promises of a better life in this world more seriously; many of them also resented pastors who complained ceaselessly about incomes that normally outstripped those of their parishioners, yet required no physical labour to earn. While only a small fraction of the population in the Habsburg lands ever formally declared itself confessionless, their numbers rose perceptibly after the turn of the twentieth century: in 1900 it had been 25,340, or 1 per cent of the population; ten years later it was 49,448, or 7 per cent. The most educated ethnic communities of the empire led the way: German speakers and Czechs. Hungary followed the pattern, though not down to the last detail. Here rural folk remained truer to traditional Christian behaviour patterns than their Austrian counterparts, but religious indifference flourished among the middle classes and intellectuals. Evangelical sects that were always suspect to Habsburg regimes had made inroads in Hungary as well, among them the Jehovah's Witnesses and Seventh Day Adventists.[5]

Religious behaviour within the House of Habsburg itself also became more idiosyncratic. One member's devoutness killed him: Archduke Charles Louis, a younger brother of Franz Joseph, would die in 1896 of an ailment he picked up in Palestine after drinking holy water fresh from the River Jordan. A scattering of Franz Joseph's nearest relatives, however, took very different confessional tacks. A second brother, Archduke Maximilian, executed in 1867 by republican rebels in Mexico where he had gone with imperial ambitions of his own, was comparatively liberal in his religious views. So was Archduke Rudolph, born in 1858 and Franz Joseph's heir apparent.

The Catholic social mission in the Habsburg lands renewed itself vigorously in the last decades of the nineteenth century and the beginning of the twentieth. Its inspiration, however, came not from the House of Habsburg but from a competitive, and therefore divisive, political organization. The followers of the Christian Social Party, led by the locally popular Viennese mayor Carl Lueger, loudly professed its loyalty to the emperor and his house at ceremonial public occasions. Its main purpose, however, was to question the patriotism of liberals and Marxists rather than committing themselves to the monarch and his agenda. Franz Joseph, in fact, disapproved of the anti-Semitism that became a rhetorical staple for many parish clergymen associated with the movement. Such homilies only stirred up the social and political antagonisms that the emperor hoped to minimize in his realms.[6]

For their part, Franz Joseph and his governments conspicuously respected all confessions that the government officially recognized. He retained enough of his public Catholic presence to ward off charges of hypocrisy. His devotion to his family's traditional religious practice was well advertised in a variety of newspapers and other mass periodicals. As late as 1908 the popular *Das Illustriertes Blatt* carried a photo of the visibly aged ruler performing the pre-Easter foot washing. Flagrant bigotry, however, had no place in Habsburg public policy. Those same newspapers, especially in the latter decades of the nineteenth century, reported his occasional visits to Eastern Orthodox, Greek Catholic, Armenian Catholic, Jewish, even Islamic services. The gesture may have lost some meaning for a society that increasingly discounted what it heard from pulpits, especially in urban areas.[7] Yet, in view of the historical ties between the dynasty and Roman Catholicism, it was a noteworthy change, regardless of the pressures that drove it. In fact, such behaviour won Franz Joseph widespread loyalty among the religiously observant.[8]

Nevertheless, the emperor and his advisers realized that religion could be only one way of tying his peoples to himself and his house. Even traditional rites could go wrong in embarrassingly exposed popular settings. In 1857, for example, the Primate of Hungary led 27,000 pilgrims to Mariazell, presumably for the good of their souls, but also as a demonstration of support for Hungary's national independence. Close watchers of similar occasions elsewhere might also have detected another sign of weakening commitment to the House of Habsburg, this time in more rarefied social circles. The ruling house had once encouraged noble participation in spectacular penitential displays to confirm the unity of its peoples, from the most exalted classes to the more modest. Even before 1848, the numbers of aristocratic participants in these functions had been dropping, in part as priorities in their homelands were absorbing more of their political energies and time.[9]

The Omnipresent Habsburgs

No longer able to rely on religious bonds to bring ruler and subject together, Franz Joseph and his officials turned to a strategy used by several contemporary monarchs who were facing a similar problem: focusing public attention directly on the person of the ruler and his or her dynasty, then turning both into emblems of a polity's greatness from past to present. Such associations, when internalized, might make people forget the missteps of ruling houses, including the insider manoeuvring that had brought Franz Joseph to his throne. The House of Habsburg-Lorraine and its advisers also revived a tactic that Maria Theresa had used to underscore her political legitimacy: associating a ruler with illustrious and approving Habsburg ancestors. The reliable Leopold Kupelwieser produced a watercolour showing the young emperor's mother and great-grandmother, Maria Theresa, leading him to the throne as he mounts it for the first time. Connecting him to the legendary piety of his family was another tactic. In the same year that his uncle stepped aside for him, Franz Joseph was incorporated pictorially into the well-known image of Emperor Rudolph I dismounting his horse to present it to the priest bearing the Host. In 1852 he was the centrepiece of a scene in which he re-enacted the episode all by himself. Within his regime, confidence in the new ruler was sufficiently high to begin striking medals and raising public memorials celebrating his victory over revolution.[10]

Reminders of the emperor's immediate ancestors, who had explicitly dedicated themselves to bettering the lives of all their subjects, were built, installed, renovated, photographed and reproduced throughout the monarchy until it collapsed in 1918. Maria Theresa and Joseph II were again especially serviceable. The representation of the former as mother-empress, an identity that she had cultivated during her reign, appeared throughout the Habsburg lands. The idea found a place in the all-male precincts of the armed forces as well; a statue of her in the inner court-yard of the imperial military academy turned her into the mother of future officers and the troops they would command. In the press and in school texts she appeared as a nurturer of infants and small children, roles that she indisputably knew at first hand. Her image was spun to soothe political antagonisms, too. The unveiling of her statue in 1888 between Vienna's museums of art and natural history, west of the Ringstrasse, was calculated to win the approval of every social and national community in the empire. For once, hope conformed to reality. At the insistence of Hungarian members of the advisory committee, she bore no territorial crown on her head, but a generic diadem. Nevertheless, supplements in the German and Hungarian press covered the event extensively. Prague celebrated the occasion with an opera on the subject of the empress-queen.[11]

Monument upon monument turned Joseph ii into a kind of cult figure, a testimonial to Habsburg concern for the well-being of their populations, even when progressive policies were the answer to their problems. Francis i had led the way here with the immense bronze equestrian statue of his uncle unveiled in 1807, the same one that Vienna's liberals would rally around in 1848. Francis and his regime were hoping to promote the notion that the Habsburgs could be 'people's emperors'; the general public had been urged to attend the ceremony. His grandson's regime had the same idea in mind and pursued it relentlessly. Joseph's major and minor reforms were extolled; the winding down of serfdom and the introduction of religious toleration were arguably the most important, but others were mentioned too. Positive things were said about his character as well. Such testimonials were more common in German-speaking areas of the empire, but also familiar in the Czech-speaking regions of Bohemia and Moravia. Etchings and engravings showed him in benevolent settings. If the subject of all this adulation had ever heard half of the posthumous praise lavished on him, he would have died a happier man.[12]

Franz Joseph himself had far fewer monuments of scale. It was very hard to draw, paint or sculpt the Habsburg in quite the same way for every nation in his *imperium*, most of whom differed sharply among themselves on their views of the dynasty. His two most prominent statues stood in the University of Vienna and in what is today the city's Technical University. None were on sites exposed to mass public viewing. Maria Theresa's figure had been installed in the courtyard of the Military Academy in 1862; Franz Joseph was not similarly honoured until 1908. Unlike his great-grandmother, however, he attended the occasion. When the two statues were aligned with one another in 1912, cadets pledged their loyalty to both in an elaborate ceremony.[13]

Nevertheless, the emperor was widely on view in many other public settings. His regime made heavy use of ritualized events, fastidiously observed and repeated, that invited mass participation. The technique easily lent itself to written and visual propaganda; it was also one of the fastest ways to impress the most vulnerable audiences, largely, though not exclusively, schoolchildren.[14] All of these appearances were well choreographed to minimize political slip-ups. Their overall goal, however, was dictated by mutually exclusive imperatives and therefore difficult in the extreme: bringing Franz Joseph closer to his peoples while restoring the uniquely exalted status of an office that the 1848 upheavals had tried to qualify. His uncle Ferdinand I's court had protected the status of their unpredictable ruler by keeping him out of the public eye. The problem with Franz Joseph was to make him appear emotionally and psychologically immediate to his peoples without compromising his singular office.[15] That some of the artifices employed might occasionally be out of fashion was no drawback. Should they link the grace of God to Habsburg rule, few were eager to oppose the link in public. Many accepted the connection quite sincerely. Moreover, to ensure that none of these affairs lessened dynastic majesty, Franz Joseph's deeply conservative cousin Archduke Albert administered the protocols.

Ceremonial tours throughout the various lands of the monarchy had long been a routine feature of the Habsburg dynastic programme. Franz Joseph and his close relatives followed the practice as actively as any of their ancestors, and then some. With questions about his succession widely in circulation, the new emperor spent the first two years of his reign in a round of travels to associate himself with his office and appear to be worthy of it. Physical demeanour counted: both he and his advisers hoped that his normal youthful vigour would help to offset the liberties he and his supporters at court had taken with local constitutions and dynastic formalities. He passed this particular test for stamina brilliantly, visiting Hungary, Trieste, Bohemia, Moravia, Tyrol, Vorarlberg, Venice, Galicia and Bukovina. His councillors were most pleased with the turnout for his first trip to Polish Galicia in 1851, heavily attended by peasants whom he had freed from required labour obligations in 1848, and who continued to think that Franz Joseph was a central element in their lives. They certainly expected him to perform benevolently again: during the three weeks that the emperor spent in the province, he received 3,500 petitions for favours.[16]

On the whole, Franz Joseph pulled off his contradictory mission remarkably well. On his side was the serene dignity that never seemed to desert him when acting either as a head of state or simply a concerned father. Pictures showed him time and again combining his singular powers with personal concern for the welfare of his peoples, regardless of social and economic status. He probably gave around 100,000 audiences during his reign. He tirelessly accepted invitations from various institutions – academic, cultural, commercial – all of which were eager to have him grace their galas and ceremonies. He encouraged people to imitate the dynasty in certain behaviours and express their loyalty to the ruling house at the same time. Expensive Habsburg anniversaries were turned into charitable events that solicited contributions from his peoples, affirming their respect for the monarch and their public spiritedness at the same time. Some traditional festivities associated with dynastic anniversaries were converted to public charitable causes into which the emperor's subjects poured ever more energy and money. The most elaborate of these would be the celebration of his birthday on 18 August. Observances at the court were scaled down to a chapel service followed by a military parade. His subjects' contributions to the occasion, however, were another matter. Franz Joseph urged them to make charitable donations as tokens of allegiance to him, and many did. Religious leaders did their part, pledging the loyalty of their confessions to the monarchy.

With the emperor's encouragement, voluntary public festivities on his behalf continued to move ever further beyond the confined circles in which he lived and worked. Thirteen jubilees marking milestones in the emperor's exceptionally long career took place between 1854 and 1909. All were accompanied by appeals for charitable contributions throughout the monarchy. So that everyone understood the message, in 1898, the 50th year of his reign, solicitations in appropriate local languages went to organizations of peasants, workers and artisans. None of this reduced Franz Joseph's commitment to personal giving, and not only for festive occasions. By the 1870s, the popular press had often depicted him aiding flood victims and wounded military veterans, as well as endowing public facilities to care for and to feed the poor. For all this, he drew from his private resources.[17]

For subjects denied contact with their emperor in the flesh, there were convenient vicarious substitutes. His likeness peered from the walls of countless public buildings far removed from Vienna or Budapest: the medieval coronation church of Suceava, in Habsburg Bukovina, had a portrait of the emperor dressed as a member of the Order of the Golden Fleece. The explanatory text was in Romanian. A vast variety of periodicals and other forms of literature also alerted the entire empire to the details and significance of these occasions, often with financial support from outside the court. Typical was Franz Isidor Proschko's *Pearls from the History of the Austrian Fatherland: On the Occasion of the Fortieth Jubilee Celebration of His Majesty Kaiser Franz Joseph I.* Published in 1888 for the 40th anniversary of Franz Joseph's accession, it was bound in sumptuous Morocco leather, the costs of which were borne by the 'Austrian Patriotic Circle of Vienna'. Perhaps encouraged by the availability of such subsidies, the publisher's foreword declared that there could not be too many books with such 'patriotic-religious' tones. The imperial family, which had appreciated the author's reverent take on their status as early as 1861, thought enough of *Pearls* to find space for it in their private library.[18]

Where imperial stereotypes appropriately reminded viewers of Franz Joseph's status, he appeared in line-ups of great rulers from classical antiquity. At Bad Deutsch-Altenburg, near Carnuntum, a major excavation of a Roman military encampment in Lower Austria, he stands on a pedestal before the entrance to the museum, flanked by two towering Ionic columns capped with busts of Marcus Aurelius and Augustus. Mindful that the emperor was part of a more egalitarian age, however, painters usually showed him in far simpler circumstances, at least by the standards of the times. His stationary poses were generally natural, completely stripped of the grandiose Baroque gestures and settings that were familiar until the mid-nineteenth century. The emperor was dressed as a well-to-do civilian or, more characteristically, in military uniform. Background material was often minimal. Many pictures of him in informal natural scenes, outfitted to match these settings, further humanized him. He especially liked to be shown as a hunter. A widely circulated likeness, made by Joseph Kriehuber around 1858, showed the emperor in a mountainous landscape, his head surrounded by a nimbus-like cloud, holding a climbing stick in the manner of a sceptre. Distinctive formalities befitting his status, however, were also reinforced. A castle in Upper Austria, which had once been the headquarters of a Hubertus Club, dedicated to the patron saint of hunters, was reconsecrated as the Franz Joseph Home for the children of impoverished hunters. Here they learned, among other things, how to behave properly should they be called upon to present the emperor with a bouquet of flowers. Franz Joseph's people formally marked his love of nature in built environments too. Some planted 'imperial' oak trees, even in urban Vienna and its outlying districts, as tributes to their sovereign and his family.[19]

15 Koloman Moser, frontispiece for Max Herzig's *Viribus Unitis. Das Buch vom Kaiser* (1898).

The emperor's family worked at making him more human too. For the fiftieth-year jubilee of his reign in 1898, Archduchess Valerie, one of his daughters, sponsored *Viribus unitis: das Buch vom Kaiser* (*With United Strength: The Emperor Book*), illustrated with photographs of the emperor and grandchildren together with gatherings of a wide variety of the social groups that made up the empire: courtiers and government officers, the middle classes, workers and peasants. Both he and his relatives dressed in regional costume, if necessary. Franz Joseph detested the modernist design of the title page; sexually ambiguous men and

200

diaphanous women had no place in his aesthetic economy (illus. 15). Nevertheless, he allowed the work to appear, presumably because local artists had done it and patrons in his empire admired it.[20]

Even where grandeur was altogether in place, egalitarian touches appeared. One of Franz Joseph's more spectacular appearances was in the gaudy Vienna pageant that celebrated the 25th year of his marriage. Modelled on Maximilian I's Renaissance *Triumphzug*, participants were costumed as figures from the sixteenth century, the moment at which Emperor Charles V came as close as any member of the family ever would to being a world ruler. Such backward looks at past greatness were familiar to rulers of Franz Joseph's time, and from that standpoint, were quite unexceptional. Nevertheless, the entire programme also reflected Habsburg acknowledgment of current social realities. The procession was open to people of all kinds, from artists, to butchers, to miners, whose professional and benevolent societies paid for temporally authentic clothing. It was hard to distinguish aristocrats from the moneyed bourgeoisie by costume. If anyone profited from the affair, it was the proprietors of the 41 photographic studios to which pageant marchers flocked to memorialize their presence at the occasion.[21]

Adjusting to Politics, 1848–68

Public graciousness and the sentimental public response that it encouraged did not completely drive away memories of 1848 and some of that year's revolutionary goals.[22] Nevertheless, eruptions of violent opposition to the regime were very unlikely. Franz Joseph's advisers therefore had reason to hope that they could restore something like the centralized and quasi-absolute rule that had prevailed under Francis I. The architect of this policy was Prince Felix von Schwarzenberg, a court insider who was committed both to the monarchy's territorial integrity and to 'freedoms granted by the emperor' rather than through compromises with unruly mobs. He had vigorously promoted Franz Joseph's immediate accession to imperial office. In fact, a complex gathering of liberal interest groups – loyal civil servants and officials, some nobles, members of the army, even the public at large – willingly tolerated a measure of autocracy and administrative centralization in Vienna if the trade-off was orderly government in the monarchy. Proven revolutionary elements such as organized political parties or national movements might disturb the system all over again; by repressing them, the regime was doing its general public a favour. Some continued to think that there should be a constitutional provision for some public oversight of fiscal affairs. A more efficient bureaucracy would help as well. Nevertheless, the most deeply held conviction among the well-to-do in the middle class was that only a rationally organized state would continue the economic advances they had made in post-Napoleonic Europe. The policy had precedents: Joseph II and Leopold II had governed in much the same way to reach the same goal: serious material progress.[23]

Manoeuvring within these parameters, Schwarzenberg was sufficiently open to administrative and economic experiments to reassure recently dissident communities that the dynasty might accept changes that furthered the general welfare. The youthful emperor would probably have accommodated himself to such throughout his reign, if the prince had stopped there. The latter was, however, as strong an advocate of ministerial responsibility as Metternich had been; such men had reputations for questioning the will of monarchs. Behaviour like this did not fit Archduchess Sophie's vision of her son as a ruler and her plans to stay close to him. Franz Joseph and Schwarzenberg soon drifted apart. Sophie was much relieved when the minister died in 1852. Minister of the Interior Alexander Bach, who took over the practical direction of the government, was of a bourgeois background. He was also a '48er' and a programmatic statist. Such was his faith in central administration that he envisioned it as a self-sufficient entity that reformed itself when needed. Principled liberals quickly labelled him a traitor to their cause. Under military and political pressure domestically and abroad, Franz Joseph dismissed Bach from his regime in 1859. For the next few years the emperor would struggle to balance centralization and decentralization in governing his lands. He would also put far more trust in bureaucrats collectively than in strong-minded individual officials.[24]

Indeed, although absolutist principles were the hallmark of Franz Joseph's first years as a ruler, the greater part of his career was devoted to placating the diverse constituencies that expected the emperor's support even as he defended the formal powers required to maintain the position of his house. His policies changed according to the way he shuffled these priorities. National causes and nationally orientated agitation sparked many episodes of intergroup tension within the monarchy from 1850 until 1918, some of which complicated the business of governing inordinately. The Italian peninsula was the first ominous example of what local agitation, an ambitious and tactically flexible local ruler, in this case Victor Emmanuel II of Savoy, and helpful foreign intervention could do.

A humiliating defeat of the Habsburg army in 1859 sent a distraught Empress Elisabeth in flight to Madeira, one of several ruptures in her marriage to the emperor.[25] An independent kingdom of Italy, which included the Habsburg secundogenitures in Lombardy and Tuscany, was in place by 1862.

Concerned that he might lose the support of his other peoples, Franz Joseph tinkered with experiments in constitutional monarchy. One in 1860 re-provincialized political and administrative procedures; those who wanted a rationally unified state, including business interests, were not pleased at all. The next year an Imperial Assembly (Reichsrat) was installed, empowered to initiate legislation and pass on the crown's budget proposals. The latter was a notable concession, given Franz Joseph's determination to retain ultimate control over military affairs, and quietened liberal critics of the 1860 arrangement. National partisans, however, disliked it intensely, especially the Hungarians, who had given up on national independence after 1848 but continued to take alarm at any strengthening of top-down government from Vienna. Indeed, they resisted it so loudly and consistently that when Prussian chancellor Otto von Bismarck manoeuvred Franz Joseph into war in Germany in 1866, to erase what formal influence the Habsburgs still exercised in the German Confederation, he gave some thought to enlisting Hungarian help.

Bismarck never pushed that idea too far. Yet even with an intact empire behind the Habsburg forces, Prussia's crushing victory persuaded Franz Joseph that he had to mollify the Hungarians in order for the dynasty's *imperium* to survive. Even in Vienna, people had lined the streets to heckle the defeated emperor, going so far as to call for his abdication, when he travelled from Schönbrunn to the Hofburg.[26] The result was the Compromise (*Ausgleich*) of 1867, or Dual Compromise, which effectively divided the Habsburg lands into autonomous halves: Hungary, including Croatia, and its associated crown lands; and Austria, which included everything else. Each half had a constitution and parliament: the same person ruled them; the House of Habsburg was uniquely charged with generating legitimate rulers for both polities. Franz Joseph was emperor in Austria and king in Hungary; there was a common army and common foreign policy. Common fiscal affairs were resolved in bilateral meetings every ten years. The disputed phrase 'imperial and royal' (*kaiserlich und königlich*, k.u.k.) would be applied to common affairs and offices, 'imperial-royal' (*kaiserlich-königlich*, k.k.) to offices in the Austrian half and 'royal' (*königlich*, k.) to Hungarian institutions alone. Not everyone liked this arrangement; Czech nationalists forever begrudged the privileging of the kingdom to their south. 'Emperor' reminded them all too much of the Habsburg ruler who had suppressed their ancestors in the seventeenth century. 'We have our own fatherland and king', the great Czech Romantic poet Karel Hynek Mácha had written; his compatriots would revive the claim after 1867.[27]

Unlike its immediate predecessors, however, the 1867 agreement did have some staying power. True to form, the emperor adjusted his personal preferences to the conditions specified in the agreement. Aside from within his house, his absolute authority was significantly constrained, both in Hungary and the non-Hungarian or Austrian part of the monarchy.[28] In 1868 the latter received a genuinely progressive constitution that mandated equality before the law, freedom of the press and other basic civil liberties. Property and educational requirements continued to limit the right to vote for local representative bodies, but they were gradually loosened in elections for the imperial parliament. By 1908 the vast majority of adult males could vote. In Hungary, however, the nobility that dominated the kingdom's assembly restricted the franchise far more selectively.

Franz Joseph also had to trim his notions of dynastic monarchy and the tactics that would position it within the social and economic realities of his time. Industrial capitalism, with all of its advantages and its drawbacks, had taken a firm foothold in several regions of his empire, most notably in eastern Austria and several locations in Bohemia. A substantial entrepreneurial class had developed as well. With banks to extend credit and guide investment strategies, their owners and shareholders had amassed sizeable profits for funding urban building booms that altered cityscapes, not only in Vienna and Prague, but more modest locations too. The court itself cooperated with some of these projects. From 1867 to 1896 Franz Joseph authorized his major-domo (*Oberhofmeister*), Prince Constantine Hohenlohe-Schillingsfürst, to intervene in major land use projects. From 1867 to 1896 he frequently consulted with planners of Vienna's Ringstrasse, the circumferential thoroughfare that replaced the medieval walls still separating the centre of the city from the surrounding outer districts. Franz Joseph himself endorsed the design.[29]

That same prosperous and educated middle class, however, had sparked the mid-century revolutions. The emperor's greatest concern, therefore, was to reconcile himself with its individual leaders and the political constituencies for whom they spoke. The bourgeois students of 1848 had demanded a formal voice in formulating government policy, especially where finances were concerned. They were also interested in government jobs. Maria Theresa and Joseph II had admitted commoners into the higher reaches of their administrations and the privileges that went with such positions. Franz Joseph both followed the policy and expanded it. Though he restored a stricter dress code than Joseph had developed, he bestowed the title of Privy Counsellor (*Geheimrat*), previously associated with the nobility, on middle-class officials as well. For its part, the public happily collected state distinctions of any kind, even though the privileges attached to them had vanished with the formal installation of equality before the law. A new and generously distributed title, *Hofrat* (Court Counsellor), was also available for members of the middle class who reached the higher ranks in state and court bureaucracies. Basic rules of direct access to the court (*Hoffähigkeit*) continued to depend upon extensive and high-born lines of familial descent, but it was clear that performance and not social background would determine most of Franz Joseph's hiring decisions.[30]

Although strong parliamentary systems never took hold in either half of the Dual Monarchy, the civil liberties guaranteed in the Austrian Constitution of 1868 had been on revolutionary middle-class agendas throughout most of Europe for decades. Where Franz Joseph's position and that of his house were not directly in question, he respected them. He personally moved forward progressive policies such as expansion of the railways, the adoption of the metric system and education for women, all of which helped to rearrange traditional societies and economic behaviours in his lands. Those with property continually received exquisite consideration in the monarchy's post-1848 constitutional experiments. Delegates to the Imperial Council (Reichsrat), in place for a short time after 1861, were chosen by provincial estates organized in four divisions based upon the size of the imposts levied on each member. Those who owned little or nothing were largely exempt from direct taxes, but they had no one who spoke primarily for them in Vienna.[31]

Alterations to the political landscape of the Habsburg lands, however, especially in the Austrian half, did not end with the recognition of the middle classes as serious political players. Throughout the later nineteenth century the parliament in Vienna, under liberal leadership, was badly divided. Parties were little more than opportunistic factions and national disagreements, especially over language policy, occasionally brought the entire institution to a standstill. Far more dynamic were two more ideologically driven mass movements, both of which had begun to speak for the disadvantaged classes in the Austrian half of the Habsburg empire. Arguing for the appallingly housed and meagrely paid proletariat were the Marxist Social Democrats. For the artisan, seriously disadvantaged by the mass merchandise coming to market thanks to industrial capitalism, there was the Christian Social Movement that took its doctrinal cues from Roman Catholicism. The central concern of its founders was that Marxist calls for the abolition of private property would drown out alternative positions in the growing debate about social and political inequality throughout the empire. Rural common folk, enjoying free use of their lands after the end of serfdom, would add significant support to the cause in the near future.

Neither party was willing to abandon the Habsburg *imperium*. The Social Democratic dream of spreading their programme throughout central Europe was predicated on the existence of a large working class that the empire had conveniently united. Doing military service between 1889 and 1898, Carl Renner, one of Social Democracy's leading and most enduring voices, was astonished to hear a Hungarian conscript say that Franz Joseph's idea of a unitary monarchy was fiction. The Christian Social Movement also had some loudly patriotic voices. Nevertheless, regardless of the stand either group took on the existence of Habsburg rule, Franz Joseph and his governments could not afford to ignore their manoeuvres. They could, on occasion, be usefully played off against one another or against other troublesome actors in the Habsburg realms. They could also, however, create unwelcome tensions. Here, contrary to his behaviour in economic and educational matters, Franz Joseph did his best to keep his distance. His answer to party politics was to place himself above their controversies. It was a pose that the press picked up and publicized lavishly in his lifetime.[32] It also walled off him and his successor from some of the pressing issues of their time.

The Emperor in the Lives of Others

By 1910 the total population of Franz Joseph's empire was close to 50 million people.[33] Neither he nor members of his dynasty, who stood in for him more frequently as he aged, could be everywhere at once. The emperor himself was legendarily attentive to government papers; images showing him working in his study were among the most widely circulated from the end of the nineteenth century though to the First World War. As scandalous speculation raced through the empire after his son, Archduke Rudolph, killed himself and his teenage mistress on 30 January

1889, the father immersed himself in documents at his desk and dispatched government business as if nothing had happened.[34]

Conscientious though he was, Franz Joseph could not master the volume of material by himself, much less digest and act on it. By the second half of the nineteenth century, however, he could make himself felt in his lands through his bureaucracy, the closest that most people would ever come to the imperial presence.[35] It took centuries for the delegation of responsibility to act as surrogates for rulers to take hold in the Habsburg domains; it took just as long for the people whom they ruled to accept the practice. Throughout the eighteenth century provincial estates in the dynasty's lands insisted that a ruler appear before them personally to discuss affairs of state in which they had some constitutional role, fiscal affairs and taxation above all.

After 1848, however, the practical responsibilities of governance were increasingly in the hands of officials charged with specific administrative portfolios and supervision of their subordinates. Most salaries were far from remunerative; with eleven grades after 1873, there were substantial differences in pay between the lowest and highest ranks. Promotion was slow at best and limited at worst. The process itself could be a Kafkaesque nightmare; candidates might be evaluated not only on the formal requirements of their job descriptions, but on criteria that had not been disclosed to them. Few minor officials ever became ministers and provincial governors (levels one and two). Those whose education never went beyond primary school would never go far. The great majority of civil servants (*Beamten*) were in ranks ten and eleven, and more than a few could not live on their incomes.[36]

Nevertheless, even these positions in the Habsburg monarchy had positive features, beginning with open access. Though practice could fall short of principle, criteria for appointment and advancement were engineered to rule out political, personal and local considerations. Those in government position, regardless of rank, also acquired a social status far above the one into which many had been born. Some would eventually join the so-called second society, people who were near the court, if not automatically entitled to direct entry. Franz Joseph was not beyond acknowledging officials with whom he had personal contact if he spotted them on the street. He also involved even the lowliest among them into celebrations of himself and his house. At Langenlebarn in Lower Austria, where Habsburg forces had once prepared to meet the Turks embarking on their last siege of Vienna, an obelisk was erected in 1882 to commemorate 600 years of Habsburg rule in Austria itself. It was dedicated by

Franz Menschiga, the stationmaster of the imperial-royal railway in the town, along with the imperial-royal postmaster, Emil Hollitzer, and the builder, one Bruno Grossman.[37]

The strict educational qualifications required to rise in the bureaucracy brought greater opportunities for schooling among the Habsburg peoples as well. University enrolments increased steadily after 1857. In Hungary, where public schooling had a later start than in the Austrian provinces and Bohemia, the process took longer to take hold, but once off the ground it moved quickly, especially at its higher levels. By 1914 the University of Budapest was the second largest institution of its kind in the monarchy and the fifth-largest university in Europe.[38] With better-trained personnel readily at hand, the bureaucracy of the Austrian half of the Dual Monarchy alone grew exponentially. Excluding low-level functionaries in the railway and postal services, it numbered 136,000 persons by 1890; ten years later it had grown to 201,000 and by 1910 to 247,000. Bohemia had an especially sharp increase, even though no major offices of central government were headquartered there.[39]

Absolute loyalty was a condition of employment; after 1849 criticizing the Habsburg regime risked dismissal. Franz Joseph's subjects were always clear on whose behalf his civil servants were acting. Few were as explicit as the resident of Linz who put an enamelled plaque on the front of his home telling passers-by that an 'Imperial-Royal Provincial and Superior Provincial Justice and Court Councilor' (*K.k. Landes-bzw. Oberlandesgerichtsrat und Hofrat*) was within. But bureaucrats large and small were expected to behave at all times as representatives of a man who held uniquely high office. Even if they chose to remain silent, the emperor expected them to look the part.[40] Dress codes were strictly monitored, regardless of the fiscal strain they put on some lower officials, who had worn uniforms provided by their sovereign since 1814; green was the required colour, with different coloured frogging to distinguish between ranks. Franz Joseph limited mandatory use of his prescribed court dress to special occasions and holidays, but his officials were nonetheless expected to outfit themselves as befit a government professional, regardless of their income. The poorer among them borrowed to cover the cost of suitable clothing, promising creditors that future salary increases would cover their debts. Those who were caught hurrying repayment along by taking bribes lost their chance for promotions and the larger salaries that went with them. As government-chosen role models for the mass of society, bureaucrats and their families were also expected to maintain appropriate households, again a costly undertaking in expensive cities like Prague. Even when settled in comfortable quarters, family life was not easy. Frequent postings and repostings to sites throughout the monarchy found these people often setting up new households. Children were especially disadvantaged as they were shunted from one school to another well into their teens.[41]

By the beginning of the twentieth century, the behaviour of civil servants was becoming more difficult to control. Coming to marriage with more education, wives, for example, were increasingly curious about what their husbands did all day to require such sacrifice and supervision.[42] For those on the receiving end of bureaucratic imperatives from afar, Vienna's regulations could seem an unnecessary and sometimes ludicrous intrusion on traditional practice. Joseph Roth, born in Habsburg Czernowitz, now in Ukraine, conjured up such a scene in his 1937 satirical novel *Das falsche Gewicht* (*The False Weights*). Into a remote village on the easternmost fringes of Habsburg Europe comes a bureaucrat charged with supervising the veracity and accuracy of weights and measures. Residents had always made these calibrations through approximations to body parts: hands, feet and the like. Everyone roughly accepted a system that allowed for a little flexibility, otherwise known as cheating. Now, however, real scales would be used. The change arouses fear and resentment rather than support and understanding; total uniformity is especially threatening. As local folk spend more time circumventing regulations rather than observing them, the master of weights and measures (*Eichmeister*) disintegrates psychologically. A man of genuine goodwill, he cannot tolerate a nagging antinomy: laws have to be broken in order for people to live happily. Moreover, his assistants happily drink with local people, take the little bribes they offer and communicate with them in ways that the master of weights and measures cannot.[43]

For all the indignities, however, that employment in the Habsburg bureaucracy brought with it, its functionaries remained true to the dynasty privately and publicly, even well into the First World War. It had given them a more secure life, along with improved social standing, than many would have had in earlier times. It also had its pleasures. Moving from post to post over the polyglot ethnic map of the empire proved to be an educational experience that young people never forgot. That the niceties of child-raising went ignored was almost beside the point. The unsettled world of central Europe after 1918 would give such people even more reason to think kindly about Franz Joseph, and his family, perhaps for longer than they should have. The same feelings took hold among the general population of the monarchy. Lethargic, insensitive, even ridiculous though Franz Joseph's ministers and minor functionaries might have been at times, their flaws were often the outcome of poor organization.[44] Even as the monarchy came to its contested end, its bureaucracy retained its reputation for integrity. This was one of the kinder judgments among the many handed down about Habsburg rule.

Enlisting the Young

The reach of public media into all levels of society in the nineteenth-century Habsburg empire greatly eased Franz Joseph's task of legitimizing his rule. The emperor's forerunners, especially Francis I, had already experimented with several of the themes that were developed and stressed after 1848, and the Habsburg subjects were spared the hard work of internalizing an unfamiliar message.[45] Government-sponsored publications that argued for Habsburg sovereignty in perpetuity continued to appear, often in eye-catching formats. The most elaborate of these ventures was the lavishly illustrated *Die österreichisch-ungarische Monarchie in Wort und Bild* (*The Austrian-Hungarian Monarchy in Word and Picture*), which came out between 1885 and 1902. One of its strongest initial supporters was Archduke Rudolph, who had hoped, or at least had informed his father, that the project would both further scholarship and promote the sense of oneness among all the dynasty's peoples. Subscriptions were kept inexpensive enough to be within the means of a broader public. Audiences of scale could now receive venerable stories of dynastic benevolence and military triumph in illustrated newspapers and popular journals as well as by attending occasional open-air ceremonies.[46]

A vast body of commercially available literature followed suit, with Proschko's *Perlen aus der österreichischen Vaterlands-Geschichte* (*Pearls from the History of the Austrian Fatherland*) a typical product. Though some of his text is more explicitly Catholic than dynastic, its focus is on the House of Habsburg from Rudolph I to the reign of Franz Joseph. Embarrassingly awful verse cameos extol each ruler, each of whom appears at least once in the book. Joseph II, epitomized as 'Mankind's Hero', performs good deeds such as writing chemists' prescriptions for the ailing. Francis I is hailed as the First Bureaucrat and Arch Financial Custodian of his lands. Helped along by the strong support of Vienna, he is lauded as the man who steered his lands through Napoleon's occupation of the city in 1805–6 and restored order once the French left.

Recent Habsburgs are charitable too; Proschko points out that heir apparent Archduke Rudolph had given money to an impoverished family in Prague. Advances in art, science, industry and material infrastructure under the rule of Franz Joseph are glowingly acknowledged; family members themselves turn up in remote places on scientific excursions. A riff on the flora and fauna of Madeira claims inspiration from Empress Elisabeth, whose alleged passion for natural history (and not her distress over her husband's military embarrassments in Italy) had taken her to the island. Such passages were intended to inspire the love of learning among the young. The dynasty also offered examples of life's terminal realities. Proschko gives a riveting account of Empress Maria Theresa gasping futilely for breath in her last moments. The story had real staying power; it also appeared in Jordan Kajetan Markus's *Historical Pictures from the Austrian-Hungarian Monarchy for School and Home.*[47]

Nevertheless, audiences for both images and the printed word were normally self-selected and unpredictable. Not everyone appeared at celebratory occasions; not everyone participated in arranging these events, even when urged to do so; not everyone scanned the same newspaper at the same time. To last in popular memory over time, the dynasty's preferred vision of itself and its rule had to be articulated, heard and repeated in an optimally didactic setting.[48] It was therefore in public-school classrooms that loyalty to the House of Habsburg could be most effectively developed and learned. A law issued in 1869 had made eight years of basic education mandatory throughout the empire. The number and variety of secondary schools grew substantially as did the size of the student population enrolled in them. More than 90 per cent of all children in the monarchy were receiving elementary education by the beginning of the twentieth century.[49] The most vulnerable captive audience of all was now available for dynastic indoctrination.

Franz Joseph figured actively in the educational culture of his lands. His signature, along with those of two of his officials, appeared on the table of organization drawn up for the Technical College (Technische Hochschule) in Graz in 1872. With the state the final authority in edu-cational matters after 1868, he laid down the general parameters for those charged with carrying out policies he endorsed. Upon recommendations from responsible ministers, the monarch named university professors; the former alone were responsible for appointing faculty members at lower ranks. Their sovereign's habit of reading documents closely forced all of his high officials, including those administering academic affairs, to think twice about what they set before him in writing.

Franz Joseph generally tolerated radical academics and teachers, so long as they expressed such views in private. The details of individual disciplines did not interest him, but he was familiar enough with new subjects to recommend adding them to curricula. He financed some schools out of his own funds. The emperor or his family surrogates opened and celebrated countless educational facilities at all levels. Museums put the dynasty on show too. Making the point as clearly as he could, the emperor stood before a statue of himself at the opening of the Graz Technical College in 1888.[50]

Education in the Habsburg lands changed greatly in the second half of the nineteenth century; new schools for females and trade academies were only two of several examples. The dynasty was not always able to capture this new audience as completely as it wished. Two consistent sources of contention were the role of religion in primary instruction and the teaching language at all levels. Especially in the Austrian half of the monarchy, national preferences were increasingly respected. Mother tongues replaced German in secondary school classrooms and in university lecture halls throughout the monarchy. In Bohemia, the use of Czech as an instructional language reached even beyond native users. In some regions of the country all pupils could be taught in Czech, so long as the majority in a given district spoke it.[51] Nor were curricula completely immune to the political pressures that had become a fixture in the monarchy in the second half of the nineteenth century. National and social-democratic educational perspectives crept into classrooms throughout the monarchy as they did in Europe as a whole.

Neither of their messages, however, touched youthful minds quite as relentlessly as the propaganda about an allegedly depoliticized ruler and family, which was concocted in Vienna, then promoted by Franz Joseph's governments through closely monitored school texts, even after 1869, when commercial firms were allowed to publish them. Teachers had some discretion in their choice of materials, thereby introducing a degree of competitiveness into the marketplace, but it was in no one's interest to cast doubts on the legitimacy and quality of the emperor, his family, or those who served them in any way.[52]

The educational bureaucracy, therefore, remained true to the basic purpose of the system in that it managed to assure continuity of a pan-imperial and centralized system turning out people ready to work in the occupations for which they had been trained. They were also to be loyal to their land, their emperor and the house that had generated him, aside from whatever subordinate identity – religious, ethnic or political – that they might acquire. Though the ideal was sidelined occasionally as the teaching staff bickered over job security and compensation, its basic substance remained intact.[53]

If Franz Joseph expected formal loyalty from teachers, he wanted unqualified approval from pupils and students. Both groups were encouraged immediately after the revolutions of 1848 to read the history of the dynasty that ruled them as the House of Habsburg wished it to be known. Books awarded to especially industrious young people abounded in praise for the emperor and his family. Classroom experience underscored the message. Hung just below a crucifix on the wall behind a teacher's desk, the emperor's portrait scrutinized boys and girls throughout the empire. From the time they started school they sang 'Gott erhalte': its text and the monarch's name were to be found at the back of children's primers. History entered the curriculum by the third year. Content varied from land to land to conform to local experience, but lavish helpings of Habsburg biography were routine.[54]

Although the text of the approved Habsburg narrative was simple, it did require serious, sometimes nuanced thought. Graphic technologies created and refined between 1850 and 1914 enabled students to learn about the dynasty's virtues and heroic past without turning a printed page. Reproductions of wall paintings were placed in schools throughout the monarchy to help youngsters follow their teacher's presentation. A great deal of expert time and attention went into the content and design of these materials. Academics, painters, publishers and bureaucrats wrestled with philosophical challenges such as striking a credible balance between fact and aesthetic imagination in historical imagery.[55]

The tone and content of schoolbooks were even more problematic. While primarily intended to shape the beliefs and thinking of children, they were likely to be read by parents and other family members. Texts, therefore, had to take account of adult scepticism. The *Manual of General History* (*Lehrbuch der allgemeinen Geschichte*) by Anton Gindely, a noted and erudite Czech historian, was as dull as the title promised. It was, however, factual and impartial, qualities that might persuade mature readers to accept the dynastic narrative behind the text. It was widely used not only in academic *Gymnasien*, but in vocational schools. It was also translated into the various languages of the Habsburg lands. For those of all ages looking for a more 'lively understanding' of their ruling house, the regime in 1884 recommended biographies. Maximilian I, Maria Theresa and Joseph II were again favourite figures.[56]

Teaching manuals were also designed to tell the story of the Habsburgs and their lands positively, but even-handedly. A history of the Austrian-Hungarian monarchy published in 1906 for future classroom instructors balanced hard, and sometimes embarrassing, data with the celebratory. The author, Theodor Tupetz, allowed that the dynasty had been often humiliated by Napoleon I, but there was much in the dynasty's history to offset such dark moments, especially in the eighteenth century and after. Maria Theresa received accolades for bringing her lands out of the Middle Ages, Joseph II for his abolition of serfdom. In fact, the book lavished attention on the monarchy's political advances over more than a century. Schoolbooks in the Habsburg lands continued to stress this theme down to 1918 and in the Austrian republic after the First World War.[57]

Boys and girls learned the history of the monarchy and the ruling house quite differently, especially at higher levels. Once they reached secondary school, young men studied 'dynastic' history, meaning war and politics. Females were assigned more culturally orientated material, a practice that distressed some young women who thought they should know something about politics and military affairs too. In fact, children of either sex were equally likely to want to know more about their monarch and his house, especially when their parents reinforced the attitude by example. Scenes of adult loyalty to individual members of the dynasty were enacted in the homes of civil servants before offspring who never forgot what they saw. One girl, Claire Mollik-Stransky, recalled how much she was moved by her father's emotional report of standing face-to-face before the emperor to receive the Order of the Iron Cross, Third Class. A wealthy industrialist from Bohemia, who had a second successful career in finance, he once told his family that he took a bank post in Vienna rather than St Petersburg or London 'because of his [elderly] mother and because of a certain Franz Joseph!' Nor was the latter the only Habsburg who shaped his behaviour. His daughter also had vivid memories of a ritual he observed each time he cantered into the Imperial Riding School, which he was permitted to use. Following required protocols, he raised his hat and his whip to the portrait of Charles VI, who had commissioned the hall, before beginning his routine.[58]

School vacations did not remove the emperor and his house from children's lives. Lorle Schinnerer-Kamler, another daughter of a civil servant, reported that the only time that she and her siblings got out of dirndls and lederhosen at her family's summer quarters in Lienz in the

East Tyrol was to mark Franz Joseph's birthday in August. The monarch himself was physically far away, usually at his own summer residence in Ischl, but the youngsters nevertheless knew that they had to be on their best behaviour all day: for the celebratory Mass and homily, speeches at the family dining table and other ceremonial moments. Dressed in summer white, they also had to keep themselves spotless. The absent emperor put his stamp on climatic conditions as well; because the event almost always took place on a bright and sunny day, it was repeatedly deemed *'Kaiserwetter'*. Children even fantasized about their ruler. A little girl in Hermannstadt (Sibiu in modern Romania) dreamed that Franz Joseph personally sent her a school stipend she received twice a year. She laughed at her behaviour years later, but said that she firmly believed it at least once in her life.[59] Thus, as a close student of Franz Joseph's era has eloquently put it,

> As the decades passed, generation after generation of Habsburg citizens read of the emperor's childhood generosity, his bravery in battle, his family tragedies, and his eternal commitment to improving the welfare of all his peoples. Millions attended local celebrations of the emperor's birthdays and bought commemorative publications lauding the deeds of the emperor.[60]

Whatever reservations critics of Habsburg purposes and their manipulative strategies have expressed over time, it could never be said that the House of Austria neglected cultivating the admiration and respect of their peoples. Indeed, they saturated the environment of their lands with their past, present and even future in ways that more than a few could not forget.

Inspiring Adults

The innocent plasticity of young children made them vulnerable to what they heard in their schoolrooms about their emperor and his family. Such flexibility endured through adolescence, but with one important change: the discovery that one could think for one's self. Not only in schoolbooks did Franz Joseph's regime confront the problem of shaping a positive image of itself that mature people could accept. In the past, the dynasty's close connection with a widely accepted religious faith added extra-dynastic reinforcement to the monarchy's political legitimacy. Franz

Joseph himself recognized that the effectiveness of this relationship had passed its peak. His bureaucracy, of course, did become an institutional emblem of his reign. Nevertheless, for all of their conscientiousness and steadfast loyalty to their ruler, officials great and minor lacked the charisma that nurtured permanent commitment to the ruling house in Vienna of Habsburg-Lorraine among its subjects.

Franz Joseph had but one overarching institutional ally to speak for his unifying duty to his peoples: his armed forces. They were ideally suited for the assignment. If nothing else, their presence assured the degree of order in the monarchy's lands that many longed for after 1848, when compromise and persuasion did not always dampen unwelcome popular demands. Officers from the eighteenth century on were often very close to the court, proof positive to the public that the two worked hand in hand. Like the bureaucracy, the Habsburg military was supraregional. Unlike the bureaucracy, however, it drew upon the entire male population of the monarchy, the largest audience for indoctrination a government could possibly capture. Military activities were reliably photogenic, ideal for the pictorial propaganda that all classes of society understood. Indeed, the possibilities for public visual encounters with the army were ubiquitous in exhibitions and other displays of Habsburg military uniforms, military insignia and emblems, medals and similar distinctions. Many of these were reproduced in a variety of publications, all of which embodied Habsburg military culture for most of the monarchy's subjects. Military service also offered what the dynasty considered useful moral lessons: self-sacrifice, loyalty, courage, obedience and, never to be trivialized, fear of God. The Habsburgs also had a proven knack for using both victory and defeat to enlist the support of their peoples: the dynasty lost as many battles against the Ottomans as it won and the Seven Years War ended with Vienna yielding control of Silesia to Frederick II of Prussia.[61] In each case, however, the monarchy's hold on its peoples was solidified. Moreover, Franz Joseph did not have to invent demonstrations of his closeness to his armed forces and his need for them. The shifting political environment within his monarchy and Europe generally favoured wholehearted support of military infrastructures. Italy and influence in Germany, after all, had been lost to him in combat. Even without any propagandistic intent at all, the young emperor from youth to old age had little choice but to make his army a central institution of his regime and to fix it centrally in the larger culture of the empire.

Visuals underscoring this message appeared even before the insurrections of 1848–9 had ended. Images of the dynasty and its rulers in military settings and costumes quickly became as common as accounts of Habsburg benevolence in schoolbook history. The transfer of power to Franz Joseph in the company of his three counter-revolutionary generals – Radetzky, Windischgrätz and the Croatian commander Joseph Jelačić – was a favourite pose. A reactionary journal, *Die Geissel*, published a version in 1848 that showed the new emperor and his three commanders standing resolutely over a grovelling worker and a member of the student Academic Legion.[62]

Guided by such principles, Franz Joseph's regime transformed the army into the epitomes of order and supranationality that the dynasty wished the domestic and foreign audiences to see. Even the erratic Archduke Rudolph agreed. Writing in 1886 to his uncle Albert, a veteran of military service to the house, the heir apparent called the armed forces the last institution that held the empire together. Whether any civilian agent could have accomplished the task without the coercive discipline of the officer–conscript relationship remains an open question. But the goal of turning the armed forces into a source of universal pride and admiration throughout the monarchy was relentlessly pursued. Monuments to military heroes, from the ruling family to other, and far greater, commanders, were erected throughout Vienna. An equestrian statue of Archduke Charles appeared near the Hofburg in 1860; Eugene of Savoy would be standing close by after 1865; Prince Carl Philip Schwarzenberg, who led the Coalition armies to victory over Napoleon at Leipzig in 1814, was installed on an eponymous square in the city centre in 1867. By the end of the century, Radetzky and Archduke Albert had their monuments too. Franz Joseph himself was universally recognized throughout his lands as a ramrod-straight man in a military uniform.[63]

Publications galore explained Habsburg military culture and its history to the general public. One of the most elaborate examples, warmly received by the emperor himself, was First Lieutenant Querin Leitner's *Gedenkblätter aus der Geschichte des kais. kön. Heeres vom beginn des dreissigjährigen Krieges bis auf unsere Tage* (*Memorial Pages from the History of the Imperial Royal Army: From the Beginning of the Thirty Years' War until the Present*), which went through two editions, the first in 1865. Its chief attractions were 42 lithographs. These, said the proud publisher H. Martin, were largely reproductions of pen and ink drawings by earlier artists that were now housed in the galleries of 'important people'. Almost all of them were battle scenes; those featuring the anti-Ottoman campaigns in Hungary and Balkans in the seventeenth century were especially dynamic. Habsburgs themselves appeared in only six of the scenes, no surprise since the family had produced few major battlefield commanders. The dynasty's famous generals, however, were prominently positioned in 23 of the plates. With no apparent objections about the secondary status accorded to the House of Habsburg-Lorraine from the current ruler, Martin worked overtime inventing ways to circulate the work as widely as possible. Prospective readers did not have to buy all of the illustrations at once; less well-to-do subscribers could purchase one lithograph a month for three florins. An explanatory text would be supplied for a price still to be set.[64]

Field Marshal Radetzky became the embodiment of military best behaviour; young cadets were advised to take him as their role model. Books and illustrated calendars devoted to him were coming out by 1859. Not everyone bought the message; on the Italian peninsula, where he had once crushed resistance to the Habsburg regimes, Radetzky and his troops were parodied in a publication with a picture captioned 'the fatherly Austrian regime'. The irony was not altogether misplaced. Nevertheless, Franz Joseph did develop some reputation for paternal regard for the men who served in his armies, especially officers whose debts he occasionally paid off from his private incomes.[65]

He also used his well-promoted fatherly relationship with military men as leverage in mending his relations with regions of the monarchy he had punished during the 1848 turmoil and after. Royal coronations in Hungary and Bohemia had historically been moments for new monarchs to extend amnesties. Once the Dual Monarchy was agreed upon in 1867, Franz Joseph accepted the Hungarian crown and the ceremony that went with it in Buda. The affair itself was breathtakingly opulent. Nevertheless, the now official ruler took time to remember the situations of Hungarians who had served in the military. He set up a charitable foundation for Hungarian veterans in his armies and for widows and orphans of men who fought in defence of Hungary's reform and revolutions in 1848–9. As king, he took the opportunity to grant pardons to Hungarian revolutionaries who had fled abroad in the immediate aftermath of the tumult.[66]

One of Franz Joseph's subjects memorialized the ties of army and dynasty in a uniquely spectacular form. Joseph Pargfrieder, a supplies contractor to the Habsburg forces in 1848, donated a substantial portion of his income to developing the Heroes Mount (Heldenberg) in Kleinwetzdorf, the Lower Austrian village where Radetzky was entombed. Both the park and its display of military statuary were tributes to the common army and the supranational Habsburg state. Coming hard upon the suppression of northern Italy and Hungary in 1848 and 1849, however, it could easily be construed by visitors as a testimonial to the dynasty's triumph in a civil war, one that made plain that the Habsburgs would uphold that communality by force when more conciliatory tactics failed.[67] Read either way, the Heldenberg underscored the centrality that the military had assumed in the dynasty's self-imaging, even in the eyes of a man with only marginal connections to the court.

With so much at stake, Franz Joseph's regime outdid itself to ensure that the army would remain loyal both to ruler and the house that produced him. The introduction of formal military conscription throughout the Dual Monarchy in December 1868 maximized the dynasty's opportunities to drill men from all regions and classes of society in 'patriotic socialization'. The Army Law called for an annual troop levy of 95,000; this number was raised to 103,100 in 1889. The normal period of service would be three years. People with money, education and influence were soon able to cut that back by two years. The new rank of 'one-year volunteer' (Einjährige-Freiwilliger) was made available to men with secondary and higher education certificates. To qualify, however, they had to volunteer to serve that single year rather than waiting to see if they were drafted. But even short training periods were enough to indoctrinate the more privileged in the lessons of fealty to the emperor and his house. Like all soldiers, they wore 'the Emperor's uniform'. They took oaths of personal loyalty to the monarch, they obeyed commanders who were their sovereign's officers. They were also unlikely to forget the message once they left the working army for the reserves. The dynasty actively intervened in veterans' associations to bolster loyalty to the monarch and the message was repeated time and again.[68]

Many young men were delighted to escape such duty, even when major physical disability was truly the reason. But, as was the case with positions in the civilian bureaucracy, military service in the emperor's forces had potential advantages that made the indoctrination more palatable, even credible. Advancement for most in the officer corps depended not on nationality, religion or social class, but on universally available education. Quick-witted and ambitious conscripts from modest corners of the provinces occasionally turned their service to professional good use. Young František Kašek from Moravia toured much of the European and Mediterranean world, courtesy of the imperial-royal navy. Technically and musically gifted, he was assigned to a music division that gave him the opportunity to learn several instruments. His experience brought him jobs wherever he went throughout his life.[69]

Through such policies, the dynasty went far towards realizing the political goal that it had hoped to reach through a standing army drafted from all the lands of the monarchy. The ethnic make-up of the Habsburg army at the beginning of the twentieth century reflected the diversity of its peoples. Out of every 100 men in an army regiment, there were, on average, 25 Germans, 23 Magyars, thirteen Czechs, eight Poles, eight Ruthenians (Ukrainians), nine Serbs and Croats, seven Romanians, four Slovaks, two Slovenes and one Italian, a mix that the Vienna regime quite intended. A few 'national regiments' did exist, but they were not the rule. Some concessions were made to native tongues; while German remained the idiom of command, officers whose regiments had ethnic minorities of 20 per cent or more were expected to have some facility in their languages.[70]

Wars and the negotiated peaces that followed had dulled some of the Habsburg monarchy's lustre. Nevertheless, over the decades between 1848 and the beginning of the twentieth century, Franz Joseph and his governments had done a great deal to secure his rule through strategic, if grudging, compromise, a measure of attention to the material needs of the monarchy's peoples, and a relentless programme of keeping itself public. Real or vicarious, the emperor's constant sovereign presence throughout his lands quieted all questions about his unorthodox accession to power. The support he had cultivated in his bureaucracy, the armed forces and the educational system not only identified him with three widely respected institutions of his regime, but brought him closer to the thousands of people who were active in them as agents of the emperor himself or simply beneficiaries of his programmes in the schoolroom. That he and his advisers were committed to retaining as much as they could of the Habsburg ceremonial tradition in no way interfered with publicizing them through modern techniques such as photography. The emperor was also willing to soften the image of his house as a bulwark of Roman Catholicism, a step that was positively received by religious minorities, even though they never quite lost their second-class cultural presence under Habsburg government.

The loyalty to himself and his house that Franz Joseph was promoting through such policies had clearly solidified since 1848. It had yet, however, to be rigorously tested. No one had probed to learn how deeply the common soldier had internalized, rather than just heard, the message of house and unitary state before nation. How persistently could Franz Joseph's administrators throughout his lands, at both high and low levels, turn a deaf ear to the concerns of local interest groups when pressures from central government became unusually intense? Propagandized schoolchildren could always change their minds in the face of political, social and economic circumstances that gave the lie to what they had heard long ago in schoolrooms. More importantly still, Franz Joseph and his regime might not yet have identified all of the monarchy's important constituencies or, if they had, were ignoring on principle those they disliked or simply did not understand.

SEVEN

ALTERNATIVE NARRATIVES, COMPETING VISIONS

Rumbles in the House of Habsburg

Conflict between rulers and their heirs apparent on matters of policy and behaviour was routine in dynastic monarchies. Most Habsburg monarchs marked time patiently for the day they would become emperors and kings, but some could not wait to get started. Maximilian I and Maximilian II openly criticized their fathers' cautious stewardship of their realms; Joseph II chafed under the supervision of his mother for the same reason. Franz Joseph, however, soldiered twice through much anguish with incompatible successors, only to see both of them die horrifically. The bizarre deaths in 1889 of his son, Archduke Rudolph, and the latter's sexually precocious inamorata Mary Vetsera at a hunting lodge in Lower Austria, became one of the dynasty's tawdriest public scandals. Adultery was bad enough – Rudolph was married – but suicide and/or homicide were worse. Christianity strictly proscribed such behaviour.

The court worked hard to rewrite, or at least heavily edit, the story that got out to the public. Doctors who autopsied the archduke's corpse eventually fell into line, reporting that the emperor's heir apparent had been out of his mind when he killed the girl. The diagnosis was toxicologically credible: Rudolph drank heavily and took lethal doses of opiates. Few accepted such a flimsy exoneration and the dynasty had every reason to keep the affair out of the headlines. Authorities hastily buried Mary in the cemetery at Heiligenkreuz, not far from where her life had ended. Nevertheless, continued evasiveness in official circles only heightened the insatiable Viennese appetite for gossip, especially about men and women in high places. Coverage of the affair would remain sketchy in the local public press; foreign periodicals, however, were under no local constraints. It was not long before their accounts of the crime and their commentary reached the Habsburg lands, where they circulated widely.

Franz Joseph was shocked and deeply hurt by his son's behaviour, but relations between the two men had always been strained. The emperor had often identified himself with progressive policies, but generally out of necessity rather than conviction. Known to harbour some liberal sympathies, Rudolph lived in constant fear that his father would one day learn what he occasionally thought. Open support of political programmes from a member of the house ran counter to the suprafactional public persona that the emperor was cultivating. The heir apparent also criticized his relatives. Scornful remarks about the bureaucratic mannerisms of an uncle, Archduke Albert, who had dedicated much of his mature life to keeping the Habsburgs morally and militarily fit, were especially unwelcome.[1] About the only advantage Franz Joseph managed to draw from the affair was the outpouring of sympathy from his subjects, many of whom had also lost sons from natural causes or in military service.

Archduke Rudolph's death forced another consultation of the family genealogy to locate an heir apparent. The emperor still had two living younger brothers, both of whom were clearly unacceptable, though for different reasons. The first of them, Archduke Charles Louis, was deemed unfit for the job in just about every important respect. He was inflexibly conservative, especially in religious matters, and had no interest in military affairs. Next in line was Archduke Louis Victor, who was, if anything, a greater public embarrassment than Archduke Rudolph. A habitué of brothels and seedy drinking establishments, his family had banished him to an out-of-the-way castle near Salzburg.[2] The role of heir apparent thus fell to Archduke Franz Ferdinand, Louis Victor's eldest son and Franz Joseph's senior nephew. Unlike his pious father, he was very energetic and interested in the job. His morals and confessional practice were all that his house could have asked for. As a future ruler, however, he turned out to be as emotionally and politically problematic for his uncle as the late Archduke Rudolph. Franz Ferdinand tried hard to avoid disagreeing openly with the emperor. Nevertheless, he firmly believed that Franz Joseph's stolid reliance on temporizing to relieve conflicts small and large throughout his lands might postpone doomsday for the House of Habsburg-Lorraine, but not prevent it. Franz Ferdinand was also highly critical of the lumbering bureaucracy that was now the central arm of the emperor's government. He cultivated a circle of men who increasingly believed that the monarchy needed proactive leadership ready to shake up established administrative structures that impeded change of any kind. Such ideas and Franz Ferdinand's identification with them unsettled the emperor's court officials. Diagnosed with tuberculosis in 1895, the archduke suspected that some of these men were secretly pleased that he might be out of the way very soon.

Nevertheless, it was the heir apparent's marital preference that most soured his relations with his uncle. By 1898 Franz Ferdinand had made plain that he was determined to wed Countess Sophie Chotek, the daughter of a reputable Bohemian noble house, but lacking the number of bloodlines that qualified her to be the wife of a Habsburg emperor-king. In a heated letter to Franz Joseph, the archduke declared that he could not marry any other woman. Early personal experience had taught Franz Joseph much about the trouble that succession controversies could bring to his family. He reluctantly consented to the union, but only after his obstinate nephew swore on 28 June 1900 an Act of Renunciation that removed his children from the line of future Habsburg rulers. The nuptials took place four days later. Sophie was honorifically titled Princess of Hohenberg, but the episode strained relations between her husband and his uncle even more.[3]

Franz Ferdinand would also take partisan positions in the empire's national squabbles, about the worst thing he could do to a ruling house supposedly serving as hereditary mediators-in-chief for peoples competing for territory, public space and government preference. Charges that the Habsburgs were undermining their subjects' indigenous political and cultural traditions and languages had grown even louder by the end of the nineteenth century. Close observers of political life in the monarchy noted that the dynasty might be falling prey to the same process that by 1878 had ended Ottoman control of Greece, Serbia, Bulgaria and Romania. Disputes about language and language usage were ceaseless.

German remained the nearest thing to the lingua franca of the Dual Monarchy lands until 1918.[4] Even in Bohemia, where the two large and linguistically defensive communities rubbed up against one another continually, significant numbers of Czechs and Germans remained stubbornly bilingual, often out of economic and social necessity.[5] Still, common sense was no obstacle to wrangling over administrative and instructional languages, especially when nationalist ideologues drove the discussion. Rancorous debate on mandatory use of Czech and German in the Kingdom of Bohemia perverted legislative life in the Austrian half of the monarchy until its dissolution. In 1897 the Reichsrat, or lower house of parliament, reached an impasse over ordinances applicable to Bohemia that gave Czech linguistic parity with German in certain bilingual districts of the kingdom. With all efforts at compromise failing, the controversies over the issue ruled out interfactional cooperation, much less majority government. After 1907 Franz Joseph chose ministers regardless of the party for which they spoke, conducting the business of state, in effect, largely from the throne. Measures were enacted through ministers who brokered the cooperation of elected representatives. The latter, in turn, came away with useful favours in return for their vote.

These issues troubled Franz Ferdinand as much as anyone who had a stake in the monarchy's survival. He was also quite sure that he had identified the chief cause of national dissent in the Habsburg lands: their division into Austria and Hungary, Franz Joseph's most far-reaching compromise to keep the Habsburg *imperium* intact. The privileging of Hungary above all other peoples angered many, especially Czechs who had long sought the same status for the historic kingdom in which they lived. The archduke characteristically judged people, groups and states on the basis of their attitude towards Habsburgs and the Habsburg monarchy; he admired Romanians after the kind reception given to him and his wife when they visited the new King Charles. Hungarian magnates, on the other hand, some of whom had supported anti-Habsburg sedition, were, in his words, on the same level as 'Jewish, Masonic elements'.[6] He was also very critical of Hungarian determination to force their tongue on other linguistic communities in the kingdom: Romanians in Transylvania, Serbs in the southeast and Croats in the southwest. Most menacing of all to nationalists, both in Budapest and the countryside, was Franz Ferdinand's alleged sympathy for federalizing the monarchy, a step that would have reduced Hungary to one among many states under Habsburg rule.

Reconciling Hungary

Just what would have persuaded ardent Hungarian patriots, who ranged from great magnates to the country gentry and a number of bourgeois intellectuals, to renounce constitutional exceptionalism in the Habsburg empire remains a historical unknown. Hungarian politicians knew well that their homeland was not the only part of the empire to have serious differences with the dynasty that ruled them. Even as regimes in Budapest tirelessly defended their national and historic identity and the symbols that bespoke it, their Czech counterparts were behaving in much the same way. Having removed the paraphernalia associated with the Crown of St Wenceslaus to Vienna in 1848, supposedly for safekeeping, the Habsburgs repatriated it when the political situation in Bohemia became calmer. Nevertheless, Franz Joseph would never consent to a coronation in Prague, a stance that opened him up to repeated charges that he was neglecting his prescribed duties in the kingdom.[7] Czechs, Poles and Italians also had arguable linguistic grievances that arose from the same nineteenth-century romanticism that inspired Hungarian national radicalism.[8]

Each of these nations, or those who served as their surrogates, started by assuming that their land was 'exceptional' in their own opinion and in the mind of their sovereign. Nevertheless, the litany of Hungarian complaints about Habsburg misrule was somewhat longer, more deeply felt and culturally omnipresent. Most prominent among them were the suppression of Protestantism, the dynasty's enduring ambition to curb the powers of historic estates through greater administrative centralization and the vicious suppression of the Hungarian 1848 revolt. Resentment of Habsburg behaviour worked its way subtly into the nomenclature of urban subdivisions. Vienna's eighth district is the Josephstadt, Budapest's eighth district the Józsefváros. The eponymous 'Josephs', however, are two men and not one. The Vienna version refers to Emperor Joseph I, who brought the Rákoczi uprising to an end; the Budapest counterpart was Archduke Joseph, a son of Leopold II, who was Emperor Francis I's popular and progressive Hungarian regent in the first half of the nineteenth century.[9]

Hungarians would reach a modus vivendi with the other Habsburg peoples and the ruling house, especially in non-political settings. The Hungarian national novelist Maurice Jókai and Vienna's Waltz King, Johann Strauss, collaborated on the text and music for *The Gypsy Baron* (*Der Zigeunerbaron*), a melody-packed operetta first performed in Vienna in 1885. It drew on not only the Austrian waltz and the Hungarian slow-fast *csárdás*, country-tavern dance music that Strauss had already exploited in *Die Fledermaus* (1874), but Bohemian polkas and Polish mazurkas too. A proscribed political tune crept in as well. The 'Rákóczi March', composed by a Hungarian, János Bihár, in 1809 and then rearranged for maximum firepower by Hector Berlioz in *The Damnation of Faust*, had taken on associations with several Hungarian uprisings against Habsburg rule. The Vienna regime forbade any performance after 1848. Diluted a tad by some softer Viennese strains, it met no official objections; *The Gypsy Baron* was an instant and lasting success: by 1900 there had been 300 performances in the Austrian capital and 100 more in Budapest.[10]

An equally benign take on Hungary dominated Imre Kálmán's *Die Csárdásfürstin* (*The Gypsy Princess* or *Csárdás Princess*), which confirmed early nineteenth-century Austrian stereotypes of Hungary as an idyllic rural outpost free of the uglier side of industrialization. A melange of Viennese sentimentalism and propulsive Hungarian rhythms, it played in both capitals of the Dual Monarchy throughout the First World War, even as local commitment to the dynasty's war efforts faltered. The production also crossed enemy borders, in this case to stages in St Petersburg and Moscow, between 1915 and 1917.

The monarchy's dominant composer of operettas, Franz Lehár required no collaborator to authenticate the pan-imperial status of his work. Indeed, he personified what has unofficially been called Habsburg 'nationality'. Born in Moravia, probably of Slavicized German extraction, he was the son of a military bandmaster whose postings took him from Komárno (Hung. Komárom; Ger. Komorn) to Cluj (Hung. Kolozsvár; Ger. Klausenburg) to Prague to Sarajevo. The young Franz initially followed in his father's footsteps, leading instrumental groups assigned to towns and garrisons in Hungary and in Vienna. Like other army musicians and conductors, he was required to be familiar with various styles of popular music throughout the empire and to be alert to shifts in public tastes. All of this training was put on display in *The Merry Widow* (*Die lustige Witwe*), which opened in Vienna in 1905. Though notes of social and political criticism ran through its text, the score gave the monarchy a kind of unity that had defied its politicians. Waltzes, polkas and mazurkas were effortlessly harmonized; dance music imported from the ballrooms of Paris made an appearance too. Clearly Lehár's masterpiece, it had been performed 400 times in Vienna and 150 in Budapest by 1915.[11]

Hungarians were never without some sense of political and social commonality with the Habsburgs. Relations between individual members of the dynasty, other than Maria Theresa, and the Hungarian political class were sometimes even cordial. A cardinal example was Archduke Joseph, who as governor of Hungary received the traditional title *nádor* (palatine) the following year. His progressive outlook paralleled views held by some influential members of the nobility in the kingdom; like them he recommended new transportation technologies and promoted Hungarian cultural facilities such as the National Museum, National Library and National Theatre. Joseph's advocacy of partial sovereignty to the kingdom would eventually be realized in the 1867 compromise. Following his death on 13 January 1847, he was designated an honorary Hungarian. A committee immediately came together to sponsor the statue of him that was unveiled in 1869 in Pest, an area that he had wished to see developed. No regime since then has removed it.

Though it snubbed other national movements in the monarchy, the Dual Compromise did in fact stabilize Hungarian–Habsburg relations considerably. With control of domestic affairs largely in their hands, the influential few who shaped Hungarian politics now had reason to become committed monarchists: many among them recognized that they owed their social, economic and political positions to their ruler. Franz Joseph and his successor Charles I (IV of Hungary) actually increased their numbers. By the last two decades of the nineteenth century, between them they had handed out 200 patents of nobility and 4,000 honorific service titles. In rural areas where kings had sometimes acted as the protectors of peasants, support of the dynasty continued to be strong.[12]

Direct criticism of the monarch remained illegal in Hungary. Nevertheless, Franz Joseph actively worked to develop more positive impressions of himself and his family with his ethnic Hungarian subjects. All the traditional symbolic gestures available to him as king were called upon to erase bad memories of his rule, especially his crushing of the revolution in 1848–9. His gaudy coronation in Budapest in 1867, an event made possible only by the Dual Compromise, was a high point of his career. He took the opportunity to atone for his earlier behaviour. Amnesties were granted to Hungarian prisoners of war taken in the mid-century upheaval; exiled revolutionaries who pledged loyalty to their now-legal sovereign were offered repatriation. Franz Joseph and Empress Elisabeth also redirected the 50,000 gold coins, traditionally presented to new monarchs by the 'nation', to invalids, veterans, the widowed and orphaned. For a Hungarian millennial exhibition in 1897, he commissioned ten historical paintings associated with Hungarian history, though one, the defence of the fortress of Szigetvár against the Turks in 1566, stressed the loyalty of Hungarians to the Habsburgs, and not the larger history of Hungary.[13]

Nevertheless, Franz Joseph's greatest asset in winning the goodwill of Hungarians was neither history, himself, nor his office, but his immediate family. Archduke Rudolph had acquired a cult-like nimbus throughout the kingdom, especially among its woefully downtrodden peasantry, who believed he sympathized with their plight. His death in 1889 ended those hopes, but by that time his mother, after 1867 the queen of Hungary, had long since pre-empted him front and centre in

Hungarian imaginations. Familiarly known to posterity as 'Sisi', Elisabeth was nature's gift to Habsburg public relations. The persona she acquired encouraged even the humblest of her husband's subjects to read their own joys and sorrows into hers. Seen in retrospect, she ranks among the foundational figures of European celebrity monarchy. Habsburg Galicia, for example, an area that Elisabeth never visited, reacted with notable collective intensity to news of her assassination in 1898. But it was in Hungary where a cult-like admiration for her really took hold. Hungarians converted their queen's rushed return to Vienna from the kingdom in 1857 to be with her dying eldest daughter into a national family tragedy. Her name and image in Hungary would become an unavoidable element in everyday life. Bridges, charitable institutions and public square statuary commemorated her in town after town and in cities. Hotels and restaurant signs bore her name, as did utilitarian facilities such as grain elevators. More widespread still were likenesses of her and her husband on trinkets and pictures hung in even remote countryside homes. Reproductions of Franz Xaver Winterhalter's stunning portrait of her (1864) were found throughout Hungary and the entire monarchy.[14]

Strikingly beautiful as a young woman, Elisabeth battled the inroads of age at least to a draw. Franz Joseph was certainly witness to the effect she could work on Hungarians during the visit the couple made to the kingdom in 1857. Daughter near death or not, Elisabeth appeared in Hungarian national costume cut low enough in the bodice to challenge all known laws of gravity. Still, a note of remoteness that appeared in many of her portraits was perhaps a way of signalling that she had more on her mind than her physical appearance. She was sincerely curious about Hungary in ways that local political and cultural leaders endorsed and respected. A committed amateur in the Hungarian language, culture and history, she read serious books in Hungarian and named her second daughter Gisella after the wife of Hungary's first Christian king, Stephen I. Even without constitutional powers, she developed important informal contacts with major Hungarian political figures such as Julius Andrássy, who had helped to cobble together the Dual Compromise and from 1871 to 1879 was Franz Joseph's foreign minister. The emperor assigned her the job of discouraging Hungarian cooperation with Bismarck during the humiliating Austro-Prussian War of 1866. The birth in 1868 of the royal couple's last child, Archduchess Valerie, took place at the mother's request in the Buda royal palace. The little girl was taught Hungarian; she came to be known as 'the Hungarian child'.[15]

Sisi's person and presence thus played a major role in restoring good-will towards Habsburg rule among Hungarians. The general feeling, however, was never extended to her husband. Some obstacles to such ties were beyond Franz Joseph's control. While Hungary's situation under Habsburg rule may have been something short of 'exceptional', ethnic Hungarians were indeed distinctive enough to argue that they were in fact a community apart and should be governed that way. Their language was unique, even in the polyglot Habsburg lands. A Finno-Ugric tongue, it has a handful of vocabulary borrowings from various European idioms, but is grammatically and morphologically quite different.[16] Surrounded in their central European heartland by the far more numerous Germans and Slavs, Hungarians had reason to believe that their language and national identity could go extinct. They read their constitutional position among the Habsburg lands somewhat differently too. Charles VI's Prag-matic Sanction of 1713, which assured that the Habsburg lands would pass undivided through both males and females of the dynasty, was recognized by the Hungarian estates as a treaty of mutual defence, with their kingdom on one side and the rest of the Habsburg patrimony on the other. The provisions for hereditary succession to the Crown of St Stephen were also more qualified than in the dynasty's other holdings.

Moreover, Franz Joseph had done enough in his early career for Hungarians to continue thinking about alternatives to his rule. Lajos Kossuth, the chief spokesman for the Hungarian Revolution of 1848–9, took the Hungarian cause abroad, to be followed by several national partisans from the Habsburg empire to plead their individual causes in Europe and North America. Despite all that the king did to make amends for his punishment of the Hungarian national army and Hungarian revolutionary leaders in 1849, it was hard for many to forget. Not every-one was as extreme as a Hungarian apprentice tailor, János Libényi, who tried to assassinate the young monarch on 18 February 1853 (illus. 16). He apparently acted alone, but said that he was responding to Franz Joseph's draconian chastisement of Hungary and Hungarians four years before. His execution followed swiftly. The episode was taken as not only a sign of Hungarian bitterness against the emperor but of persistent revolutionary thinking in the kingdom.[17]

The Dual Compromise also left local power in Hungary where it had always been: in the hands of the landed Hungarian high nobility, which Archduke Franz Ferdinand mistrusted so deeply along, with the country gentry. Both groups were typically hostile to significant social reforms and eager to exercise as much control over Hungarian troops

16 J. J. Reiner, *The Attempt on the Life of Kaiser Franz Joseph 1 on 18 February 1853*, 1853, oil on canvas.

in the common army as they could. Such ambitions put the Hungarian parliament at odds with Franz Joseph more than once. An exemplary confrontation took place in 1907 over proposed military reforms. The Hungarians finally cooperated, but only after their king threatened to introduce the universal manhood suffrage recently granted for parliamentary elections in the Austrian half of the monarchy. The gesture won Franz Joseph some points among Hungarian socialists, who had been demanding reform of the very limited franchise in Hungary. It was anathema, however, to the kingdom's aristocratic political chieftains. They were equally alarmed by the Habsburg annexation in 1908 of Bosnia. Technically still a part of the Ottoman Empire, it had a large population of ethnic Slavs who would only increase the non-Hungarian speaking element in the empire.

Such tensions also persuaded Hungary's middle-class nationalists and many intellectuals to keep their emotional and critical distance from their ruler and his governments. A few politicians and bureaucrats refused to wear the medals that the government had bestowed upon them, even when they were expected to do so on special occasions. Display of the dynasty's black and gold flag on Hungarian public buildings and in public ceremonies was always contested, as was the singing of the imperial 'Gott erhalte'. Some of the forms in which Franz Joseph's name was incorporated into Hungarian daily life and conversation was a far cry from the Hofburg ideal. His Hungarian nickname, Ferenc Jóska, was incorporated into innumerable crude verses and songs. Pictures of 'Ferenc Jóska' showed him indulging in coarse pastimes, such as penny ante poker, or using vulgar Yiddishisms quite out of keeping with his august station.[18] More refined negative male stereotypes of the German in nineteenth-century Hungary had scrawny physiques topped by the doleful, elongated faces characteristic of several contemporary Habsburgs.[19] Correctly but not well dressed, they appear to have been inoculated against fun at birth.

Discontents Elsewhere

Hungarians may have had a more complex list of anti-Habsburg grievances than the monarchy's other peoples, but they were not alone in questioning long-standing relationships with Habsburg rule. In the Kingdom of Bohemia, speakers of Czech and speakers of German often disagreed publicly in evaluating the Habsburg contribution to their homeland. Each community had begun reading its own agenda into statues and monuments of Joseph II that they funded and erected throughout their land in the late nineteenth century and the early twentieth. Although both sides acknowledged his role in bringing necessary reforms to legal procedures and economic life in the kingdom, Germans came to identify with his controversial support of their language as the administrative idiom for the entire empire; Czechs criticized him for the same reason, along with his other centralizing policies. Sites memorializing him in Bohemia would remain flashpoints for conflict between Czechs and Germans after the end of the First World War and the founding of a newly minted Republic of Czechoslovakia. František Palacký, a founder of the Czech school of national history, had once declared that his nation's relationship with Germans had been a story of perpetual conflict and nothing would change it.[20] Such firmly fixed lines between peoples were wholly antithetical to the polity that Franz Joseph and his regime had in mind.

That German was the mother tongue of modern Habsburg rulers did not in itself win the dynasty automatic support from their natural linguistic community. Following Prussia's defeat of Austria in 1866, many ethnic Germans in the Austrian lands and elsewhere in the monarchy had growing misgivings about a house that did not always observe the liberal political ideals that many in the German upper middle classes still endorsed.[21] Moreover, in matters of public policy the Habsburgs held firmly to the position that Germans were just one among the dynasty's peoples with no claim to preferential treatment simply because they spoke the same language as their sovereign. The more vocal among them looked increasingly to Berlin for political and cultural cues. A large number of the empire's *Gymnasium* students joined various German national movements. Although most of these did not expand into full-blown public opposition to the dynasty, they reflected serious dissatisfaction with Habsburg reluctance to identify their house with the community to which it bore the closest ethnic affinity.[22] There were also hints that the indoctrination in the history of the dynasty prescribed in classrooms was turning some of them into critics, rather than supporters, of Habsburg rule, particularly in national matters. In 1887 a secondary schoolteacher from Styria told the Ministry of Religion and Education that such history could hardly pass as 'truth'. Uncritical celebration of the dynasty, he said, was just as unwise as dismissing criticism of it out of hand. Punishing such views – he appears to have tried it – was equally counterproductive.[23]

Franz Joseph thus still stood above his peoples, but the unity he sought to bring to them remained elusive. Political life in the Dual Monarchy remained perversely fractious, manageable, perhaps, only because it was routine. Efforts to win general support through cultural accommodation to the regime's nations had disappointing outcomes too. The most successful of the government's larger projects was the Imperial Museum of Fine Art. Opened on the Ringstrasse in 1891, it was planned as a monument to the care that the dynasty had lavished on a collection that was ecumenical from the beginning. Secondarily, it was to further scholarly research and the work of contemporary and future artists. All people with artistic tastes and talents could enjoy and learn from the facility, regardless of ethnic background. Experience with similar museums in other parts of the empire told different stories. Intended by Habsburg governments to advance the understanding of local national cultures, they ended in underscoring the divisiveness that challenged the monarchy as a whole. The Hungarian and Bohemian National Museums became not only repositories of regional artefacts but centres for promoting national identification.[24]

A small Academy of Art had existed in Prague since 1799, established by Francis I and funded by local patrons of high culture. Historical subjects that alluded to greatness and past independence soon became delicate themes. Some painters synchronized national concerns and those of Habsburg governments quite adroitly. Antonín Maček (1755–1844), for example, produced a series of small woodcuts depicting all the Bohemian kings down to Ferdinand V. Each was outfitted in a historical costume appropriate to the dates of their reigns. At the same time, the context in which they appeared was the Biedermeier-like family grouping that prevailed in Habsburg iconography after the Napoleonic wars.

Generally speaking, however, images taken from legends about the medieval royal Czech house of the Přemyslids, on view in the 1820s and '30s, bothered the government in Vienna considerably. So did venerable themes that were popular after the 1848 revolt in Bohemia had been stifled. Anti-papal Bohemian Hussites and Protestants became favourite subjects not only for Czech historical painters but their contemporaries in other countries of Europe throughout the last half of the nineteenth century.[25] Tensions between the Vienna and Czech schools of historical art increased correspondingly over the place of the dynasty in their work. Especially contested was the programme for fourteen paintings in the upper gallery of the sixteenth-century Belvedere Palace in Prague, which were completed between 1851 and 1865. The chosen subjects from Bohemian history had to suggest links to the Habsburgs and needed the approval of Franz Joseph himself. Acceptable themes included *Rudolph II Contemplating the Torso of a Classical Statue* and *Joseph II Distributing Alms during a Famine in Prague, 1772*. A depiction of the defence of Prague against the Swedes towards the end of the Thirty Years War looked reassuringly like views of the defence of Vienna against the Turks in 1683. For the fiftieth anniversary of Franz Joseph's accession, the Czech history painter Václav Brožík did a widely copied painting of Maximilian I's marriage to Mary of Burgundy. Intended as an allegory of the oneness of the Habsburg lands throughout the centuries, it pleased Franz Joseph enough for him to order it hung in the imperial painting gallery, available for all to see after the opening of the Art History Museum.[26]

National styles of architecture were also contentious. Long after Prussia's humiliating defeat of Franz Joseph in 1866, Habsburg regimes found North German 'Brickstone Gothic' (*Backsteingothik*) distastefully provocative. In Liberec (Reichenberg), a town in northern Bohemia with a large German-speaking population, the outcome of the Austro-Prussian War inspired construction of a town hall in a recognizably German historicist style that had unwelcome triumphal connotations for the local Czech population and the ruling dynasty. Progressive intellectuals and religious minorities throughout the empire did not like buildings that they connected to medieval Catholic obscurantism.

Objections could fade away spontaneously. Friedrich von Schmidt, the architect for the immense City Hall in Vienna, was heavily criticized for the Gothic Revival design of the building, which was completed in 1883: some said that it was openly anti-Habsburg. Nevertheless, it had important defenders among the city's liberal bourgeoisie, some of whom thought that it represented the freedoms allegedly found in medieval urban society.[27] The building stands as a striking testimony to Schmidt's personal vision, to what the Habsburg government frowned upon and to the role inertia plays in suppressing public controversy.

Political compromises could also be arranged in the building styles of the Habsburg monarchy, for example in the design of a social centre for Czech speakers in Brno, the capital of Moravia. The city had a large and prosperous German population, and its residents had often commissioned architects from Vienna (between four and eight hours away, depending on the railway timetable). The decision to go ahead with the project was taken in 1868; Theophilus Hansen, the Danish architect whose structures were lining the capital's new Ringstrasse, was hired to realize it. His models were the London clubhouses that he had designed, along with some of his residential structures in Vienna itself. Local contractors in Brno modified all of that. In the end, the exterior of the building was bland enough to disguise the fact that Czech culture was being promoted inside.[28] Its official name was the generic 'Club House' (*Besední dům*), although Germans called it the 'Slavic Club' (*Slavisches Vereinshaus*). Its close neighbour on one of the city's central squares was the German Gymnastics Club or *Turnverein*. At least from the outside, both fit comfortably into the inherited architectural styles of the city and many of the social values that it reflected.

After 1880, however, new controversies erupted for every compromise struck between nationally focused art and architecture in Bohemia and the supranational imagery that the dynasty in Vienna preferred. While the Prague territorial museum was structurally similar to the great museums of art and natural history in Vienna, the spirit in which each building was conceived and decorated could not have been more different. The cupola in the Vienna building celebrates Habsburgs from Maximilian to Franz Joseph. The Young Czech Movement and the artistic circles close to it began by demanding that only Czech sculptors and artists be commissioned for the work. Austrian history painters of the time could not have been more politically untrustworthy: *Rudolph of Habsburg Contemplating the Body of Přemysl Otakar* was a frequent subject in their work. The issue reached the Bohemian provincial legislature in the 1890s, with some members acidly pointing out that Vienna had better artists and museum holdings than Prague because art in the former was supported by the state and the ruling house. Overlooked were the contributions of leading Czech artists and sculptors to the Arsenal and the Parliament, both in Vienna. The walls, ceilings and staircase of the Prague museum would be devoted exclusively to Czech history and art. The style was extended to the inner pantheon, although busts of Franz Joseph and Empress Elisabeth were displayed in the Pantheon as patrons of Bohemian arts and learning. Nevertheless, a nearby lunette window depicting the mythic founding of the Kingdom of Bohemia by the Přemyslids created a palpable tension between the dynasty that once ruled the kingdom and the one embodied by the current occupant of the throne.[29]

Construction and reconstruction of the Czech National Theatre also turned into a contest between Czech and Habsburg identities that would shape the direction of Czech national art generally. The first building took 40 years to complete, but it was badly damaged by fire in 1880, soon after it opened. True to family custom, Franz Joseph donated 20,000 Gulden to the repairs; other members of the dynasty also gave substantial sums. Their gestures did little to resolve politicized disputes about the decor of the box reserved for the emperor and his house. The emperor's stubborn resistance after 1867 to an official coronation had sparked a prolonged debate in nationalist circles about the propriety and ornamentation of the space. The Bohemian provincial legislature eventually followed the path of least resistance, in part, perhaps, because it promised to cost less. The original decoration in the imperial box had withstood the conflagration quite well and it was decided to restore it, while acknowledging both the need to celebrate Czech culture and to confirm the realm's loyalty to the dynasty. The relevant political agendas, however, received their due: some images were bland tributes to peace to which no one could object, the imperial dynasty included; still others were allegories inspired by the Bohemian crown. National bias, however, was not altogether absent, however subtle its expression. Several visual references were made to the kingdom's independent historical past: the mythic Bohemia, a study of the royal Přemyslids in their era, an image of Emperor Charles IV. The paraphernalia of Bohemian statehood decorate each of them. But symbols of royal sovereignty are missing in the lone picture of a Habsburg Emperor, Rudolph II. In Spanish dress, he stares at a globe. The skyline of Prague is in the background, but his mind is on realms far from the one he supposedly governs.[30]

Stylistic disagreements between Czechs and Germans were even more rancorous in the construction of the Prague Rudolfinum, which opened in 1885. The model was the Vienna Künstlerhaus, which had been completed seventeen years earlier. Its Bohemian equivalent was intended as a mixed-use space for concerts, contemporary art exhibitions and a gallery with a permanent display arranged on historical principles. There was also a conservatory. The chief sponsors of the project were mostly Prague Germans and the board of directors of the Bohemian State Bank, who wished to commemorate their institution's 50th anniversary. Czech national spokesmen, however, resented the plan bitterly, calling it competition for the National Theatre. The eclectic facade of the building was said to be an insult to specifically Czech aesthetic standards.[31]

Ambiguities connected to association with the Habsburgs were even more pronounced in Hungarian architecture and art, and the sites where such artefacts could be seen. The kingdom did not have an academy for fine art until 1871. Once established, however, it became the gathering place for numerous history paintings, many of which were executed in the two decades after the suppression of the Hungarian uprising of 1848–9. Many of them not only downplayed the Habsburg role in the kingdom's history, but left it out completely. The discovery of the body of King Louis II after the Battle of Mohács in 1526 was frequently depicted, for example by Soma Orlai Petrichs (1822–1880), to suggest a form of grieving for the loss of the kingdom to the Habsburgs who followed. Franz Joseph himself tried to highlight moments when Hungarians had performed heroic deeds for his house through commissioning ten history paintings for the Hungarian millennial celebration of 1897. The gesture, though well meant, ignored local readings of the past.[32] Scenes of cooperation between dynasty and doomed Hungarian commanders like Miklós Zrínyi at Szigetvár never dispelled Hungarian convictions that it was they, and not their rulers, who freed them from Ottoman occupation.

In fact, even the military, the institution on which Franz Joseph was banking to embody and defend the unity of Habsburg rule, had a fractious side. Although Austria–Hungary's common army comprised men from a substantial cross-section of the monarchy's peoples, important segments of the society as a whole were abandoning lives of military service to their ruler and his house. Careers in business, finance, parliamentary politics and the learned professions had become increasingly attractive to even the great historical nobility who had once given the Habsburgs several significant commanders. Some aristocrats in Hungary, for example, had become spokesmen for patriotic causes including the development of a national militia, the Honvéd. Habsburg policy may have also accelerated the shift. The dynasty's long-standing campaign to open up high army ranks to merit rather than birth had compromised the aura of exclusivity that distinguished the nobility from other social constituencies. Every retired and pensioned officer received a hereditary noble title, even though this was legally meaningless after 1868.[33] Such distinctions, however, still played a serious role in the civilian pecking order of the Habsburg monarchy, leaving the 'common' army open to the charge of discouraging an influential part of society from military careers.

Nor did Franz Joseph's civilian subjects always share his construction of the common army as an agent and symbol of a united polity. Resentment of the Vienna regime was sometimes strong in towns where officers commanding garrisons differed ethnically from the local population. Some saw general military service strictly in terms of their own political advantage. Social Democrats coupled universal military obligations with demands for universal manhood suffrage. Others objected to armies on principle. Bohemian-born Bertha von Suttner, author of the worldwide best-seller *Die Waffen Nieder! (Disarm!)*, published in 1889, was a powerful voice in the international pacifist movement. Resentful of a regime that had drafted them in the first place, conscripts were often kept in line by brute force. Such feelings would become one source of dissent among troops during the First World War.[34]

Divisive wrangling also afflicted cultural undertakings that the dynasty hoped would remind its peoples of their long ties to the House of Habsburg-Lorraine and its armed forces and persuade them to let it continue. In 1863 Theophilus Hansen was commissioned to design and supervise construction of a museum on the grounds of the Vienna Arsenal. In addition to celebrating the feats of men at arms and those who led them, it was to memorialize Habsburg rule over the collected nations that the dynasty governed in good times and in bad. Military events would be frequently tied to individual commanders who had dedicated themselves to the dynasty's service.[35] The martial focus displaced the long-employed theme in past Habsburg iconography that many of Franz Joseph's subjects in the mid-nineteenth century could no longer swallow: the dynasty's close connections to the Catholic faith. Benevolent despotism was not stressed either. The Arsenal's permanent exhibitions covered historical weapons, battlefield mementos and the personal effects of military men.

Aesthetically and didactically, however, the central element of the concept was to be an intimidating Hall of Fame. Such a space would give 'judgmentally competent' (*urtheilsfähig*) persons from all classes of society the means to visualize the history that the planners wanted to convey. The purely decorative, wall-size history paintings and monumental sculpture would all play a role in the effort. Printed explications would be available for those who could not penetrate the symbolic or allegorical rhetoric of the installation.[36]

Completed by 1877, the interior of the museum stands today as a spectacular memorial to battles fought defending the Habsburg monarchy and its peoples. The process of realizing this vision, however, said more about fissures in Habsburg society than the solidarity that Franz Joseph was promoting. Although the official patron of the project, the emperor may have realized very soon that the goal was beyond his reach. He quickly delegated the oversight of details to appropriate ministers and other subordinates. They, in turn, seized every possible opening to advance their official and personal agendas: scholarly, political, military and national. Almost every constituency consulted for the scheme found fault with it, both in its planning stage and the finished product that eventually emerged.[37] The monarch himself and the historians who were advising him had crucial reservations about the first suggestions for a Hall of Fame. These came from the atelier of Carl Rahl, a well-known painter who made heavy use of classical and Romantic models. Anachronisms such as Habsburg forces in Greek and Roman battle dress bothered him not in the slightest. Neither did counter-realistic imagery. Facing his end before a sword-wielding Rudolph I, Otakar of Bohemia bares a buffed torso totally unlike the effeminate build and face that a medieval illustrator gave him. Franz Joseph's tastes ran towards the realistic; this was just the kind of imagery he deplored.[38]

Rahl's contribution to the museum was cut back to some ceiling frescoes. The emperor continued to ask for material that explicitly 'celebrated the history of Austria and its army', especially its exemplary suppression of the 1848 uprisings. Historians argued over that one too. All agreed that the exhibition should reflect the rigorous standards of documentation that Austrian historiography espoused in the latter decades of the nineteenth century. But they differed sharply on the qualities that made depictions of past people and events true to life. The 56 statues of major Habsburg commanders that line the vestibule of the building, the Feldherrnhalle, are an impressive reminder of persons who served the dynasty nobly.[39] They do not, however, exactly replicate the men whom they supposedly represent. And what should be made of Carl Blaas's gripping mural of Eugene of Savoy's crushing victory over the Ottoman forces at Zenta in 1697 (see illus. 7)? Do the agonized faces of the sultan's troops reflect their suffering and fear of imminent death or the artist's conviction that they should have felt that way?

Most off-message of all, however, was some of the imagery in the upper chambers of the museum. The central cupola in the great hall of the entrance focuses far more on the history of the Austrian lands than on the Habsburgs and the internal histories of realms that the dynasty had brought under its rule after 1526. The medieval Babenbergs, not the Habsburgs, dominate the panels in the dome: Leopold the Glorious founding the Ostmark; Leopold III, the patron saint of Lower Austria after 1663; Heinrich II Jasomirgott receiving the *Privilegium minus* from German Emperor Frederick Barbarossa in 1156. Modest pictorial references to Hungary and Bohemia have niches in the hall, but none are as eye-catching as those stretching over the central ceiling arched above.

High Aesthetics Go their Way

Until the mid-nineteenth century popular culture in Vienna, both high and low, respected the hierarchy of God, king, nobility and the varied commonality below as an existential norm. Although the themes for entertainment beyond the Habsburg court later grew increasingly independent of traditional authority, they continued to amuse people from all classes of society.[40] The dynasty had no reason to question seriously a model of society that placed it in the political category it believed it deserved. It certainly reinforced the idea that monarchs were entitled to cultivate aesthetic programmes that expressed the singularity of their positions, regardless of common tastes. Ruling houses generally expected the many artists, sculptors, composers and writers they engaged to accept this system and to realize the preferences of those who commissioned them.

From the fifteenth century on, the House of Habsburg had patronized leading artists and architects knowingly and lavishly – too lavishly at times for its resources. The Spanish branch of the family outstripped their Austrian cousins in taste and in funding truly great painters, but the Vienna Habsburgs did have some first-rate commissions to their credit. The latter also bought widely on markets throughout Europe. Their patronage of major musical talents, composers and instrumentalists alike, set standards aped by aristocrats and small circles of the wealthy middle class throughout the monarchy. By the end of the eighteenth century prestige-hungry instrumentalists and vocalists were begging for engagements at the Habsburg court. The dynasty's capital city would endure as a premier site – some would say *the* premier site – for music and musical performance from then until after the First World War.

Through the first half of the nineteenth century new styles in history painting, along with more socially broad-based themes, found their way without trouble into artwork supported by the dynasty. Not only did Habsburgs buy it, but they also exhibited it in the Upper Belvedere palace where the first imperial gallery was housed. The Imperial Academy of Fine Arts regularly mounted displays of new art. Yet, as Franz Joseph's long reign wore on, sophisticated outside observers such as the historian Heinrich Friedjung were noting that the court no longer had an influential advocate for the contemporary arts.[41]

Habsburg involvement with high literature had, in fact, always been spotty. Maximilian I had done all he could to immortalize himself in prose and verse. Daniel Casper von Lohenstein, arguably the leading dramatist of the German Baroque, dedicated some of his work to Emperor Leopold I and threaded allusions to the dynasty into both his plays and a posthumously published novel, *Grossmütiger Feldherr Arminius* (*The Brave General Arminius*, 1689–90).[42] Joseph II was a serious reader of both prose and poetry. Major writers worked and were published in the Habsburg lands, even in the intellectually restrictive years between the end of the Napoleonic Wars and 1848. But high literature flourished thanks to the support of the middle classes throughout the empire rather than the dynasty, its court and its administration. Francis II was more informed about his censors than he was about authors who worked during his reign. As Franz Grillparzer stood before him in an imperial audience, he asked the playwright if he was indeed the man whose play the imperial theatrical watchdogs had turned down. Thoroughly intimidated, the author grew ever more politically cautious as he aged. Whatever citations he received from the Habsburgs were decidedly second-hand. In 1865, two years before Franz Josef's brother Emperor Maximilian of Mexico was executed, he awarded the dramatist the Cross of the Order of Guadalupe.[43]

The word in printed form spreads more widely ideas ranging from the trivial to the hermetically exclusive. At the same time, it provides a platform from which readers can criticize, rethink, even reject those ideas. While censors find written materials easier to supervise than speech, the sheer quantity of what they must scan can be overwhelming.[44] Nevertheless, Habsburg rulers never quite gave up on controlling writers rather than identifying and rewarding outstanding ones. Ecclesiastical and secular authorities had begun watching with varying degrees of rigour over what was written in the dynasty's lands in the sixteenth century; their secular counterparts were still at it in 1918. Even as the Austrian constitution of 1868 affirmed freedom of speech and the press, Habsburg governments kept a close eye on what publishers were marketing, especially in popular newspapers and periodicals.

As a result the bourgeois turn in German literature and the liberal values it typically embodied came more slowly to Austria than the rest of German-speaking Europe. Programmatic statements of egalitarianism, especially of the political kind, were formally unwelcome at Habsburg courts. The dynasty's censors had been acutely sensitive to the radical implications found in several plays of the great German dramatist Friedrich Schiller. His *Wilhelm Tell*, drawn from a legendary story of a rebellion in rural Swiss cantons against Habsburg rule, was first performed in Weimar in 1804. It was several years before it reached Vienna, and only after it had been considerably sanitized – anonymously.[45]

Where the work of writers reflected some sympathy for the dynasty, the ruling House of Habsburg did, on occasion, recognize it. For a statue of Franz Grillparzer, who dramatized the coming of Rudolph I to the Austrian lands, the official patron was Franz Joseph's other-worldly brother, Charles Louis. Along with officers and people associated with the court, the archduke dominated the executive committee and evaluated the more delicate aspects of the project, which depicted the seated author surrounded by a series of reliefs drawn from his plays. These include the moment in *König Ottakars Glück und Ende* (*King Ottakar's Fortune and Fall*) when the kneeling king of Bohemia accepts his enfeoffment from the Habsburg emperor. Some official concerns about offending Bohemian national sensibilities still existed, but in the end the court gave in. Dynasty-related themes abounded in speeches delivered at the installation of the work in 1889.

By the last decades of the eighteenth century, however, ideas of universal civil rights had settled on Vienna and survived despite Franciscan obscurantism and decisive repression in 1848. The idea that the monarchy's peoples, particularly the educated among them, deserved some political role in the regime endured, and authors who represented these ideas became bourgeois moral and cultural heroes. In these circles, the House of Habsburg was increasingly marginalized. Celebrating Schiller in 1859, the Viennese *Bildungsbürgertum* (intellectual bourgeoisie) made clear how little they associated their sovereign with the liberal ideas the poet-dramatist continued to represent. Though the affair was officially under Franz Joseph's patronage, the opening remarks lacked the conventional professions of loyalty to the emperor or his house. The entire affair came off as a tribute to German culture and the values of the people who had contributed to it. The emperor did attend the unveiling of a Schiller monument in 1876, but Vienna's moneyed and educated citizenry once more set the tone of the festivities. One pavilion was reserved for the court; several for middle-class 'notables'. The two busts that flanked the statue after 1898 are of Anastasius Grün, a rogue aristocrat from the Auersperg family, who was a committed liberal, and Nikolaus Lenau, a Romantic poet and anti-clerical figure who had lived in Hungary for part of his life. The middle classes also made the politically idiosyncratic Beethoven their own. For all that the composer's major patrons were aristocrats and one extremely generous Habsburg, Archduke Rudolph, the youngest son of Leopold II, Beethoven's statue in Vienna, unveiled in Vienna in 1880, was a citizens' initiative.[46]

In fact, music, up to now one of the monarchy's least controversial diversions, was acquiring a partisan tone. Whatever messages it had sent in the past had been comparatively easy to supervise. The vast number of scores written for the Church followed prescribed texts and compositional rules. The expense of mounting operas and engaging trained instrumental ensembles could be met only by Habsburg courts themselves or great aristocrats such as Joseph Haydn's Hungarian patrons, the Eszterházys. Nobles were also typically eager to model their own musical entertainments on those played for their monarch and his family. Composers, librettists and performers had only limited control over their work: patrons could reject it quickly. Both professionally and psychologically, it was a trying environment for the truly creative. At the same time, the results said something about the sophisticated requirements of the institutions and men for whom composers turned out everything from Masses, symphonies and operas, down to supper music and garden

divertissements. That Gluck, Haydn, Mozart and Beethoven thrived in such a demanding environment is a tribute not only to the genius of these artists but the discerning tastes of their employers. The considerable talents of secondary figures such as Antonio Salieri, whose works were programmed throughout the nineteenth century in the imperial chapel of the Hofburg, says something about the musical acumen of their audiences too.

Public debates over musical styles were never unknown in the Habsburg lands, especially in major cities. Still, only in the second half of eighteenth century did national affinities come up in discussions of programming and performance practice. Even then it did not divide the

17 Hans Makart, *Emperor Charles v Enters Antwerp*, 1878, oil on canvas.

communities concerned. In Bohemia, both speakers of Czech and their German counterparts objected to the court's continued support of dominant Italian musical fashions. The cultivation of 'national' musical styles throughout much of the nineteenth century, however, would only underscore the divisions among its peoples that Habsburg regimes wished to downplay. Class sensibilities intruded subtly into musical life too. The wealthy and educated bourgeoisie of Vienna joined aristocrats and even the dynasty in sponsoring public concert houses: the stately building of the Society of the Friends of Music, which opened in 1871, and the Vienna Concert House, finished between 1912 and 1913, were underwritten by middle-class families, aristocrats and the dynasty alike. Nevertheless, when those same Viennese middle classes endowed their first statue for the newly constructed Ringstrasse, it was a likeness of the indisputably common-born Franz Schubert, who did not write for the court.[47]

Modernist thrusts in music also had publicly disruptive powers. On 31 March 1913 the auditorium of the Society of the Friends of Music offered a concert that included the chromatic and often craggily atonal work of Arnold Schoenberg, Alban Berg and Alexander Zemlinsky. Its sponsor was the Akademischer Verband, an alliance of avant-garde intellectuals, musicians, students, artists and architects, dedicated to 'doing things that no one else in Vienna dares to do', the only way, they contended, that art of the future would flourish. Not everyone in the audience, however, shared these convictions: the performance ended in a brawl that spilled onto the street.[48]

None of these disputes disturbed Franz Joseph unduly. Visual art, however, came much closer to touching his self. His private tastes ran to the realistic and representational, yet he was not the aesthetic reactionary some have made him out to be.[49] Beneath his unflappable public bearing lurked an experimental streak. He was a key supporter of Hans Makart, who designed and choreographed the imperial couple's silver wedding anniversary in 1879. Indeed, the emperor invited the painter to the city when advised by an aristocratic friend that Makart would liven up the art scene in Vienna. The monarch also arranged a workshop for Makart in the grounds of a one-time imperial cannon foundry in Vienna's Third District. Brilliantly coloured, audaciously sensual and sometimes very beautiful, his huge canvases covered the walls of the Viennese wealthy and their counterparts throughout the world, including New York and Philadelphia (illus. 17). One piece was awarded a gold medal at the latter city's centennial celebration in 1876.[50] Leopold I, the emperor who had scoured Europe vainly for a renowned artist to ornament his court, would have been a happy man, for all that Makart's frank eroticism might have strained his moral convictions.

Franz Joseph was also as committed as his predecessors to exploiting any aspect of the pictorial, both contemporary and traditional, that linked him and his subjects more tightly. For its part, the popular press, the great 'representer' of public life in his day, owed a great debt to the dynasty. It provided subject-matter for pictures galore and the respectful texts that accompanied them, provoking and satisfying ceaseless curiosity about the privileged, the powerful and the accomplished. Nevertheless, independent writers, painters, sculptors, musicians and even architects were cultivating new paying audiences elsewhere in the monarchy, especially among its high bourgeoisie. Such people were making it easier for artists in all areas of serious culture to live quite adequately without the dynasty's subsidies and the aesthetic constraints that often went along with them. Dependence upon the ruler-as-patron dwindled accordingly. Even when they enjoyed the support of the court, the most successful painters and sculptors felt secure enough to trivialize their monarch's attributes of power. Hans Makart's admirers once awarded him a mock sceptre that made him 'Ruler of Vienna'. In Habsburg Galicia, the history painter Jan Matejko was named 'Ruler of Kraków'.[51] For all of his sensitivity to the visual possibilities that the public media provided, along with countless official celebrations, appearances and the like, Franz Joseph's long reign would mark the waning of the dynasty's central presence in the high cultural activities of the empire. Moreover, many of the most creatively original minds among his subjects were preoccupied with themes and images that often challenged tradition, familiar historical themes and even the formal properties of the arts themselves. Very little of this promoted the bonds between the Habsburgs and their peoples.

The *Fin de siècle* Effect

Just why late nineteenth-century Vienna became an epicentre of aesthetic radicalism remains a debate in progress.[52] The phenomenon was not unique to the Habsburg capital. The sense of foreboding, the decadence of venerable political systems, the inadequacies of post-revolutionary institutions such as parliaments, and the effort to encapsulate these themes into art, music and literature, as well as to develop alternatives to what was vanishing, could be found throughout Europe.[53] Writers in Budapest, and more famously in Prague, struggled with these feelings in the newly inward forms of literature as much as their counterparts in Vienna. The existential anxiety that still unsettles readers of Kafka's *The Castle*, first published in German in 1926, probably haunted some Habsburg bureaucrats whose promotions were being decided on criteria they could only imagine. Conventional tonality in music was challenged by younger composers, not only in Franz Joseph's empire but also in France and the distant United States by Charles Ives.

Indeed, the extraordinary side of Vienna's emergence as a centre of progressive art and design may lie less in its originality than in surprise at its mere existence. Conventional stereotypes of Habsburg government in western Europe and North America had never been flattering. European liberals had sniffed mightily over the repressiveness of Francis I's government, which, rightly or wrongly, was often linked to Catholic obscurantism. That Charles Sealsfield (the pseudonym of Karl Postl) wrote in English as well as German widened the audience for his scathing criticism of the Vienna regime. Republican advocates on either side of the Atlantic deplored the brutal suppression of the revolutions in 1848–9 throughout the Habsburg *imperium*. Lajos Kossuth, the Hungarian radical spokesman, took his agenda not only to London but to the United States. There, counties and towns were named after him as a latter-day victim of the same type of colonial rule that had allegedly tormented colonial North America.

Nevertheless, much in the aesthetic and cultural context of Habsburg history foreshadowed colouristic experimentalism, the sinuous lines and the increasingly explicit eroticism found in high art in the later years of Franz Joseph's reign. Catholicism, particularly as renewed by the Counter-Reformation, translated sensory experience into a form of religious experience as a way of persuading Protestant defectors to rejoin the Church they had abandoned. Through Church-sponsored high art, Christians were to bond themselves emotionally to their Creator and the martyrs who had suffered in His name. The tactic was also useful in keeping the still-faithful true. The flowing lines of Baroque art were ideally suited to such subjects. Out of all of these tactics, it was hoped a human mind psychologically attuned to the goals of Church and state would emerge.

The idea that high art might perform that mission once again for the Habsburg monarchy never wholly vanished in the reign of Franz Joseph. An evening supplement to the moderately liberal *Neue Freie Presse* in 1865 argued that artists could help to solve a pressing problem in large and diverse states. The more heterogeneous a polity, the more necessary it was to create images that fostered communities of ideas, feelings and convictions within an existentially diverse public.[54] Like Francis I's regime, his grandson's government had tried to develop these sentiments through history painting and the museums they established, only in the end to find that the policy accentuated ethnic and national particularism. In the 1890s Franz Joseph's ministry of culture decided that aesthetic modernism could complement the universalistic aspirations and traditions of the House of Habsburg. The movement transcended national identification; artists and designers, in Vienna, for example, were following models taken from colleagues in Great Britain. Especially influential was the work of William Morris and the Scottish architect Charles Rennie Mackintosh.

Art and architecture would thus reinforce the process theoretically taking place in a conscript army: making many peoples one. An Arts Council that the government had created in 1899 heartily endorsed the styles of the contemporary visual avant-garde as a tool for promoting cultural unity. So did Wilhelm von Hartel, the responsible minister in the regime, who was a noted academic classicist. He believed sincerely in the programme and worked diligently from 1900 to 1904 to realize it. Significant writers offered their services. One was Hermann Bahr, among the most active public intellectuals and commentators of his time. Another was a versatile poet-dramatist, Hugo von Hofmannsthal, who was especially partial to the work of the Vienna Secession, which was at the forefront of pictorial modernism in the Habsburg lands. He had reservations about making the culture of the empire coextensive with the state, but put them aside, at least for the time being.

The Habsburg regime's relations with the more artisanal side of aesthetic modernism were generally cordial and mutually supportive. For Franz Joseph's Jubilee of 1908, the Imperial Ministry of Commerce invited Koloman Moser, one of the luminaries working in the Wiener Werkstätte, to design a series of postage stamps bearing the emperor's image. Moser's name appeared in the lower margin.[55] The interactions of avant-garde painting and sculpture and the crown, however, were far crankier. The emperor's preferences were no secret; even books that tried to bring him closer to his subjects mentioned his dislike of pictorial modernism.[56] In all likelihood, many of his subjects probably agreed. Archduchess Valerie had a hard job persuading her father to accept Moser's diaphanous males and females on the frontispiece of his jubilee book in 1898 (see illus. 14). He liked pictures, above all portraits, that faithfully reproduced what their subjects wore and how they appeared in real life. Painterly embellishment of these images was acceptable only when it improved already attractive features. He much admired the style and technique of Nikolaus Schattenstein, a Russian-American artist who earned his living by making good-looking people yet more handsome. His success, claimed the anonymous author who introduced a small catalogue of Schattenstein's work, came from his ability to please his clients. A picture mounted directly across from Franz Joseph's desk in the Hofburg epitomized his tastes: an elaborately framed Winterhalter likeness of Empress Elisabeth, which showed off her beauty but also her reluctance to commit all of herself to anyone.[57]

The emperor had no problems with the early work of one of Vienna's first and greatest Secession painters, Gustav Klimt. Between 1886 and 1888 he worked with his brother and a third partner on designing and executing the ornamentation for the interior of the new imperial court theatre, the Burgtheater. Although brilliantly adapted to indoor use, their models were still consistent with the neo-Romanesque or neo-Baroque facades that dominated the new Ringstrasse. The finished product brought Klimt a *Goldenes Verdienstkreuz* (Golden Service Medal) in 1888, the highest civilian order the emperor could bestow.[58]

From a practical perspective, however, it is difficult to understand how Minister Hartel persuaded himself that the highly allusive new aesthetic would bring large numbers of the poverty-challenged Viennese proletariat or rural labourers closer to the idea of the Habsburg state.[59] Even the most educated of the elite found radical reconceptions of human and natural form hard to swallow. Klimt himself brought the problem into broad public focus. By the time he was commissioned to decorate the ceiling in the Great Auditorium of the University of Vienna's new building, also on the Ringstrasse, he had jettisoned historicizing artistic conventions altogether for an explicitly contemporary imagery. He began the project in 1898. The finished work, which took six years, jolted the moral and professional sensibilities of numerous significant constituencies. Dominated by gossamer yet erotic female figures, the entire concept as realized was too undignified for the professorate. The German national Right and the Catholic Social movement both found it morally offensive. The vehement reactions from so varied a public shattered all hope that non-representational art might create a culture beyond factionalism and the passionate criticism that often went with it. That many remained silent as they viewed the work of Klimt and other aesthetic progressives did not mean they liked it. The Habsburg regime gave up. Speaking before the Reichsrat, culture minister Hartel dissociated the government from the work, leaving it up to the public to pass judgment.[60]

Klimt was not the only major artist to gain Franz Joseph's support, only to reject his sovereign's underlying political purposes. An impressive new Croatian sculptor, Ivan Meštrović was the son of a shepherd. He had, however, studied in Vienna and developed contacts with the Secession. On a visit to Zagreb in 1905, Franz Joseph had been pleased enough by a plaster group of a mother and child to order a copy in Belgian granite for his private collection. The emperor even lent it to the Secession for an exhibition in 1906. For all of his ruler's approval, however, in 1911 Meštrović refused to show his work in the section allocated to the Habsburg monarchy at an exposition in Rome. Rather he demanded that a space be created to display the art of South Slavs, his pieces included. When that condition was turned down, he and other Croatians asked that their work be exhibited in the Serb pavilion. Meštrović would spend most of the First World War in Italy and England, actively promoting the establishment of a South Slavic state.[61]

Franz Joseph occasionally saw eye to eye on aesthetic matters with the more discriminating members of Vienna's high bourgeoisie. One of Meštrović's most generous patrons was the industrialist Charles Wittgenstein.[62] Nevertheless, influential individuals and wealthy families took Hartel's advice to heart; they judged the value of modernist art and architecture independently of whatever they thought about Habsburg rule politically, socially or economically. That it caused the controversy and factionalism that were anathema to the regime was the government's problem and not theirs. It was Vienna's upper middle classes and their social counterparts throughout the empire and Europe that made Klimt and his two immediate successors, Egon Schiele and Oscar Kokoschka, eminent figures on the contemporary art scene domestically and abroad. Klimt was a favourite of the middle-aged and late-in-life wealthy. The same people patronized Kokoschka and Schiele too, although they sold their work to somewhat more varied audiences. Schiele had a somewhat younger following of his own generation that included art critics, academics, even railway civil servants. Kokoschka's early backers and advocates were largely intellectuals and other artists in the Habsburg lands, but also, very importantly, in Berlin. The relations of all three men and the circles within which they worked were anything but free of controversy. Convinced that great art was grounded in austere simplicity, the architect Adolf Loos held up Oscar Kokoschka as an example of how to paint without the heavy ornamental detail that made Klimt famous. All of them, however, circulated in an environment in which major artists no longer routinely served the court, along with the nobility historically tied to it, and the Church.[63]

Franz Joseph may have disliked Secession-influenced art, but he expressed himself politely on the subject. Archduke Franz Ferdinand frankly detested it, even when local artists did it. His own aesthetic was implacably traditionalist. He used Baroque models when he renovated the shabby interior of the Belvedere palace, which became his urban headquarters.[64] Whether he actually said, as some have claimed, that every bone in Oscar Kokoschka's body should be broken for some of his artwork, remains to be proven. Nevertheless, such a comment certainly came close to the spirit of his feelings. He blocked faculty membership at the Vienna Academy of Art for Albin Egger-Linz, who actually conformed to some of the archduke's criteria for good art; he had won a couple of state prizes for his uncommonly elegant renderings of rural life on canvas. He was, however, also a colleague of Kokoschka's in the Hagenbund, a group of artists who had rejected the intricate fussiness in some Secession imagery. By the time his appointment to the Academy had come up, his focus was on the drama and symbolism of line alone, in which human figures appear as schematic designs. Bitterly disappointed, Egger-Linz abandoned the imperial capital. Though he received considerable recognition in Austria after the war, he never forgot the insult.[65]

For all its efforts to distance itself from domestic partisan wrangling, the imperial government would be drawn in. Increasingly explicit erotic themes on stage and the moral outrage they aroused in some segments of the public forced authorities to tighten censorship. Monitoring theatres for crudity of all kinds was nothing new in Habsburg administrative and cultural history; Maria Theresa and Joseph II had done it programmatically in the eighteenth century. But the plays they were blacklisting were largely popular entertainments not to be confused with high culture. Franz Joseph's regime allowed an avant-garde troupe, the New Vienna Stage, to put on sexually controversial plays by the German Frank Wedekind, but only in closed performances. It flatly rejected the proposal for a Wedekind Week. In 1913 it also forbade performance of Oscar Kokoschka's *Mörder, Hoffnung der Frauen* ('Murder, the Hope of Women'), a brutal snippet of sadomasochistic histrionics that horrified many when it was given at the Vienna Art Show in 1909. Now that four years had elapsed, the authorities had enough time to decide it was pornography; appeals to reverse the decision were fruitless.[66]

Music and its texts, while less openly contrarian, often skipped mention of the monarchy altogether, even in contexts where it lurked in the background. Hugo von Hofmannsthal's tender look back on the Old Regime in his libretto for Richard Strauss's *Der Rosenkavalier* first and foremost dramatizes relations among the multinational commoners and nobles of the time in Vienna, its environs and the Austrian provinces. The Marschallin's dignified submission to generational and biological realities may seem more poignant because of her implicitly high social station, but rare is the woman of any class who has not been tugged by similar regrets.[67] Operettas, the entertainment staple of lower and middle classes alike, often poked quiet fun at sclerotic government bureaucrats, thick-headed police officials and monarchical establishments. Lehár's seductive *Merry Widow* is set in the Parisian embassy of the fiscally challenged court of Pontevedro, in all likelihood a fictional conflation of the Balkan mini-kingdom of Montenegro with Franz Joseph's operation in Vienna. Different though they were in size, they resembled each other strikingly after 1900. The coats of arms of each ruling house bore a double eagle; both polities were being sucked into the orbit of a united Germany; their parliaments were quasi-functional at best; and their foreign policies opaque to all but insiders. Political parties in the Austrian half of the monarchy were making many of these points quite openly, so they were all the easier to grasp when encapsulated in Lehár's seductive musical style. Debates over the expansion of the franchise in the Habsburg lands at the beginning of the twentieth century are briefly touched on as well.[68]

Expressions of radical dissent with the Habsburgs and the Habsburg system came especially often out of Hungary. Though writers in the kingdom did not directly challenge the monarchy, they criticized, and often despaired of, the class structure on which it rested. A frequent target was an aristocracy that relied upon kings to uphold its status. Even poets joined the chorus. Endre Ady, the master Hungarian lyricist, was also a prominent journalist. By 1914 he concluded that the Dual Monarchy was thoroughly corrupt both in Vienna and in Budapest.[69] The pessimism of his Austrian literary counterparts was more diffuse. Nevertheless, the inner lives of the self-absorbed people whom the very popular Arthur Schnitzler created both in fiction and for the stage are shaped by a social and political environment that they understand only in personalized terms. Many struggle with crippling indecisiveness; commitment to one another, much less to a political system, is alien to their make-up. Canards about the unity of Franz Joseph's lands are a minor element in the static that disturbs their minds and cuts off their willpower. The popular Viennese monologist Karl Kraus would say that he lived in the 'experimental station of the end of the world'.[70]

High literature, therefore, had less than ever to offer to a monarch and house that hoped to use the contemporary arts to explain its style of rule and validate the polity it liked to think it was ruling. Most dissonant of all, however, were changes in avant-garde painting and architecture that put both fields at odds with the representational imagery that the Habsburgs had long favoured in artworks and grand buildings. Erotic urges and demon-haunted psyches defined the men and women whom Klimt, Schiele and Kokoschka portrayed, and not their place in the political and social order that was part of their historical interaction with the dynasty. Indeed, the inward focus of their imagery had levelling implications quite at odds with the august public standing Franz Joseph wanted to maintain for himself and his house. Should artists depict a psychologically fragile member of the ruling house, such as Archduke Rudolph, in the same agonized postures as Schiele's more commonplace subjects, pretences of absolute difference between them would fade. More radical yet, artists and models with equally chaotic lives might come together in emotional transference, breaking through political and social distinctions between people, including those between rulers and the ruled. Schiele exemplified the threat. Neurotically self-absorbed, he was known to have drawn himself when he was ill at ease. He thus had little trouble in understanding the equally egocentric, but far richer, young Erich Lederer, whose family supported both Klimt and Schiele generously and commissioned a portrait of their son from the latter.[71] Unlike Maulbertsch, however, facing a much-reduced income without the patronage of Joseph II, Schiele would not be depending on the ruling dynasty for his compensation.

It was, however, in contemporary architecture where the images of power that Habsburgs had traditionally cultivated and new theory parted their ways most radically. Champions of Gustav Klimt and progressive architects disagreed on several issues, first and foremost the role of ornamentation in painting and building design. But the great challenge to the imperial house's preferences in building style and the message they conveyed came from Adolf Loos. Though professionally an architect, he was at war with everything that called upon history for inspiration but ended as what Germans so eloquently call *Kitsch* (trivial junk). Austrian arts and crafts, he said, had become utterly ridiculous 'by manufacturing Gothic suitcases, Renaissance hatboxes and Greek cigarette cases'. State schools for the applied arts had only encouraged this work. Modifications of old objects in order to adapt them for modern uses 'should cease and desist'. Loos respected great Austrian architects of the past, but on his own terms. In 1898 he praised his seventeenth-century predecessor Johann Bernhard Fischer von Erlach in the *Neue Freie Presse* for creating great structures from clay, limestone and sand when granite was not available to him. He was a '*king*' (Loos's emphasis) in the realm of materials, for he had mastered the use of them all.[72] Unmentioned was the Baroque architect's goal of creating buildings that would recall the power and grandeur of their owners in any age, rather than the technical ingenuity of the designers they employed. The author of a history of imperial architecture in world history that begins in the Near East and ends in Vienna, Fischer also had reworked any number of styles from centuries gone by into his own buildings.[73]

Time spent in Britain and especially in the United States had introduced Loos to using structural elements of buildings to express their function in their own time rather than remind viewers of past inhabitants and their status. He endorsed Franz Joseph's austere private habits, which met his standards of functional simplicity. Commenting on the exhibition planned for his emperor's jubilee in 1898, however, he wrote:

> The strong wind of America and England has . . . stripped me of all prejudices against the products of my own time. Totally unprincipled men have attempted to spoil this time for us. We were always supposed to look back; we were always supposed to take another age as our model. But all of this has now retreated from me like a bad dream. Yes, our time is beautiful, so beautiful that I could not see living in any other.

Such notions were a direct assault on the historicizing structures that the dynasty had commissioned throughout the centuries as memorials to itself, most recently on the Ringstrasse, where neo-Romanesque reminiscences of classical antiquity's greatest empire marked building upon building along the boulevard. All new architecture, he said, should be free of any personal and historical allusions that might divert eyes and minds from appreciating a structure as an autonomous aesthetic statement.[74]

Leading contemporary artists in the past had happily accepted commissions to configure the Habsburg programme visually, dramatically and musically; their counterparts in the late nineteenth and early twentieth centuries made the form of art itself and the inner lives of humankind generally the core of their work. Pictorializing the social, political, even the economic positions of patrons continued, but images now reflected the inner idiosyncrasies of subjects rather than their external persona. Distorted body lines and garishly pigmented skin and clothing were not the products of malicious artistic imaginations. What to Franz Ferdinand was insultingly ugly only reflected what was going on in the heads of artists' subjects. The archduke's reaction to Kokoschka and his colleagues was atypically forthright for a Habsburg speaking publicly. It did, however, make plain that a highly important member of the dynasty had little use for such work, regardless of who praised and bought it.

Readers only needed to leaf occasionally through Vienna's numerous daily papers or their equivalents throughout the monarchy to appreciate the variety of media that gave the Habsburgs public visibility. Surrogates throughout the monarchy published much the same material. Nevertheless, the dynasty was fast breaking its cultural associations with major artists and architects, whose counterparts in the past had been crucial to creating images of the ruling house. As Franz Joseph's regime had less use for them, they had less need of his patronage.

Adolf Loos went so far as to criticize buildings dedicated to the emperor and his house not only when they neglected his prescriptions for simplicity and contemporaneity, but also when they degraded natural landscapes. The construction of the Habsburgwarte, a faux medieval defence tower in the coniferous hills on the outskirts of Vienna, grated on all of his professional sensibilities. Commissioned by the Austrian Tourist Club in recognition of the fortieth year of Franz Joseph's reign in 1888, it became the orientation point for all surveyors working in the Austrian provinces.[75] That the structure was dedicated to his sovereign seemed not to bother Loos in the slightest. For him, along with other spokesmen for the progressive aesthetics of his day, the integrity of their work was their highest priority. They had alternative patrons ready to commission and pay them. That the dynasty was using other outlets to present itself to its peoples was welcome to popular journals and photographers, perhaps to the creatively gifted as well for the creative freedom it granted them. Now that one subset of subjects had decided that the dictates of their profession and the very integrity of their being were more important than cultivating relations with an establishment for which they had worked productively in centuries past, might not others with equally long associations with those close to the monarchy have reason to think the same? There were broad hints by the beginning of the twentieth century that some constituencies in the monarchy were doing just that, though not always with a clear sense of what might follow. The best possible policy for the House of Habsburg was to avoid provocative situations altogether.

EIGHT

BOSNIA AND AFTER

When Ceremonies Go Wrong

The assassination of Archduke Franz Ferdinand and his wife in the Bosnian city of Sarajevo on 28 June 1914 is the most widely known episode in the long story of Habsburg rule (illus. 18). People otherwise innocent of history will often refer to an 'archduke' whose murder, they think, set off the First World War. Journalists, scholars and politicians have yet to decide conclusively who actually inspired the crime, why the dynasty's heir apparent was killed, and how a good part of the known world would be drawn into what unfolded as one of the deadliest conflicts that Europe would ever impose on humankind.

Naive causal connections drawn between Franz Ferdinand's murder and the outbreak of the hostilities are actually not all that off the mark. Indeed, they suggest the context in which Franz Joseph and his closest advisers thought their way through to the declaration of war late in July. The ageing emperor neither forgave his nephew's morganatic marriage nor endorsed the latter's suggestions for reform of the monarchy. But the two men saw eye to eye on three crucial matters: both were devout Roman Catholics, both were committed to strengthening and preserving a unified Habsburg military force, and they were both wholeheartedly dedicated to the survival of Habsburg rule. Franz Ferdinand put personal preference ahead of bloodline obligations in choosing his spouse. Nevertheless, his decision had some bearing on his usefulness to his house. He could never, he said, adequately serve the dynasty without the woman he loved beside him.[1] Writing to Emperor Wilhelm II of Germany, Franz Joseph blamed the episode on anti-Habsburg Serb nationalism. Should the movement continue, it would 'represent a permanent threat to my House and my lands'.[2]

The archduke died carrying out one of the most familiar of all Habsburg rites: sharing their sovereign presence with their public. Franz

18 The assassination in Sarajevo of Archduke Franz Ferdinand and his wife, 28 June 1914, depicted in a contemporary Austrian newspaper.

Joseph had never abandoned the practice; by the end of the nineteenth century, his visits to urban centres were following a fixed script. Municipal officials welcomed him under a triumphal arch and often presented him with the keys to the city. He would then go into the main district to accept accolades from schoolchildren and civic organizations. Passing down the street lined by ranks of young girls scattering flowers before him, he would proceed to his local quarters. There he would meet other civil, military and religious authorities and hear a further tribute. If the empress was absent, he would appear at a few social and cultural facilities. If Elisabeth was with him, she would stop at hospitals, girls' schools and charitable establishments while he reviewed military installations or held audiences. Evening festivities would include banquets, musical events and torchlight parades, particularly if he stayed in the town for more than one or two nights.[3]

Now and again, however, the raucous local politics that the emperor sought to minimize throughout the monarchy intruded on the ceremonies. Writing from Zagreb in Croatia in 1895, Franz Joseph noted that a rough student demonstration had taken place. Nevertheless, his reception at the city train station, his appearance at the laying of a foundation stone for the new Croatian national theatre, a serenade performed for him and even a stop at the university had gone off without incident. What he did not see and hear, or chose not to see and hear, were the details of the protest. Some Croatian youths had burned a Hungarian flag in defiance of Hungarian banners appearing on their soil. Such incidents were clear signs to observers that the emperor's realms were unified more in theory than in fact. Among them was Charles Khuen-Héderváry, Franz Joseph's governor in Croatia, who thought that such behaviour came close to mocking the formal ceremony itself.[4]

Political nastiness surfaced during the emperor's occasional appearances in Bohemia too. A barrage of preparatory literature on Franz Joseph and the symbolism of his presence anticipated a visit he made to Prague in 1891 to open a provincial jubilee exhibition on 100 years of industrial and cultural progress in the kingdom. Younger Czech radicals, however, used the event to circulate pamphlets that charged the king with ignoring their state rights. Increasingly frequent attacks upon Habsburg-themed statuary and other visual representations of Habsburg rule in the kingdom were also sharpening tensions between Czechs and Germans in the kingdom.

Worse yet from the emperor's point of view, his visits inspired both communities to rehearse their contentious debate over which of them was more loyal to the ruler. Czech nationalists used the occasions to turn essential symbols of sovereignty, like the Bohemian crown, into embodiments of the nation rather than of an office held by someone whose authority was conferred through his lineage. Czechs boycotted Franz Joseph's 1908 jubilee parade in Vienna completely. When the anniversary of his accession to the Bohemian throne came around in December of that year, edgy national interactions and ethnic rowdiness in the kingdom again implied that the emperor had a way to go before he could claim that his person unified his lands.[5]

In setting off to do his dynastic duties in Bosnia, Franz Ferdinand certainly knew that ritual appearances had not always gone off smoothly of late. He was keenly aware that he was entering a part of the monarchy where Serb national appeals were stoking hostility to rule from Vienna, especially among young men. The government in Belgrade did not want to complicate its relations with Franz Joseph's regime by associating itself directly with nationalist agitators. Nevertheless, activists within the general staff of the Serbian army were cooperating with civilian groups in whipping up as much anti-Habsburg feeling in the south Slavic Balkans as possible. A core of these officers made up the terrorist 'Unity or Death' (Ujedinjenje ili Smrt) bloc, a sinister Serb national cell with few compunctions against assassinating princes to further Serbian territorial interests. Unity or Death had a cohort of young supporters in Bosnia, who had trained in Belgrade before slipping westward over the boundary with Serbia, helped along by sympathetic border guards.

In all likelihood, the archduke also realized that some of his thoughts about reforming the Habsburg monarchy did not sit well with the government in Belgrade. The archduke's alleged interest in a scheme for raising the status of Croatia within a reorganized Habsburg state ran counter to Serb dreams of a much larger realm, known by some as Greater Serbia. Some of his views on international affairs affected Serb interests too. Habsburg relations with Russia had soured badly over the last decades of the nineteenth century, largely because of conflicting ambitions in the Balkans, but the archduke wanted to avoid outright war. Desirable though such a rapprochement might have been for Europe generally, the prospect worried patriots in the fledgling Serb kingdom. St Petersburg had long been an unofficial protector of Orthodox Catholic peoples in Europe's southeast, and Belgrade was loath to have anything in that relationship compromised. Any change in Russian foreign policy, especially more cordial relations with the Habsburg monarchy, might do just that.[6]

Given these conditions and private forebodings of his own, Franz Ferdinand might have rethought the choice of 28 June for a public ceremonial appearance in Sarajevo. It was the date on which the Ottoman army destroyed the medieval kingdom of Serbia at the Field of the Blackbirds (Kossovo Polje) in 1389, thus extinguishing Serbian independence for centuries thereafter. It also marked the fourteenth anniversary of one of his worst experiences: accepting morganatic status for his marriage. The morning began ominously. On the first leg of the appearance, the couple followed Franz Joseph's practice of proceeding in a motorcade to Sarajevo Town Hall. Along the way, a bomb thrown from the spectators who lined the street ricocheted off the rear of the imperial couple's vehicle and hit the street, injuring those in the car following behind. Two wounded men were removed to a garrison infirmary and the procession came to an end. Before leaving the city later in the day, however, Franz Ferdinand decided to follow another family practice and visit the beds of the injured. Though an alternative route had been planned, his party mistakenly retraced the same path it had followed that morning. The assassin, Gavrilo Princip, a Bosnian Serb student, was waiting. His bullets hit his major target – the archduke – but also Princess Sophie, whom he had apparently not intended to kill. She died almost instantly, and Franz Ferdinand followed shortly after.[7]

As a demonstration of Serbian national extremism, the couple's murder shocked Habsburg officials in Vienna and Budapest. Uncomfortable with his nephew though he had been, Franz Joseph was visibly rattled by the horrific nature of both deaths.[8] The funeral arrangements for the couple, however, fell far short of the standards normally observed for deceased members of the dynasty, especially heirs apparent to sovereign titles. There was no entombment in the Crypt of the Capuchins; Franz Ferdinand had disallowed that himself, and court officials readily obliged. The corpses were quickly removed to Lower Austria for burial in the grounds of Schloss Artstetten, a private property of the Hohenberg family, a name bestowed upon Sophie and her offspring in 1910. All responsible figures advising Franz Joseph in both halves of the Dual Monarchy agreed that some retaliation was in order. Princip was dealt with swiftly. He and his accomplices were captured, but because Austrian law forbade capital punishment for people under twenty, he was sentenced to prison. There he died, probably of tuberculosis, two years later.

The government in Vienna had been thinking about trimming back Serbian ambitions in the Balkans for some time. One faction had gathered around Franz Conrad von Hötzendorff, the army general chief of staff, who had long argued that pre-emptive war against Serbia was a precondition of the Habsburg monarchy's survival. Foreign minister Leopold Berchthold would eventually come around to his view. Not everyone agreed. Franz Ferdinand had discouraged war in any form, and those close to him continued to oppose it. Arguing that the monarchy was unprepared militarily and politically for large-scale hostilities, they feared it would collapse altogether when put to such a test. Count István Tisza, the Hungarian prime minister, fretted over the timing of such a strike and the negative foreign reaction that might follow. Proof that the Serb government instigated the assassination had yet to emerge. Speaking as a Hungarian, he wanted no conflict that might end with even more Slavs in an empire where together they outnumbered all other ethnicities, most conspicuously his own. In return for supporting a declaration of war, Tisza required that the monarchy disclaim all thoughts of taking over Serbia. Should other Balkan states pick away at the kingdom's lands, they could go right ahead.[9]

Many Bosnians had joined local protests against the assassination but in the end the voices for war in the emperor's regime prevailed. Franz Joseph endorsed the terms of a deliberately provocative ultimatum to Serbia and allowed it to go forward on 23 July. It effectively demanded that the government in Belgrade discipline open and clandestine anti-Habsburg action groups in the kingdom, even if high military officers had to be brought into line. Austria–Hungary would have a direct role in adjudicating suspects. The Serbs would not tolerate such intrusions on their sovereignty, just as the war party in Vienna had expected. The emperor realized that he might be putting his monarchy in danger but, having survived so many crises, he was prepared to do so again. His sturdy faith in a pro-Habsburg Providence reassured him too. Experience after experience had indicated that a higher power had sustained both himself and his monarchy as they weathered private tragedies and humiliating military defeats.

His explanation to 'his peoples', as he called them to war on 28 July 1914, could not have been simpler and more authentic: 'to maintain the honour of my monarchy, to protect its reputation and position, to secure its possessions'. Serbia had long been committed to challenging the territorial integrity of the Dual Monarchy and 'the hatred against me and my house rages higher and higher, the attempt to tear loose inalienable territories of Austria–Hungary becomes more and more apparent'. While he made one brief reference to the damage the Serbian challenge might do to the economic, political and military progress of his lands, his heaviest grievance was Serbia's unrepentant wish 'to unsettle the loyalty of the people . . . to the ruling house and to the fatherland', as well as to himself personally and his government.

One month to the day since Franz Ferdinand's murder, the strike against Serbia began as a limited manoeuvre to protect the integrity of the Habsburg monarchy. For Franz Joseph, it stayed that way. When, in the early years of the war, he was advised to consider making territorial concessions in South Tyrol and Trieste that Italy was demanding as its price for remaining in a formal alliance with Austria–Hungary, the emperor said that he would rather die than accept such an insult to his honour. Such conditions were, in his opinion, 'brigandry'.[10] That keeping his monarchy together had converted a regional military operation into a global cataclysm may have disappointed him, but never convinced him to modify his goal.

Bosnia's Habsburg Back Story

Told narrowly from the perspective of Habsburg policy, the month-long run up to war reads as a series of dreadful miscalculations, with Franz Ferdinand hazarding his life in Sarajevo as one of the worst. But taken by itself, his assassination in Bosnia, and not elsewhere in the monarchy, had grave implications for the future of his house and the entire cultural-political system that supported them. Princip's bullet not only opened the way to war, it also emblematically closed down the final, unusually organized effort of the dynasty to do what it had done for more than 300 years: persuade one people after another that its rule was beneficial enough to learn to live with. Programmes to incorporate Bosnia into the monarchy may have come as close to systematic imperialism as Habsburg regimes ever did, at least in the modern era.[11] But however short they may have fallen by British or French standards, the dynasty, its officials and its chosen supporters had indeed tried hard.

Transparent geopolitical thought drove the transfer of the administration of Bosnia–Herzegovina from the Ottomans to the Habsburg monarchy in 1878 at a conference in Berlin that reset the political structure of the Balkans. The same considerations applied to the decision in Vienna to annex the two provinces in 1908. Serbia's expansion towards the Adriatic had to be stalled. With the decline of Constantinople's influence, Austria–Hungary had become a serious economic and naval presence along the Dalmatian and Istrian coasts and in parts of the Mediterranean.[12] Once the move took shape as a fait accompli, however, the government in Vienna realized that much work lay ahead before their new subjects believed that Habsburg rule, overseen by the finance ministry in Vienna, was good for them.

The Dual Monarchy's overall plans for Bosnia had been clear for some time: to build and secure rail connections that would promote the monarchy's economic and strategic interests throughout the Balkans. Realizing their goal through sheer force could be counterproductive, on public relations grounds alone. The imperial army's ruthless suppression of resistance by Orthodox Serb and Muslim elements in the province in 1878 had drawn unwelcome criticism from Russia and Britain, who were increasingly wary of Habsburg ambitions in the Adriatic and the Mediterranean. The 1908 annexation had made Belgrade's anti-Habsburg propaganda in Bosnia more virulent; claims that Vienna and Budapest both wished to denationalize and exploit South Slavs generally were typical.[13]

Persuading Bosnians to think more positively about Habsburg rule was a delicate mission. They were an exceptionally diverse population, confessionally, ethnically and economically. Any major policy announced by an administration in distant Vienna and its local deputies was certain to antagonize a sizeable constituency. Religion was especially touchy. As late as the nineteenth century, Habsburg emperors were internationally recognized as protectors of fellow Roman Catholics in eastern and south-eastern Europe. Open defence of Roman Catholicism in Bosnia was bound to stir up confessional tensions among Eastern Orthodox Christians, Muslims and even Jews, something that the dynasty's regimes wanted to avoid whenever possible. All faiths, at least officially, were to be respected, regardless of formal responsibilities that the ruling house had to its own faith.[14]

Policy makers in Vienna and Budapest agreed that to win the loyalty of a population that was largely agricultural and among Europe's most impoverished, Bosnia should be configured as a model of economic and social progress, courtesy of Habsburg rule. In fact, noteworthy improvements took place up to 1914. New and growing industries came quickly to Sarajevo, along with an elaborate transportation infrastructure to support them. Railway connections multiplied exponentially.[15] But local indifference towards the dynasty and even open criticism of it persisted. Parochial politics and economic issues dominated civic discussion, and Franz Joseph and his officials did not always fare well in these.[16] To persuade such a public that Vienna and Budapest were working for the common good, people had to hear and/or read about it, the more frequently the better.

By the beginning of the twentieth century Habsburg governments were long rehearsed in justifying their agendas in the various corners of their empire and enlisting the public media to help them.[17] In Bosnia, however, they hesitated. Press campaigns could offend ethnic and confessional sensibilities and their spokesmen. That readership in the heavily illiterate province was quite small may have been an added consideration. By 1907 and 1908, however, editorializing on behalf of Serb and Croatian territorial causes was growing more strident, and the government in Vienna started to worry about countering it. The Litterarisches Bureau (Press Bureau) of the foreign office and the Presseleitung, its equivalent under the prime minister, guided the discussion, joined eventually by representatives of the finance ministry. Their exchanges ended in a scheme to establish and co-opt a local daily, preferably one written in a European *Kultursprache*, that is, German, to promote the Habsburg case in Bosnia. The editor would be Hermenegild Wagner, currently holding that position at the *Bosnische Post*.[18]

Born in Vienna, Wagner grew up largely in the Balkans. His mother was Croatian, his father an Austrian engineer who worked most of his life in Bulgaria. Their journalist son spoke Serbo-Croatian and Bulgarian fluently; as a reporter for the *Reichspost*, an influential Catholic-oriented Vienna daily, he took great pride in the access he had to people whom less polyglot, and sometimes envious, western colleagues could not interview. His dispatches during the Balkan Wars of 1912–13 were reprinted in London in *The Times*. Professionally innovative as well, he urged war correspondents to move from their traditional posts on battlefields to headquarters where they could question field commanders on the contents of incoming orders. Military officers were also part of his family background; Wagner himself would be an army lieutenant.[19]

A close observer of radical Balkan nationalism, Wagner thought that Bosnia's Serbs could be assimilated into a Habsburg-governed land, but only on the monarchy's terms. His thinking, in this respect, echoed the opinions of the monarchy's first governor in the province, Benjamin Kállay, who wrote of 'occidentalizing eastern peoples', while at the same time strengthening Bosnian local patriotism. Wagner promised to take up this mission in his new daily, devoted to illuminating the purposes and accomplishments of what he called the 'powerful and illustrious' Habsburg empire in the Balkans. His commitment to the task was so complete that he volunteered his services without the subsidies that Bosnian political associations normally gave out to supportive journals.[20]

The masthead of his new paper, the *Sarajevoer Tagblatt*, promised frankly to uphold 'Austrian-Hungarian interests in the Balkans'. It faithfully echoed arguments for the expansion of Austria–Hungary to the south and southeast that the government and metropolitan press rooms had been developing since 1878: the monarchy needed outposts to defend the Dalmatian coast from the rear; the monarchy had to maintain itself as a great territorial power in order to survive; the monarchy was obligated to uphold historic rights of the Hungarian crown in Bosnia; the monarchy had to prevent new states from forming on its Balkan borders; the monarchy needed to promote trade more aggressively in the area, and on and on. Wagner's columns also took as fact the internationally contested proposition that Austria–Hungary had sovereign rights in Bosnia by virtue of Article 25 of the Berlin accord. Residual Ottoman claims to the area did not trouble him. Nor did the reservations that Russia, Great Britain and Italy had about the move. He did not rule out using force to counter extremist national propaganda coming out of Belgrade, something Serbs did not like to hear, nor did all local Croatians, with whom Wagner was generally on good terms.[21]

His main editorial strategy, however, was to take every opportunity that arose to remind readers of the man and the family who governed them. Birthdays of the emperor and rare appearances of the dynasty in Bosnia for whatever purpose were treated in print with impeccable reverence. But the *Tagblatt* also carried stories that humanized Franz Joseph. A typical effort reported him calming a panicky crowd in a theatre at his summer residence in Ischl when the electricity failed.[22] But Wagner's chief editorial theme was economic progress in Bosnia under Habsburg rule. Such material, factually presented, would do more to convince Bosnians that the monarchy was working in their interests than heavy-handed, anti-Serb broadsides ever could. Indeed, from the outset he planned to dedicate a section of the paper to matters of interest to tradesmen, bankers, industrialists and their employees.[23] Wagner was fascinated and impressed by technology and its contributions to human well-being. Column after column of his paper covered material improvement in Bosnia under Habsburg rule. Even as war with Serbia threatened briefly in 1909, 'proven pioneers of Austrian-Hungarian culture' were laying down a 'new work of progressive civilization': railway lines to Bosnia's granary in the northwest that would link the region with the rest of the world. Editorials begged administrations in Vienna and Budapest to install more public lighting, better telephone connections within Bosnia and with the monarchy's two capitals, and ever more rail connections.[24]

Firm monarchist though he was, Wagner brought to his journalism an informed liberalism that helped him to pinpoint features in Franz Joseph's policies that Joseph ii would have supported had rail transport existed in his reign. For all the stress that the *Tagblatt* placed on the Catholic virtues of the dynasty and the patriarchal attributes reserved for its rulers, frequent mention was also made of contributions that the House of Habsburg-Lorraine could make to turning Bosnia into a more progressive place. Representative government, Wagner declared, could come about in Bosnia, but the protective aegis of the Habsburg monarchy was needed to help it along. With the emperor as sole source of law and order, all communities in Bosnia would be more secure politically as well as economically. Without the full force of the emperor's rule, radical Serbs and their allies might gain a majority in any provisional assembly and position themselves to control the body in perpetuity.[25]

Bosnia, in Wagner's editorial hands, also exemplified the inclusiveness that the dynasty was promoting as a hallmark of its rule. He reported what he could about every religious, ethnic and economic community in the region, even if it was only a short notice or brief account of meetings and other activities. The tone of these pieces was invariably upbeat. To read the *Tagblatt* was to read about Sarajevo in 1908 as a place that fostered the well-being and prosperity of all groups. Furthermore, they respected each other's particular qualities. The Sarajevo Men's Chorus sang the works of German, Slovene and Croatian composers. A capacity audience for one such programme danced to a gypsy ensemble after the formal concert ended. Germans, Slavs, Hungarians, a Pole and a Muslim belonged to the committee overseeing horse racing in the resort of Ilidže. People from all ranks of society were invited to contribute to imperial celebrations. For Franz Josef's birthday in 1908 railway workers offered job-themed music: 'Irrfahrten' ('Travelling in No Particular Direction'), a *Potpourri*, and the more professional *Orient Express Galopp*. A glance through the paper's advertisements was enough to persuade all but the most sceptical that Habsburg rule had brought social harmony and prosperity to the city. Although a few items were in Serbo-Croatian, the majority were in German. Regardless of the purveyors' names, the variety of wares and services they offered indicate the general vigour of the city's diverse financial and mercantile communities and the discretionary income at their disposal. Local needs were addressed, but so were the tastes of the well-to-do: British fabrics, Singer sewing machines and men's garters from the United States were readily available.[26]

Nevertheless, as suddenly as Wagner had been called into editorial service for the dynasty, he abandoned the job. The sale of this paper was announced on page three of the *Tagblatt* of 21 August 1909, along with the press shop associated with it. Wagner's name disappeared from the masthead on 16 November; he had apparently severed his connections with the enterprise two days earlier. He admitted that he had financial problems, along with implacable enemies, meaning Serbs and those south Slavs who supported them. The integrity and accountability of the *Tagblatt* seem to have come into question as well. Whatever the problem, however, his replacement, Felix Schulz, was on the way from Vienna and the paper continued to argue for the Habsburg presence in southeastern Europe until 1918.[27]

Wagner had relentlessly criticized sclerotic state bureaucrats pre-occupied with passing memoranda on crucial questions back and forth among themselves. His particular whipping boy had been the cautious finance minister István Burián, who, Wagner said, refused to take Serb radicalism seriously and was disengaged intellectually and emotionally from the land he administered. He had also deplored ministerial wrangling in Vienna over permanent constitutional status for Bosnia–Herzegovina within the Dual Monarchy.[28]

The most likely reason for his hurried departure, however, may have been his editorial rhetoric. The measured tone that he had brought to the *Tagblatt* in its first months was straying radically from the impartial posture that the monarchy had been cultivating in its newly annexed province. The Vienna press office attached to the Council of Ministers had been watching the paper; an order was given to prepay a subscription for 1909 and 1910 'as quickly as possible'.[29] Wagner's criticisms of Serb national polemics, particularly when coming from Bosnian locals, had become increasingly intemperate. He was convinced that their purpose was to deny civil rights to so-called 'foreigners'. The reference was to people like himself: educated and largely German-speaking civil servants, entrepreneurs and articulate journalists. *Kulturträger* ('civilizing agent'), he called them; it was they who paid the bulk of the taxes in the province and had the learning to train a population in ways that would make it more materially secure.[30]

Wagner's celebration of German institutions and his blatant endorse-ment of German cultural superiority in Bosnia was yet another example of the provocative public language that Vienna wanted to avoid. Worse yet, on 23 July 1909, speaking 'as a child of the west and a child of the Habsburg monarchy', he had recommended that Bosnia–Herzegovina be dynastically incorporated into the kingdom of Croatia. This new arrangement would create a South Slavic unit, Bosnia–Herzegovina included, equal to Austria and Hungary. He had pointed out in prior editorials that large numbers of South Slavs were already under Habsburg sway. It was time, he said, for the Roman Catholic Croatians to acknow-ledge that they had more to gain by strengthening their ties to the dynasty and ignoring Belgrade's propaganda about a Greater Serbia.[31] Flawlessly pro-Habsburg though the writer's sentiments were, they once again ran counter to Vienna's purposes. The interior ministry was committed to keeping all hints of discord in Bosnia out of the news; not until 1910 were English, French and German wire services allowed to report from Sarajevo.[32]

Abortive though it was, Wagner's editorial career at the *Tagblatt* had major implications for the future of Habsburg rule in the Balkans. The house had hoped to quieten internal political and social tensions in Bosnia by developing its economy along modern European lines. Progress had certainly taken place – Wagner was not wrong to emphasize that in his pages – but Franz Joseph's government had oversold these policies badly, to itself and to Bosnians. The social, economic and educational reforms proposed from Vienna would have taken decades for their effects to be felt broadly. Factional interests strained administrative operations in the province, regardless of how well-educated and apolitical civil servants allegedly were. Despite orders to avoid controversy, these men often succumbed to the political and cultural conflicts going on around them. Ethnic status sometimes dictated personnel decisions. In fact, the Habsburg bureaucracy was resented for what it was: a foreign presence. Even Wagner knew that.[33] The dynasty's promised golden age for a backward Balkan stretch of land was a thing of the distant future, not a journalist's imminent reality. With Bosnia's present as politically and economically problematic as it was, the outlook for tomorrow was uncertain, to say the least.

Worse yet, a newspaper that promoted the dynasty's goal of mediating among fractious peoples in order to perpetuate dynastic authority over them had abandoned the position for active combat in the venomous ethnic and confessional hostilities of the Balkans. Wagner's swift transformation from a convinced but reasonable spokesman for Habsburg rule in Bosnia to a partisan critic of Serbs, both in Bosnia and in Belgrade, was the very political trajectory that the government in Vienna had wished to minimize. While the strategic advantages of a foothold in the province were obvious, the dynasty was eager to prove to the world and its own peoples that its latest territorial acquisition had taken place without great resistance and had brought living standards in the region to levels familiar elsewhere in Europe. Princip's bullets at Sarajevo abruptly, but plainly, ended that vision. Many Serbs wanted nothing to do with a dynasty that ruled both from Vienna and Budapest and still believed in confirming the fact through parades and local appearances.

Wagner had never rejected the military option as a way of preserving Habsburg economic and strategic interests in the Balkans. In his opinion, Franz Joseph's willingness to rattle his swords in Bosnia in 1909 had finalized the annexation domestically and abroad. It had also turned the elderly emperor into the leader of 'Young Austria', individuals eager to realize the centuries-old dream of Austrian pre-eminence in the region.[34] The night that the news of the assassination arrived in Vienna, Wagner was on Heroes' Square in front of the Hofburg, demanding instant retaliation against Serbia. Unlike many of the monarchy's aesthetes, artists and intellectuals, Wagner went back into the army immediately. He was killed on 12 June 1915 fighting on the eastern front, a war zone where thousands upon thousands would die, suffer debilitating wounds or languish in enemy captivity in the service of their emperor or king and the house that had generated their kind.[35]

Dynastic Rule and an Angry Polity

In some parts of Franz Joseph's realms a number of his subjects had decided that the Habsburgs should exit the political stage as quickly as possible. A young journeyman from the Kingdom of Bohemia, who had left the monarchy for a better life abroad, came back to perform his prescribed military service because every Czech soldier was obligated to see that 'Austria was the first to lose the war'.[36] Yet regardless of the national bickering that had plagued the Habsburg monarchy for decades, Franz Joseph's summons to arms found thousands of takers, albeit for different reasons. The political grandees in Budapest saw something to be gained in a swift put-down of the regime in Belgrade. Serbs were a troublesome minority in southern Hungary; trimming the wings of their national kingdom to the south might tame them a bit. Russia's entry into the war to assist Serbia would also give Hungarians a chance to avenge Tsar Nicholas I's contribution to suppressing their national revolution in 1849.[37] Nor had all Habsburg subjects scattered throughout the world completely cut their ties to the monarchy. On 26 July 1914 Franz Joseph ordered émigré reservists to return home for duty. In the United States, where more than 200,000 of them worked, many as waiters, the response was immediate. They flocked to the Austrian consulate in New York and requested repatriation to their regiments.[38]

Nevertheless, the conflict went badly in ways that the late Archduke Franz Ferdinand had predicted. Serbia was brought down, but not in

1914 as had been widely anticipated, but a year later, and only with massive German help against unexpectedly stubborn local resistance. Moreover, the conflict had become generalized along the Habsburg eastern front, with Russia as the primary opponent. When Italy decided to throw in its lot with the western Allies in 1915, Habsburg forces had to be deployed to the south as well. The common army was visibly stretched way beyond its limits. It also proved to be horrifically vulnerable. At the beginning of the war the most loyal newspapers in Vienna, notably Frederick Funder's *Reichspost*, regularly published casualty lists that covered military personnel regardless of rank. As the toll quickly rose to sickening levels, only the names of officers were made public. About one-third of the male population in the Dual Monarchy, 8 million men, served in the conflict along with about 100,000 women. At its end the dead numbered 1,016,200 and a further 1,691,000 were missing or captured. Thousands of prisoners of war would never be accounted for: around 480,000 probably perished in Italian, Serbian and Russian captivity.[39]

Thus it was clear from the outset that hostilities would extend far beyond the time frame that Vienna had set for them. Sustaining public support in the Habsburg lands for the duration was even more important than it was in comparatively settled times. It was somewhat easier in those few cases where military objectives corresponded to traditional local interests. Opening the southern front in 1915 was popular among the Tyrolese, who were quite ready to activate their centuries-old privilege of self-defence to keep Italian forces out of the province. Croatians worried about Italian designs on Trieste, and along the Dalmatian coast and its nearby islands they welcomed an excuse to push Rome as far back to the west as they could. More conservatively inclined communities in the monarchy, including many observant Catholics and country people generally, also remained true to the emperor even after the military and economic situation worsened appreciably in 1916.[40]

A military dictatorship in all but name, the wartime regime in Vienna was long familiar with the visual and editorial tools that forged sympathetic publics. They had also mastered the canonical texts that gave content to such appeals, regardless of Princip's brutal dismissal of them in Bosnia. Familiar slogans and the historically resonant terminology that expressed them were updated in sites where people were likely to encounter them. A plaque reminded residents at Weissgerberstrasse 19 in Vienna's Third District that their emperor was part of an alliance with Wilhelmine Germany and the Ottoman sultan. Reliefs of Franz Joseph and Wilhelm II signifying the partnership of 'Germania' and 'Austria' were to be seen at Peter Jordanstrasse 86 in the Eighteenth District. The new medium of film was now bringing images to screens throughout Vienna; the government co-opted the technique quickly. Printed propaganda became voluminous as segments of it were carefully calculated to the requirements of specific audiences, children included: *Let's Play World War! A Contemporary Picture Book for Our Little Ones* came out in 1916. Manufacturers and artisans turned out dynastic war kitsch galore. Coffee house patrons were handed a receipt with Habsburg black and gold on it when they added two Heller to their bills. The most lavish single effort to explain to the public how they were fighting, and why they should continue to do so to the end, was the Vienna War Exhibition of 1916–17. Set up, ironically, in the Prater, the city's famous amusement park, it drew more than 1 million visitors in the course of the year. There they could inspect military equipment, play war games and absorb visual lessons about the dynasty's military history through the ages. One divisive note belied the overall impression of Habsburg power: the Hungarians, characteristically, declined to participate in the project. But the numbers alone of viewers and participants amply offset their absence.[41]

Where propaganda fell short, official and private censorship kept public thinking in line. Its application was not uniform. The Austrian half of the monarchy was monitored rigorously, Hungary far less so. During the first two years of the war, articles in relatively radical Hungarian journals such as *Nyugat* (*The West*), which published the work of some of the kingdom's leading intellectuals at the beginning of the twentieth century, openly criticized Hungarian writers who approved of the war. They also mentioned the ebbing morale of Habsburg troops as they experienced a long string of defeats. In Croatia, censorship was even lighter. Events celebrating the idea of a south Slavic polity went ahead there as early as 1917 without significant government interference. On the other hand, Carniola (Ger. Krain), today in Slovenia, was more closely monitored, probably because it was situated in the Austrian half of the monarchy. The very pro-Habsburg *Illustrated Weekly* in Ljubljana (Ger. Laibach) had much government support as well. Like many other journals eager to stay on the right side of authority, it ceased printing obituaries in 1916, presumably because the news was too depressing. Public spaces were also kept under tight control. The prominent Czech national patriot Tomáš Masaryk declared war on Austria on 6 July 1915, the day that marked the 500th anniversary of Jan Hus's martyrdom at the Council of Constance. Imperial authorities quickly took down a recently installed statue of Hus on the Old Town Square,

19 Oskar Kokoschka, *The Errant Knight*, 1915, oil on canvas.

along with a plaque commemorating the execution in 1621 of men who organized the kingdom's rebellious estates against Habsburg rule.[42]

The government made a final serious attempt to enlist leading artists, writers and intellectuals in support of the dynasty's cause in the war. Few made themselves available for active duty. Egon Schiele combined rare frankness with insufferable arrogance in declaring that the lives of men like himself were too important to put them at risk. Patriotism was clearly low among his priorities, if it was on his list at all. In 1915 he was photographed in his atelier in front of a knick-knack cabinet on which stood a small British Union Jack. More telling still, he apparently had sympathizers in the government. The intervention of a well-connected patron spared him frontline service. Called up in 1915, he was posted to Vienna where he sat out sinecures in the Army Commissary and the Military Museum. His pro-forma stabs at inspirational official painting fell flat, yet his superiors allowed him to travel with art exhibits to Stockholm and Copenhagen.[43]

Although he claimed to be more committed to the war effort than some fellow artists, Oscar Kokoschka dodged being drafted until 1915. When he did volunteer for one year in 1915, he was not in a pro-Habsburg frame of mind. His current project was *Der irrende Ritter* (*The Lost Knight*), an image of an exhausted knight in an indeterminate landscape (illus. 19). Quite clearly weary of battle, he is fully prostrate. The image contrasts sharply with the glamorized scenes of military valour that the government preferred. It was also strikingly unlike the brilliantly armoured chivalric St George that Emperor Maximilian I once mimicked to express his readiness for battle against Ottoman Islam. Kokoschka may have anticipated his coming physical fate; he was badly wounded on the

Isonzo front, where he had been posted as a war artist. Leaving the army in 1917, he went to Dresden for therapy in a sanatorium run by pacifists. Viennese art galleries also demurred at supporting government-sponsored war visuals. Asked in 1917 to include artwork commissioned by the War Press Bureau to be sent to exhibitions abroad, dealers were reluctant to make room for items of questionable aesthetic value.[44]

Though few leading writers actively opposed the war, they, like major artists, ducked battlefield service when they could. The poet Rainer Maria Rilke was well connected to the aristocracy; he found an assignment in the literary department of the War Archives. Arthur Schnitzler, whose plays probed the dynamics of the monarchy's society high and low, was characteristically more nuanced. He hoped that the Central Powers would be victorious, but his encounters as a physician with the injured quickly made him a hard-core critic of armed conflict, at least privately. He saw no reason to differentiate between atrocities committed by the Central Powers and the western Allies.

Some authors volunteered their services for government efforts to control the public narrative of the monarchy's history and its current struggles. A few may have been driven by the guilt over avoiding combat service that had troubled Kokoschka. Others were sincerely committed, at least at the outset. Hermann Bahr wrote in 1915 that the evident unity with which the monarchy went to war suggested that it was still a vital state. 'The Austrian Miracle' he called it in the article's title. Intellectual luminaries whose reputations flourished after the war ended – Arnold Schoenberg, Robert Musil, Ludwig Wittgenstein, Stefan Zweig – all came down with the form of patriotic fever that Franz Joseph's government wished to spread.[45]

Among the most deeply persuaded was Hugo von Hofmannsthal. An exquisitely precocious creative spirit, whose his first poetry came out under the pseudonym Lauris to evade a law forbidding minors to publish, he had quickly become prominent among the aesthetes of German-speaking central Europe. French literary Symbolism had influenced him too. The subtleties he coaxed from language had meaning for the broadly literate alone. For all of his hermetic inclinations, however, Hofmannsthal grew increasingly sensitive to the social and political problems of his time. The ageing of Franz Joseph, a cause of growing concern to his closest ministers and advisers, distressed Hofmannsthal too. His characterization of a dying artist in *Tizian's Tod* (*The Death of Titian*), an early work for the stage, echoes feelings about the emperor that many had held for some time:

it seemed . . . that he had tried,
To give declining strength some form,
By clinging to each ironclad norm;
Declaring that his life force had not wavered;
With strong words, as his voice quavered.[46]

Hofmannsthal was caught up in the patriotic celebrations that annex-ation of Bosnia in 1908 set off in many areas of the Dual Monarchy. Just how much of his feeling was the result of a foreign policy coup and how much of it came from the emotional high he was on during successful rehearsals of *Elektra*, his first operatic collaboration with Richard Strauss, is an open question. Like most of his literary counterparts in Vienna, he used every political contact that he had to avoid combat in 1914. Never-theless, he felt compelled to serve the monarchy productively. Until 1917 he threw himself into some of the government's more ambitious propa-ganda campaigns, both as a writer and lecturer. Emblematic of his efforts, and the one that came to real fruition, was the *Österreichische Bibliothek*, a set of 26 pocket-size books celebrating the lives and deeds of some of the empire's most notable figures, particularly military heroes such as Radetzky and Eugene of Savoy. The series was sold in Germany and distributed gratis to troops, officers and military support staff. For those in the empire whose native tongue was not German, he developed a never-implemented scheme for pictorializing historical sites throughout the monarchy that would remind all whom the dynasty ruled of the history that they shared.[47]

Nevertheless, Hofmannsthal soon found that the Habsburg-orientated thrust of the *Bibliothek* was competing with national readings of cultural affinity throughout the monarchy. Czech intellectuals, artists and writers as a group rebuffed his quite sincere efforts to recruit them for the project. He was also unaccustomed to the criticism that some of his views provoked. Even fellow Austrian intellectuals were thinking about a homeland of their own. On the way to becoming an eloquent spokesman for Austria as a small, but independent, nation, the poet Anton Wildgans turned down Hofmannsthal's request to write a paean to the diversity of the Habsburg empire. Though he had brought out several patriotic poems at the outset of hostilities, Wildgans would sing the praises of the dynasty's rule only when it was run by and for the German-speaking population. In *Österreich*, a new periodical focusing on the specifically Austrian past, historian Wilhelm Bauer recommended in 1917 that contributors keep traditional patriotism at a bare minimum to avoid linking the magazine with the current regime.[48]

Hofmannsthal withdrew from the propaganda front lines even before the war ended, redirecting himself to more narrowly cultural enterprises. By the middle of 1918 he had begun to think that the tradition-encrusted Burgtheater and other stages could be used to strengthen the monarchy by representing what would come to be called 'the Austrian idea'. The imperial theatre, which had lost some of its pre-eminence in German-speaking Europe to livelier houses in Berlin, would be opened to plays from the classical to the experimental written in all the languages in the empire. He was now at work on a new comedy, *Der Schwieriger* (*The Difficult Man*), which was to be staged by the Burg, a first for one of his theatrical pieces. His friend and close political collaborator, Leopold von Andrian, who had served in important positions in the foreign service, was the director. He too had put much thought into the scheme. Hofmannsthal also wrote a memorandum on establishing festival performances that followed the same programme; the notion lingered to be built into the concept of the Salzburg Festival after the war ended. Emperor Charles, who succeeded Franz Joseph in 1916, supported the proposal, although the end of the monarchy itself in 1918 forced much rethinking of the whole idea. By 1917 Hungarian writers, too, were beginning to redirect their attention from the war.[49]

Two years before the conflict ended, however, the Habsburg empire had one last opportunity to experience fully a spectacle that recalled for its peoples their ties to the house that was ruling them. Emperor Franz Joseph was aware that the lives of civilians and troops alike were not going well. In July 1916 he told Alexander Margutti, his aide-de-camp, that his people would not put up with privation much longer.[50] He stubbornly continued working at his desk until the end, which came for him on 21 November in that year.

The routine gloom of late autumn Vienna accentuated the foreboding solemnity of a funeral that mobs of people, for whatever reason, thought they should see. So many swarmed into the city for the public procession that some had to watch it from the ramps of the Schwarzenberg Palace, around half a mile from the Ringstrasse. Many probably saw nothing, but they could hear the music. Whatever they missed, however, filled newspapers the following day, including pictures of the late emperor reposing in his coffin, prepared to meet his maker in the uniform of an imperial-royal *Feldmarschall*. It was the garb that identified him in his lifetime when he was still ramrod-erect; it was the way he would be remembered by the generations that followed his passing.[51] One spectator claimed to have hung out of a window above his father's shop at the age of seven to see the cortège as it moved up the Rotenturm-strasse, near St Stephen's Cathedral. The sight, he said, left him with a lifelong sense of the meaning of the monarchy. The daughter of the master chef of the Hotel Sacher, a man who was exempt from military service because Anna Sacher, proprietress of the fashionable hotel, wanted it that way, remembered how the emperor had figured in her childhood. In the first year she and her classmates had learned and sung the imperial anthem 'Gott erhalte.' Along with a schoolfriend, she had once stood with a crowd in the central courtyard of the Hofburg, where popular entertainments were sometimes allowed, to catch a glimpse of her sovereign. Promptly at 10.30 a.m., a white-bearded man with a bald head had appeared on a stone balcony and waved his hand to acknow-ledge a crowd below crying 'Hoch, hoch!' The two children, however, were disappointed: they had hoped to see someone in a red, ermine-trimmed robe with a gold crown on his head. Nor were the obsequies confined to Vienna; memorial services took place in schools throughout the monarchy conducted by clergymen from all three recognized confessions: rabbis, priests and ministers.[52]

But even the mournful solemnity that marked the passing of a man whose longevity had convinced much of Europe that it would always have to reckon with the presence of a Habsburg monarchy did not over-ride growing public anger at wartime hardship and the various ways people were feeling it. One small girl watching the procession make its way eastward from Schönbrunn down to Vienna's First District remem-bered grumbling in the crowd about the use of expensive gas lighting for the occasion.[53] Among artists and intellectuals, where support for the war had been mixed at best, criticism had become ever more pointed. In 1915 Albin Egger-Lienz, the painter whom Franz Ferdinand had blocked from teaching at the Academy of Fine Art, was producing *Die Helden* (*The Heroes*), an image of confident and firmly aligned troops moving to confront an enemy. A year later, his most famous work, *Die Namenlosen* (*The Nameless Ones*), shows those same soldiers now advancing far more tentatively. Even as he continued to turn out propaganda for the monarchy and its military efforts, Stefan Zweig wrote *Jeremias* in 1917. A reworking of the biblical story of Nebuchadnezzar to underscore its parallels with the war, it featured an aged king Zedekia who, like Franz Joseph, allowed himself to be swayed by pro-war advisers and personal concerns for his honour. For all the critical qualities of his theme, the author received permission from his supervisor in the War Archives to attend the premiere of the play in Zürich, perhaps because it supported officials in Vienna who wanted to make public their interests in peace. Zweig did not return, staying in Switzerland until the war ended.

Closer to home, writer and monologist Karl Kraus was pouring himself into what was arguably the most biting commentary on the war. Like many of those who had believed that the monarchy could be reformed, he had once held out great hopes for Archduke Franz Ferdinand. He had moved from this to skewering the brutal cynicism and abiding hypocrisy that inspired the war's exponents and managers, including members of the dynasty itself. The first part of his gargantuan theatrical epic *Die letzten Tagen der Menschheit* (*The Final Days of Humankind*) came out in his self-published and -edited journal *Die Fackel* (*The Torch*) in 1918; the rest after the conflict had ended. Though accidental, the timing gave his audiences not only reasons to stop fighting, but to think about the larger forces that had brought about the plight many of them were in.[54]

Popular culture took an anti-war and anti-Habsburg turn as well. In Prague, where the Vienna regime had never mounted large-scale propaganda campaigns, a student cabaret group, the Red Seven, reworked a comic scenario known at least to Austrians since the late seventeenth century. A song told of the brave Austrian-German soldier Huber who had lost one part of his brain after another under enemy fire. Having finally had the inside of his head thoroughly reamed out, his skull is stuffed, reattached to his body, and sent back home where he asks to go to the front once again. Having heard the story, the emperor visits him and makes him a general. By the spring of 1918 more serious major writers in Bohemia were firmly united behind the drive for national independence.[55]

The monarchy, in fact, had slipped up badly, not only on the battlefield but also in the imagery it chose to justify the war to its peoples and the personnel charged with carrying out this mission. Responsibility for generating much of the propaganda was in the hands of military men, whose primary focus was inevitably on combat events. While the pictorials for such materials could be gripping, the overall impact of these scenes required successes rather than reverses. Unfortunately for the regime, there were far more of the latter than the former. Efforts to cover this up only weakened public support for the entire enterprise. Widespread awareness of censorship made army-issued accounts of the war increasingly suspect, even contemptible. Rumour had become as credible as truth, and the government could not reliably distinguish one from the other. By 1917 disbelief was routine as soldiers back from the front and other alleged eyewitnesses claimed that defeat was all but imminent.[56]

In fact, an alternative popular discourse about the war was circulating among Vienna's 2 million or so residents that was far closer to Karl Kraus's rants about official hypocrisy than to Wildgans's and Hofmannsthal's ruminations about the Austrian spirit or dramaturgy at the Burgtheater. It was also very dangerous. Communal loyalty in any polity depends in part on how credibly a regime identifies itself with the collective sense of social justice. The Habsburg regime seemed to many to have forgotten this as it put more of the war's burdens on the underprivileged than the moneyed and the titled. Preferential treatment for some classes at the expense of others gave the lie to all claims that the dynasty's monarchs embodied the oneness of their peoples.[57]

Spontaneous anger at Franz Joseph himself popped up in many sites, including the hugely popular cinemas where audiences diverted themselves from their troubles, at least for a little while. When in 1915 he appeared on a screen in the working-class Fifth District, a nine-year-old boy blurted out that the emperor should be killed because the boy's wounded father was bedridden in a hospital. Trundled off with his mother to the local police headquarters, the culprit confirmed officially that he had said this.[58] Impromptu though it was, the remark had deeply worrisome implications both for the present and the future of the monarchy. The government in Vienna had intensified its indoctrination of children even before war broke out. At his Jubilee in 1908, Franz Joseph had declared his support of a general European initiative to make the new twentieth century the 'Century of the Child'. His desired end product, at least within his lands, was to be the 'imperial child', someone who identified with the empire as a whole rather than the ethnic or national culture in which he or she grew up. Should the programme alone fail to persuade, boys and girls could simply model their behaviour on the emperor himself. The verses of *Unser Franzi: Wahre Geschichten aus der Kinderzeit unseres lieben Kaisers Franz Joseph I. (Our Little Franz: True Stories from the Childhood of Our Beloved Emperor Franz Joseph I)* showed them how to do it. Published in 1908, it abounded in exhortations to study and testimonials to the goodness and omniscience of the emperor. Children were also asked to keep their sovereign in mind as they prayed: supplications from the innocent would more likely incline the Almighty towards his monarchy than similar entreaties from more sinful adults. The public media loved all of this, particularly when emotionally sensitive boys and girls responded appropriately. A good example was the letter of one Josephine Lederer to her emperor. Concerned by his preoccupation with the ongoing conflict, she hoped to brighten him up with a poem she had written.[59]

But the reason that had driven the nine-year-old to wish his emperor dead had exposed the clumsiest of all the miscalculations in Habsburg wartime propaganda. Over the centuries, the house had never abandoned the idea of the emperor as a father writ large, whose family was the entirety of his peoples. In private, the emperor did not always live up to such magnanimous billing; he could be quite peevish about keeping popular dissidence out of sight. Reading in 1911 about street rioting over excessive rents in Ottakring, one of Vienna's rougher underclass suburbs, he noted curtly that it should be suppressed as quickly as possible.[60]

Nevertheless, direct appeals to territorial rulers for help had a long history in the Habsburg lands; treasury financial records from the sixteenth century are packed with them. The custom lived on unbroken. Franz Joseph was getting 30,000 of these supplications every year by the 1870s. The ones the emperor actually read usually came from government employees of one kind or another. Many simply asked for money, others for assistance in state procedures such as legal cases. After 1914 expectations that people could look to him to ease their privations were, if anything, even higher. The government did nothing to stop it, even promoting patriarchy as a public virtue that deserved some compensation in families bereft of their menfolk through death in combat or captivity. Grief over the loss of a husband and a father had struck the House of Habsburg too. The mixed personal and political reputation of the late Archduke Franz Ferdinand turned more positive in a press that published and republished images of his distraught children receiving the news of his death. Such scenes, however, proved to be as dissonant with reality as were reports of battlefield bravery calculated to erase public memories of defeats. If Franz Ferdinand's uncle had cared for his subjects as children, he would have sent them to war more reluctantly. The emperor's lack of significant response further undercut claims of paternal connections between emperor and people.[61] The dynasty's long association with public charity was also fading. By 1915 spokesmen for German and Czech communities in Bohemia had taken over management of the Imperial Widow and Orphans' Fund, a move that highlighted pressures for ethnic parity in the division of public relief services rather than the emperor's concern for his peoples collectively.[62]

The clash of image and reality grew even more strident under Franz Joseph's nephew and successor, Emperor Charles I in the Austrian half of the Dual Monarchy, King Charles IV in Hungary. Though the uncle had been far more at ease with his third heir apparent than his first and second, the young man had much in common with archdukes Rudolph and Franz Ferdinand. Like both, he realized that the monarchy needed reform if it were to survive. He echoed Franz Ferdinand's thoughts on modifying the primacy of Germans and Hungarians in the Dual Monarchy so that all historical nations under Habsburg rule would receive equal treatment. Indeed, Charles was prepared to federalize the dynasty's whole territorial complex if necessary. Like his late cousin, he wanted to increase the dynasty's role in the business of governing at the expense of ministers and bureaucrats. As deeply Catholic as Franz Ferdinand, the new sovereign also abhorred secular ethical models embedded in brutal capitalism and political liberalism. Again like the murdered archduke, he mistrusted the Prussian-German Empire, an attitude that would lead him into one of the worst blunders of his hapless reign. His relations with his wife and children exemplified marital probity, which many considered a welcome change from his father, Archduke Otto, a compulsive womanizer. The latter's appetites brought considerable grief upon his devoutly religious wife; her marital principles and her intense Catholicism marked her son for life. Indeed, some commentators felt that Charles's deference to Empress Zita, his pious and ambitious spouse, qualified as uxoriousness.[63]

All of these notions had serious advocates among various constituencies throughout the Dual Monarchy. Nevertheless, in a culture well conditioned to respect the image of an erect Franz Joseph on horseback even in old age, Charles had none of the external attributes of an emperor. He was short, slender and narrow-faced; visiting his troops he was all but smothered in his military greatcoat. His foreign minister, Count Otakar Czernin, occasionally called him the 'poor little Kaiser'. Boulevard wits in Vienna developed an assortment of quips about his unprepossessing bearing. Some called him a twenty-year-old (he was born in 1887) who thought and behaved like someone ten years younger. Unfair though all of these digs may have been, the critics were not entirely wrong. A picture of him with Empress Zita and their eldest son Otto, taken at his coronation in Budapest in 1916, was both sad and comical. The Crown of St Stephen was too big for the new king; the photographer caught it teetering just above Charles's eyebrows.[64] Indeed, his advisers had to tweak the paternal image of their sovereign to give it greater public credibility. The august stature of his office was played down; his qualities as a model family man were stressed, rather than those of straightforward paternal authority. The principle was meant to carry over to his peoples as well. Various amnesties that he granted to political prisoners in 1916 and 1917 supposedly followed the lines of forgiveness a father extended to wayward wives and their children. Zita soon appeared in schoolbooks as the maternal counterpart of her benevolent husband.[65]

Necessary to circumstances though this ploy may have been, it only worsened the dynasty's relations with its peoples, at least in Vienna. Authoritarian wartime governments in both halves of the Dual Monarchy had left the public little choice but to look to the state to relieve life's daily discomforts; now Charles and his wife were targets for such appeals. Letters recounting assorted miseries started coming to Zita. The bulk of these supplications, however, continued to go to Charles himself and in mounting numbers. They chronicled the accumulation of everyday troubles: dwindling supplies of food, clothing and shoes; too little money for rent and heating; and, occasionally, simple poverty. Others complained about bureaucratic slights or even warned of assassination plots.

In keeping with the parental analogy of the imperial couple were requests for Charles and Zita to assume guardianship of children. Far more frequent after 1917, a few were granted, particularly for cases where a father's military service was outstanding. Unsuccessful petitioners received a token payment and a bracelet with the emperor's initials on it. But the Charles-as-father figure started crumbling too. Though approaching the emperor closely without authorization was illegal, the government hesitated to punish such acts for fear of undercutting the emperor's humane self-image. By 1917 his motorcades were occasionally being stopped, more often than not by women begging for his help. Women were also preparing to march on Laxenburg, now Charles's residence, to beg him for relief from the shortages of food and fuel that they faced every day. While such people possibly still considered him a patriarch, as a mundane provider he was failing abysmally.[66]

Opinion in Hungary was taking the same turn, but with a more overtly political edge. From 1916 onward currency devaluation, shortages of basic goods and strong doubts about the quality of military leadership were eroding domestic commitment to the war. A year later, censors were intercepting letters from ordinary folk in the kingdom who made plain that they cared very little about who won or lost on the battlefield, so long as the conflict ended. With starvation an imminent threat, personal survival was the overwhelming concern. A couple of writers declared that having lost all respect for a monarchy that was treating them so shabbily, the Lenin-style Bolshevism now on display in Russia seemed preferable. Hungarian Social Democrats were especially critical. Large workers' demonstrations organized by the movement began in 1917, and even more extreme left-wing groups were forming. A sympathy strike in the kingdom, coordinated with a similar protest among workers in a Viennese munitions factory in 1918, intensified opposition even more broadly. After some stabs at political concessions, the conservative aristocrats controlling the royal government in Budapest tried outright force and suppression. Work stoppages only continued, now further reinforced by scattered mutinies within the army.[67]

By the summer of 1918 loss upon loss had all but destroyed the morale among the Dual Monarchy's troops, the late Franz Joseph's emblem of the unity of his lands. Men deserted outright; others, on temporary furlough, simply decided not to go back. Many took refuge in rural corners of the empire or even in the new Russia.[68] Emperor Charles manoeuvred to the end in the hope of saving his position and that of his dynasty, but his lands were not buying it. Every attempt to remake him as a 'Peoples' Emperor' (*Volkskaiser*), all his public appearances, and all the orders and awards citations he gave out to honour those who had worked to save him and his house, had failed to win the respect and loyalty of his subjects. Sincere though his concerns for his peoples may have been, his administrative style by itself often undercut his more positive qualities. His inborn modesty never compromised his belief that he ruled by the grace of God and had the right to act that way. Within this context, he could make the abrupt shifts in policy that annoyed his advisers. His impatience with bureaucracy in general kept him from delegating work, of which he had far more than he could handle effectively. By March 1918 soldiers on the streets of Vienna were overheard exchanging nasty wisecracks about the dynasty; riders on tramways were also telling disrespectful jokes. Nor did Charles and his government ever fully control the flow of enemy propaganda that reached Vienna and various sites in the empire. Hoping to expand their own kingdom in the postwar settlement, Italians opened up a vigorous anti-Habsburg campaign among other nationalities in the Habsburg lands, especially in Croatia and along the Dalmatian coast. The most technically imaginative of their efforts went broadly public on 9 August 1918 when the nationalist poet Gabriele D'Annunzio flew over Vienna and scattered leaflets to crowds below.[69]

Convinced that the war was a lost cause, Charles scrambled to save some position for himself. On 16 October 1918 he declared his intentions to federalize the Austrian half of the monarchy. Two days later, however, the Czechs issued a Declaration of Independence that cut straight to the sovereignty of the House of Habsburg: the dynasty was deemed

20 The funeral cortège of Emperor Franz Joseph, 1916.

'unworthy of leading our nation'. Echoing the sentiments of that journeyman who returned to serve the Dual Monarchy in order to destroy it, the
document sanctioned anything that the Czech people were doing to rid
the world of rule by the House of Habsburg-Lorraine. The beneficiaries
would be humankind and civilization as a whole. They quickly began
recovering the public space in Bohemia from statuary that reminded
local people of their rulers from Vienna; a likeness of the late Franz
Joseph was among them. The programme continued vigorously well into
the 1920s.[70] Hungary, to which the federalization decree did not apply,
began a contested life as a republic on 16 November.

Charles had waited to go until the armistice was signed on 11 November 1918. He resisted abdicating until the end, insisting that he could
not abandon duties that heredity had entrusted to him. When he did
agree to give up, he would only withdraw personally from government
and not in the name of his family. But the mood in Vienna had become
very unfriendly. Fear that a local version of the recent Russian revolution
was at hand gripped many, including the now ex-emperor. Some looked
upon every man returning from the eastern front as a possible Communist agent, eager to spread Bolshevism to the west. Considerable
unrest in the city buttressed these suspicions, although most of it stemmed
from food shortages and not programmatic left-wing activism.[71]

Towards evening on 11 November, the emperor and his family were
swiftly transported to the hunting lodge of Eckartsau on the Marchfeld,
recently renovated by Archduke Franz Ferdinand. It lay roughly 20 km

south of Dürnkrut, the burial site of King Otakar II, the Bohemian king whose defeat by Rudolph I had begun the Habsburgs ascent to greatness. Among the various perversions of imagery that had plagued the regime's management of the war, it was clearly the most ironic. Charles would soon regret his hasty departure. He had already fathered an heir to his thrones, Archduke Otto. Born in 1912, the boy had been repeatedly photographed in characteristically dynastic settings: with his ageing great-uncle Franz Joseph; walking between his father and mother in the emperor's funeral cortège (illus. 20), with his parents in their official picture for the Hungarian coronation and visiting airfields and other localities in Austria during the war. But broad popular internalizing of such performances had halted. The time that the Habsburgs could present themselves as defenders of a Christian faith to which both they and their subjects looked for salvation had long passed. The domestic miseries inflicted by the dynasty's latest self-protective war were absurdly at odds with any history it had of fostering the general welfare. Worst of all, the military, the last institution that dynasty had called upon to exemplify its sole sovereign power, had faltered abysmally in crucial moments. Nevertheless, thinking of the future even as he trembled before the present, Charles took his leave to protect his children.[72]

NINE

One Goodbye, Several Farewells

Return Appearances

Relief was the dominant mood in central and east-central Europe once a general armistice was declared. That much trouble would follow the redistribution of the Habsburg *imperium* in 1919 at the Paris Peace Conference occurred to very few. Regrets about the end of the dynasty's formal political life came largely from economic dislocations that Austria–Hungary's collapse brought with it and not the exit of its rulers.

Ex-emperor Charles botched whatever opportunities were left to restore himself to a throne. Under British military escort, he left Eckartsau for Switzerland on 23 March 1919. Before crossing the border the next day, he issued a manifesto that suggested he might contest the republican regime taking shape in a territorially redefined Austria: 'In war I was called to the throne of my fathers, in peace I wanted and want to be a just and genuinely caring father.'[1] The language was familiar, but it had lost all traction with the peoples he once governed. Other than among some aristocrats, devout Catholics, bureaucrats, students and, counter-intuitively, front-line veterans, the house was unwelcome in the new country.[2] The most strident opposition came from urban socialists, but many rural folk had given up on the monarchy too. To remove any chance of a Habsburg political resurrection, the assembly of the First Austrian Republic passed a Habsburg Exclusion Act on 3 April 1919 that abolished whatever sovereign rights the house might claim. Charles and his heirs could not set foot in the country unless they took an oath of citizenship that effectively ruled out monarchy as they understood it. The new regime swiftly confiscated most of the property that the dynasty and its cadet lines still owned in the country along with other assets. Income derived from these measures would go towards support for people disabled in the war and families whose chief provider had died in wartime military service.

A few Hungarian aristocrats remained loyal to Charles, tempting him to exploit a loophole in the Compromise of 1867 that opened a way for him to hang on as a monarch in Budapest. Constitutionally speaking, the Kingdom of Hungary still existed, and Charles's withdrawal from active government had applied only to the Austrian half of the Dual Monarchy. Miklós Horthy, an admiral in the erstwhile imperial-royal navy who had taken control of the realm in the midst of a wrenching social and economic civil insurrection that broke out at the end of the war, was technically a regent for a yet-to-be named ruler.

Charles ventured into the kingdom twice in 1921 to assume the position. Both times the former Habsburg officer rebuffed him. For all of Charles's benevolent assurances, Horthy feared that the dynasty's return would set off a bloody domestic conflict in a fragile state that could ill afford it. Foreign governments ranging from Hungary's central European neighbours to the governments of western Europe were also eager to keep the Habsburgs off the international scene. Charles's claims were formally dismissed under Hungarian law. There would be no more Habsburg rulers in Hungary. He died in 1922 in Madeira, where he had landed under British escort, following a brief captivity in the state he thought he could rule. With eight offspring to care for, ex-empress Zita remained on the lookout for thrones that would give them adequate livings. She was especially active in the cause of her eldest son, ex-archduke Otto.

By the end of the 1920s monarchist groups were recovering some public presence in Austria. In 1934, with the heavily pro-Catholic Fatherland Front controlling the government, the imperial double eagle once again appeared on an Austrian flag. Otto was made an honorary citizen of 1,600 Austrian communities. In 1935 Federal Chancellor Kurt von Schuschnigg lifted the republic's exclusion of the former ruling house. A devout jurist from the conservative Tyrol, he sympathized with the dynasty generally; some discussion took place about restoration of a monarchy in Austria alone. Once again, however, international opposition argued the idea down. Spokesmen for new sovereign states in central Europe such as Czechoslovakia were predictably adamant; bystanders were linguistically more inventive. The American journalist John Gunther had declared the previous year that 'the Habsburgs are more than a family, they are a sort of organism – a resplendent fungus long attached to the body politic of Europe. They are as prolific as mice and as international as counterfeiters . . . The family was always superior to the state.'[3]

Otto flirted briefly with National Socialism, but Hitler repelled him. As a student in Berlin from 1931–2 he refused two invitations to meet with the future dictator and turned to countering a threatened Nazi takeover in Austria. By 1936 he had strong support in the legitimist ranks of the Fatherland Front. Hitler returned the favour by moving him up a notch or so on his hit list.[4]

Otto also had good contacts with William C. Bullitt, the American ambassador in Paris, who had the ear of Franklin Delano Roosevelt in the United States; he urged the president to abandon the latter's republican inclination to think of the Habsburg monarchy as a 'Prisoner of peoples'. In 1940 Otto fled Belgium to the United States at Roosevelt's invitation. The u.s. State Department toyed with the idea of returning him as ruler of an independent and non-Nazi Austria once the Second World War came to an end. Emigrés from the former monarchy with keen memories of Habsburg-inflicted sufferings from 1914 to 1918 were still hearing nothing of it. Otto certainly had remembered how to behave like a monarch: in 1949 he bestowed noble titles on two families. In 1961, however, he declined when the Spanish dictator Francisco Franco offered him a throne in Spain. His family, said the one-time archduke, had long lost connections with its former Iberian outpost. He also renounced his claims to a monarchy in Austria, largely because he wanted to visit the land of his birth. The gesture did not, however, end Otto's troubles in his family's one-time patrimony. The Austrian State Treaty of 1955 had formally revoked the exile of the dynasty's members from the new Second Republic, but his criticism of the Austrian Socialist Party's membership in the new government had offended many. Once again, he was barred from the country. The ban was lifted only in 1966.[5]

Otto was not the only member of his far-flung house casting about for a throne. There was, for example, Archduke William, a cadet descendant of Archduke Charles, the Habsburg who temporarily checked Napoleon not far from Vienna in 1809. Fighting with the Dual Monarchy's forces against the Russians in the east, he tried to create a crown for himself in a briefly independent Ukraine. When that move imploded he emigrated to Spain and Paris, where he divided his time between speculative fiscal operations, sexual adventures with partners male and female, and hoping that he might yet find an appropriate political niche. The Nazis found him suspect; the Soviet Secret Police even more so: they kidnapped him from Vienna in 1947. His death place remains uncertain. The Red Cross reported that it was in Kiev; others said that it was in a gulag. Otto was in no way so adventurous; he clearly gave up on ruling any part of his family's former holdings. He never, however, lost the traditional Habsburg commitment to political supranationalism. For years he held a seat in the European parliament as a representative from Germany, his residence for much of the time.[6]

Second Thoughts among the Cultured

European politicians after the First World War found the Habsburgs a nuisance at best and dangerous at worst. Intellectuals who had criticized the dynasty's performance in the war continued their attacks after the conflict ended. Karl Kraus, whose polemics were a commentary on Franz Joseph's management of the war rather than a critique of dynastic monarchy as such, was relentless. His reworking of the lyrics of the still familiar imperial anthem was typically caustic:

> God preserve us, God protect us,
> From a kaiser in our land,
> Powerful without religion,
> Safe without his guiding hand;
> Out from underneath his crown,
> We firmly stand our ground;
> No more with any Habsburg throne,
> Will Austria's fate be bound.[7]

The master Czech satirist Jaroslav Hašek dismissed his one-time emperor through droll mockery of the Habsburg's beloved army and its cumbersome bureaucracy in the four-volume *The Good Soldier Švejk*, which appeared between 1920 and 1923.[8] At the core of Austrian composer Alban Berg's opera *Wozzeck*, first performed in 1925, is a searing depiction of the brutalities and hypocrisies in imperial-royal army life.

By 1927, however, the general spleen directed towards the dynasty had started to ebb, at least in Austria. Prettified Habsburg kitsch appeared on shelves and display counters in knick-knack and antiques shops. Those working to give the new state a viable historical identification began to look more dispassionately at what would come to be known as the *Kaiserzeit*. The Habsburgs themselves received kinder treatment. Bruno Brehm, who had been born in Ljubljana (Ger. Laibach), heard schoolchildren disparaging Franz Joseph after 1918. Convinced that the emperor might have done better if he had been younger and more energetic during the war years, the writer made fictionalized rehabilitations of the Habsburgs his lifetime mission.

The stage became more Habsburg-friendly too. *White Horse Inn* (*Im Weissen Rössl*), a fanciful version of the imperial past around Salzburg in operetta form, was derived from an 1897 play by Oscar Blumenthal and Gustav Kadelburg. The operetta was first performed in Berlin in 1930 and then transferred to Vienna, where it was strikingly successful, with some 700 performances there alone between 1931 and 1933. A white-bearded caricature of Franz Joseph had been part of the operetta's original text. Paul Hörbiger, a famous Austrian actor who was cast in the part, insisted that his former emperor deserved more respectful treatment. Some rewriting took place, but audiences apparently did not mind in the slightest.[9] The theatrical stereotype of Franz Joseph the Benevolent endured through the twentieth century. A Burgtheater performance in 1963 of Ferenc Molnár's *Liliom*, a tale of a hot-tempered but well-meaning carnival roustabout, featured a soft-spoken, elderly police magistrate with the white facial mutton chops that were one of the ex-emperor's prominent features.

But it is Joseph Roth who comes most immediately to mind in any search for the literary emblem of the pro-Habsburg turn in cultural circles, and not only for the skill and passion that he put into his work. Just as significant were the ideological twists and turns he took as he produced it. One should probably not entirely discount the fact that he was a working alcoholic who, by 1939, would effectively poison himself to death by drinking. At the same time, he was also the author of *Das falsche Gewicht* (*The False Weights*), a subtle but critical satire of bureaucratic intrusion upon customary life in rural Bukovina. As a young man he was a socialist and he never lost his ambivalent feelings towards the Habsburg monarchy generally, and towards Franz Joseph in particular.[10]

Roth, however, came to appreciate the depth of respect and affection for the old monarchy that it had elicited for centuries and which still lingered in some. His signature novel *Radetzkymarsch* (*Radetzky March*), published in 1932, explores the levels of professional and psychological interaction of members of the Trotta family with Franz Joseph's regime. Of Dalmatian origins, they serve the emperor as military officers and civil servants through the nineteenth century and into the twentieth. Their loyalty stretches from the battlefield to their private lives; some members identify so closely with a portrait of Franz Joseph in their home that they copy it in their clothes and physical demeanour. Generations of Trottas stand by as witnesses or contribute to the gradual breakdown of Habsburg rule and the ideals that sustained it.[11] An aura of romantic nostalgia hangs over the story, but Roth's deeper inspiration is clearly the aching sadness that comes with the realization that familiar things are gone forever.

Roth also had an uncommon flair for enlivening dynastic pageantry in print, a welcome distraction from the drabness of central and east-central Europe after the First World War. Such antics also took minds off the ideological power struggles among an array of movements ranging from the most globally inclusive Marxists to the most exclusionary nationalists, which fuelled vicious ethnic, racial and class antagonism. The most graphic example was the programmatic anti-Semitism found in varying degrees almost everywhere, but richly represented among the peoples once ruled by the Dual Monarchy.

Warm feelings in Europe towards the monarchy reappeared after the Second World War as well. The conflict left vast stretches of the continent as a whole in material ruin; authoritarian fascist regimes east of the Elbe were replaced almost uniformly by exploitative communist regimes, enforced by the Soviet army. Whatever calm and prosperity Franz Joseph's regime brought to parts of the region looked good by comparison. Forgotten in both republics and Soviet versions of them was that Franz Ferdinand's and Emperor Charles's impatience with bureaucratic and legislative procedures often fostered authoritarian regimes.

By 1963 at least one serious critic was questioning the historical benevolence of the monarchy. Claudio Magris, an Italian scholar and general man of letters, argued in *The Habsburg Myth in Austrian Literature* that writers who accepted idealized visions of Habsburg rule were themselves only condoning rigid social structures and moral timidity. The German translation of the book, which came out in 1966, heavily influenced two very important contrarian literary movements in Austria, the Graz group and the Vienna group.

Yet the realization that the peoples of central and east-central Europe had a shared, though not identical, pre-Marxist history continued to fuel interest in the dynasty. Calling for the comparative study of east central European literatures, the Hungarian scholar Tibor Klaniczay suggested in 1963 that he and many of his colleagues represented two political and cultural commonalities, one Soviet, the other Habsburg. Both polities had linked Slav and non-Slav alike. In fact, he went on, solidarity among the Habsburg peoples had a long history. Amid ritual nods to the contributions of Marxist-Leninist precepts and Russian scholarship, he recalled Conrad Celtis's late fifteenth-century Sodalitas Litteraria Danubiana (Danubian Society of Letters), which, sponsored by Emperor

Maximilian I, acknowledged the accomplishments of a wide range of contemporary academics and literati.[12]

A yet greater step towards rehabilitating the dynasty locally and internationally also had its roots in the culturally turbulent 1960s. Like other positive turns in the monarchy's history, it was laced with irony. Young counter-cultural radicals of the day, denouncing the intellectual timidity and social conformity that marked their parents' generation, located antecedents in the visual, musical and literary aesthetics of *fin de siècle* Vienna. The frank eroticism of Klimt, the emotional transcendence that Gustav Mahler hoped to achieve orchestrally, Karl Kraus's vitriolic contempt for mismanagement and hypocrisy in high places, all fed into the post-adolescent longing for personal freedom through membership in alternative societies.

Neglected for roughly three decades, these artefacts of the late nineteenth-century Habsburg metropolis quickly caught the attention of older people as well, but for quite different reasons. Such people read Vienna's culture and history far more reflectively than did radicalized youth, seeing it in a context of memory and experience rather than a longing for personal liberation in newly constructed alternative societies. Factual reinforcement for mature reflections on the subject came from three massive, and quite different, multimedia exhibitions on pre-war Vienna held in Paris, New York and the Austrian capital. These, in turn, had been inspired from an improbable, but very crucial, quarter. Once eager to escape Habsburg rule in any form, Italians were rethinking their views of the dynasty. Craving an alternative to the domestic terrorism and intractable political corruption of the 1970s and '80s, they looked to the orderliness with which the Habsburgs allegedly ran their governments. Out of such curiosity came the *fin de siècle* Vienna exhibition for the Venice Biennale in 1984, which would serve as a prototype for the larger events that followed in 1985 and 1986. What was once a highly contested region for governments in both Rome and Vienna was now the site of a noteworthy reconciliation. The doughtily republican French, once enemies of hereditary monarchy in any form, were also finding the Habsburgs more sympathetic. Linguistic discontents in Brittany, the Basque regions and the Languedoc had sensitized scholars and politicians alike to the challenges faced by a government that France had helped to dismantle in 1919.

In New York City a large and articulate community of Jewish émigrés, whose departure from Austria, Hungary and Czechoslovakia was an act of personal preservation rather than a quest for opportunity in the New World, put the exhibition to many uses. Most importantly it gave them a chance to explain to themselves and younger family members alike why a small bust of Franz Joseph still sat on a bookshelf or mantelpiece. A polity with a culture that produced a Klimt, a Kokoschka, a Mahler, and a Sigmund Freud, not to mention a Franz Lehár, was still a polity with a positive identification.

Unsurprisingly, the Austrian response was the most complex. The local Nazi regime had, perhaps unwittingly, agreed with Franz Joseph and Archduke Franz Ferdinand that the art of figures like Kokoschka was 'degenerate'. The second Austrian Republic made some effort to make up for lost time in the aesthetic educations of local young people, whose notions of modern art outside central Europe were still sketchy. The Vienna version of the exhibition, however, brought several basic facets of a bygone culture together in an exceptionally vivid way. That the student cohort among Austrian viewers spoke for their local counter-culture added to the ideological intensity of the entire scene; the 'culture' they were protesting against had yet-to-be examined associations with Nazis, who had suppressed the work of Kokoschka and others in the first place. Whatever feelings the last Habsburgs had about modernism in any form was beside the point; the art, architectural and design movements, and the music that was provoking imaginations throughout the world, had appeared on Franz Joseph's watch and that was enough. Christian Brandstätter, a prolific publisher of coffee-table books and other Vienna-oriented material, said in 1985 that he could produce six volumes about the former emperor annually and expect them to sell themselves.[13]

Moderate forms of dynastic rehabilitation continued. After the Soviet departure from Hungary in June 1991, the government renovated Empress Elisabeth's retreat at Gödöllő. Foreigners aplenty have come to ramble through the complex, but many Hungarians have explored it too. The Serbs, who get sizeable amounts of investment capital from Austrian banks, seem to be softening their opinions of the dynasty as well, at least officially. A historical museum in Sarajevo, near where Princip stood to shoot Franz Ferdinand, has a photograph of the young man that makes him look like a criminal. A monument to the archduke is due to be built in 2014 close to the site of his death.[14] The European Union's struggle to devise a comprehensive fiscal infrastructure in the early decades of the twenty-first century has prompted serious reflections about the dynamics that kept the Habsburg monarchy together for so many different peoples and for so long.[15]

Individual Habsburgs still maintain some public presence where they can find one. Roughly 600 of them are scattered throughout the world, living in a wide variety of circumstances. The two daughters who were Franz Joseph's direct heirs came into a considerable fortune that the Austrian state did not confiscate after 1918. Their children have lived quite comfortably. The current representative of this line, Markus Habsburg, who manages the imperial summer villa in Bad Ischl and calls himself 'archduke' on ceremonial occasions, is among them. He insists, however, that he has no political interests, probably a good thing as far as his house is concerned. A monarchist movement in Austria, the Black-Yellow Alliance, wants to make the Austrian presidency hereditary in the House of Habsburg. Such a person would be constitutionally empowered to veto parliamentary legislation and to call plebiscites. It is the only way, advocates say, that political reform will come to a system in which support for traditional governing parties has dropped sharply. The average age of the group's members is 35, a hint that they are more committed to change than to restoration of monarchy on historical grounds. Around 70 historic military regiments in Austria retain uniforms from the *Kaiserzeit* in storage, ready to be worn for funerals and other memorial occasions: the men who appear dressed in them, however, are not uniformly monarchist.

Some members of the house seem more ready to provoke controversy. Now that the prohibition against Habsburgs holding public office is no longer in force, Ulrich Habsburg may offer himself as a candidate for the Austrian presidency in 2016. Descended from the cadet line of his house once seated in Tuscany, he now resides in Carinthia. While his dynasty's instincts for the politically opportune appear to be soldered into his genes – he has considered running on the Green Party line and might accept a nomination from the Socialists if the party will have him – he is more a maverick than an authentic spokesperson for the traditional values of his family. One finds it hard to imagine him admiring the Order of the Golden Fleece with the enthusiasm of Charles Habsburg, the current head of the house.[16] The latter does, however, know that such authority is limited, even when privately exercised. Even though he could order his outspoken relative to stay out of high-profile national politics, he seems to be ready to let Ulrich go his own way.

Archduke Otto, the direct heir of the last emperor and his wife Zita, spent much of his life in comparatively straitened circumstances, living largely from an income generated by his books and public lectures. In 1951 he improved the fortunes of his house by marrying Regina, Princess of Saxony-Meiningen; they had five daughters and two sons. Family finances remained tight, however. Only after the 1970s, when he was drawn into active work for the Bavarian Christian Social Union party (CSU), did he have anything resembling a steady salary. Lawsuits over Habsburg property claims are still being pursued in Austria. Nevertheless, Otto's successor as the head of the house will probably have fewer fiscal worries than his father. In 1993 Charles married the enormously wealthy Francesca Thyssen-Bornemisza, her lack of equivalent heraldic status notwithstanding.

The couple has also produced a son, Ferdinand Zvonimir; Charles says, however, that his main concerns are shepherding the interests of his house and keeping its members on good terms with one another. Should he ever become more engaged politically, he is prepared to follow liberal principles. In fact he heartily endorses freedom of speech and freedom of movement for all. He also has no intention of compelling anyone in matters of faith. Charles is a keen supporter of the European Union. Like others in his extended family, he sees the arrangement as an updating of Habsburg pan-national aspirations. His siblings have already tried out their political wings in smaller contemporary settings: one sister, Walburga, is a member of the Swedish parliament; Gabriela, an art historian, now serves as the ambassador of Georgia to the Federal Republic of Germany; their other brother, George, is the Hungarian Special Envoy to the European Parliament.[17]

But for all of the circumspection with which the dynasty now conducts its affairs, it still retains a niche in the Austrian imagination and memory that allows it on occasion to recall what people once saw, thought and, above all, felt when the House of Habsburg-Lorraine appeared before them. The funeral and entombment of former empress Zita in 1989, at the peak of the world's fascination with *fin de siècle* Vienna, recalled to both friends and critics of the dynasty the Baroque solemnity that had once accompanied the dynasty's members as they joined their ancestors forever. Despite the events that followed Sarajevo, one of the most practised ceremonial ploys in the Habsburg public relations template still moved audiences deeply.

Her eldest son, Archduke Otto, died on 4 July 2011, at the age of 98. Several funeral services or obsequies followed: in the town of Pöcking in Bavaria where he had lived; at the pilgrimage site of Maria Zell in Styria and, for close relatives only, in the Benedictine abbey of Pannonhalma, near Győr in Hungary. His heart was entombed there as well. The metal urn suggested a piece of barbed wire: a reminder of his efforts to open the boundaries of Hungary for East Germans to cross in 1989. In Vienna, much of the house turned out, as did the ever-thinning ranks of European royalty. Sizeable crowds lined the streets of the Austrian capital on Saturday 16 July to watch the procession. True to tradition, it followed the route from St Stephen's Cathedral, where the Mass for the dead had taken place, to the Capuchin crypt. Here most of Otto's physical remains were deposited beside his ancestors. The honour guard that accompanied the coffin came from all regions of Austria: Tyrolean *Schützen* (Sharpshooters) and representatives from military units dressed in red, gold and white, with red or white feathered headdresses, the Franz Joseph-style *Stulphut*. The public, which numbered in the thousands, was deeply impressed for many reasons ('such a beautiful corpse' was one comment). Complaining is an art form in Vienna and soon there were sour references to public funds lavished on the event. But that was a familiar component of the Habsburg experience too. Like many of his forebears, Otto had left this earth memorably, regardless of cost.[18]

Genealogy: The House of Habsburg

The House of Habsburg (1273–1519)

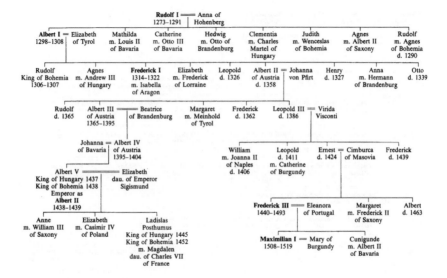

The House of Habsburg–Lorraine (1493–1780)

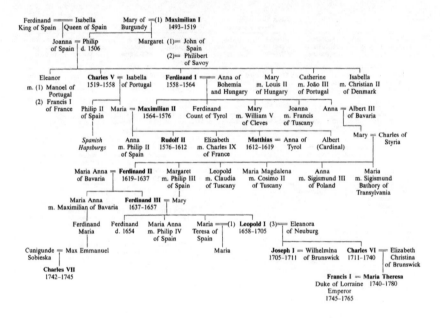

The House of Habsburg (1740–1918)

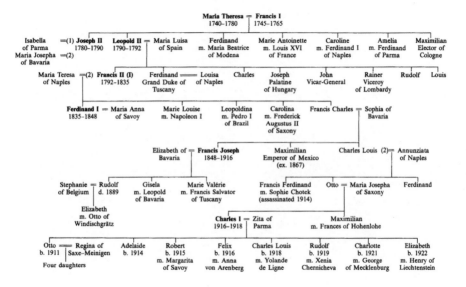

References

Introduction

1 Geoffrey Wheatcroft, 'Hello to All That', *New York Review of Books*, LVIII/2 (2012), p. 32; obituary of Paul Fussell, *New York Times*, 24 May 2012, A29.
2 Alan Sked, *The Decline and Fall of the Habsburg Empire*, 2nd edn (Harlow, 2001), p. 3. The Spanish side of the Habsburg story is well told and illustrated in Andrew Wheatcroft, *The Habsburgs: Embodying Empire* (New York, 1995).
3 For example, Gary Cohen, 'Nationalist Politics and the Dynamics of State and Society in the Habsburg Monarchy, 1867–1914', *Central European History*, XL (2007), pp. 241–78; Peter Urbanitsch, 'Pluralist Myth and Nationalist Realities: The Dynastic Myth of the Habsburg Monarchy – a Futile Exercise in the Creation of an Identity?', *Austrian History Yearbook*, XXXV (2004), pp. 101–14; Ernst Bruckmüller, 'Was There a "Habsburg Society" in Austria–Hungary?', *Austrian History Yearbook*, XXXVII (2006), pp. 1–16; Pieter M. Judson, 'L'Autriche-Hongrie était-elle un empire?', *Annales. Histoire, Sciences Sociales*, LXIII/3 (2008), pp. 164, 565–6, 583. See also, more generally, Pieter M. Judson, *Guardians of the Nation: Activists on the Language Frontiers of Imperial Austria* (Cambridge, MA, 2007) and Tara Zahra, *Kidnapped Souls: National Indifference and the Battle for Children in the Bohemian Lands, 1900–1948* (Ithaca, NY, 2008). A good summary of these arguments is Pieter M. Judson and Tara Zahra, 'Sites of Indifference to Nationhood', *Austrian History Yearbook*, XLIII (2012), pp. 21–7.
4 Daniel L. Unowsky, *The Pomp and Politics of Patriotism: Imperial Celebrations in Habsburg Austria, 1848–1916* (West Lafayette, IN, 2006), is exemplary. See also Nancy Wingfield, *Flag Wars and Stone Saints: How the Bohemian Lands Became Czech* (Cambridge, MA, 2007), pp. 108, 110–11, which has a vivid account of these occasions in nineteenth-century Bohemia.
5 See the commentaries in Jutta Schumann, *Die Andere Sonne: Kaiserbild und Medienstrategien im Zeitalter Leopolds I* (Berlin, 2003), pp. 16–17, 19–20, 25, 32, 34; Jan Assmann, *Das kulturelle Gedächtnis: Schrift, Erinnerung und politische Identität in frühen Hochkulturen* [1992] (Munich, 2007), pp. 17, 19–21, 29, 133, 141; Jan and Aleida Assmann, *Schrift und Gedächtnis: Beiträge zur Archäologie der literarischen Kommunikation* (Munich, 1983), pp. 265, 267, 270, 275–6; Jan and Aleida Assmann, 'Schrift und Kultur', in

Zwischen Festtag und Alltag: Zehn Beiträge zum Thema 'Mündlichkeit und Schriftlichkeit', ed. Wolfgang Raible (Tübingen, 1988), pp. 29–33.

6 Larry Wolff, *The Idea of Galicia: History and Fantasy in Habsburg Political Culture* (Stanford, CA, 2010), pp. 1, 4.

1 Getting Started

1 Sabine Weiss, 'Das Bildungswesen im spätmittelalterlichen Österreich. Ein Überblick', in *Die Österreichische Literatur: Ihr Profil von den Anfängen im Mittelalter bis ins 18. Jahrhundert (1050–1750)*, ed. Herbert Zeman (Graz, 1986), I/1, p. 228.

2 Friedrich Krieger, *Rudolf von Habsburg* (Darmstadt, 2003), pp. 32–7, 59, 63, 67–9,78–9; Günther Hödl, *Habsburg und Österreich, 1273–1493: Gestalten und Gestalt des österreichischen Mittelalters* (Vienna, 1988), pp. 19–20.

3 Krieger, *Rudolf*, pp. 3–5, 55–8, 99; Thomas Ebendorfer, *Chronicon Austriae*, *Scriptores Rerum Austriacarum*, ed. R.D.P. Hieronymus Pez (Leipzig, 1725), II, col. 913.

4 Krieger, *Rudolf*, pp. 78, 99, 108; Jiří Kuthan, *Premysl Ottokar II. König Bauherr und Mäzen: Höfische Kunst im 13. Jahrhundert*, trans. Petronilla Cemus, Lenka Reinerová and Ursel Sedmidubská (Vienna, 1996), pp. 14, 16, 34–7.

5 Kuthan, *Ottokar*, p. 17.

6 Krieger, *Rudolf*, p. 99.

7 Kuthan, *Ottokar*, pp. 27, 56–87; Mario Schwarz, 'Die Baukunst in Österreich zur Regierungszeit Ottokars II. Premysl (1251–1276)', in *Ottakar-Forschungen*, ed. Max Weltin and Andreas Kusternig (Vienna, 1979), pp. 453–8; Heinrich Appelt, 'Verfassungsgeschichtliche Grundlagen der Herrschaft König Ottokars von Böhmen über die österreichischen Länder', in *Ottokar-Forschungen*, p. xiv.

8 Krieger, *Rudolf*, pp. 127–54.

9 Max Weltin, 'König Rudolf und die österreichischen Landherren', in *Rudolf von Habsburg 1273–1291*, ed. Egon Boshof and Franz-Reiner Erkens (Cologne, 1993), pp. 106–9.

10 Krieger, *Rudolf*, pp. 131–7, 143; Max Weltin, 'Landesherr und Landherren: Zur Herrschaft Ottokars II. Přemysl in Österreich', *Ottokar-Forschungen*, pp. 168, 186, 197, 215.

11 Krieger, *Rudolf*, pp. 145–6, 149–150. Cf. Maurice Keen, *Chivalry* [1984] (New Haven, CT, 2005), p. 169.

12 Krieger, *Rudolf*, pp. 151–3, 238, 254; Kuthan, *Ottokar*, pp. 7–8, 34.

13 Hödl, *Habsburg*, pp. 25–6.

14 Krieger, *Rudolf*, pp. 243–6.

15 Ernst Bruckmüller, *Sozialgeschichte Österreichs*, 2nd edn (Vienna, 2001), pp. 63–83, 72–4; Appelt, 'Grundlagen', pp. ix–xii; Weltin, 'König Rudolf', pp. 110–11, 113, 115.

16 Friedrich Polleross, 'From the *exemplum virtutis* to the Apotheosis: Hercules as an Identification Figure in Portraiture: An Example of the Adoption of

Classical Forms of Representation', in *Iconography, Propaganda, and Legitimation*, ed. Allan Ellenius (Oxford, 1998), pp. 37–52; Fernando Checa Cremades, 'Monarchic Liturgies and the "Hidden King": The Function and Meaning of Spanish Royal Portraiture in the Sixteenth and Seventeenth Centuries', in *Iconography*, p. 98

17 Thomas Brockmann, 'Das Bild des Hauses Habsburg in der dynastienahen Historiographie um 1700', in *Bourbon-Habsburg-Oranien: Konkurrierende Modelle im dynastischen Europa um 1700*, ed. Christoph Kampmann, Katharina Krause, Eva-Bettina Krems and Anuschka Tischer (Cologne, 2008), p. 30; Peter Burke, 'The Demise of Mythologies', in *Iconography*, pp. 245–54.

18 Krieger, *Rudolf*, pp. 229, 234, 236, 239–40, 250.

19 Marie Tanner, *The Last Descendant of Aeneas: The Habsburgs and the Mythic Image of the Emperor* (New Haven, CT, 1993), pp. 208, 222.

20 Krieger, *Rudolf*, pp. 3–5; Thomas M. Martin, 'Das Bild Rudolfs von Habsburg als "Bürgerkönig" in Chronistik, Dichtung und moderner Historiographie', in *Blätter für deutsche Landesgeschichte*, CXII (1976), p. 215.

21 Ibid., pp. 204, 207, 209 and n. 4, 210–11, 229, 250.

22 Ibid., pp. 216–20, 223–6.

23 Brockmann, 'Bild', pp. 30–34; Harald Kleinschmidt, 'Das ostasienbild Maximilians I: Die Bedeutung Ostasiens in der Kaiserpropaganda um 1500', *Majestas*, VIII–IX (2000–2001), pp. 117–20; Paula Sutter Fichtner, *Emperor Maximilian II* (New Haven, CT, 2001), p. 107.

24 Johann Franzl, *Rudolf I: Der erste Habsburger auf dem deutschen Thron* (Graz, 1986), pp. 215–18, Weltin, 'Rudolf', pp. 117–22.

25 Hödl, *Habsburg*, pp. 40–46.

26 Karl-Friedrich Krieger, *Die Habsburger im Mittelalter: Von Rudolf I bis Friedrich III*, 2nd edn (Stuttgart, 2004), pp. 139–40; Hödl, *Habsburg*, pp. 75–92.

27 Krieger, *Habsburger*, pp. 132, 137; Wilhelm Baum, *Rudolf IV der Stifter* (Graz, 1996), pp. 13–16.

28 Krieger, *Mittelalter*, pp. 142–3; Markus Reisenleitner, *Frühe Neuzeit, Reformation und Gegenreformation: Darstellung, Forschungsüberblick, Quellen und Literatur* (Innsbruck, 2000) p. 20; Baum, *Rudolf IV*, pp. 242–76, 338.

29 Krieger, *Habsburger*, pp. 144–5; Baum, *Rudolf IV*, pp. 169–71, 176–86.

30 Weiss, 'Bildungswesen', pp. 239–40.

31 Krieger, *Habsburger*, pp. 145–6.

32 Ibid., pp. 23, 148, 155; Günther Hödl, 'Das Zeitalter der habsburgischen Teilungen 1379–1411', in *Regionale-Identitätsfindung durch Herrschaft-steilung im spätmittelalterlichen Österreich?*, ed. Otto Fraydenegg-Monzello (Graz, 1997), p. 20.

33 Krieger, *Habsburger*, pp. 156, 158–9.

34 Hödl, *Habsburg*, pp. 161, 165–6; Krieger, *Habsburger*, pp. 168–9, 170–71; Otto Frass, ed. *Quellenbuch zur österreichischen Geschichte* (Vienna, 1956), vol. I, p. 199.

35 Frass, *Quellenbuch*, I, pp. 195–6.

36 Karl Vocelka and Lynne Heller, *Die Lebenswelt der Habsburger* (Graz, 1997), p. 13; Hödl, *Habsburg*, p. 17.

37 Friedrich, *Habsburger*, pp. 132, 144–5.

38 Krieger, *Mittelalter*, p. 133; Hödl, *Habsburg*, pp. 115–18.

39 Krieger, *Habsburger*, p. 135; Francis Dvornik, *The Slavs in European History and Civilization* (New Brunswick, NJ, 1962), p. 66; Hödl, *Habsburg*, pp. 120–21, 160–62.

2 The Habsburgs Regroup

1 Karl-Friedrich Krieger, *Die Habsburger im Mittelalter: Von Rudolf I. bis Friedrich III.*, 2nd edn (Stuttgart, 2004), pp. 172–3, 185–6, 199–205.

2 Ibid., pp. 180–82, 188–92; Aeneas Sylvius Piccolomini [Pope Pius II], *Commentaries*, ed. Margaret Meserve and Marcello Simonetta, The I Tatti Renaissance Library (Cambridge, MA, 2003, 2007), vol. XII, p. 113.

3 Arno Strohmeyer, 'Geschichtsbilder im Kulturtransfer: Die Hofhistoriographie in Wien im Zeitalter des Humanismus als Rezipient und Multiplikator', in *Metropolen und Kulturtransfer im 15./16. Jahrhundert*, ed. Andrea Langer and Georg Michels (Stuttgart, 2001), p. 80; Sabine Weiss, 'Das Bildungswesen im spätmittelalterlichen Österreich. Ein Überblick', in *Die Österreichische Literatur: Ihr Profil von den Anfängen im Mittelalter bis ins 18. Jahrhundert (1050–1750)*, ed. Herbert Zeman (Graz, 1986), p. 230.

4 Hermann Wiesflecker, *Kaiser Maximilian I* (Vienna, 1986), vol. I, p. 66.

5 Report of Casper Enenkel von Albrechtsberg, in *Quellenbuch zur österreichischen Geschichte*, ed. Otto Frass (Vienna, 1956), vol. I, pp. 217–26; Krieger, *Habsburger*, pp. 170–72; Paul-Joachim Heinig, *Kaiser Friedrich III. (1440–1493): Hof, Regierung und Politik* (Cologne, 1997), vol. I, pp. 1–18; vol. II, pp. 1321–6, 1330–32, 1339–40; Manfred Holleger, *Maximilian I (1459–1519): Herrscher und Mensch einer Zeitenwende* (Stuttgart, 2005), p. 24.

6 Jakob Unrest, in Frass, *Quellenbuch*, I, p. 250; Günther Hödl, *Habsburg und Österreich, 1273–1493: Gestalten und Gestalt des österreichischen Mittelalters* (Vienna, 1988), pp. 214, 216; Krieger, *Habsburger*, p. 178.

7 Krieger, *Habsburger*, pp. 194, 199–200; Günther Hödl, *Habsburg*, p. 225; Frass, *Quellenbuch*, I, p. 250.

8 Heinig, *Kaiser Friedrich III*, vol. II, p. 1322.

9 Krieger, *Habsburger*, pp. 172–3.

10 Alfons Lhotsky, 'AEIOU. Die Devise Kaiser Friedrichs III. und sein Notizbuch', in Alfons Lhotsky, *Aufsätze und Vorträge*, ed. Hans Wagner and Heinrich Koller (Vienna, 1971), vol. III, p. 199.

11 Cf. Hödl, *Habsburg*, p. 224.

12 Paula Sutter Fichtner, *Protestantism and Primogeniture in Early Modern Germany* (New Haven, CT, 1989), p. 22; Hödl, *Habsburg*, p. 224; Wiesflecker, *Maximilian I*, vol. I, p. 66.

13 Hödl, *Habsburg*, pp. 222–3.

14 Heinig, *Friedrich III*, vol. II, pp. 1339–40; Jakob Unrest, *Österreichische*

Chronik, Monumenta Germaniae Historica. Scriptores, n.s. (Weimar, 1957), vol. II, p. 75.

15 Hollegger, *Maximilian I*, p. 288; Peter Niederhäuser and Raphael Sennhauser, 'Kaiser Maximilian I. und die Eidgenossen: Kunst und Propaganada des "letzten Ritters"', in *Vom 'Freiheitskrieg' zum Geschichtsmythos: 500 Jahre Schweizer-oder Schwaben Krieg*, ed. Peter Niederhäuser and Werner Fischer (Zürich, 2000), pp. 75, 77–8; Frass, *Quellenbuch*, I, p. 258.

16 Piccolomini, *Commentaries*, XII, pp. 117–18.

17 Hermann Wiesflecker, *Maximilian I: Die Fundamente des habsburgischen Weltreiches* (Vienna, 1991), p. 80.

18 Weiss, 'Bildungswesen', p. 236.

19 Cited in Stephan Füssel, 'Dichtung und Politik um 1500: Das "Haus Österreich" in Selbstdarstellung, Volkslied und panegyrischen Carmina', in *Die Österreichische Literatur*, ed. Zeman, p. 803, n. 2.

20 Piccolomini, *Commentaries*, vol. XII, p. 3; Gerhard Benecke, *Maximilian I, 1459–1519: An Analytical Biography* (London, 1982), p. 11.

21 Larry Silver, *Marketing Maximilian: The Visual Ideology of a Holy Roman Emperor* (Princeton, NJ, 2008), p. 3; Harald Tersch, ed., *Österreichische Selbstzeugnisse des Spätmittelalters und der Frühen Neuzeit (1400–1600)* (Vienna, 1998), p. 112.

22 Tersch, *Österreichische Selbstzeugnisse*, pp. 112, 135; Hollegger, *Maximilian I*, p. 247; Weiss, 'Bildungswesen', p. 233.

23 Jan-Dirk Müller, *Gedechtnus: Literatur und Hofgesellschaft um Maximilian I* (Munich, 1982), p. 274; Silver, *Marketing Maximilian*, p. 122; Füssel, 'Dichtung', pp. 815–31; Harald Kleinschmidt, 'Das ostasienbild Maximilians I: Die Bedeutung Ostasiens in der Kaiserpropaganda um 1500', *Majestas*, VIII–IX (2000–2001), pp. 116–17.

24 Füssel, 'Dichtung', p. 812; Dieter Mertens, 'Maximilians gekrönte Dichter über Krieg und Frieden', in *Krieg und Frieden im Horizont des Renaissance-humanismus*, ed. Franz Josef Worstbrock (Weinheim, 1986), p. 109.

25 Thomas Brockmann, 'Das Bild des Hauses Habsburg in der dynastienahen Historiographie um 1700', in *Bourbon-Habsburg-Oranien: Konkurrierende Modelle im dynastischen Europa um 1700*, ed. Christoph Kampmann, Katharina Krause, Eva-Bettina Krems and Anuschka Tischer (Cologne, 2008), pp. 30, 67; Niederhäuser and Sennhauser, 'Eidgenossen', p. 81; Kleinschmidt, 'Ostasienbild', pp. 125, 128–9, 134–5; Marie Tanner, *The Last Descendant of Aeneas: The Habsburgs and the Mythic Image of the Emperor* (New Haven, CT, 1993), pp. 103, 107, 124.

26 Tanner, *Last Descendant of Aeneas*, pp. 103, 107, 109, 208, 210–12; Brockmann, 'Bild', p. 39; Silver, *Marketing Maximilian*, p. 125.

27 Franz Matsche, *Die Kunst im Dienst der Staatsidee Kaiser Karls VI* (Berlin, 1981), vol. I, p. 60; Karl Vocelka, 'Höfische Feste als Phänomene sozialer Integration und internationaler Kommunikation: Studien zur Transfer-funktion habsburgische Feste im 16. und 17. Jahrhundert', in *Metropolen und Kulturtransfer*, ed. Langer and Michels, p. 150; William McDonald, 'Maximilian I of Habsburg and the Veneration of Hercules: On the Revival

of Myth and the German Renaissance', *Journal of Medieval and Renaissance Studies*, VI (1976), pp. 139–71.

28 For example Hannes Kästner, 'Meister der Kurzweil und Liebhaber des Saitenspiels: zur Literarischen Selbstinszenierung Maximilians I. in seinen pseudo-autobiographischen Werken', in *Musik und Tanz zur Zeit Maximilians I*, ed. Walter Salmen (Innsbruck, 1992), pp. 9–20.

29 Weiss, 'Bildungswesen', p. 232; C.J.A. Armstrong, 'The Golden Age of Burgundy', in *The Courts of Europe: Politics, Patronage, and Royalty, 1400–1800*, ed. A. G. Dickens (New York, 1977), p. 64.

30 Silver, *Marketing Maximilian*, pp. 231–5.

31 Paula Sutter Fichtner, 'Maximilian I and His Others: A Dialogue of the Fantastic and Real', in *Maximilian I. 1459–1519: Wahrnehmung, Übersetzungen, Gender*, ed. Heinz Noflatscher, Michael A. Chisholm and Bertrand Schnerb, Innsbrucker Historische Studien, XXVII (2011), p. 31.

32 Paula Sutter Fichtner, 'Actionable Propaganda and Communities of Memory: Austrian Historians in the Renaissance and Islam', revised from paper delivered at University of Copenhagen conference, 'Turks', September 2010. See also Fichtner, 'Maximilian I and His Others', pp. 31–44.

33 Tanner, *Last Descendant of Aeneas*, p. 124.

34 Inge Wiesflecker-Friedhuber, 'Maximilian I. und der St. Georgs-Ritterorden', *Archiv für vaterländische Geschichte und Topographie*, LXXVIII (1997), p. 434.

35 Kleinschmidt, 'Ostasienbild', pp. 137–9.

36 Marx Treitzsauerwein von Ehrentreitz, *Theuerdank* (Nuremberg, 1517), n.p.

37 Mertens, 'Maximilians gekrönte Dichter', pp. 108–9.

38 Giesela Goldberg, 'Das Gebetbuch Maximilians I. und der St. Georgs-Ritterorden', *Archiv für vaterländische Geschichte und Topographie*, LXXVIII (1997), pp. 461–5.

39 Silver, *Marketing Maximilian*, p. 118.

40 Dieter Mertens, 'Europäische Friede und Türkenkrieg im Spätmittelalter', in *Zwischenstaatliche Friedenswahrung in Mittelalter und Früher Neuzeit*, ed. Heinz Duchhardt (Cologne, 1991), pp. 80–82.

41 Ibid., pp. 85–6.

42 Tersch, *Österreichische Selbstzeugnisse*, p. 146; Wiesflecker, *Maximilian I*, vol. V, p. 483.

43 Holleger, *Maximilian*, pp. 111–12, 175; Wiesflecker, *Maximilian I*, vol. IV, p. 207.

44 Stanley Appelbaum, *The Triumph of Maximilian I* (New York, 1964), pp. 18–19; Kleinschmidt, 'Ostasienbild', pp. 142, 146–68; Harald Kleinschmidt, *Ruling the Waves: Emperor Maximilian I, the Search for Islands and the Transformation of the European World Picture, c. 1500* (Utrecht, 2008), pp. 185–9, 192. Cf. Sanjay Subrahmanyam, 'Holding the World in Balance: The Connected Histories of the Iberian Overseas Empires, 1500–1640', *American Historical Review*, CXII (2007), p. 1371.

45 Thomas Schauerte, *Die Ehrenpforte für Kaiser Maximilian I.* (Munich, 2001), pp. 151, 216–17 and n. 61, 389; Mertens, 'Europäische Friede', pp. 84–5, 90.

46 Most importantly, Anastasius Grün [Count Anton Alexander Auersperg], *Der Letzte Ritter*, 8th edn (Vienna, 1875).

47 For the tortuous story of the Innsbruck cenotaph, see Hubertus Günther, 'Das Projekt Kaiser Maximilians für sein Grabmal', in *Les Funérailles à la Renaissance*, ed. Jean Balsamo (Geneva, 2002), pp. 77–111; Elisabeth Scheicher, 'Das Grabmal Kaiser Maximilians I. in der Hofkirche', in *Die Kunstdenkmäler der Stadt Innsbruck: Die Hofbauten*, ed. Johanna Felmayer and Karl Oettinger (Vienna, 1986), pp. 355–426.

3 Champions of Faith and Family

1 James D. Tracy, *Emperor Charles V, Impresario of War: Campaign Strategy, International Finance, and Domestic Politics* (Cambridge, 2002), pp. 27–8; John Headley, *The Emperor and His Chancellor* (Cambridge, 1983), p. 131.

2 Alfred Kohler, *Ferdinand I, 1503–1564: Fürst, König, und Kaiser* (Munich, 2003), pp. 35–59. On Charles's Burgundian advisers, see Tracy, *Charles V*, p. 24.

3 Paula Sutter Fichtner, *Ferdinand I of Austria: The Politics of Dynasticism in the Age of the Reformation* (Boulder, CO, 1982), pp. 20–21, 28–9; Christopher F. Laferl, *Die Kultur der Spanier in Österreich unter Ferdinand I, 1522–1564* (Vienna, 1997), pp. 66–76.

4 Cf. Peter Niederhäuser and Raphael Sennhauser, 'Kaiser Maximilian I. und die Eidgenossen: Kunst und Propaganada des "letzten Ritters"', in *Vom 'Freiheitskrieg' zum Geschichtsmythos: 500 Jahre Schweizer-oder Schwaben Krieg*, ed. Peter Niederhäuser and Werner Fischer (Zürich, 2000), pp. 86, 88.

5 Arno Strohmeyer, 'Geschichtsbilder im Kulturtransfer: Die Hofhistoriographie in Wien im Zeitalter des Humanismus als Rezipient und Multiplikator', in *Metropolen und Kulturtransfer im 15./16. Jahrhundert*, ed. Andrea Langer and Georg Michels (Stuttgart, 2001), pp. 69–70.

6 Karl Vocelka, 'Höfische Feste als Phänomene sozialer Integration und internationaler Kommunikation: Studien zur Transferfunktion habsburgische Feste im 16. und 17. Jahrhundert', in *Metropolen*, pp. 141–4; Paula Sutter Fichtner, *Emperor Maximilian II* (New Haven, CT, 2001), p. 27. See also Kohler, *Ferdinand I*, pp. 118–29.

7 'Am Ersten Decembris geen Wienn khomen, das mir gegen der vorigen gestallt frembd anzusehen was. Alle vorstet, die nit vill minder gewest sein dann die Recht Stat, warn all geschlaipfft unnd ausgeprenndt, damit der Veindt sein bequemblichait darinn nit haben möcht, unnd aller maist, damit die Wörn in ein Ennge eingezogen worden. Darzue das Lanndt derselben Ennden alles durch den veindt verprennt unnd selten uber aines Armbrust schuss weit, das nit ain Todt mennsch, Phärdt, Schwein oder Khue gefunden gelegen. Von Wienn hintzt der Newstat unnd neben umb allenthalben. Es war Erbärmlich zusehen . . .'; Sigismund von Herberstein, *Selbst Biographie, 1486–1553*, Fontes rerum austriacarum. Scriptores (1855), I, p. 290.

8 Hans Sachs 'Der türkischen belägerung der stadt Wien mit handlung beider

teil auf das kürzest ordentlich begriffen', in *Die historischen Volkslieder der Deutschen vom 13. bis 16. Jahrhundert*, ed. Rochus von Liliencron (Leipzig, 1865–9), vol. III, pp. 587–94, 607; Georg Kirchmair, *Denkwürdigkeiten seiner Zeit*, Fontes rerum austriacarum. Scriptores (1855), I, p. 484; Wolfgang Lazius, *Vienna. Austriae* (Basel, 1546?), p. 7.

9 Sachs, 'Der türkischen belägerung', pp. 587–94.

10 *Del Gran Turco la Obsidion sopra Vienna d'Austria. Le horre[n]de crudelta et inauditi torme[n]ti usati da Turchi contra Christiani , et ancho la bestial fierezza co[n]tra animali domestici et cose i[n]animate. Mine, Strategemi, furibondi assalti de Turchi, et descrittione del potentissimo esercito loro . . .*, in *Turcica*, ed. Carl Göllner (Bucharest and Baden Baden, 1961–78), vol. I, pp. 202–3.

11 Ibid., pp. 174, 180, 184, 199, and plates 334, 342.

12 Ibid., p. 219.

13 Ibid., p. 206.

14 Lazius, *Vienna*, pp. 117, 150.

15 Ferdinand to Charles, 17 March 1531, in *Die Korrespondenz Ferdinands I*, ed. Herwig Wolfram and Christiane Thomas (Vienna, 1977), vol. III, pp. 76, 79. See also Paula Sutter Fichtner, 'Aber doch ein Friede: Ferdinand I., Ungarn, und die Hohe Pforte', in *Kaiser Ferdinand I: Ein mitteleuropäischer Herrscher*, ed. Martina Fuchs, Teréz Oborni and Gábor Ujváry (Münster, 2005), pp. 235–48.

16 '. . . que al juyizio de algunos por la mayor parte plebeyos y de baxa condicion que aun no tienen noticia de la potencia del Turco . . .'; Ferdinand to Charles, 17 March 1531, *Korrespondenz*, vol. III, p. 76.

17 Paula Sutter Fichtner, 'Actionable Propaganda and Communities of Memory: Austrian Historians in the Renaissance and Islam', revised from paper delivered at University of Copenhagen conference, 'Turks', September 2010; Paula Sutter Fichtner, *Terror and Toleration: the Habsburg Empire Confronts Islam, 1490–1850* (London, 2008), p. 52; Otto Frass, ed., *Quellenbuch zur österreichischen Geschichte* (Vienna, 1959), vol. II, p. 37.

18 'Wahrhaffte Gründtliche und aygentliche Beschreibung, welcher gestalt die Belägerung, so der Erbfeindt der gantzen Christenheit des Sultani Murath, Constantinopolitanischen Türkischen Kaysers, Sinan Bassa Obrister Vesier, nach Auffgebung der Stadt Raab, gegen der Kayserlichen Grainistz Vesstung Comorn in Nidern Hungern fürgenomen'; quoted in Helmut Lang, 'Die Neue Zeitung des 15. bis 17. Jahrhunderts – Entwicklungsgeschichte und Typologie. Unter besonderer Berücksichtigung der österreichischen Neuen Zeitungen', in *Die Österreichische Literatur: Ihr Profil von den Anfängen im Mittelalter bis ins 18. Jahrhundert (1050–1750)*, ed. Herbert Zeman (Graz, 1986), pp. 681, 683, 685, 689.

19 Strohmeyer, 'Geschichtsbilder', pp. 74–5.

20 Ferdinand to Charles, 17 March 1532, *Korrespondenz*, vol. III, pp. 76–7.

21 For an extended excerpt of the text see Karl Vocelka, *Die politische Propaganda Kaiser Rudolfs II. (1576–1612)* (Vienna, 1981), pp. 303–4.

22 Paula Sutter Fichtner, 'Of Christian Virtue and a Practicing Prince: Emperor Ferdinand I and his Son Maximilian', *Catholic Historical Review*, LXI/3

(1975), pp. 412–13.

23 See generally Howard Louthan, *The Quest for Compromise: Peacemakers in Counter-Reformation Vienna* (Cambridge, 1997).

24 Paula Sutter Fichtner, *Ferdinand I*, pp. 246, 249.

25 Ibid., p. 237; Fichtner, *Maximilian II*, p.114.

26 Vocelka, *Propaganda*, p. 253.

27 Fichtner, *Maximilian II*, p. 107.

28 Ibid., p. 218; Adam Wandruszka, *Das Haus Habsburg* (Vienna, 1956), p. 123; Peter H. Wilson, *Europe's Tragedy: A History of the Thirty Years War* (London, 2009), p. 65; Vocelka, *Propaganda*, pp. 143–5.

29 For the general picture of Rudolph and his court, see R.J.W. Evans, *Rudolf II and his World* (Oxford, 1973).

30 Thomas DaCosta Kaufmann, *Court, Cloister, and City: The Art and Culture of Central Europe, 1450–1800* (Chicago, 1995), p. 186; Vocelka, *Propaganda*, pp. 102–3.

31 Vocelka, *Propaganda*, pp. 140–41, 200–01, 206, 208; Paula Sutter Fichtner, 'A Community of Illness: Ferdinand I and his Family', in *Kaiser Ferdinand I. Aspekte eines Herrscherlebens*, ed. Martina Fuchs and Alfred Kohler (Münster, 2003), pp. 214–15; Arno Strohmeyer, 'Wahrnehmungen des Fremden: Differenzerfahrungen von Diplomaten im 16. und 17. Jahrhundert: Forschungsstand-Erträge-Perspektiven', in *Wahrnehmungen des Fremden: Differenzerfahrungen von Diplomaten im 16. und 17. Jahrhundert*, ed. Michael Rohrschneider and Arno Strohmeyer (Münster, 2007), pp. 22–3; Thomas DaCosta Kaufmann, *Variations on the Imperial Theme: Studies in Ceremonial, Art and Collecting in the Age of Maximilian II* (New York, 1978), pp. 105ff; Kaufmann, *Court, Cloister*, p. 59; Selma Krasa-Florian, *Die Allegorie der Austria: Die Entstehung des Gesamtstaatsgedankens in der österreichisch-ungarischen Monarchie und die bildende Kunst* (Vienna, 2007), p. 32; Evans, *Rudolf*, pp. 116–61.

32 Wilson, *Tragedy*, p. 105.

33 Vocelka, *Propaganda*, p. 168.

34 Ibid., pp. 90–95, 160–61.

35 Ibid., pp. 239–45.

36 Joseph F. Patrouch, *Queen's Apprentice: Archduchess Elizabeth, Empress María, the Habsburgs, and the Holy Roman Empire, 1554–1569* (Leiden, 2010), p. 20; Fichtner, *Terror and Toleration*, pp. 46–57.

37 Juliusz Chrościcki, 'Ceremonial Space', in *Iconography, Propaganda, and Legitimation*, ed. Allan Ellenius (Oxford, 1998), pp. 202–3.

38 I am grateful to Professor Robert Bireley sj of Loyola University in Chicago, who shared with me his insights on these matters and others throughout this work in his study of Ferdinand II, now in manuscript.

39 Wilson, *Tragedy*, pp. 58–61.

40 Christoph Kampmann, *Reichsrebellion und kaiserliche Acht* (Münster, 1992), pp. 6–7; Robert Bireley, *The Counter-Reformation Prince: Anti-Machiavellianism or Catholic Statecraft in Early Modern Europe* (Chapel Hill, NC, 1990), pp. 45–6, 50–51, 54–5, 61; Giovanni Botero, *The Reason of State*, trans. P. J. Waley and D. P. Waley (London, 1956), p. 162; Ilsebill

Barta, *Familienporträts der Habsburger: Dynastische Repräsentation im Zeitalter der Aufklärung* (Vienna, 2001), p. 58; Notker Hammerstein, 'Kommentar', in *Staatslehre der frühen Neuzeit*, ed. Notker Hammerstein (Frankfurt am Main, 1996), p. 1171.

41 Wilson, *Tragedy*, p. 67.

42 Ibid., pp. 62, 68–9, 74, 104.

43 Ibid., p. 72; Grete Mecenseffy, *Geschichte des Protestantismus in Österreich* (Graz, 1956); Regina Pörtner, *The Counter-Reformation in Central Europe: Styria, 1580–1630* (Oxford, 2001), pp. 144–80.

44 Jaroslav Pánek, 'Ferdinand I. – der Schöpfer des politischen Programms der österreichischen Habsburger', in *Die Habsburgermonarchie 1620 bis 1740*, ed. Petr Mat'a and Thomas Winkelbauer (Stuttgart, 2006), p. 65.

45 Howard Louthan, *Converting Bohemia: Force and Persuasion in the Catholic Reformation* (Cambridge, 2006), pp. 20–21, 48, 160–61, 181–5.

46 Wilson, *Tragedy*, pp. 276–7, 435, 543–51, 589.

47 Geoffrey Parker, *The Thirty Years War* (London, 1984), pp. 138–9; Geoff Mortimer, *Wallenstein: The Enigma of the Thirty Years War* (Basingstoke, 2010), pp. 199–220.

48 Thomas Schroeder, 'The Origins of the German Press', in *The Politics of Information in Early Modern Europe*, ed. Brendan Dooley and Sabrina Baron (London, 2007), pp. 135, 145–6; Christoph Kampmann, *Reichsrebellion*, pp. 173, 178–80, 190, 193, 195, 201–21; Wilson, *Tragedy*, pp. 824–6.

49 Mark Hengerer, *Kaiser Ferdinand III. (1608–1657): Eine Biographie* (Vienna, 2012), p. 288; Lothar Höbelt, *Ferdinand III. (1609–1657): Friedenskaiser wider Willen* (Graz, 2008), pp. 265–86; Wilson, *Tragedy*, pp. 588, 846–7.

50 Mecenseffy, *Protestantismus*, pp. 164–5; Karl Vocelka and Lynne Heller, *Die Lebenswelt der Habsburger: Kultur- und Mentalitätsgeschichte einer Familie* (Graz, 1997), pp. 139–40; Wilson, *Tragedy*, pp. 126–7, 276–7, 435, 589.

51 Wilson, *Tragedy*, pp. 846–7.

52 Vocelka and Heller, *Lebenswelt*, pp. 17–18.

53 Ruprecht Wimmer, 'Constantinus redivivus: Habsburg im Jesuitendrama des 17. Jahrhunderts', in *Die Österreichische Literatur*, ed. Zeman, pp. 1105–6, 1109–10, 1113, 1115–16.

54 Maria Goloubeva, *The Glorification of Emperor Leopold I in Image, Spectacle, and Text* (Mainz, 2000), pp. 57–8.

55 John P. Spielman, *Leopold I of Austria* (New Brunswick, NJ, 1977), pp. 108–10.

56 Hellmut Lorenz, 'Die Wiener Hofburg im 18. Jahrhundert: Legitimation durch Tradition', in *Bourbon-Habsburg-Oranien: Konkurrierende Modelle im dynastischen Europa um 1700*, ed. Christoph Kampmann, Katharina Krause, Eva-Bettina Krems and Anuschka Tischer (Cologne, 2008), pp. 96–106.

57 Goloubeva, *Glorification*, p. 128.

58 Jörg Ulbert, 'Die österreichischen Habsburger in bourbonischer Sicht am Vorabend des Spanischen Erbfolgekriegs', in *Bourbon-Habsburg-Oranien*, p. 249; Martin Wrede, 'Türkenkrieger, Türkensieger: Leopold I. und Ludwig XIV. als Retter und Ritter der Christenheit', in *Bourbon-Habsburg-Oranien*, pp. 148–9, 152–8; Hendrick Ziegler, 'Stat Sol. Luna Fugit. Hans Jacob Wolrabs Joshua Medaille auf Kaiser Leopold I und Ihre Reception in

Frankreich', in *Bourbon-Habsburg-Oranien*, pp. 166, 169–71, 176, 179–80 n. 37, 181.

59 Mario Infelise, 'The War, the News, and the Curious: Military Gazettes in Italy', in *Politics of Information*, ed. Dooley and Baron, pp. 217–20, 225, 232.

60 Goloubeva, *Glorification*, p. 59; Jutta Schumann, *Die Andere Sonne: Kaiserbild und Medienstrategien im Zeitalter Leopolds I* (Berlin, 2003), p. 300.

61 Goloubeva, *Glorification*, pp. 50, 96–7; Wilson, *Tragedy*, p. 127; Magdelena Hawlik-Van de Water, *Die Kapuzinergruft: Begräbnisstätte der Habsburger in Wien* (Vienna, 1987), p. 132; Vocelka and Heller, *Lebenswelt*, pp. 63–4.

62 Hawlik-Van de Water, *Kapuzinergruft*, p. 132; Goloubeva, *Glorification*, pp. 45–9; Schumann, *Andere Sonne*, pp. 299–301, 305.

63 Goloubeva, *Glorification*, p. 51.

64 Ziegler, 'Stat Sol. Luna Fugit', p. 181 n. 38; Wrede, 'Türkenkrieger', pp. 148–9, 153–5; Ulbert, 'Habsburger', p. 249; Schumann, *Andere Sonne*, p. 306.

65 Schumann, *Andere Sonne*, pp. 306–15, 350.

66 Goloubeva, *Glorification*, pp. 53–4; Schumann, *Andere Sonne*, pp. 319–20.

67 Andreas Weigl, 'Die Bedeutung des Wiener Hofes für die städtische Öknomie in der zweiten Hälfte des 17. Jahrhunderts', in *Ein zweigeteilter Ort? Hof und Stadt in der Frühen Neuzeit*, ed. Claudine Pils (Vienna, 2005), pp. 62–4, 69, 75.

68 Cf. Wrede, 'Türkenkrieger', pp. 156–7.

69 Hawlik-Van de Water, *Kapuzinergruft*, p. 132; Goloubeva, *Glorification*, pp. 226–7.

70 Vocelka, 'Feste', p. 150.

4 New Tactics for New Times

1 Ernst Bruckmüller, *Sozialgeschichte Österreichs*, 2nd edn (Vienna, 2001), pp. 142–5.

2 C. A. Macartney, ed., *The Habsburg and Hohenzollern Dynasties in the Seventeenth and Eighteenth Centuries* (New York, 1970), pp. 70–74, 78; Otto Frass, *Quellenbuch zur österreichischen Geschichte* (Vienna, 1970), vol. II, p. 182.

3 Frass, *Quellenbuch*, II, pp. 178–9.

4 Ibid., p. 181.

5 An English-language excerpt of these crucial passages is to be found in Paula Sutter Fichtner, *The Habsburg Empire: From Dynasticism to Multinationalism* (Malabar, FL, 1997), pp. 123–4.

6 Michael Hochedlinger, *Austria's Wars of Emergence, 1683–1797* (London, 2003), pp. 205–8; Reed Browning, *The War of the Austrian Succession* (New York, 1993), pp. 38–9.

7 Ernst Wangermann, *The Austrian Achievement, 1700–1800* (London, 1973), p. 27; Charles Ingrao, *The Habsburg Monarchy, 1618–1815* (Cambridge, 1994), pp. 126–42, lays out these issues clearly.

8 Hubert Ch. Ehalt, *Ausdrucksformen absolutistischer Herrschaft: Der Wiener Hof im 17. und 18. Jahrhundert* (Vienna, 1980), pp. 83–113; Paula Sutter

Fichtner, *Terror and Toleration: The Habsburg Empire Confronts Islam, 1490–1850* (London, 2008), pp. 57–8; Mark Hengerer, 'Embodiments of Power: Baroque Architecture in the Former Habsburg Residences in Graz and Innsbruck', in *Embodiments of Power: Building Baroque Cities in Europe*, ed. Gary B. Cohen and Franz A. J. Szabo (New York, 2008), pp. 16–17.

9   Andreas Weigl, 'Die Bedeutung des Wiener Hofes für die städtische Ökonomie in der zweiten Hälfte des 17. Jahrhunderts', in *Ein zweigeteilter Ort? Hof und Stadt in der frühen Neuzeit*, ed. Claudine Pils (Vienna, 2005), pp. 64, 67; Franz Matsche, *Die Kunst im Dienst der Staatsidee Kaiser Karls VI* (Berlin, 1981), vol. I, pp. 375–7.

10 Salamon Kleiner, *Wahrhafte und genaue Abbildung aller Kirchen und Klöster, vieler Paläste, Monumente, Spitäler und Bürgerhäuser in Wien und seinen Vorstädten*, ed. Anton Macku, Alfred May and Hans Aurenhammer (Graz, n.d.), vol. I, p. 17.

11 Matsche, *Staatsidee*, vol. I, pp. 232, 328, 408–16.

12 Ibid., pp. 404–5, 413, 416–17.

13 Ibid., pp. 419–27; Hochedlinger, *Austria's Wars of Emergence*, pp. 138–9.

14 'Zum grössten Nutzen sowohl des Gemeinwesens wie auch dem privaten Vorteil der meisten . . .', in Matsche, *Staatsidee*, vol. I, p. 403.

15 Hellmut Lorenz, 'Die Wiener Hofburg im 18. Jahrhundert: Legitimation durch Tradition', in *Bourbon-Habsburg-Oranien: Konkurrierende Modelle im dynastischen Europa um 1700*, ed. Christoph Kampmann, Katharina Krause, Eva-Bettina Krems and Anuschka Tischer (Cologne, 2008), pp. 97–8.

16 Matsche, *Staatsidee*, vol. I, pp. 377, 386–427.

17 Thomas DaCosta Kaufmann, *Court, Cloister, and City: The Art and Culture of Central Europe, 1450–1800* (Chicago, 1995), p. 300.

18 Matsche, *Staatsidee*, vol. I, pp. 398–400.

19 Magdalena Hawlik-Van de Water, *Die Kapuzinergruft: Begräbnisstätte der Habsburger in Wien* (Vienna, 1987), p. 58.

20 Matsche, *Staatsidee*, vol. I, pp. 386–427; Paula Sutter Fichtner, *The Habsburg Monarchy, 1490–1850: Attributes of Empire* (Basingstoke, 2003), p. 141.

21 Thomas Martin, 'Mythologische Heldenapothesen in Deckengemälden Wiener Adelspaläste des frühen 18. Jahrhunderts', in *Ex fumo lucem: Baroque Studies in Honour of Klára Garas*, ed. Zsuzsana Dobos (Budapest, 1999), vol. I, pp. 318, 331, 336–7, 340–44 and n. 73, 350–52; Martin Wrede, 'Türkenkrieger, Türkensieger: Leopold I. und Louis XIV. als Retter und Ritter der Christenheit', in *Bourbon-Habsburg-Oranien*, p. 163; Ulrike Seeger, 'Herkules, Alexander, Aeneas: Präsentationsstrategien der Türkensieger Prinz Eugen, Ludwig Wilhelm von Baden-Baden und Max Emmanuel von Bayern', in *Bourbon-Habsburg-Oranien*, pp. 184–8, 190–91.

22 Ilsebill Barta, *Familienporträts der Habsburger: Dynastische Repräsentation im Zeitalter der Aufklärung* (Vienna, 2001), pp. 37, 52, 54, 149 n. 133, 153 n. 219.

23 Alfred Ritter von Arneth, ed., 'Zwei Denkschriften der Kaiserin Maria Theresa', *Archiv für Österreichische Geschichte*, XLVII/2 (1871), pp. 282–3, 285–304, 326.

24 Barta, *Familienporträts*, pp. 45–9.

25 Lorenz, 'Wiener Hofburg', p. 102.
26 Karl Vocelka and Lynne Heller, *Die Lebenswelt der Habsburger: Kultur- und Mentalitätsgeschichte einer Familie* (Graz, 1997), pp. 147–8.
27 Bruckmüller, *Sozialgeschichte*, pp. 193–5; Barta, *Familienporträts,* pp. 19, 91–116, 199; Michael Yonan, *Empress Maria Theresa and the Politics of Habsburg Imperial Art* (University Park, PA, 2011), p. 98.
28 Arneth, 'Zwei Denkschriften', p. 305.
29 Maria Theresa to Maria Amalia, end of June 1769, in Severin Perrig, ed., *'Aus mütterlicher Wohlmeining': Kaiserin Maria Theresia und ihre Kinder. Ein Korrespondenz* (Weimar, 1999), pp. 145–50; Maria Theresa to Marie Antoinette, 3 November 1780, ibid., p. 264.
30 Maria Theresa to Marie Antoinette, 30 July 1775, ibid., p. 217; Larry Wolff, 'Habsburg Letters: the Disciplinary Dynamics of Epistolary Narrative in the Correspondence of Maria Theresa and Marie Antoinette', in *Marie Antoinette*, ed. Dena Goodman (New York, 2003), pp. 28–30; *Wiener Zeitung*, 8 January 1771.
31 Maria Theresa to Count Franz Thurn, *Ajo* (tutor) to Leopold II, 1761, in *'Mütterlicher'*, p. 37; Maria Theresa to Archduke Maximilian, April 1774, ibid., p. 206; Maria Theresa to Archduke Ferdinand, 2 January 1772, ibid., pp. 181–2. See also Maria Theresa to Archduke Ferdinand, 14 May 1779, ibid., p. 251.
32 For example, Maria Theresa to Maria Christina, 4 September 1754, ibid., p. 24; Maria Theresa to Archduke Maximilian, April 1774, ibid., p. 204.
33 Arneth, 'Zwei Denkschriften', p. 287.
34 I am indebted to Franz A. J. Szabo for alerting me to this.
35 Maria Theresa to Archduchess Maria Carolina, April 1768, in *'Mütterlicher'*, p. 129; Yonan, *Empress Maria Theresa and the Politics of Habsburg Imperial Art*, pp. 173–8.
36 Derek Beales, *Joseph II: In the Shadow of Maria Theresa, 1741–1780* (Cambridge, 1987), p. 158.
37 Hochedlinger, *Austria's Wars of Emergence*, pp. 305–7, 315–16; Franz A. J. Szabo, *The Seven Years War in Europe, 1756–1763* (Harlow, 2008), pp. 26–7.
38 Ibid., pp. 64–5; Hochedlinger, *Austria's Wars of Emergence*, p. 306.
39 Maria Theresa to Albert of Saxony-Teschen, 18 April 1776, in *'Mütterlicher'*, p. 94; Yonan, *Empress Maria Theresa and the Politics of Habsburg Imperial Art*, pp. 67, 77–8, 86–7. On the use of 'Madame' in court ceremony, see Christina Hofmann-Randall, 'Die Herkunft und Tradierung des Burgundischen Hofzeremoniells', in *Zeremoniell als höfische Ästhetik in Spätmittelalter und Früher Neuzeit*, ed. Jörg Jochen Berns and Thomas Rahn (Tübingen, 1995), p. 154.
40 Yonan, *Empress Maria Theresa and the Politics of Habsburg Imperial Art*, pp. 73, 83–5, 87–8.
41 Arneth, 'Zwei Denkschriften', pp. 294–5.
42 Macartney, *Habsburg and Hohenzollern*, p. 106; James Van Horn Melton, *Absolutism and the Eighteenth-century Origins of Compulsory Schooling in Prussia and Austria* (Cambridge, 1988), p. 208; Derek Beales, *Prosperity and Plunder: European Catholic Monasteries in the Age of Revolution, 1650–1815*

(Cambridge, 2003), pp. 181, 205.

43 Beales, *Prosperity and Plunder*, pp. 182–3; Gábor Tűskés and Éva Knapp, *Volksfrömmigkeit in Ungarn: Beiträge zur vergleichenden Literatur- und Kulturgeschichte* (Dettelbach, 1996), pp. 226–7.

44 Sabine Weiss, 'Das Bildungswesen im spätmittelalterlichen Österreich: Ein Überblick', in *Die österreichische Literatur: Ihr Profil von den Anfängen im Mittelalter bis ins 18. Jahrhundert (1050–1750)*, ed. Herbert Zeman (Graz, 1986), pp. 212–24, 236.

45 Ibid., pp. 232–3.

46 Herbert Zeman, 'Die Alt-Wiener Volkskomödie des 18. und frühen 19. Jahrhunderts: ein gattungsgeschichtlicher Versuch', in *Österreichische Literatur*, ed. Zeman, p. 1366.

47 Maria Theresa to Archduke Ferdinand, 12 December 1771, 'Mütterlicher', p. 180; Maria Theresa to Archduke Maximilian, April 1774, ibid., p. 205.

48 Maria Theresa to Maria Carolina, ibid., pp. 109–10; Maria Theresa to Maria Carolina, 'beginning of April 1768', ibid., pp. 116–17; Maria Theresa to Archduke Ferdinand, 28 October 1772 , ibid., p. 189.

49 See ibid., pp. 31, 33, 35, 53, 97, 147, 175, 229; Yonan, *Empress Maria Theresa and the Politics of Habsburg Imperial Art*, pp. 108–10, 118.

50 Beales, *Joseph II: In the Shadow of Maria Theresa*, plate 7.

51 Frass, *Quellenbuch*, II, p. 343.

52 Melton, *Absolutism and the Eighteenth-Century Origins of Compulsory Schooling*, p. 186.

53 Ibid., pp. 203, 208, 222, 225; Bruckmüller, *Sozialgeschichte*, pp. 240–41.

54 Melton, *Absolutism and the Eighteenth-century Origins of Compulsory Schooling*, pp. 215–16; Frass, *Quellenbuch*, II, p. 343.

55 Bruckmüller, *Sozialgeschichte*, p. 241.

56 T.C.W. Blanning, *The Culture of Power and the Power of Culture: Old Regime Europe, 1660–1789* (Oxford, 2002), pp. 175–6.

57 Paula Sutter Fichtner, 'Print versus Speech: Censoring the Stage in Eighteenth Century Vienna', in *Freedom of Speech: The History of an Idea*, ed. Elizabeth Powers (Lewisburg, PA, 2011), p. 84.

58 Ibid., p. 2; Franz Hadamowsky, 'Zur Quellenlage des Wiener Volkstheaters von Philip Hafner bis Anzengruber', in *Die österreichische Literatur*, ed. Zeman, pp. 580–81; Hawlik-Van de Water, *Die Kapuzinergruft*, pp. 16–17; Joseph von Sonnenfels, *Briefe über die Wienerische Schaubühne* [Vienna, 1768] (Vienna, 1884), p. iii.

59 Maria Theresa to Archduchess Maria Christina, 4 September 1754, in 'Mütterlicher', p. 24.

60 Fichtner, 'Print versus Speech', pp. 80–90.

61 Beales, *Prosperity and Plunder*, p. 184; Beales, *Joseph II: In the Shadow of Maria Theresa*, pp. 482–4, 488; Maria Theresa to Joseph II, 24 December 1775, in 'Mütterlicher', p. 223.

62 Derek Beales, *Enlightenment and Reform in Eighteenth-century Europe* (London, 2005), pp. 103–5; Franz A. J. Szabo, 'Prolegomena to an Enlightened Despot? Text and Subtext in Joseph II's Co-Regency Memoranda', in *Politics and Culture in the Age of Joseph II*, ed. Franz A. J. Szabo, Antal Szántay and

István György Toth (Budapest, 2005), pp. 20–21.

63 Beales, *Prosperity and Plunder,* p. 212; Hawlik-Van de Water, *Kapuzinergruft,* p. 179; Vocelka and Heller, *Lebenswelt,* pp. 259, 262.

64 Vocelka and Heller, *Lebenswelt,* pp. 250–53, 255–6.

65 'Allen Menschen gewidmeter Belustigungsort, von ihrem Schätzer', in Johann Pezzl, *Beschreibung und Grundriss der Haupt und Residenzstadt Wien,* 3rd edn (Vienna, 1809), pp. 336–40.

66 Werner Telesko, *Geschichtsraum Österreich: Die Habsburger und ihre Geschichte in der bildenden Kunst des 19. Jahrhunderts* (Vienna, 2006), pp. 118–19; Derek Beales, *Joseph II: Against the World, 1780–1790* (Cambridge, 2009), pp. 435–6, 443; Vocelka and Heller, *Lebenswelt,* pp. 139, 259, 262; Andrea Sommer-Mathis, 'Theatrum und Ceremoniale: Rang und Sitzordnungen bei den theatralische Veranstaltungen am Wiener Kaiserhof', in *Zeremoniell,* ed. Berns and Rahn, pp. 532–3.

67 Hawlik-Van de Water, *Kapuzinergruft,* pp. 14–15; Joseph II to Leopold, 4 December 1780, in *'Mütterlicher',* p. 269.

68 Beales, *Joseph II: Against the World,* pp. 446–55.

69 Ibid., pp. 457–8, 460; Beales, *Enlightenment and Reform,* pp. 95–6.

70 Ibid.; Fichtner, 'Print vs. Speech', p. 92; Beales, *Joseph II: Against the World,* pp. 430, 465–7.

71 Ibid., pp. 475–6.

72 Hochedlinger, *Austria's Wars of Emergence,* pp. 311–12. Cf. Maria Theresa to Joseph, July 1777, in *Habsburg and Hohenzollern,* pp. 152–3.

73 Beales, *Prosperity and Plunder,* p. 185, 195–8.

74 Thomas Da Costa Kaufmann, *Painterly Enlightenment: The Art of Franz Anton Maulbertsch* (Chapel Hill, NC, 2005), pp. 56, 58, 61–4, 66–7, 73.

75 Beales, *Prosperity and Plunder,* pp. 194, 203, 227.

76 Beales, *Enlightenment and Reform,* p. 98.

77 Gerda Lettner, *Der Rückzugsgefecht der Aufklärung in Wien, 1790–1792* (Frankfurt am Main, 1988), pp. 18–19; Beales, *Enlightenment and Reform,* pp. 98, 213, 259; Maria Theresa to Joseph II, 24 December 1775, in *'Mütterlicher',* p. 223.

78 Antal Szántay, 'The Robot-Abolition in Hungary under Joseph II', in *Politics and Culture,* pp. 98–107.

79 Beales, *Joseph II: Against the World,* pp. 430, 661; Beales, *Enlightenment and Reform,* p. 262. See also Leslie Bodi, *Tauwetter in Wien: Zur Prosa der österreichischen Aufklärung, 1781–1795* (Frankfurt am Main, 1979), pp. 162–3.

80 On Ibrahim Goether and his *Joseph II. im Controlleur-Gang, oder: Allerlei Scenen aus der heutigen Regierung* (Vienna, 1782), see Bodi, *Tauwetter,* pp. 155–8.

81 Bodi, *Tauwetter,* pp. 162–3.

82 Ibid., pp. 153–4; Beales, *Enlightenment and Reform,* p. 262.

5 Revolution, Recovery, Revolution

1 'Trefflicher Bevölkerer', in Magdelena Hawlik-Van de Water, *Die Kapuziner-gruft: Begräbnisstätte der Habsburger in Wien* (Vienna, 1987), p. 231.

2 Derek Beales, *Prosperity and Plunder: European Catholic Monasteries in the Age of Revolution, 1650–1815* (Cambridge, 2003), p. 225.

3 Rolf Haaser, 'Das Zeremoniell der beiden letzten deutsch-römischen Kaiserkrönungen in Frankfurt am Main und seine Rezeption zwischen Spätaufklärung und Frühromantik', in *Zeremoniell als höfische Ästhetik in Spätmittelalter und Früher Neuzeit*, ed. Jörg Jochen Berns and Thomas Rahn (Tübingen, 1995), pp. 614–15; Hawlik-Van de Water, *Kapuzinergruft*, p. 234; Paul Bernard, *From the Enlightenment to the Police State: The Public Life of Johann Anton Pergen* (Urbana, IL, 1991), pp. 171–3.

4 Haaser, 'Zeremoniell', pp. 614–15.

5 Michael Hochedlinger, *Austria's Wars of Emergence, 1683–1797* (London, 2003), pp. 417–18.

6 Gerda Lettner, *Der Rückzugsgefecht der Aufklärung in Wien, 1790–1792* (Frankfurt am Main, 1988), p. 96.

7 Leslie Bodi, *Tauwetter in Wien: Zur Prosa der österreichischen Aufklärung, 1781–1795* (Frankfurt am Main, 1979), pp. 80–82.

8 Lettner, *Rückzugsgefecht*, pp. 36–7, 40–41; Hochedlinger, *Austria's Wars of Emergence*, pp. 417–18.

9 Lettner, *Rückzugsgefecht*, pp. 42–6, 53–5, 59, 61–2, 77–8; Hochedlinger, *Austria's Wars of Emergence*, pp. 417–18.

10 Moritz Csáky, 'Geschichtlichkeit und Stilpluralität: Die Sozialen und intellektuellen Voraussetzungen des Historismus', in *Der Traum vom Glück: Die Kunst des Historismus in Europa*, ed. Hermann Fillitz with Werner Telesko (Vienna, 1996), p. 27.

11 Hermann Fillitz, 'Der Traum vom Glück. Das Phänomen des europäischen Historismus', in *Traum vom Gluck*, p. 20; Karl Vocelka and Lynne Heller, *Die Lebenswelt der Habsburger: Kultur- und Mentalitätsgeschichte einer Familie* (Graz, 1997), p. 149.

12 Hawlik-Van de Water, *Kapuzinergruft*, p. 58.

13 Haaser, 'Zeremoniell', pp. 604, 610, 620.

14 Johann Pezzl, *Beschreibung und Grundriss der Haupt- und Residenzstadt Wien*, 3rd edn (Vienna, 1809), pp. 279–81, 469–72; Bernard, *Enlightenment to the Police State*, p. 184.

15 Paula Sutter Fichtner, 'History, Religion, and Politics in the Austrian Vormärz', *History and Theory*, X (1971), pp. 33–48; Beales, *Prosperity and Plunder*, pp. 226–7.

16 Charles Sealsfield [Karl Postl], *Austria as It Is; or, Sketches of Continental Courts by an Eye-Witness* (London, 1828), pp. 81–7; Waltraud Heindl, *Gehorsame Rebellen: Bürokratie und Beamte in Österreich, 1780 bis 1848* (Vienna, 1990), pp. 69–70; Robert Kann, *A History of the Habsburg Empire, 1525–1918* (Berkeley, CA, 1974), p. 241. Cf. Bernard, *Enlightenment to the Police State*, pp. 182–3, 189, 191–5. The office of Supreme Burgrave was the highest political position in the Kingdom of Bohemia.

17 Paula Sutter Fichtner, 'Print vs. Speech: Censoring the Stage in Eighteenth-century Vienna', in *Freedom of Speech: the History of an Idea*, ed. Elizabeth Powers (Bucknell, PA, 2011), pp. 95–6; Bodi, *Tauwetter in Wien*, p. 438.

18 Haaser, 'Zeremoniell', p. 628.

19 Csáky, 'Geschichtlichkeit', pp. 27–8.

20 Herbert Zeman, 'Die Alt-Wiener Volkskomödie des 18. und frühen 19. Jahrhunderts: ein gattungsgeschichtlicher Versuch', in *Die österreichische Literatur: Ihr Profil von den Anfängen im Mittelalter bis ins 18. Jahrhundert (1050–1750)*, ed. Herbert Zeman (Graz, 1986), p. 1367; Alfons Lhotsky, *Österreichische Historiographie* (Vienna, 1982), pp. 146–7.

21 Werner Telesko, *Geschichtsraum Österreich: Die Habsburger und ihre Geschichte in der bildenden Kunst des 19. Jahrhunderts* (Vienna, 2006), pp. 361–6.

22 Ibid., pp. 380–83.

23 Franz Grillparzer, *Sämtliche Werke* (Darmstadt, 1969), vol. I, pp. 1036–7 (trans. author).

24 Ibid., pp. 987, 1000–1001, 1021, 1028, 1030, 1038, 1043.

25 Ibid., pp. 981–7, 1000, 1315.

26 Pezzl, *Beschreibung*, pp. 222–3; Telesko, *Geschichtsraum*, p. 350.

27 Hannes Stekl, 'Der Wiener Hof in der ersten Hälfte des 19. Jahrhunderts', in *Hof und Gesellschaft in den deutschen Staaten im 19. und beginnenden 20. Jahrhundert*, ed. Karl Möckl, Deutsche Führungsschichten in der Neuzeit, XVIII (1990) pp. 22, 56–60. Cf. Eric Hobsbawm, 'Mass- Producing Traditions: Europe, 1870–1914', in *The Invention of Tradition*, ed. Eric Hobsbawm and Terence Ranger (Cambridge, 1983), p. 282.

28 Ilsebill Barta, *Familienporträts der Habsburger: Dynastische Repräsentation im Zeitalter der Aufklärung* (Vienna, 2001), p. 50; Telesko, *Geschichtsraum*, p. 194.

29 Stekl, 'Wiener Hof', p. 53; Telesko, *Geschichtsraum*, pp. 166–7, 355–6, 451. For a list of Habsburg family charities in the eighteenth and nineteenth centuries, see Alan Sked, *The Decline and Fall of the Habsburg Empire*, 2nd edn (Harlow, 2001), pp. 296–7.

30 Stekl, 'Wiener Hof', pp. 53–4.

31 Derek Beales, *Joseph II: Against the World, 1780–1790* (Cambridge, 2009), p. 438.

32 See generally, Pezzl, *Beschreibung*, pp. 213–64; Jan Dirk Müller, *Gedechtnus: Literatur und Hofgesellschaft um Maximilian I* (Munich, 1982), p. 271. On Habsburg medal production in the late seventeenth and early eighteenth centuries, see Vladimir Simić, 'Patriotism and Propaganda: The Habsburgs' Media Promotion of the Passarowitz Peace Treaty Ratification in 1718', in *The Peace of Passarowitz, 1718*, ed. Charles Ingrao (West Lafayette, IN, 2011), pp. 267–90.

33 Sabine Grabner, 'Die "Moderne Schule" in der kaiserlichen Gemäldegalerie und andere Bestrebungen zur Förderung der zeitgenössischen Kunst im 19. Jahrhundert', in *Das Museum: Spiegel und Motor kulturpolitischer Visionen, 1903–2003*, ed. Hadwig Kräutler and Gerbert Frodl (Vienna, 2004), pp. 94–5, 98–9, 102–3.

THE HABSBURGS

34 Pezzl, *Beschreibung*, pp. 323–4, 328–9; W. E. Yates, *Theatre in Vienna: A Critical History, 1776–1995* (Cambridge, 1996), p. 3.

35 Pezzl, *Beschreibung*, pp. 400, 406.

36 Barta, *Familienporträts*, pp. 48–9. Cf. Telesko, *Geschichtsraum*, pp. 174–5, 177.

37 Pezzl, *Beschreibung*, pp. 151–5, 157–8, 409.

38 Stekl, 'Wiener Hof', p. 30; Pezzl, *Beschreibung*, pp. 141–2, 160–63; Telesko, *Geschichtsraum*, pp. 186–9. For details on the private charitable activities of Francis I (II), see Monica Knopf, 'Die Wohlfahrtspolitik des österreichischen Herrscherhauses im Vormärz', PhD thesis, Vienna, 1966, pp. 88–96.

39 Stekl, 'Wiener Hof', pp. 17–20, 28–9, 36, 38.

40 Knopf, 'Wohlfahrtspolitik', pp. 163–8.

41 Telesko, *Geschichtsraum*, p. 202, 355–6.

42 Paula Sutter Fichtner, *The Habsburg Monarchy, 1490–1848: Attributes of Empire* (Basingstoke, 2003), pp. 113–15.

43 Kann, *History of the Habsburg Empire*, p. 297.

44 Francis Dvornik, *The Slavs in European History and Civilization* (New Brunswick, NJ, 1962), p. 553; Pezzl, *Beschreibung*, pp. 286, 288.

45 Fichtner, *Habsburg Monarchy*, pp. 124–8.

46 Jane Regenfelder, 'Bernard Bolzano's "revolutionärisches" Vermächtnis', in *Bewegung im Reich der Immobilität: Revolutionen in der Habsburgermonarchie, 1848–1849*, ed. H. Lengauer and P. H. Kucher (Vienna, 2001), pp. 78, 83–5.

47 Fichtner, *Habsburg Monarchy*, p. 118; Ernst Bruckmüller, 'Die österreichische Revolution von 1848 und der Habsburgermythos des 19. Jahrhunderts: Nebst einigen Rand und Fussnoten von und Hinweisen auf Franz Grillparzer', in *Bewegung im Reich der Immobilität*, pp. 2–4.

48 *EIN ALTER MANN (Graf Kolowrat)*
    Ein altes Weib (Metternich)
    Ein alter Jungesell (Erzherzog Louis)
    Die Träger unserer Krone sind.
    Als Stützen für ein altes Kind.
    Soll es da nicht beim alten bleiben,
    Wo Altersschwächen ihr Handwerk treiben.

Eduard Beutner, 'Metternich und seine elende Umgebung: Strategien der Satire auf Exponenten des "Systems" bei Franz Grillparzer im Vorfeld von 1848', in *Bewegung im Reich der Immobilität*, pp. 69–75 (capitals in original). See also Ernst Bruckmüller, 'Die österreichische Revolution von 1848', p. 6 (trans. author).

49 Wolfgang Häusler, '"Was Kommt heran mit kühnem Gange?" Ursachen, Verlauf und Folgen der Wiener Märzrevolution von 1848', in *1848: Revolution in Österreich*, ed. Ernst Bruckmüller (Vienna, 1999), pp. 26, 49.

50 Ibid., pp. 49–51.

51 Hubert Lengauer, '"Hab Achtung vor dem Menschenbild!" Zur Literatur der österreichischen Revolution im Jahre 1848', ibid., pp. 79–80; Waltraud Heindl, '"Hoch, hoch an die Laternen!" Aus dem Tagebuch der Wiener Oktoberrevolution', ibid., p. 132.

52 István Deák, *Beyond Nationalism: A Social and Political History of the Habsburg Officer Corps, 1848–1918* (New York, 1990), pp. 31–41.

53 Helmut Rumpler, '"Das neu und kräftig möge Österreichs Ruhm erstehen!" Der Thronwechsel vom 2. Dezember 1848 und die Wende zur Reaktion', in *1848: Revolution in Österreich*, ed. Bruckmüller, pp. 142–4; Telesko, *Geschichtsraum*, pp. 189–90; Stekl, 'Wiener Hof', pp. 33–5; Häusler, 'Gange', in *1848: Revolution in Österreich*, ed. Bruckmüller, pp. 49–51.

54 Rumpler, '"Neu und kräftig"', ibid., p. 149; Vocelka and Heller, *Lebenswelt*, p. 193.

55 Selma Krasa-Florian, *Die Allegorie der Austria: Die Entstehung des Gesamtstaatsgedankens in der österreichisch-ungarischen Monarchie und die bildende Kunst* (Vienna, 2007), pp. 16, 18–19, 30.

56 Bruckmüller, 'Revolution von 1848', in *1848: Revolution in Österreich*, ed. Bruckmüller, pp. 14–16, 29–30, 32–3; Lengauer, '"Hab Achtung"', ibid., pp. 72–4.

57 'Alle Revolutionselemente, alles Menschheitempörende, was sie anders im grossen haben, das haben wir hier im kleinen. Wir haben ein absolutes Regierungsformerl, wir haben ein unverantwortliches Ministeriumerl, ein Bureaukraturl, ein Zensurerl, Staatschulderln, weit über unsere Kräfterln, also müssen wir auch ein Revolutionerl, ein Konstitutionerl und endlich a Freiheiterl krieg'n', in *Nestroys Werke*, ed. Otto Rommel (Berlin, 1908?), part Two, p. 59. See also Lengauer, '"Hab Achtung"', in *1848: Revolution in Österreich*, ed. Bruckmüller, p. 77.

58 Brigitte Hamann, 'Der Wiener Hof und die Hofgesellschaft in der zweiten Hälfte des 19. Jahrhunderts', in *Hof und Gesellschaft in den deutschen Staaten im 19. und beginnenden 20. Jahrhundert*, ed. Karl Möckl, Deutsche Führungsschichten in der Neuzeit, XVIII (1990), p. 62.

59 Telesko, *Geschichtsraum*, p. 360.

60 Pezzl, *Beschreibung*, pp. 475–6.

6 Constructing Commitment

1 Hannes Stekl, 'Der Wiener Hof in der ersten Hälfte des 19. Jahrhunderts', in *Hof und Hofgesellschaft in den deutschen Staaten im 19. und beginnenden 20. Jahrhundert*, ed. Karl Möckl (Boppard am Rhein, 1990), pp. 38–9.

2 Katrin Unterreiner, *Emperor Franz Joseph, 1830–1916: Myth and Truth*, trans. Martin Kelsey (Vienna, 2006), pp. 18–27; Fritz Fellner, 'L'imperatore Francesco Giuseppe', in *Gli imperi dopo l'Impero nell'Europa del XIX secolo*, ed. Marco Bellabarba, Brigitte Mazohl, Reinhard Stauber and Marcello Verga (Bologna, 2009), pp. 351–2.

3 J. Rak and V. Vlnas, eds, *Habsburské Století, 1791–1914: Česká společnost ve vztahu k dynastii a monarchii* (Prague, 2004), p. 69; Karl Vocelka and Lynne Heller, *Die Lebenswelt der Habsburger: Kultur- und Mentalitätsgeschichte einer Familie* (Graz, 1997), p. 196; Daniel Unowsky, 'Reasserting Empire: Habsburg Celebration after the Revolutions of 1848–1849', in *Staging the Past: The Politics of Commemoration in Habsburg Central Europe, 1848 to*

the Present, ed. Maria Bucur and Nancy Wingfield (West Lafayette, IN, 2001), pp. 24–5.

4 Brigitte Hamann, 'Der Wiener Hof und die Hofgesellschaft in der zweiten Hälfte des 19. Jahrhunderts', in *Hof und Hofgesellschaft*, p. 65; Unowsky, 'Reasserting Empire', pp. 25–6; Werner Telesko, *Geschichtsraum Österreich: Die Habsburger und ihre Geschichte in der bildenden Kunst des 19. Jahrhunderts* (Vienna, 2006), p. 231.

5 Vocelka and Heller, *Lebenswelt*, p. 38; Ernst Bruckmüller, 'Was there a "Habsburg Society" in Austria–Hungary?', *Austrian History Yearbook*, XXXVII (2006), pp. 9–10; László Kutas, 'Die Magyaren', *Die Habsburger-monarchie, 1848–1914*, III/1: *Die Völker des Reiches*, ed. Adam Wandruszka and Peter Urbanitsch (Vienna, 1980), pp. 442–3 and Table 5.

6 John Boyer, *Political Radicalism in Late Imperial Vienna: Origins of the Christian Social Movement, 1848–1897* (Chicago, 1981), pp. 31–2, 128, 137–8, 147, 149, 166–83; Unowsky, 'Reasserting Empire', pp. 35–6.

7 Unowsky, 'Reasserting Empire', p. 26; Telesko, *Geschichtsraum*, p. 231; Bruckmüller, 'Habsburg Society', pp. 9–10.

8 Rupert Klieber, *Jüdische-Christliche-Muslimische Lebenswelt der Donaumonarchie, 1848–1918* (Vienna, 2010), pp. 218–19.

9 Gábor Tüskés and Éva Knapp, *Volksfrömmigkeit in Ungarn: Beiträge zur vergleichenden Literatur- und Kulturgeschichte* (Dettelbach, 1996), pp. 219, 221.

10 Telesko, *Geschichtsraum*, pp. 79, 209, 211, 280–81.

11 Ibid., pp. 83–4, 88, 91–6, 100–101.

12 Ibid., pp. 106–10, 112–13, 136–41.

13 Stefan Riesenfellner, '"*Alles mit Gott für Kaiser und Vaterland*": Der maria-theresianische Denkmalkult und das Beispiel des "nationalen" österreichischen Denkmalraumes der k. u k. Militärakademie in Wiener Neustadt', in *Steinernes Bewusstsein, I: Die öffentliche Representation staatlicher und nationaler Identität Österreichs in seinen Denkmälern*, ed. Stefan Riesenfellner (Vienna, 1998), pp. 333, 340–41.

14 Eric Hobsbawm, 'Mass-Producing Traditions: Europe, 1870–1914', in *The Invention of Tradition*, ed. Eric Hobsbawm and Terence Ranger (Cambridge, 1983), p. 282.

15 Hamann, 'Wiener Hof', p. 65.

16 Unowsky, 'Reasserting Empire', pp. 27, 32.

17 Ibid., p. 22; Telesko, *Geschichtsraum*, pp. 206, 220–21, 225–30, 238–49; Leopoldine Beck, 'Das Bild und der Mythos der Habsburger in den Schulgeschichtsbüchern und im "vaterländischen" Schrifttum der franzisko-josephinischen Ära 1848–1918', Geisteswissenschaftliche Diplomarbeit, University of Vienna, 1991, pp. 61, 79, 90, 97.

18 Unowsky, 'Reasserting Empire', p. 21; Franz Isidor Proschko, *Perlen aus der österreichischen Vaterlands-Geschichte. Zum vierzigjährigen Regierungs-Jubiläum Sr. Majestät des Kaisers Franz Joseph I* (Würzburg, 1888), pp. iii–iv.

19 Telesko, *Geschichtsraum*, pp. 216, 220–23. St Hubert is the patron saint of hunters.

20 Andrew Wheatcroft, *The Enemy at the Gate: Habsburgs, Ottomans, and the*

Battle for Europe (London, 2008), p. 258.

21 Hermann Fillitz, 'Der Traum vom Glück: Das Phänomen des europäischen Humanisus', in *Der Traum vom Glück: Die Kunst des Historismus in Europa*, ed. Hermann Fillitz with Werner Telesko (Vienna, 1996), p. 24; Ralph Gleis, ed., *Makart: Eine Kunstler Regiert die Stadt* (Munich, 2011), pp. 238, 252–4; Hermann Wiesflecker, *Kaiser Maximilian I* (Vienna, 1986), vol. V, p. 372.

22 Christiane Wolf, 'Representing Constitutional Monarchy in Late Nineteenth and Early Twentieth-century Britain, Germany, and Austria', in *The Limits of Loyalty: Imperial Symbolism, Popular Allegiances, and State Patriotism in the Late Habsburg Monarchy*, ed. Lawrence Cole and Daniel Unowsky (New York, 2007), pp. 212–13.

23 Helmut Rumpler, '"Das neu und kräftig möge Österreichs Ruhm erstehen!" Der Thronwechsel vom 2. Dezember 1848 und die Wende zur Reaktion', in *1848: Revolution in Österreich*, ed. Ernst Bruckmüller and Wolfgang Häusler (Vienna, 1999), pp. 139–41.

24 Ibid., pp. 147, 149–52.

25 Alice Freifeld, 'Empress Elisabeth as Hungarian Queen: The Uses of Celebrity Monarchism', in *Limits of Loyalty*, ed. Cole and Unowsky, p. 146.

26 András Gerő, *Emperor Francis Joseph, King of the Hungarians* (Boulder, CO, 2001), pp. 77–9.

27 '"vlastí své i svému králi"', in *Habsburské Století*, ed. Rak and Vlnas, pp. 17, 77.

28 Fellner, 'L'imperatore Francesco Giuseppe', pp. 351–2.

29 Jean-Pierre Bled, *Franz Joseph*, trans. Teresa Bridgeman, 2nd edn (Oxford, 1992), p. 212; Péter Hanák, *The Garden and the Workshop: Essays on the Cultural History of Vienna and Budapest* (Princeton, NJ, 1998), p. 10.

30 Hamann, 'Wiener Hof', p. 76; Unowsky, 'Reasserting Empire', pp. 17–20.

31 Fellner, 'L'imperatore Francesco Giuseppe', p. 351; Hanák, *Garden and the Workshop*, p. 65.

32 Fredrik Lindström, *Empire and Identity: Biographies of the Austrian State Problem in the Late Habsburg Empire* (West Lafayette, IN, 2008), p. 212; Wolf, 'Constitutional Monarchy', pp. 209, 211–12.

33 Ernst Bruckmüller, *Sozialgeschichte Österreichs*, 2nd edn (Vienna, 2001), p. 287.

34 Telesko, *Geschichtsraum*, p. 253; Brigitte Hamann, *Kronprinz Rudolf: Ein Leben*, revd edn (Munich, 2006), p. 492.

35 See generally Waltraud Heindl, *Gehorsame Rebellen: Bürokratie und Beamte in Österreich, 1780–1848* (Vienna, 1990).

36 Pavla Vošahlíková, 'Ämter und Beamte unter Franz Joseph I', in *Von Amts wegen. K. K. Beamte Erzählen*, ed. Pavla Vošahlíková (Vienna, 1998), pp. 19, 21–2, 27–9.

37 Ibid., pp. 16, 20; Telesko, *Geschichtsraum*, p. 244.

38 István Deák, *Beyond Nationalism: A Social and Political History of the Habsburg Officer Corps, 1848–1918* (New York, 1990), p. 187; Peter Urbanitsch, 'Die Deutschen in Österreich', in *Die Habsburgermonarchie*, pp. 94–5, 482; Gary B. Cohen, *Education and Middle Class Society in Imperial Austria, 1848–1918* (West Lafayette, IN, 1996), pp. 272–92.

39 Vošahlíková, 'Ämter', pp. 10 n. 5, 11, 13, 16, 25, 34.

40 Hannes Stekl and Andrea Schnöller, eds, *'Es war eine Welt der Geborgenheit'*: *bürgerliche Kindheit in Monarchie und Republik* (Vienna, 1987), p. 210.

41 Vošahlíková, 'Ämter', pp. 10 n. 6, 19, 22, 24–5, 27–9; Heindl, *Gehorsame*, pp. 241–3.

42 Vošahlíková, 'Ämter', pp. 32–5, 37.

43 Sabine Zelger, *Das ist alles viel komplizierter, Herr Sektionschef! Bürokratie-literarische Reflexionen aus Österreich* (Vienna, 2009), pp. 125–50.

44 Vošahlíková, 'Ämter', pp. 18, 32–5, 37. Cf. Waltraud Heindl, 'Bureaucracy, Officials, and the State in the Austrian Monarchy: Stages of Change since the Eighteenth Century', *Austrian History Yearbook*, XXXVII (2006), p. 55.

45 Hobsbawm, 'Mass-Producing Traditions', p. 263.

46 Wheatcroft, *Enemy at the Gate*, p. 257.

47 Telesko, *Geschichtsraum*, p. 367; Proschko, *Perlen*, pp. 27, 29–32, 36–7, 41, 45–9, 57–76, 86–98, 122–3, 136–7; Jordan Kajetan Markus, *Geschichtsbilder aus der österr.-ungar. Monarchie für Schule und Haus*, 2nd edn (Vienna, 1879), p. 361.

48 Tara Zahra, *Kidnapped Souls: National Indifference and the Battle for Children in the Bohemian Lands, 1900–1948* (Ithaca, NY, 2008), p. 93.

49 Hobsbawm, 'Mass-Producing Traditions', pp. 263–4; Eva Tesar, *Hände auf die Bank: Erinnerungen an den Schulalltag* (Vienna, 1992), p. 3; Urbanitsch, 'Deutschen in Österreich', pp. 79–80; Cohen, *Education and Middle Class Society*, pp. 64–5, 272, table 1.

50 Helmut Engelbrecht, *Geschichte des österreichischen Bildungswesens: Erziehung und Unterricht auf dem Boden Österreichs* (Vienna, 1984–6), vol. IV, pp. 8–9, 561–5, and cover illustration.

51 Ibid., IV, pp. 27–31; Cohen, *Education and Middle Class Society*, pp. 46–7.

52 Zahra, *Kidnapped Souls*, p. 104; Engelbrecht, *Bildungswesens*, vol. IV, pp. 57–8.

53 Engelbrecht, *Bildungswesens*, vol. IV, pp. 77–91.

54 Beck, 'Bild und Mythos', p. 56; Hämmerle, *'Es war eine Welt der Geborgenheit'*, p. 53; Ernst Bruckmüller, 'Patriotic and National Myths: National Consciousness and Elementary School Education in Imperial Austria', in *Limits of Loyalty*, ed. Cole and Unowsky, pp. 15–23; Tesar, *Hände auf die Bank*, pp. 64, 111, 138.

55 Engelbrecht, *Bildungswesen*, vol. IV, pp. 59–60.

56 Beck, 'Bild und Mythos', pp. 4, 59; Bruckmüller, 'Patriotic and National Myths', pp. 25–7.

57 Theodor Tupetz, *Lehrbuch der Geschichte für Lehrbildungsanstalten*, part Two, 5th edn (Vienna, 1904); Telesko, *Geschichtsraum*, pp. 393–4; Markus, *Geschichtsbilder*, pp. 416–17; Beck, 'Bild und Mythos', pp. 26–7, 31, 35–6, 38–40, 171–3, 180–88.

58 Schnöller and Stekl, *Geborgenheit*, pp. 77, 85, 250–51.

59 Ibid., p.123; Tesar, *Hände auf die Bank*, p. 108.

60 Unowsky, 'Reasserting Empire', pp. 35–6.

61 Telesko, *Geschichtsraum*, p. 385.

62 Ibid., pp. 208–9, 231, 385.

63 Christa Hämmerle, 'Die k. (u.) k. Armee als "Schule des Volkes"? Zur
    Geschichte der Allgemeinen Wehrpflicht in der multinationalen
    Habsburgermonarchie', in *Die Bürger als Soldat: Die Militarisierung*
    europäischer Gesellschaften im langen 19. Jahrhundert: ein internationaler
    Vergleich, ed. Christian Jansen (Essen, 2004), p. 180; Laurence Cole,
    'Military Veterans and Popular Patriotism in Imperial Austria, 1870–1914',
    in *Limits of Loyalty*, ed. Cole and Unowsky, p. 38; Telesko, *Geschichtsraum*,
    pp. 211–16.
64 Quirin Leitner, *Gedenkblätter aus der Geschichte des kais. kön. Heeres:*
    Vom Begin des dreissigjährigen Krieges bis auf unsere Tage (Vienna, 1865),
    unpaginated.
65 Telesko, *Geschichtsraum*, pp. 389–90, 392; Deák, *Beyond Nationalism*,
    p. 124.
66 Vocelka and Heller, *Lebenswelt*, p. 200.
67 Riesenfellner, *Steinernes Bewusstsein*, I, pp. 13–14, 25.
68 Bruckmüller, 'Habsburg Society', p. 9; Cole, 'Veterans Associations',
    pp. 37–40. For Hungary, see Tibor Papp, 'Die königliche Ungarische
    Landwehr (Honvéd)', in *Die Habsburgermonarchie*, pp. 634–86.
69 Pavla Vošahlíková, ed., *Auf der Walz: Erinnerungen böhmischer Handwerks-*
    gesellen (Vienna, 1994), pp. 218, 233–43; Deák, *Beyond Nationalism*, p. 187.
70 Hämmerle, 'Die k. (u.) k. Armee als "Schule des Volkes"?', pp. 80–81, 183.

7 Alternative Narratives, Competing Visions

1 Jean-Pierre Bled, *Franz Joseph*, trans. Teresa Bridgeman, 2nd edn (Oxford,
   1992), pp. 141–2, 252–3; Brigitte Hamann, *Kronprinz Rudolf: Ein Leben*,
   revd edn (Munich, 2006), pp. 252–63.
2 Andrew Wheatcroft, *The Habsburgs: Embodying Empire* (London, 1995),
   p. 283.
3 Bled, *Franz Joseph*, pp. 267–9; Paula Sutter Fichtner, 'Charles I (IV): War
   Leadership as Personal Leadership', in *East Central European War Leaders:*
   Civilian and Military, ed. Béla K. Király and Albert Nofi (Boulder, CO,
   1988), pp. 80–81.
4 Paula Sutter Fichtner, *Terror and Toleration: The Habsburg Empire Confronts*
   Islam, 1526–1850 (London, 2008), p. 168; Ernst Bruckmüller, 'Was there a
   "Habsburg Society" in Austria–Hungary?', *Austrian History Yearbook*,
   XXXVII (2006), p. 12; Gary B. Cohen, *Education and Middle-Class Society*
   in Imperial Austria (West Lafayette, IN, 1996), pp. 34–5, 39, 45–7, 112–13.
5 See generally, Tara Zahra, *Kidnapped Souls: National Indifference and the*
   Battle for Children in the Bohemian Lands, 1900–1948 (Ithaca, NY, 2008);
   Pieter M. Judson, *Guardians of the Nation: Activists on the Language*
   Frontiers of Imperial Austria (Cambridge, MA, 2007).
6 Paula Sutter Fichtner, 'The Habsburg Empire in World War I: A Final
   Episode in Dynastic History', *East European Quarterly*, XI (1977), p. 422.
7 Hugh Agnew, 'The Flyspecks on Palivec's Portrait: Franz Joseph, the
   Symbols of Monarchy, and Czech Popular Loyalty', in *The Limits of Loyalty:*

Imperial Symbolism, Popular Allegiances, and State Patriotism in the Late Habsburg Monarchy, ed. Laurence Cole and Daniel L. Unowsky (New York, 2007), pp. 96–7.

8 Cf. László Deme, 'Hungary and the Habsburg Monarchy', in *Hungarian History – World History*, ed. György Ránki (Budapest, 1987), pp. 181–7.

9 Péter Hanák, *The Garden and the Workshop: Essays on the Cultural History of Vienna and Budapest* (Princeton, NJ, 1998), p. 5.

10 Ibid., pp. 135–46.

11 Moritz Csáky, *Ideologie der Operette und Wiener Moderne: Ein kulturhistorischer Essay zur österreichischen Identität* (Vienna, 1996), pp. 79–80; Hanák, *Garden*, pp. 143, 145–6.

12 András Gerő, *Imagined History: Chapters from Nineteenth and Twentieth Century Hungarian Symbolic Politics*, trans. Mario D. Fenyo (Boulder, CO, 2006), pp. 62–5, 79–80, 82, 89–90.

13 Ibid., pp. 72–3, 76–7, 82–4; Werner Telesko, *Geschichtsraum Österreich: Die Habsburger und ihre Geschichte in der bildenden Kunst des 19. Jahrhunderts* (Vienna, 2006), p. 382.

14 Alice Freifeld, 'Empress Elisabeth as Hungarian Queen: The Uses of Celebrity Monarchism', in *Limits of Loyalty*, ed. Cole and Unowsky, pp. 139–40, 145–6; Larry Wolff, *The Idea of Galicia: History and Fantasy in Habsburg Political Culture* (Stanford, CA, 2010), pp. 301–2; Gerő, *Imagined History*, p. 102.

15 Freifeld, 'Empress Elisabeth', pp. 143, 146–7, 151; Gerő, *Imagined History*, pp. 91–2, 96–7, 100–101.

16 On the difficulties of Germans and Slavs mastering Hungarian, see Hanák, *Garden*, pp. 49–50.

17 Gerő, *Imagined History*, pp. 69–70; Christiane Wolf, 'Representing Constitutional Monarchy in Late Nineteenth and Early Twentieth-century Britain, Germany, and Austria', in *Limits of Loyalty*, ed. Cole and Unowsky, pp. 207–8.

18 Gerő, *Imagined History*, pp. 80–81, 86–7, 89–90, 93–4; Freifeld, 'Empress Elisabeth', p. 158.

19 Hanák, *Garden*, p. 47. For a representative illustration, see Brigitte Hamann, ed., *Die Habsburger: Ein biographisches Lexikon* (Vienna, 1988), p. 399.

20 Nancy Wingfield, *Flag Wars and Stone Saints: How the Bohemian Lands Became Czech* (Cambridge, MA, 2007), pp. 17–47; Hugh Agnew, *The Czechs and the Lands of the Bohemian Crown* (Stanford, CA, 2004), p. 113.

21 Pieter M. Judson, *Exclusive Revolutionaries: Liberal Politics, Social Experience, and National Identity in the Austrian Empire, 1848–1914* (Ann Arbor, MI, 1996), pp. 193–222.

22 Gary Cohen, 'Nationalist Politics and the Dynamics of State and Society in the Habsburg Monarchy, 1867–1914', *Central European History*, XL (2007), pp. 242–3; Ernst Bruckmüller, 'Patriotic and National Myths: National Consciousness and Elementary School Education', in *Limits of Loyalty*, ed. Cole and Unowsky, pp. 29–30.

23 Ibid., p. 30.

24 François de Capitani, 'Nation, Geschichte und Museum im 19. Jahrhundert',

in *Der Traum vom Glück: Die Kunst des Historismus in Europa*, ed. Hermann Fillitz with Werner Telesko (Vienna, 1996), pp. 33–7. See also Hermann Fillitz, 'Der Traum vom Glück: Das Phänomen des europäischen Historismus', ibid., p. 25.

25 Markéta Theinhardt, 'Historismus in der polnischen, tschechischen und ungarischen Malerei des 19. Jahrhunderts', ibid., pp. 86–91, n. 8.

26 Telesko, *Geschichtsraumm*, pp. 348–9.

27 Michaela Marek, *Kunst und Identitätspolitik: Architectur und Bildkünste im Prozess der tschechischen Nationbildung* (Cologne, 2004), pp. 290 and n. 348, pp. 311–15; Carl Schorske, *Fin de Siècle Vienna: Politics and Culture* (New York, 1980), p. 37.

28 Marek, *Kunst und Identitätspolitik*, pp. 284–5, 288.

29 Theinhardt, 'Historismus', p. 90; Marek, *Kunst und Identitätspolitik*, pp. 358–9, 363–7, 371–3.

30 Marek, *Identitätspolitik*, pp. 78, 80, 183 and n. 446, 200, 272–4, 276–7.

31 Ibid., pp. 293–4, 297–8.

32 Theinhardt, 'Historismus', p. 90; Telesko, *Geschichtsraum*, p. 382.

33 István Deák, *Beyond Nationalism: A Social and Political History of the Habsburg Officer Corps, 1848–1918* (New York, 1990), pp. 155, 163–4; Johann Christian Allmayer-Beck, 'Die Bewaffnete Macht in Staat und Gesellschaft', in *Die Habsburgermonarchie, 1848–1914*, v: *Die Bewaffnete Macht*, ed. Adam Wandruszka and Peter Urbanitsch (Vienna, 1987), pp. 37–8.

34 Laurence Cole, 'Military Veterans and Popular Patriotism in Imperial Austria, 1870–1914', in *Limits of Loyalty*, ed. Cole and Unowsky, pp. 39–40; Christa Hämmerle, 'Die k. (u.) k. Armee als "Schule des Volkes"? Zur Geschichte der Allgemeinen Wehrpflicht in der multinationalen Habsburgermonarchie (1866–1914/1981', in *Die Bürger als Soldat: Die Militarisierung europäischer Gesellschaften im langen 19. Jahrhundert: ein internationaler Vergleich*, ed. Christian Jansen (Essen, 2004), pp. 182–4.

35 Telesko, *Geschichtsraum*, pp. 367–8, 385, 394, 398.

36 Stefan Riesenfellner, 'Die "Ruhmeshalle" und die "Feldhernhalle" – das k. (u.) k. "Nationaldenkmal" im Wiener Arsenal', in *Steinernes Bewusstsein i: Die öffentliche Representation staatlicher und nationaler Identität Österreichs in seinen Denkmälern*, ed. Stefan Riesenfellner (Vienna, 1998), pp. 63–4, 73; Telesko, *Geschichtsraum*, pp. 394, 398.

37 Riesenfellner, 'Ruhmeshalle', pp. 66, 68–9; Eva Klingenstein, 'Zur Problematik eines k.k. Nationaldenkmals: Die Entstehungsgeschichte des nach-1848er Ausstellungsprogramms in den Prunkräumen des Arsenal-Zeughauses', in *Traum vom Glück*, p. 53.

38 Cornelia Reiter, *Schöne Welt, Wo Bis Du? Zeichnungen, Aquarelle, Ölskizzen-des deutschen und österreichischen Spätklazissimus* (Salzburg, 2009), pp. 124–5, 133, pl. 313; *Československá Vlastivěda* (Prague, 1932), vol. IV, p. 55 pl.

39 Riesenfellner, 'Ruhmeshalle', pp. 68–9; Telesko, *Geschichtsraum* , pp. 412–13, 416.

40 Wolfgang Maderthaner, *Die Anarchie der Vorstadt: das andere Wien um*

1900 (Frankfurt am Main, 1999), pp. 114–15.

41 Hannes Stekl, 'Der Wiener Hof in der ersten Hälfte des 19. Jahrhunderts', in *Hof und Gesellschaft in den deutschen Staaten im 19. und beginnenden 20. Jahrhundert*, ed. Karl Möckl (Boppard am Rhein, 1990), p. 55; Sabine Grabner, 'Die "Moderne Schule" in der kaiserlichen Gemäldegalerie und andere Bestrebungen zur Förderung der zeitgenössischen Kunst im 19. Jahrhundert', in *Das Museum: Spiegel und Motor kulturpolitischer Visionen, 1903–2003*, ed. Hadwig Kräutler and Gerbert Frodl (Vienna, 2004), p. 93; Brigitte Hamann, 'Der Wiener Hof und die Hofgesellschaft in der zweiten Hälfte des 19. Jahrhunderts', in *Hof und Hofgesellschaft*, p. 75.

42 Richard Newald, *Die deutsche Literatur vom Späthumanismus zur Empfindsamkeit, 1570–1750*, 3rd edn (Munich, 1960), pp. 327–9.

43 Lorenz Mikoletzky, 'Grillparzer – ein Homo Politicus?', in *Grillparzer oder die Wirklichkeit der Wirklichkeit*, ed. Bernhard Denscher und Walter Obermaier (Vienna, 1991), p. 2/9; Barbara Allmann, 'Die Leiden des Reisenden Franz', in *Wirklichkeit der Wirklichkeit*, pp. 10/8, 9.

44 Jan Assmann, *Das kulturelle Gedächtnis: Schrift, Erinnerung und politische Identität in frühen Hochkulturen*, revd edn (Munich, 2007), p. 23.

45 Paula Sutter Fichtner, 'Print versus Speech: Censoring the Stage in Eighteenth Century Vienna', in *Freedom of Speech: The History of an Idea*, ed. Elizabeth Powers (Lewisburg, PA, 2011), p. 96.

46 Stefan Riesenfellner, 'Zwischen deutscher "Kulturnation" und österreischer "Staatsnation": Aspekte staatlicher und nationaler Repräsentation in Dichter-und Musikdenkmälern der Wiener Ringstrasse bis zum ersten Weltkrieg', in *Steinernes Bewusstsein I*, pp. 270, 273–8, 289.

47 Ibid., p. 286.

48 Werner Schweiger, *Der junge Kokoschka: Leben und Werk* (Vienna, 1983), pp. 210–12.

49 For example, Christian Dickinger, *Franz Joseph I: Die Entmythisierung* (Vienna, 2001), pp. 176–84.

50 Ralph Gleis, ed., *Makart: Ein Kunstler Regiert die Stadt* (Munich, 2011), pp. 159, 170, 175–7.

51 Ralph Gleis, 'Phänomen Makart: Künstlerkult im 19. Jahrhundert', ibid., pp. 26, 28–9.

52 A good overview of this question is Stephen Beller, ed., *Rethinking Vienna 1900* (New York, 2001). Cf. Hanák, *Garden,* pp. 32–6.

53 Hanák, *Garden,* pp. 10, 64, 67.

54 Selma Krasa-Florian, *Die Allegorie der Austria: Die Entstehung des Gesamtstaatsgedankens in der österreichisch-ungarischen Monarchie und die bildende Kunst* (Vienna, 2007), p. 13.

55 Schorske, *Fin de Siècle*, pp. 236–7, 239; Fredrik Lindström, *Empire and Identity: Biographies of the Austrian State Problem in the Late Habsburg Empire* (West Lafayette, IN, 2008), pp. 114–17.

56 Anon., *Viribus Unitis: Das Buch vom Kaiser* (Budapest and Leipzig, 1898?), p. 73.

57 Katrin Unterreiner, *Emperor Franz Joseph, 1830–1916: Myth and Truth*, trans. Martin Kelsey (Vienna, 2006), p. 56; Nikol Schattenstein, *Exhibition*

of Portraits (Philadelphia, 1934), n.p.

58 Tobias Natter, *Die Welt von Klimt, Schiele und Kokoschka: Sammler und Mäzene* (Cologne, 2003), pp. 14–16.

59 Maderthaner, *Anarchie der Vorstadt*, p. 10.

60 Csáky, *Ideologie der Operette und Wiener Moderne*, pp. 67–8; Schorske, *Fin de Siècle*, pp. 227, 242–3.

61 Elizabeth Clegg, 'Mestrovic and the Moderne Galerie: Remembering the Future', in *Das Museum*, ed. Kräutler and Frodl, p. 109; Andrew Wachtel, 'Culture in the South Slavic Lands, 1914–1918', in *European Culture in the Great War: The Arts, Entertainment, and Propaganda, 1914–1918*, ed. Aviel Roshwald and Richard Stites (Cambridge, 1999), pp. 197–8.

62 Clegg, 'Mestrovic and the Moderne Galerie', pp. 110, 112.

63 Natter, *Die Welt von Klimt*, pp. 294–5.

64 Salamon Kleiner, *Das Belvedere in Wien*, ed. Hans Aurenhammer and Gertrude Aurenhammer (1731; Graz, 1969), II/2, pp. 114–15.

65 Schweiger, *Junge Kokoschka*, p. 195; Natter, *Die Welt von Klimt*, p. 265.

66 Schweiger, *Junge Kokoschka*, pp. 224, 227–8; Schorske, *Fin de Siècle*, p. 335.

67 Lindström, *Empire and Identity*, pp. 127–34.

68 Csáky, *Ideologie der Operette und Wiener Moderne*, pp. 64–5, 67–8, 74–5, 97–8.

69 Hanák, *Garden*, p. 122.

70 Ibid., pp. 67–75.

71 Natter, *Die Welt von Klimt*, p. 158.

72 Adolf Loos, *Spoken into the Void: Collected Essays, 1897–1900*, trans. Jane O. Newman and John Smith (Cambridge, MA, 1982), p. 7; Adolf Loos, *On Architecture*, trans. Michael Mitchell, ed. Adolf and Daniel Opel (Riverside, CA, 1995), pp. 9, 16, 197.

73 J. B. Fischer von Erlach, *Entwürff einer Historischen Architectur des Altherthums und fremder Völker . . .* (Leipzig, 1725); Thomas DaCosta Kaufmann, *Court, Cloister, and City: The Art and Culture of Central Europe, 1450–1800* (Chicago, 1995), p. 293.

74 Loos, *Spoken into the Void*, pp. 25–6; Unterreiner, *Franz Joseph*, pp. 56–75.

75 Loos, *On Architecture*, pp. 122–3.

8 Bosnia and After

1 Jean-Pierre Bled, *Franz Joseph*, trans. Teresa Bridgeman (Oxford, 1992), pp. 299–301; Magdalena Hawlik-Van de Water, *Die Kapuzinergruft: Begräbnisstätte der Habsburger in Wien* (Vienna, 1987), p. 286.

2 Cited in Bled, *Franz Joseph*, p. 306.

3 Ibid., p. 221.

4 Sarah Kent, 'State Ritual and Ritual Parody: Croatian Student Protest and the Limits of Loyalty at the End of the Nineteenth Century', in *The Limits of Loyalty: Imperial Symbolism, Popular Allegiances, and State Patriotism in the Late Habsburg Monarchy*, ed. Laurence Cole and Daniel L. Unowsky (New York, 2007), pp. 162, 167, 172–3.

5 Hugh Agnew, 'The Flyspecks on Palivec's Portrait: Franz Joseph, the Symbols of Monarchy, and Czech Popular Loyalty', in *Limits of Loyalty*, ed. Cole and Unowsky, pp. 98–101, 103–4, 106–7; Nancy Wingfield, *Flag Wars and Stone Saints: How the Bohemian Lands Became Czech* (Cambridge, MA, 2007), pp. 128–34.

6 Bled, *Franz Joseph*, p. 303; Samuel R. Williamson Jr, *Austria–Hungary and the Origins of the First World War* (Basingstoke, 1991), pp. 37, 105–6.

7 Bled, *Franz Joseph*, pp. 304–5.

8 Williamson, *Austria–Hungary and the Origins of the First World War*, p. 192.

9 Gabor Vermes, *István Tisza: The Liberal Vision and Conservative Statecraft of a Magyar Nationalist* (Boulder, CO, 1985), pp. 220, 228, 231–2; Robert Kann, *A History of the Habsburg Empire, 1526–1918* (Berkeley, CA, 1974), p. 419.

10 Steven Beller, *Francis Joseph* (London, 1996), p. 219; Bled, *Franz Joseph*, pp. 309–10, 314–15. Text of Franz Joseph's Manifesto of 28 July 1914 in Paula Sutter Fichtner, *The Habsburg Empire: From Dynasticism to Multinationalism* (Malabar, FL, 1997), pp. 190–91.

11 Clemens Ruthner, 'Kakaniens Kleiner Orient: Post/koloniale Lesarten der Peripherie Bosnien-Herzegowina (1878–1918)', in *Kultur-Herrschaft-Differenz*, ed. Moritz Csáky, Wolfgang Müller-Funk and Klaus R. Scherpe (Tübingen, 2006), p. 255. Cf. Pieter M. Judson, 'L'Autriche-Hongrie était-elle un empire?', *Annales. Histoire, Sciences Sociales*, LXIII (2008), pp. 563–97.

12 Peter Berger, 'Finanzwesen und Staatswerdung: Zur Genese absolutistischer Herrschaftstechnik in Österreich', in *Von der Glückseligkeit des Staates. Staat, Wirtschaft und Gesellschaft im Zeitalter des aufgeklärten Absolutismus*, ed. Herbert Mathis (Berlin, 1981), pp. 110–11; Otto Frass, ed., *Quellenbuch zur österreichischen Geschichte* (Vienna, 1959), vol. II, p. 232; Manfred Sauer, 'Aspekte der Handelspolitik des aufgeklärten Absolutismus', in *Glückseligkeit*, ed. Mathis, p. 252; Alison Frank, 'The Children of the Desert and the Laws of the Sea: Austria, Great Britain, the Ottoman Empire, and the Mediterranean Slave Trade in the Nineteenth Century', *American Historical Review*, CXVII (2012), p. 415.

13 Robert A. Donia, *Sarajevo, a Biography* (Ann Arbor, MI, 2006), pp. 8–32, 107–14; Williamson, *Austria–Hungary and the Origins of the First World War*, p. 62; Emil Palotás, 'Die Aussenwirtschaftlichen Beziehungen zum Balkan und zu Russland', in *Die Habsburger Monarchie 1848–1918*, VI/1: *Die Habsburgermonarchie im System der Internationalen Beziehungen*, ed. Adam Wandruszka and Peter Urbanitsch (Vienna, 1989), pp. 599–602.

14 Günther Ramhardter, 'Propaganda und Aussenpolitik', in *Die Habsburger Monarchie*, pp. 504–28; Donia, *Sarajevo*, pp. 8–32, 52–3, 56; Heinz Alfred Gemeinhardt, *Deutsche und österreichische Pressepolitik während der Bosnischen Krise, 1908–1909* (Husum, 1980), pp. 84–5.

15 Noel Malcolm, *Geschichte Bosniens*, trans. Ilse Strasmann (Frankfurt am Main, 1996), p. 68.

16 Donia, *Sarajevo*, pp. 8–32, 73–82.

17 See Leopold Kammerhofer, 'Diplomatie und Pressepolitik 1848–1918', in

Die Habsburger Monarchie, pp. 459–95; and Gemeinhardt, *Deutsche und österreichische Pressepolitik*, pp. 88–9.

18 Horst Haselsteiner, *Bosnien-Herzegovina: Orientkrise und Südslavische Frage* (Vienna, 1996), pp. 49–73; Srećko M. Džaja, *Bosnien-Herzegowina in der österreich-ungarischen Epoche (1878–1918)* (Munich, 1994), pp. 87–90; excerpt from a private letter of Leopold Mandl to unknown recipient, April 1907, Vienna, Haus, -Hof, und Staatsarchiv (henceforth HHStA), Ministerium des Äusserns, 1.1, Presseleitung (Literarisches Büro), Karton 107, no. 246/5; Gemeinhardt, *Deutsche und österreichische Pressepolitik*, pp. 88–90. As the correspondent from the Dual Monarchy for the Berlin *Vossische Zeitung*, Mandl would be awarded the Franz Josef Iron Cross, Third Class in 1910 for his helpful reporting on the Bosnian annexation. Vienna, Allgemeine Verwaltungsarchiv (henceforth AVA), Staatsarchiv des Innern und der Justiz, Ministerratspräsidium, Presseleitung, Karton 79b, 21 May 1910, no. 364.

19 Friedrich Funder, *Vom Gestern ins Heute*, 3rd edn (Vienna, 1971), pp. 363–4; Hermenegild Wagner, *With the Victorious Bulgarians* (Boston, MA, 1913), p. 243.

20 *Sarajevoer Tagblatt*, no. 1, 20 June 1908, p. 1; Ramhardter, 'Propaganda und Aussenpolitik', pp. 500–501; Donia, *Sarajevo*, pp. 60–66. Cf. Vienna, AVA, Staatsarchiv des Innern und Justiz, Presseleitung, 1908, Kartons 71–7. It is possible that evidence of such a subsidy might be held in contemporary archives of the Ministry of Finance, which are currently in Sarajevo.

21 *Sarajevoer Tagblatt*, no. 1, 1 January 1909, p. 1; Ramhardter, 'Propaganda und Aussenpolitik', pp. 496–8; Lothar Classen, *Der völkerrechtliche Status von Bosnien-Herzegovina nach dem Berliner Vertrag vom 13. 7. 1878* (Frankfurt am Main, 2004), pp. 61–75.

22 *Sarajevoer Tagblatt*, no. 15, 7 July 1908, p. 5; ibid., no. 174, 13 July 1909, p. 1.

23 Ibid., no. 1, 20 June 1908, p. 1; ibid., no. 52, 18 August 1908, pp. 2–3; Vienna, AVA, Ministerium des Innerns, Ministerratspräsidium, Presse-leitung, Karton 74, no. 1136, 21 December 1908; ibid., Karton 79b, 25 March 1910, no. 301; Džaja, *Bosnien*, pp. 89–90, 93.

24 *Sarajevoer Tagblatt*, no. 4, 24 June 1908, p. 3; ibid., no. 5, 25 June 1908, p. 5; ibid., no. 78, 25 March 1909, p. 1.

25 Ibid., Extraausgabe, no. 98, 7 October 1908, pp. 1–2; ibid., no. 52, 2 December 1908, pp. 1–2.

26 Ibid., no. 1, 20 June 1908, pp. 7–8; ibid., no. 4, 24 June 1908, p. 3; ibid., no. 53, 19 August 1908, p. 4; ibid., no. 122, 22 October 1908, p. 1; ibid., no. 6, 26 June 1908, p. 3.

27 Ibid., no. 208, 21 August 1909, p. 3; ibid., no. 241, 29 September 1909, p. 1; ibid., no. 282, 16 November 1909, p. 1; ibid., no. 287, 21 November 1909, pp. 1, 3; Džaja, *Bosnien*, p. 94. I have not been able to identify Felix Schulz. A person of that name resurfaced after the First World War as the editor and publisher of two populist right-wing journals in Vienna, *Der Turm* and *Freiheit*, both dedicated to supporting a national Austria.

28 Kammerhofer, 'Pressepolitik 1848–1918', pp. 483–91; *Sarajevoer Tagblatt*, no. 54, 20 August 1908, pp. 1–2; ibid., no. 57, 23 August 1908, p. 1; ibid., no. 180, 20 July 1909, p. 1.

29 'mit tunlichster Beschleunigung', Vienna, AVA, Ministerium des Innerns, Ministerratspräsidium, Presseleitung, Karton 77, 14 May 1909, no. 514.

30 *Sarajevoer Tagblatt*, no. 39, 18 February 1909, p. 1; ibid., no. 44, 24 February 1909, p. 1; ibid., no. 169, 7 July 1909, p. 2; ibid., no. 147, 9 June 1909, p. 1; ibid., no. 180, 20 July 1909, p. 1; ibid., no. 196, 7 August 1909, p. 1.

31 Vienna, AVA, Ministerium des Innerns, Ministerratspräsidium, Presse-leitung, Karton 84, no. 680, 8 July 1911; *Sarajevoer Tagblatt*, no. 172, 18 December 1908, p. 1; ibid., no. 181, 22 July 1909, pp. 1–2; ibid., no. 182, 23 July 1909, p. 2.

32 Vienna, AVA, Ministerium des Innerns, Ministerratspräsidium, Presseleitung, Karton 79a, no. 32, 9 January 1910.

33 Pavla Vošahlíkova, 'Ämter und Beamte unter Franz Joseph I', in *Von Amts wegen. K. K Beamte Erzählen*, ed. Pavla Vošahlíkova (Vienna, 1998), pp. 32–5, 37.

34 *Sarajevoer Tagblatt*, no. 123, 23 October 1908, p. 1; ibid., 4 April 1909, p. 1; ibid., no. 97, 10 April 1909, p. 1; ibid., no. 134, 23 May 1909, p. 1; ibid., no. 205, 18 August 1909, p. 1; ibid., no. 217, 1 September 1909, p. 11.

35 Funder, *Vom Gestern ins Heute*, p. 364; Vienna, Kriegsarchiv, TK Vagenho, no. 994 gives Wagner's death date as 12 June 1915 in a battle in Žežanow on the Russian front.

36 Pavla Vošahlíková, ed., *Auf der Walz: Erinnerungen böhmischer Handwerksgesellen* (Vienna, 1994), p. 172.

37 András Gerő, *Emperor Francis Joseph, King of the Hungarians* (Boulder, CO, 2001), pp. 227–9; Jörg K. Hoensch, *A History of Modern Hungary, 1867–1994*, trans. Kim Traynor, 2nd edn (London, 1996), p. 78.

38 I am grateful to Professor James Oberley of the University of Wisconsin-Eau Claire, who pointed me to this information in an email communication, 10 January 2011.

39 Beller, *Francis Joseph*, p. 220; István Deák, *Beyond Nationalism: A Social and Political History of the Habsburg Officer Corps, 1848–1918* (New York, 1990), pp. 192–3.

40 Bled, *Franz Joseph*, pp. 316–17, 320.

41 Werner Telesko, *Geschichtsraum Österreich: Die Habsburger und ihre Geschichte in der bildenden Kunst des 19. Jahrhunderts* (Vienna, 2006), p. 252; Steven Beller, 'The Tragic Carnival: Austrian Culture in the First World War', in *European Culture in the Great War: The Arts, Entertainment, and Propaganda, 1914–1918*, ed. Aviel Roshwald and Richard Stites (Cambridge, 1999), pp. 131–2; Maureen Healy, *Vienna and the Fall of the Habsburg Monarchy: Total War and Everyday Life in World War I* (Cambridge, 2004), pp. 88–91, 106, 108.

42 Joseph Held, 'Culture in Hungary during World War I', in *European Culture in the Great War*, ed. Roshwald and Stites, p. 191; Andrew Wachtel, 'Culture in the South Slavic Lands, 1914–1918', ibid., pp. 199–201, 203, 207–8; Wingfield, *Flag Wars*, pp. 137–8.

43 Tobias Natter, *Die Welt von Klimt, Schiele und Kokoschka: Sammler und Mäzene* (Cologne, 2003), pp. 143, 151; Beller, 'Tragic Carnival', pp. 140–41.

44 Agnes Husslein-Arco and Alfred Weidinger, eds, *Kokoschka: Träumender*

Knabe-Enfant Terrible (Weitra, 2008), pp. 250, 254–6; Marx Treitzsauerwein von Ehrentreitz, *Theuerdank* (Nuremberg, 1517); Beller, 'Tragic Carnival', pp. 131–9.

45 Beller, 'Tragic Carnival', pp. 131–54; Vermes, *István Tisza*, p. 237.

46 *Und vieles mehr, mir wars, also ob er strebte,*
    schwindenden Vermögen zu gestalten,
    Mit überstarken Formeln festzuhalten,
    Sich selber zu beweisen, dass er lebte,
    Mit starkem Wort, indes die Stimme bebte.

    Hugo von Hofmannsthal, 'Tizian's Tod', *Ausgewählte Werke* (Frankfurt am Main, 1957), vol. I, p. 61 (trans. author).

47 Fredrik Lindström, *Empire and Identity: Biographies of the Austrian State Problem in the Late Habsburg Empire* (West Lafayette, IN, 2008), pp. 124–5, 134–6, 138–9.

48 Ibid., pp. 139–41; Paula Sutter Fichtner, 'Schorske's Garden Transformed Again: War Propaganda, Aesthetics, and the Conservative Revolution', in *Essays on World War I: Origins and Prisoners of War*, ed. Samuel T. Williamson (Boulder, CO, 1983), p. 98.

49 Lindström, *Empire and Identity*, pp. 156–9; Held, 'Culture in Hungary during World War I', p. 191.

50 Beller, *Francis Joseph*, p. 223.

51 Bled, *Franz Joseph*, p. 320. Cf. Christian Dickinger, *Franz Joseph I: Die Entmythisierung* (Vienna, 2001), p. 206.

52 Christa Hämmerle, *Kindheit im Ersten Weltkrieg* (Vienna, 1993), p. 53; Hannes Stekl and Andrea Schnöller, eds, *'Es war eine Welt der Geborgenheit'* *– bürgerliche Kindheit in Monarchie und Republik* (Vienna, 1987), pp. 53, 185–6; Bled, *Franz Joseph*, p. 320.

53 Hämmerle, *Kindheit im Ersten Weltkrieg*, pp. 184–5.

54 Beller, 'Tragic Carnival', pp. 135–54.

55 Joseph Anton Stranitzky, *Ollapatrida des durchgetriebenen Fuchsmundi* (n.p., n.d.), pp. 19–21; Claire Nolte, 'Ambivalent Patriots: Czech Culture in the Great War', in *European Culture in the Great War*, ed. Roshwald and Stites, pp. 172–4, 390, n. 4.

56 Beller, 'Tragic Carnival', p. 132.

57 Jan Assmann, *Das kulturelle Gedächtnis: Schrift, Erinnerung und politische Identität in frühen Hochkulturen* (Munich, 2007), pp. 232–3.

58 Healy, *Vienna and the Fall of the Habsburg Monarchy*, pp. 21–2, 24, 103.

59 Hannes Leidinger, *Das Schwarzbuch der Habsburger: die unrühmliche Geschichte eines Herrschergeschlechtes* (Vienna, 2003), p. 227; Healy, *Vienna and the Fall of the Habsburg Monarchy*, pp. 216–17, 223, 225.

60 Wolfgang Maderthaner, *Die Anarchie der Vorstadt: das andere Wien um 1900* (Frankfurt am Main, 1999), pp. 20–21.

61 Healy, *Vienna and the Fall of the Habsburg Monarchy*, pp. 218–19, 260, 280–82; Paula Sutter Fichtner, *Emperor Maximilian II* (New Haven, CT, 2001), p. 86.

62 Tara Zahra, *Kidnapped Souls: National Indifference and the Battle for*

Children in the Bohemian Lands, 1900–1948 (Ithaca, NY, 2008), pp. 98–9.

63 Friedrich Oberkofler, *Von Gottes Gnaden: Karl von Habsburg-Lothringen (1887–1922), Kaiser von Österreich und König von Ungarn (1916–1922)* (Kisslegg, 2006), pp. 24–5, 27–8; Leidinger, *Schwarzbuch der Habsburger*, p. 250; Paula Sutter Fichtner, 'Charles I (IV): War Leadership as Personal Leadership', in *East Central European War Leaders: Civilian and Military*, ed. Béla K. Király and Albert A. Nofi (Boulder, CO, 1988), pp. 75–83.

64 Mark Cornwall, 'Disintegration and Defeat: the Austro-Hungarian Revolution', in *The Last Years of Austria–Hungary: A Multi-national Experiment in Early Twentieth-century Europe*, ed. Mark Cornwall (Exeter, 2002) pp. 169–71; Leidinger, *Schwarzbuch der Habsburger*, p. 252.

65 Healy, *Vienna and the Fall of the Habsburg Monarchy*, pp. 294–6.

66 Cornwall, 'Disintegration and Defeat', pp. 181–3; Healy, *Vienna and the Fall of the Habsburg Monarchy*, pp. 282, 287, 289–92, 294–6.

67 Péter Hanák, *The Garden and the Workshop: Essays on the Cultural History of Vienna and Budapest* (Princeton, NJ, 1998), pp. 85, 204; Hoensch, *History of Modern Hungary*, pp. 79–80.

68 Cornwall, 'Disintegration and Defeat', pp. 172–3.

69 Leidinger, *Schwarzbuch der Habsburger*, pp. 251–2; Cornwall, 'Disintegration and Defeat', pp. 167–8, 178–9.

70 Hugh Agnew, 'The Flyspecks on Palivec's Portrait', p. 86; Wingfield, *Flag Wars*, pp. 145–69.

71 Paula Sutter Fichtner, 'The Habsburg Empire in World War I: A Final Episode in Dynastic History', *East European Quarterly*, XI (1977), p. 457; Healy, *Vienna and the Fall of the Habsburg Monarchy*, pp. 275–7; Leidinger, *Schwarzbuch*, pp. 255–6.

72 Hawlik-Van de Water, *Kapuzinergruft*, p. 306; Fichtner, 'Habsburg Empire in World War I', p. 457; Karl Vocelka and Lynne Heller, *Die Lebenswelt der Habsburger: Kultur- und Mentalitätsgeschichte einer Familie* (Graz, 1997), p. 200; Erich Feigl, ed., *Kaiser Karl: Persönliche Aufzeichnungen, Zeugnisse und Dokumente* (Vienna, 1984), pls 33, 34, 35, 52.

9 One Goodbye, Several Farewells

1 'Im Kriege wurde Ich auf den Thron Meiner Väter berufen, zum Frieden wollte und will Ich ihnen ein gerechter und treubesorgeter Vater sein.' Hannes Leidinger, *Das Schwarzbuch der Habsburger: die unrühmliche Geschichte eines Herrschergeschlechtes* (Vienna, 2003), pp. 259–60.

2 Leopold R. G. Decloedt, *Imago Imperatoris: Franz Joseph I. in der österreichischen Belletristik der Zwischenkriegszeit* (Vienna, 1995), pp. 36, 38, 192.

3 Paula Sutter Fichtner, 'Americans and the Disintegration of the Habsburg Monarchy: The Shaping of an Historiographical Model', in *The Habsburg Empire in World War I: Essays on the Intellectual, Military, Political, and Economic Aspects of the Habsburg War Effort*, ed. Robert A. Kann, Béla K. Király and Paula S. Fichtner (Boulder, CO, 1977), p. 225.

4 Gerhardt Plöchl, *Willibald Plöchl und Otto Habsburg in den USA: Ringen um Österreichs 'Exilregierung' 1941/42* (Vienna, 2007), pp. 12–13.

5 Ibid., pp. 17–19; Leidinger, *Schwarzbuch der Habsburger*, p. 262.

6 On Archduke William, see Timothy Snyder, *The Red Prince: The Secret Lives of a Habsburg Archduke* (New York, 2008). See also Bruce Pauley, 'Otto von Habsburg, 1912–2011' (Obituary), *Austrian Studies Newsletter* (Autumn 2011), p. 23; Leidinger, *Schwarzbuch der Habsburger*, pp. 260–63.

7 Decloedt, *Imago Imperatoris*, pp. 55–6 (trans. author).

8 Walter Schamschula, 'Die Literatur der Tschechen', in *Die österreichische Literatur: Ihr Profil von den Anfängen im Mittelalter bis ins 18. Jahrhundert (1050–1750)*, ed. Herbert Zeman (Graz, 1986), p. 778.

9 Decloedt, *Imago Imperatoris*, pp. 83, 85 and n. 365, 224.

10 Ibid., pp. 143–9, 166–7.

11 Ibid., pp. 156, 163–4, 168–9.

12 Tibor Klaniczay, 'Die Möglichkeiten einer vergleichenden Literaturgeschichte Osteuropas', in *Vergleichende Literaturforschung in den sozialistischen Ländern, 1963–1979*, ed. Gerhard Kaiser (Stuttgart, 1980), p. 46.

13 Paula Sutter Fichtner, 'Fin-de-siècle Vienna: Creators, Critics, and Audiences', *Annals of Scholarship*, VII/1 (1990), pp. 19–21, 23–5.

14 *Die Presse*, Spectrum, 23 July 2011, p. iv.

15 Alan Sked, *The Decline and Fall of the Habsburg Empire*, 2nd revd edn (Harlow, 2001), p. 3; István Deák, 'Where's Charlemagne When We Need Him?', *New York Times*, 30 June 2012, Sunday Review, p. 4.

16 'Der Name Polarisiert Noch', interview with Charles von Habsburg conducted by Dietmar Pieper and Johannes Saltzwedel in their *Die Welt der Habsburger* (Munich, 2011), p. 33.

17 *News* (Vienna), no. 28, 14 July 2011, pp. 10–19; Pieper and Saltzwedel, *Welt der Habsburger*, pp. 30–32, 34.

18 'So a scheene Leich', *News* (Vienna), no. 29, 21 July 2011, pp. 118–19.

Select Bibliography

Agnew, Hugh LeCaine, *The Czechs and the Lands of the Bohemian Crown*
  (Stanford, CA, 2004)
Barta, Ilsebill, *Familienporträts der Habsburger: Dynastische Repräsentation
  im Zeitalter der Aufklärung* (Vienna, 2001)
Baum, Wilhelm, *Rudolf IV: Der Stifter* (Graz, 1996)
Beales, Derek, *Joseph II: Against the World, 1780–1790* (Cambridge, 2009)
——, *Joseph II: In the Shadow of Maria Theresa, 1741–1780* (Cambridge, 1987)
Beller, Steven, *Francis Joseph* (London, 1996)
Bernard, Paul, *From the Enlightenment to the Police State: The Public Life of
  Johann Anton Pergen* (Urbana, IL, 1991)
Bireley, Robert, *The Counter-Reformation Prince: Anti-Machiavellianism
  or Catholic Statecraft in Early Modern Europe* (Chapel Hill, NC, 1990)
Bled, Jean-Pierre, *Franz Joseph*, trans. Teresa Bridgeman (Oxford, 1992)
Bodi, Leslie, *Tauwetter in Wien: Zur Prosa der österreichischen Aufklärung,
  1781–1795* (Frankfurt am Main, 1979)
Browning, Reed, *The War of the Austrian Succession* (New York, 1993)
Bucur, Maria, and Nancy Wingfield, eds, *Staging the Past: The Politics of
  Commemoration in Habsburg Central Europe, 1848 to the Present*
  (West Lafayette, IN, 2001)
Cohen, Gary B., *Education and Middle-class Society in Imperial Austria*
  (West Lafayette, IN, 1996)
——, and Franz A. J. Szabo, eds, *Embodiments of Power: Building Baroque Cities
  in Europe* (New York, 2008)
Cole, Laurence, and Daniel L. Unowsky, eds, *The Limits of Loyalty: Imperial
  Symbolism, Popular Allegiances, and State Patriotism in the Late Habsburg
  Monarchy* (New York, 2007)
Coreth, Anna, *Pietas Austriaca*, trans. William D. Bowman and Anna Maria
  Leitgeb (West Lafayette, IN, 2004)
Cornwall, Mark, *The Last Years of Austria–Hungary: A Multi-national Experiment
  in Early Twentieth-century Europe* (Exeter, 2002)
——, *The Undermining of Austria–Hungary, 1914–18: The Battle for Hearts and
  Minds* (Basingstoke, 2000)
Csáky, Moritz, *Ideologie der Operette und Wiener Moderne: Ein kulturhistorischer*

Essay zur österreichischen Identität (Vienna, 1996)

Deák, István, *Beyond Nationalism: A Social and Political History of the Habsburg Officer Corps, 1848–1918* (New York, 1990)

Decloedt, Leopold R. G., *Imago Imperatoris: Franz Joseph I. in der österreichischen Belletristik der Zwischenkriegszeit* (Vienna, 1995)

Evans, R.J.W., *Rudolf II and his World: A Study in Intellectual History, 1576–1612* (Oxford, 1973)

Fichtner, Paula Sutter, *Emperor Maximilian II* (New Haven, CT, 2001)

—, *Ferdinand I of Austria: the Politics of Dynasticism in the Age of the Reformation* (Boulder, CO, 1982)

—, *The Habsburg Monarchy, 1490–1848: Attributes of Empire* (Basingstoke, 2003)

—, *Terror and Toleration: The Habsburg Empire Confronts Islam, 1526–1850* (London, 2008)

Fillitz, Hermann, ed. with Werner Telesko, *Der Traum vom Glück: Die Kunst des Historismus in Europa* (Vienna, 1996)

Gerő, András, *Imagined History: Chapters from Nineteenth and Twentieth Century Hungarian Symbolic Politics*, trans. Mario D. Fenyo (Boulder, CO, 2006)

Goloubeva, Maria, *The Glorification of Emperor Leopold I in Image, Spectacle, and Text* (Mainz, 2000)

Hamann, Brigitte, *Kronprinz Rudolf: Ein Leben*, revd edn (Munich, 2006)

Hanák, Péter, *The Garden and the Workshop: Essays on the Cultural History of Vienna and Budapest* (Princeton, NJ, 1998)

Hawlik-Van de Water, Magdelena, *Die Kapuzinergruft: Begräbnisstätte der Habsburger in Wien* (Vienna, 1987)

Healy, Maureen, *Vienna and the Fall of the Habsburg Monarchy: Total War and Everyday Life in World War I* (Cambridge, 2004)

Heindl, Waltraud, *Gehorsame Rebellen: Bürokratie und Beamte in Österreich 1780 bis 1848* (Vienna, 1990)

Heinig, Paul-Joachim, *Kaiser Friedrich III (1440–1493): Hof, Regierung und Politik*, 3 vols (Cologne, 1997)

Hochedlinger, Michael, *Austria's Wars of Emergence, 1683–1797* (London, 2003)

Hoensch, Jörg K., *A History of Modern Hungary, 1867–1994*, trans. Kim Traynor, 2nd edn (London, 1996)

Hollegger, Manfred, *Maximilian I (1459–1519): Herrscher und Mensch einer Zeitenwende* (Stuttgart, 2005)

Judson, Pieter M., *Exclusive Revolutionaries: Liberal Politics, Social Experience, and National Identity in the Austrian Empire, 1848–1918* (Ann Arbor, MI, 1996)

—, *Guardians of the Nation: Activists on the Language Frontiers of Imperial Austria* (Cambridge, MA, 2007)

Kampmann, Christoph, Katharina Krause, Eva-Bettina Krems and Anuschka Tischer, eds, *Bourbon-Habsburg-Oranien: Konkurrierende Modelle im dynastischen Europa um 1700* (Cologne, 2008)

Kann, Robert, *A History of the Habsburg Empire, 1526–1918* (Berkeley, CA, 1974)

Kaufmann, Thomas DaCosta, *Court, Cloister, and City: The Art and Culture of*

Central Europe, 1450–1800 (Chicago, 1995)

——, *Painterly Enlightenment: The Art of Franz Anton Maulbertsch* (Chapel Hill, NC, 2005)

Kohler, Alfred, *Ferdinand I, 1503–1564: Fürst, König und Kaiser* (Munich, 2003)

Krasa-Florian, Selma, *Die Allegorie der Austria: Die Entstehung des Gesamtstaats-gedankens in der österreichisch-ungarischen Monarchie und die bildende Kunst* (Vienna, 2007)

Krieger, Karl-Friedrich, *Die Habsburger im Mittelalter: Von Rudolf I. bis Friedrich III.*, 2nd edn (Stuttgart, 2004)

Langer, Andrea, and Georg Michels, eds, *Metropolen und Kulturtransfer im 15./16. Jahrhundert* (Stuttgart, 2001)

Lindström, Fredrik, *Empire and Identity: Biographies of the Austrian State Problem in the Late Habsburg Empire* (West Lafayette, IN, 2008)

Louthan, Howard, *Converting Bohemia: Force and Persuasion in the Catholic Reformation* (Cambridge, 2006)

Magris, Claudio, *Il mito absburgico nella letteratura austriaca moderna* (Turin, 1963)

Marek, Michaela, *Kunst und Identitätspolitik: Architectur und Bildkünste im Prozess der tschechischen Nationbildung* (Cologne, 2004)

Maťa, Petr, and Thomas Winkelbauer, eds, *Die Habsburgermonarchie, 1620 bis 1740* (Stuttgart, 2006)

Matsche, Franz, *Die Kunst im Dienst der Staatsidee Kaiser Karls VI*, 2 vols (Berlin, 1981)

Möckl, Karl, ed., *Hof und Hofgesellschaft in den deutschen Staaten im 19. und beginninden 20. Jahrhundert* (Boppard am Rhein, 1990)

Mortimer, Geoff, *Wallenstein: The Enigma of the Thirty Years War* (Basingstoke, 2010)

Natter, Tobias, *Die Welt von Klimt, Schiele und Kokoschka: Sammler und Mäzene* (Cologne, 2003)

Patrouch, Joseph F., *Queen's Apprentice: Archduchess Elizabeth, Empress María, the Habsburgs, and the Holy Roman Empire, 1554–1569* (Leiden, 2010)

Pörtner, Regina, *The Counter-Reformation in Central Europe: Styria, 1580–1630* (Oxford, 2001)

Riesenfellner, Stefan, ed., *Steinernes Bewusstsein I: Die öffentliche Representation staatlicher und nationaler Identität Österreichs in seinen Denkmälern* (Vienna, 1998)

Schorske, Carl, *Fin-de-siècle Vienna: Politics and Culture* (New York, 1980)

Schumann, Jutta, *Die andere Sonne: Kaiserbild und Medienstrategien im Zeitalter Leopolds I* (Berlin, 2003)

Schweiger, Werner, *Der junge Kokoschka: Leben und Werk* (Vienna, 1983)

Silver, Larry, *Marketing Maximilian: The Visual Ideology of a Holy Roman Emperor* (Princeton, NJ, 2008)

Sked, Alan. *The Decline and Fall of the Habsburg Empire*, 2nd revd edn (Harlow, 2001)

Snyder, Timothy, *The Red Prince: The Secret Lives of a Habsburg Archduke* (New York, 2008)

Spielman, John P., *Leopold I of Austria* (New Brunswick, NJ, 1977)

Szabo, Franz, *The Seven Years War in Europe, 1756–1763* (Harlow, 2008)

Tanner, Marie, *The Last Descendant of Aeneas: The Habsburgs and the Mythic Image of the Emperor* (New Haven, CT, 1993)

Telesko, Werner, *Geschichtsraum Österreich: Die Habsburger und ihre Geschichte in der bildenden Kunst des 19. Jahrhunderts* (Vienna, 2006)

Unowsky, Daniel L., *The Pomp and Politics of Patriotism: Imperial Celebrations in Habsburg Austria, 1848–1916* (West Lafayette, IN, 2006)

Unterreiner, Katrin, *Emperor Franz Joseph, 1830–1916: Myth and Truth*, trans. Martin Kelsey (Vienna, 2006)

Vocelka, Karl, and Lynne Heller, *Die Lebenswelt der Habsburger. Kultur- und Mentalitätsgeschichte einer Familie* (Graz, 1997)

—, *Die politische Propaganda Kaiser Rudolfs II., 1576–1612* (Vienna, 1981)

Wheatcroft, Andrew, *The Enemy at the Gate: Habsburgs, Ottomans, and the Battle for Europe* (London, 2008)

—, *The Habsburgs: Embodying Empire* (London, 1995)

Wilson, Peter H., *Europe's Tragedy: A History of the Thirty Years War* (London, 2009)

Wingfield, Nancy, *Flag Wars and Stone Saints: How the Bohemian Lands Became Czech* (Cambridge, MA, 2007)

Yonan, Michael, *Empress Maria Theresa and the Politics of Habsburg Imperial Art* (University Park, PA, 2011)

Zahra, Tara, *Kidnapped Souls: National Indifference and the Battle for Children in the Bohemian Lands, 1900–1948* (Ithaca, NY, 2008)

List of Illustrations

Schönbrunn, Vienna. Reproduced © and courtesy Schloss Schönbrunn Kultur- und Betriebsgesellschaft m.b.h.

13 Franz Joseph I (*r.* 1848–1916) in a Corpus Christi procession, 1900. Photo © and courtesy Österreichische Nationalbibliothek, Vienna.

14 'A Pauper after Maundy Thursday Foot Cleansing', from Max Herzig, *Viribis Unitis. Das Buch vom Kaiser* (Budapest and Leipzig, 1898). Photo © and courtesy Österreichische Nationalbibliothek, Vienna.

15 Koloman Moser, frontispiece to Max Herzig, *Viribus Unitis. Das Buch vom Kaiser* (Budapest and Leipzig, 1898). Photo © and courtesy Österreichische Nationalbibliothek, Vienna.

16 J. J. Reiner, *The Attempt on the Life of Kaiser Franz Joseph I on 18 February 1853*, 1853, oil on canvas. Historisches Museum der Stadt Wien. Reproduced courtesy Museen der Stadt Wien, Vienna.

17 Hans Makart, *Emperor Charles V Enters Antwerp*, 1878, oil on canvas. Kunsthalle Hamburg.

18 The assassination in Sarajevo of Archduke Franz Ferdinand and his wife, 28 June 1914, depicted in a contemporary Austrian newspaper. Photo © and courtesy Bildarchiv of the Österreichische Nationalbibliothek, Vienna.

19 Oskar Kokoschka, *The Errant Knight*, 1915, oil on canvas. Copyright © 2014 Fondation Oskar Kokoschka/Artists Rights Society (ARS), New York/ProLitteris, Zürich. Image courtesy Solomon R. Guggenheim Museum, New York.

20 The funeral cortège of Emperor Franz Joseph, 1916. Photo © and courtesy Bildarchiv of the Österreichische Nationalbibliothek, Vienna.

Acknowledgements

Rare is the scholarly publication that goes forth without expert advice from others; this one is no exception. I am much indebted to Janet Wolf Berls, Robert Bireley, Peter Judson, Robert David K. C. Johnson, Howard Louthan, Paul Miller, Joseph Patrouch, Elizabeth Powers and Franz A. J. Szabo for taking some of their precious time to read parts of my manuscript critically, but always constructively. Edward G. Fichtner faithfully provided technical assistance and an audience for my endless oral rehearsals of the book as it came together. Jay Barksdale always willingly extended my privileges in the Allen Writing Room of the New York Public Library, where many of my books could be held and where one could work through them undisturbed. The years of hospitality that Waltraud Heindl and Walter Langer gave me in Vienna will never be forgotten.

I have also received exemplary cooperation and counsel from the staffs of Austrian collections that have provided almost all of my illustrations. Matthias Böhm in the Bildarchiv of the Austrian National Library and Johannes Stoll of the Belvedere Palace Gallery went out of their way to find materials that I wanted and to get them to me promptly. Reinhard Gruber, the archivist of St Stephen's Cathedral in Vienna, did the same. Elfriede Iby from the Schloss Schönbrunn Kultur- und Betriebsgesellschaft also gave me very useful advice. Responsible figures at the Wien Museum and the Kunsthistorisches Museum were also quick to answer my requests. I also owe a thank you to Kim Bush of the Guggenheim Collection in New York for coming up with a picture I very much wanted, even as the museum's business office was underwater following one of the most severe episodes of coastal flooding that New York City had ever seen.

Index